The Legend From Bruce Rock
THE WALLY FOREMAN STORY

The Legend from Bruce Rock

The Wally Foreman Story

G E Foreman

FFPRESS

info@ffpress.com.au

www.ffpress.com.au

Copyright © 2017 by Glen Foreman

'The Five People You Meet In Heaven', written by Mitch Albom. © 2003 Hyperion. All rights reserved. 'The Hardest Part', by Guy Berryman, Jonny Buckland, Will Champion and Chris Martin. © 2006 Parlophone. All rights reserved. 'The Legend from Bruce Rock', written by Mick Colliss. © 2006. All rights reserved. Used by permission. 'The Magic Strings of Frankie Presto', written by Mitch Albom. © 2015 HarperCollins. All rights reserved.

All rights reserved. Apart from any fair dealing for the purposes of private study, research, criticism, or review, as permitted under the *Copyright Act 1968*, no part may be reproduced by any process without the written permission of the author.

Printed in Australia

First Printing, 2017
ISBN: 978-0-6480408-0-4
Available from the National Library of Australia, Canberra

Edited by Tim Clarke

Artwork designed by Ashley Storey/Ashley Storey Creative Digital Media

Typesetting by Christian Komnick/iKOM Creative Solutions

Proudly supporting the Wally Foreman Foundation.

www.wff.org.au

For Charlotte and Jonathon.
I'd like to introduce you to your
grandad, who would have loved you dearly.
He was an amazing man. This is why …

The Legend from Bruce Rock
By Mick Colliss

Another Aussie icon. A West Australian great.
Chosen well before his time to walk through Heaven's gate.
The man we all admired, respected and adored
Was placed into the draft and was hand-picked by the Lord.
He was passionate and humble, courteous and fair
Loyal and good-humoured, both on and off the air.
The consummate professional, a master of his trade
His reputation's one that time itself will never fade.
A fiercely proud ambassador for all sports in our State
His easy going nature made him everybody's mate.
Not afraid to have his say and give his point of view
He was the man that every West Australian felt they knew.
Olympic Games, Davis Cups and all things in between
He'd start with "I suspect..." and then go on to paint the scene.
His colourful descriptions made us feel like we were there
Without a hint of ego which – in roles like his – is rare.
He never chased the spotlight, he never courted glory
He always knew, no matter what, the athletes were the story.
Totally unbiased and guided by the facts
To callers he was welcoming, engaging and relaxed.
His anecdotes were famous and held listeners in a trance
Like when he used dynamic lifter on his indoor plants.
The way he hated mobile phones, despised those ATMs
Technologically inept, right to the very end.
The news that he had passed away – it came as such a shock.
I thought he was invincible. The Legend from Bruce Rock.
And even now it's something I find hard to comprehend
We've lost a colleague, workmate, mentor. And we've lost our friend.
And still our hearts are heavy and our tears are not yet dry
We wish we had just one more chance so we could say goodbye.
We'll reminisce, remember. We'll cry, we'll laugh, we'll grieve.
But most of all we'll miss him. More than he'd believe.

Foreword

THE AUSTRALIAN OPEN OF 2003 is probably best remembered for its marathon quarterfinal match between Andy Roddick and Younes El Aynaoui in the men's singles. Roddick finally prevailed, but only after winning the 40th game of the fifth set.

Yet, it's another quarterfinal played that same year – one that was over in straight sets – that remains one of my most vivid memories in sport.

I remember it was a hot day in Perth and I was headed for home after a meeting in the city. I flicked on the radio hoping to catch a few cricket scores but instead found myself listening to tennis and the unmistakable, raspy voice of my good friend Wally Foreman in full flight.

If the game between Wayne Ferreira and Juan Carlos Ferrero was forgettable, the broadcaster was not. In many respects, his commentary that day was part sobriety test, part masterpiece. The tongue-twisting rallies between Ferrero and Ferreira were fraught with danger at every stroke, but Wal was unfazed.

If ever a country town had reason to be proud it was Bruce Rock that day. Within minutes of turning on the radio I found myself parked under a tree outside Queens Park Gardens listening to the entire match, not for the result, but for the broadcaster.

I rang Wal the next day to congratulate him. It was a phone call that helped rekindle our friendship. Fair to say the two young men who first met then shared an office and a dream at the ABC in 1975 had, by 2003, gone from being inseparable, to being friends who always had a lot to catch up on. In the last few years before his death we made sure we caught up on a lot.

Wally Foreman was my friend and a friend who made friends easily. Wal's mate from his army days Kevin Harrison got it right when he said Wally was "just a larrikin", but, like all of us, he showed himself in different shades to different people. For my part, the mention of Wally's name makes me smile. He was feisty, he was driven but, most of all, he was fun.

The ABC building in Adelaide Terrace has recently been demolished and, with it, the office Wal and I shared just inside the front door.

In its way, this book is about time travel; from a son, to his daughter and son, about their grandfather. I know that if I could travel back through time, there are few places in my life I would enjoy re-visiting more than that little office on the terrace.

Dennis Cometti
Iconic sports broadcaster. And West Australian.

Author's Note

Dear Reader,

"I never met Wally Foreman, but ..."

That was how many of the beautiful tributes for dad written by the public began, before ending with lines such as "I felt I knew him", "I feel like I've lost a mate", or "Gee, I miss him".

This biography will unlikely resemble any you've read before. It's even less likely to be what you expect. As I go on to explain in the Introduction, I have written this in the first-person to my daughter, Charlotte, who I expect to pass on the stories to her brother Jonathon. As such, the name Wally Foreman rarely appears in these pages and has instead been substituted with "your grandad".

I wanted to clear that up early.

I also wanted to make something else clear: this book is for you, as much as it is my daughter and son. That is true whether you are family, friends of the family or have never met any member of our family. This is for you.

I wrote this story the way I did for two reasons.

Firstly, because I am Wally Foreman's son and to attempt to write it in any other way than a participant in the story would have ended in a jumbled mess. In fact, it did so when I attempted to do just that at the start of this project. So, why write it to Charlotte in particular? She would have been dad's first grandchild and, as such, will be the first of the next generation to hear about her grandad.

Secondly, because I truly feel comfortable sharing dad's life and story with the public in such a personal and intimate way. Dad did not have an on-air/off-air persona; the man you enjoyed listening to, who felt like a mate, was the same man we knew and loved.

My family was inundated by the sincerest sentiments imaginable following dad's death – mostly from people who never knew him, or us. We still have those notes. Thousands of them.

My hope is that the way in which this story is written does not alienate you, but I also acknowledge that it's a possibility it will. In those moments, I want you to know that is not my intention.

I have written this story the way I have as a way of welcoming you into our family as you read it. It was the sincerest form of writing I could conjure. The same sincerity dad employed as he addressed you through the airwaves and the same sincerity with which you comforted us after we lost him.

Thank you for caring. And thank you for helping Wally Foreman's name live on.

GF

Contents

Part One
Introduction: Dear Charlotte
Chapter 1: Always Remember Where You Came From
Chapter 2: Family and Friends Matter
Chapter 3: Make the Most of the Hand You're Dealt
Chapter 4: Never Give In, Never Give In (Never, Never, Never)
Chapter 5: Always Follow Your Dreams
Chapter 6: Dreams Can Come True
Chapter 7: The Legend from Rivervale
Chapter 8: Sometimes the Grass is Greener

Part Two
Chapter 9: The Western Australian Institute of Sport
Chapter 10: There's Always Another Way
Chapter 11: 'Good Facilities Only Help the Good People'
Chapter 12: When Two Worlds Collide
Chapter 13: There is More to Life than Results
Chapter 14: Actions Have Consequences
Chapter 15: Sometimes, We Must Let Go

Part Three
Chapter 16: Follow Your Heart
Chapter 17: Take Time for Family
Chapter 18: Regrets, You'll Have a Few
Chapter 19: The Hardest Part is Letting Go
Chapter 20: Always Keep a Sense of Humour
Chapter 21: People Come First
Chapter 22: Always Look After Your Mates

Part Four
Chapter 23: Every Ending has a Beginning
Chapter 24: Every Beginning has an End
Chapter 25: Endings Are Contradictions
Chapter 26: A Thousand Words Paint a Picture
Chapter 27: The Legend from Bruce Rock

Appendix
Acknowledgements
Interviews

Everyone joins a band in this life.
You are born into your first one. Your mother plays the lead.
She shares the stage with your father and siblings. Or perhaps
your father is absent, an empty stool under a spotlight.
But he is still a founding member.
… Everyone joins a band in this life.
And what you play always affects someone.
Sometimes, it affects the world.

Mitch Albom
The Magic Strings of Frankie Presto

PART ONE

Introduction

Dear Charlotte

Dear Charlotte,

THOSE TWO WORDS WERE A lot easier to write than the ones that follow. That's because this book was not always titled as it is. And it did not always read the way it does.

It was always dedicated to you, but it took an entirely different form. It was a form that had me attempting to tell the story of your grandad as a normal biography. I had written seven chapters, totalling 57,000 words, but the manuscript read like someone trying to write a biography objectionably, yet from a position of journalist, son and participant in the story. A local publisher helped me understand that, but it knocked me down.

Your grandad taught me resilience. The fact there is this completed book for you to read is testament to that and it's a lesson I hope he also helps your mum and me teach you. But while the publisher helped me understand that the story was confused, it was you, Charlotte, who helped me see what it needed to become.

I had spent three years researching and interviewing and one year writing a book that tried to be everything to everybody and ended up just being confusing. I was so focused on trying to produce something that would be appreciated by people he knew and who respected him within the industries he worked. People such as Ric Charlesworth, Dennis Cometti, Kim Hughes and Justin Langer. And then there were my colleagues in the media; what would they think when the book was finally released?

The irony is that one of those people, Dennis Cometti, said to me when I interviewed him: "People don't want a normal biography; they want to read a biography about a man, written by his son". That is why the foreword is written by Dennis; he could see what this book needed to be even before I could.

I was so clouded by thoughts of what others would think that I let drift the one name that should have been at the forefront of my mind: yours, Charlotte Anne Foreman. The reason is simple: your grandad would have loved you so much. More than anything in the world. Even more than sport.

Had he had the opportunity to sit with you and tell you a story while you balanced on his knee, a knee that for once in his life would not have been jigging up-and-down at a million miles an hour, you would have been the only thing that existed to him in the world at that moment. The Australian Broadcasting Corporation, the Western Australian Institute of Sport and everything before, in between and after, would have meant nothing at that moment.

That was because your grandad had a heart of gold. It was what made him so well-respected by so many people, be they well-known names, those he worked with, those he helped, or those he had never met in person.

He never let profile bother him and he respected people and took them as they came, regardless of where they came from. He had a very clear understanding of right and wrong and fought with every bit of his essence for the former, no matter who those battles were against or how he may have appeared throughout them. He was not perfect, but most of the 3000 people who attended his memorial service after he passed away would probably say that he was as close as they come.

Had you had the opportunity to sit on his knee, listening to him talking in what would have been that uplifting tone that comes naturally to anyone when they speak with a beaming smile, he would have told you stories to make you laugh and tales to teach you lessons and it's important for you to know the life that they came from.

So, I say thank you, Charlotte, because from this moment, there is no more confusion. This book, this biography of your grandad, is written for you. Sure, it's not for your eyes only and I sincerely hope that others enjoy reading it and learning about a man that was special to them, too. But it is written to you, to help you get to know a grandad you'll never meet in person.

However, with that comes some responsibilities.

You were the first grandchild of Wally Foreman, but in the time it took to complete this project, we welcomed your brother Jonathon and, undoubtedly, your Uncle Mark would hope to give you some cousins. As the first grandchild, this book might be written for you, but it will also belong to them and it will be your responsibility to introduce them to their grandad. My hope is that is not a burden for you, but a gift that you feel privileged to give.

My thanks to you goes deeper than that, because you've also given me a gift. I didn't have the strongest relationship with your grandad when I was growing up, for a variety of reason. We loved each other, but we argued a lot. Especially when I was a teenager, who thought he knew better. I will forever be thankful that my relationship with your grandad began to mend in the months leading up to his passing, but we had only just begun to get to know each other.

As a result of writing this book, I've had the opportunity to get to know my dad in ways I otherwise never would have, even if he was still around today. I've had the opportunity to realise just how similar we were. You and I share a loss that is immense, but we also share this journey.

I should probably explain to you how this project begun, because it did so at a time when you were just a thought and not the driving force for it. I had conducted a lecture in journalism at a university in about 2011 and was approached by one of the students. He said that your grandad was the reason he was taking that course. They were kind words, but they also made me realise that there would be a generation of West Australians that at some stage no longer recognised the name, Wally Foreman.

I made a public comment to that effect, which was met with a reply from editor of *The West Australian* Brett McCarthy: "You should write his biography". And so began my stumble along an unknown path with fractured purpose until the moment you were born, three years later.

There's also a couple of technical points I need to mention before you start reading. Being written to you, I've referred to your grandad as just that, "your grandad", throughout. However, he was also my dad and I was the one doing the interviews. So, you'll come across quotes from people that say, "your dad" or "your father". Don't get confused; they're the same person and still your grandad. I just don't like changing quotes.

There's also some bad examples that will be contrary to what your mum and I have taught you, such as swearing and drink-driving. I'm going to assume you'll first pick up this book when you're nearing the end of your teenage years, so you'll understand that those incidents are mentioned and happened in a context and time. I trust your mum and I have helped you to understand the difference between right and wrong.

So, where should we start?

Well, considering you never met your grandad, we should probably start at the beginning and, for him, that was the Western Australian wheatbelt. He was born in Kalgoorlie, but grew up in a town named Bruce Rock. The latter was a place that forever held his heart and one that you have visited.

You were barely three months old and you joined your mum and me as I needed to interview two of your grandad's childhood friends, Ray Williams and Bryan Kilminster. We joined them for dinner that night at the local club and you had your photo taken with them. It was a touching moment at the time – they were meeting the first grandchild of one of their closest mates, who never got to meet you himself – but it is now an even more significant memory.

Bryan passed away before this book was released, but that night you helped to paste a big smile all over his face. It was a smile that resembled the one your grandad would have beamed whenever he held you. He would have beamed, because you would have filled him with the same sense of beauty and nostalgia, wholeness and peace that made him love the way he did the town of Bruce Rock and the childhood he spent there.

It would have been the same sense of peace that made him escape to the country at every opportunity. The sense that made him inhale deeply the clean, unspoilt air, with eyes closed, listening to nothing but the whisper of the wind through the wheat fields, remembering the journey from country to city of both that breeze and his own life.

Bruce Rock and the country had the unique ability to bring calm to a life you will learn was very busy. To bring clarity. To bring a proud sense of identity with every deep breath taken and every whisper heard.

So, close your eyes. Deep breath. And listen to the whispers.

It's time to meet your grandad.

Chapter 1

Always Remember Where You Came From

"The ball spills to Medhurst. He collects on the run. He might not have the size, this Medhurst, but he's quick."

There was no green field of perfectly mown turf. There were no floodlights making the area at least semi-visible. And this was no weekend clash-of-the-titans. It was midweek. Which day? It didn't matter; they often played out the same.

And the words could have been those that blared through the wireless from a 6WF broadcast, spanning the 250km from city to regional WA, describing the movements of West Perth rover Peter Medhurst as he helped the club end a nine-year drought in its surge towards the 1960 Western Australian National Football League (WANFL) Premiership.

Those words could have been all of that, but they weren't.

They were the words – paraphrased as they are – of 12-year-old Lindsay "Wimpy" Moroney as he described 10-year-old upstart Wally "Wallygog" Foreman ducking and weaving around his taller opponent of the same age, Trevor "Red" Riley. The light was dimming early, as it often did in a wheatbelt winter. Houses and nearby trees became silhouettes. To the west, streaks of golden sunlight burst over the horizon, trying desperately to claw to the crisp, clear black that was rapidly engulfing the east.

It would have meant the end to most games.

Yet the sound of crunching, dusty red gravel, twisting underfoot filled the air in harmony with Moroney's commentary. The game was not over. Not until it was an optical impossibility for these two friends and bitter rivals to see the ball. Or until your great grandparents – Norma or Eric Foreman – issued a stern ultimatum from across the main road that was effectively the western wing boundary line.

The boundary of the eastern wing was the tracks of the railway, which carried steam-powered trains past the match, puffing out the smoke of burning Collie coal. The southern grandstand was the wheatbin sentinels that stood guard a short distance away. The goalposts were rocks, tin cans and anything else that would suffice.

The facilities might not have been state of the art, but they were exceptionally versatile, because every summer, as Jim Fitzmaurice called the first delivery of the Sheffield Shield season and Alan McGilvray described the performances of Australia in the post-Bradman era, that football field rapidly transformed into the perfect cricket pitch.

Of course, location is crucial for the success of any sporting facility – as one of those 10-year-olds would repeatedly point out later in life to whichever government controlled the state – and this particular ground was ideal: directly across the road from the "Foreman Clubrooms" of No.6 Johnson Street, with a major access route – the back lane – making The Vacant Block a natural convergence point.

Winning meant the world. And it meant nothing, because they'd be back tomorrow. It was Bruce Rock, 1958, and it was the perfect place for your grandad and his friends to spend their childhood.

A typical weekday went something like this: wake up, have breakfast, take The Back Lane to walk to school; at lunchtime, sneak out of the school grounds and head to Ray "Bozo" Williams' house to play table tennis while listening to the wireless; sneak back into school until the bell went; stop past home – or someone else's home – to refuel, before beginning the final session of play at The Vacant Block. Weekends were similar, just with organised sport replacing school and sneaking out during the lunchbreak replaced with supporting the local football team.

Our family comprised at that time of your Great Grandad Eric, your Great Grandma Norma, your grandad and your Great Aunty (or, "Grunty", as you prefer) Sandy. They arrived in Bruce Rock in 1950 from Kalgoorlie and remained there until 1960, leaving the country behind them and ending a decade in a town that would become such a great part of them all.

Your grandad and the town of Bruce Rock are practically synonymous. That is, of course, largely due to the unrivalled reach of the ABC – the national broadcaster that he used frequently to trumpet the merits of the town. Yet, your grandad was born in Kalgoorlie in 1948 – Sandy arrived two years later in the same town – and the family spent only 10 years in "The Rock".

Some of the most memorable moments of your grandad's life occurred during his time in the city and he forged some of his closest and longest-running friendships away from the country. He joined the army, became a media figure recognised by name in print, voice and image and later founded a vision for, then steered the direction of, high performance sport in Western Australia for almost two decades.

Some of your grandad's greatest accomplishments were based in Perth. Yet, he and Bruce Rock are practically synonymous.

Bruce Rock, on first glance, is the polar opposite of the life that your grandad later led. The town you visited with your mum and me when you were just a baby resembled a ghost town in a way: many shops were closed, it was quiet with only the occasional passing car and there certainly were no signs of children playing football or cricket on any block, let alone a vacant one.

I've been back a couple of times since by myself and it was a similar sight. It made it easy to wonder what it was about Bruce Rock that was so endearing to your grandad. It was – and remains – a beautiful town and its stillness brings an infectious sense of peace, with the sound of rattling ute trays in the distance and barking kelpies often the only disturbances to the wispy sound of an easterly through the gum trees.

That peace is a hallmark from the generations of the past, but there are also major differences to the town that existed six decades ago. The Vacant Block is no longer vacant. A deserted, automated petrol station was positioned in the centre square and would have made an awkward obstacle in the middle of a cricket pitch come summer.

That is, if there was no chain-link fence preventing access to the land. And if there were children left to play.

The population of the town has dwindled from about 2300 to less than a thousand and the demographic has changed greatly. The changes began when companies and government agencies began "consolidating assets": the modern-world's way of describing a march to the future that requires the abolition of relics from the past. Rightly or wrongly, that period rapidly reeled in the growth of Bruce Rock throughout the 1970s.

Bruce Rock still has its beauties, but they are different beauties to those that existed six decades ago and it might not be obvious as to why the town held such a special place in your grandad's heart. That's because Bruce Rock is not as it once was. The abandoned monolith in the middle of one of the most important sites of your grandad's childhood stands as a reminder of that. A shrine to consolidated assets.

"That block there, we would get a stack of kids there," said Ray Williams, who your grandad first met at school in Bruce Rock and with whom he remained close friends throughout life.

"There was Trevor Riley, Reg Napier – he was Wally's neighbour – the two Baker boys, Wimpy Moroney and there was always a game of footy going on there. We'd have goals set up with tins and what-not. There wasn't a lot of room there and the footy was as round as a basketball, because we were kicking it until it was just about bloody popping.

"Wally, because he was the runt of the pack and a West Perth man, he always thought he was Peter Medhurst, their No.1 rover. Every day after school and every bit of daylight you could get; we'd be out there. It'd be dark-as and you'd still be kicking the ball around."

This was the foundation of your grandad.

Every trait found in him later in life could be found in that town and its people. Bruce Rock of the 1950s resembled a younger, raw version of what your grandad's life would become: a version without the spit-and-polish, but with the same underlying foundations and values. The same work ethic. The same grit and determination.

Bruce Rock was booming. It was a central hub and it was a place of pride for all its residents. Vehicle traffic was frequent, people were bustling to and from the buildings along the main road of Johnson Street, while the neighbourhood's 100-strong children were rarely indoors and were seen playing on all corners of the town.

The world you were born into is vastly different to the one into which your grandad arrived. Television did not arrive in Bruce Rock until the late 1950s, when the transmitter was erected at Mawson and, even then, TV sets were not prolific.

"You'd be battling to find a kid indoors at that period of time," said Bryan Kilminster, another childhood friend of your grandad's. "Out on the farm, we'd always have to do the chooks, or collect firewood, or do something; we never, ever were allowed to be indoors."

Elders Smith had a seven-man workforce and the Co-Op employed about 20 staff, while the post office required a four-person team and two railway gangs worked the train line. Telephones operated only during Exchange Hours and the exchange rivalled the Elders workforce. What is now the Op-Shop on Johnson Street was then the Court House, where your great grandad and Clerk of Courts Eric Foreman worked, just five doors down from the family home.

There was a farming family every 6000 acres, roughly, and every Friday they would converge on the town centre for shopping day, which would then evolve into the adults meeting at the Club and the children either entertaining themselves or taking in a movie at Lonsdale's Durham Hall Theatre for one-and-sixpence a head. One-and-sixpence a head: even currency was different.

The weekends provided the reverse opportunity and your grandad was often an extra pair of hands on the Kilminster property, halfway between Bruce Rock and Merredin. Whether those hands were helping-hands or not was debatable.

"There's two incidents I remember clearly: one weekend, we were out in the paddock and dad used to get me to steer the truck. We called it driving, but it wasn't really, we just steered it around while dad fed the sheep," Kilminster said.

"This one time, dad wanted us to go up the race and do a left-hand turn, because he was trying to tease the sheep up to another paddock. I'm driving up the track and Wally says to me, 'Hey, Bryan, can I drive?' and I say, 'Sure, hop over'. The corner was coming up and I said he better turn the wheel, but he turned it too sharp and the strainer post has gone down.

"The old man went right off his rocker, 'Bryan you blah-blah-blah', but then I piped up and said, 'I wasn't driving dad, it was Wally'. Absolute dead silence and nothing else was ever said.

"The other time was a bit later on, when we were walking through a paddock. We told my brother we'd meet him further along; I think we were trying to trap some rabbits or something. As we walked down towards the gate, my brother – probably 200, 300 metres away – dragged out his .22 (rifle) and thought, 'I'll scare these little bastards', and had a pot at us.

"He had his gun pointed up, thinking it was going to go over the top of us, but it didn't; it landed about 25, 30 metres on Wally's side and zinged passed his head. Wally hit the deck, clutching his head and I looked up, I tell you what; my brother's face went absolutely white. He absolutely shit himself, he thought he'd bloody drilled Wally.

"Wally talked about it on the radio. He wasn't specific, but my brother Les rang me and said, 'Did you hear that? Wally just mentioned that incident'. I said it served him bloody right."

The distance between the bullet and your grandad's head got smaller with every retelling of the story and Bryan's older brother Les – the one who fired the gun – explained the scenario differently.

His recollection involved firing the rifle in the opposite direction to the younger pair, but such was the state of guns in the 1950s that the unharnessed reverberations that followed caused ripples to spread throughout a pool of salt water near Bryan and your grandad, causing both to drop to the ground clutching their heads, thinking the bullet had come their way.

You didn't know your grandad, so let me give you this piece of advice: anyone who did know him would be inclined to enjoy his humorous retelling of the story, while believing Les'.

Back in the town, grand ballroom dances were held in the Community Hall on Saturday nights and were not only a point of pride for Bruce Rock, but were a sight to behold as an entire room would dip in unison. The dances held such pride of place mainly due to neighbouring town Narembeen having in its possession the former Embassy dance floor from Perth.

Sibling rivalry is a powerful force. It meant every layer of kerosene-soaked woodchips and every buffering from the chaff bag of the Bruce Rock floor was performed meticulously to better the big or little brother (depending which town someone was from), Narembeen.

The churches – plural – garnered strong attendances, particularly the Catholic congregations. A highlight of Anglican services was often your Great Grandma Norma playing the organ in just one of the many ways the Foreman family was deeply embedded into the town's life.

And then, of course, there was the pillar of the community and probably its true religion: sport. Not only did it thrive – Bruce Rock itself had two football teams: Towns and Magpies – but it was the glue that bound people together. The Grade 5 teacher, for example, was the doubles-partner of a farmer whose daughter he taught. That sort of relationship served as an example as to why country towns are such tight-knit communities.

The opening of the swimming pool in 1958 even gave rise to water polo competitions and a swimming club; something that might initially sound out of place in the middle of the wheatbelt.

The infectious passion of sport was everywhere and it was

inevitable that it seeped into your grandad from an early age. His school projects became about sport and he collected scrapbooks and autograph books and, of course, listened intently as history was etched in living rooms around the country.

"We had this huge wireless in the lounge room. I can remember vividly listening to the Olympic Games from Melbourne in 1956 ... I can remember listening to the Test matches from England where you could hardly hear what the commentator was saying," your grandad told *The West Magazine* in 2001.

Bruce Rock was alive.

It nurtured your grandad into the sports enthusiast he became, but it also had lessons to teach him about those who lived around him. Everyone had a story and everyone had a role to play.

Let's start with his mum and dad: your great grandma and great grandad.

"Mum and dad were obviously a huge influence in the direction my life took," your grandad said in a 2001 interview with then-ABC broadcaster Liam Bartlett for *WA Story*.

"They were heavily involved in sport in Bruce Rock and in the community, generally, and there is absolutely no doubt that had a bearing."

Your grandad could be dogmatic. Relentless. Take my word for it.

His sisters have their moments, too. Your great grandma and great grandad never stood a chance. They finally succumbed to the urgings of their children and had their life stories penned in 2002 by a lady named Trish Robinson. While the bulk of those stories are best delivered in their own words, their influences began building the personality of their only son: your grandad.

The witty and self-effacing preface of Eric George Foreman's biography might as well have been a preface to your grandad's. They were that similar in personalities.

"Please note: I am no Albert Facey, nor did I have to battle the difficulties which beset that gentleman whose fortitude I admire and whose book I deeply appreciated," your great grandad wrote.

"If you become bored, I will understand. I add a disclaimer that boredom is wholly the responsibility of the said Sandra, Jill and Wally."

The preface was, of course, modest, because from the first page the story of your great grandad is captivating and we are fortunate that you had the opportunity to meet each other. That's right: you never met your grandad, but you met your great grandad. You hadn't turned one-year-old yet, but he was on his way to 99. He never made it to the ton, but the partnership you shared ensured you combined to get over the line.

And he made the most of every one of those years.

He was the third of three sons – the runt of the pack not expected to survive childhood – born to a restaurant keeper and a guesthouse manager, with all three orphaned and separated at a very early age.

Eric Foreman lived with an aunt in North Fremantle and was raised in a strict and regimented Methodist household, with everyone having to earn their keep in financially challenging times. Your grandad was known as a quick thinker well before his time as a journalist or broadcaster and your great grandad was no different as he went through life in the 1920s.

"Pocket money was an unheard of luxury – picture theatres were well and truly a luxury," your great grandad wrote.

"My pride would not allow me to admit that I had not gone to the popular Friday night picture session, so I picked the brains of those who had, then boasted of the incidents that occurred in the film."

Your Great Grandad Eric began life in blue collar society and remained amongst the working class, even when he began climbing the ranks of government employees, beginning with the Harbour Lights Office as a Messenger in 1931 and ending as Chief Electoral Officer upon his retirement in 1980.

In between that almost 50-year service to government was a service to his country as a Wireless Air Gunner in the Royal

Australian Air Force through World War II. It was a time that had him earn the Caterpillar Badge, having survived a parachute escape from his plummeting bomber.

However, it was through Eric Foreman's service to government that he found himself as Clerk to the Inspector of Mines in 1936 Kalgoorlie, where he met a young lady named Norma Lyle Regan, whom he described as "definitely the most gorgeous looking lass" in the town. Norma was not a product of the same blue-collar upbringing Eric was. They were both one of three children, but Norma was a twin alongside her brother Walter James Regan, with whom she had a special relationship that was tragically cut short when he died during the war.

Your grandad was renowned for his nostalgic musical tastes – his passing of that to me is the reason why the first "nursery rhyme" you fell in love with was *Forty Shades of Green*, by Johnny Cash – and if there was a seed planted early in life that gave rise to that love, it was likely planted by his mother and your great grandma, who was also an accomplished national dancer.

Norma was working as a junior clerk for a public accountant when she met Eric and the couple's future son had no chance of escaping a life in sport. The courtship began through Eric convincing Norma to join the badminton and tennis clubs so that he could spend more time with her. They officially became your great grandparents when they were married nine years later, just 13 days after Eric returned from the war on 18 October 1945.

Any luxuries the Foremans had in later life were earned through an unflappable and determined work ethic from your great grandad and an equally determined resilience and love from your great grandma. There was no car to speak of and the couple was living with Norma's family in the early stages after marriage. Their consolation of at least being together after four-and-a-half years of war was short-lived, as your great grandad was transferred to Wiluna for three month's relief work with the Crown Law Department.

There was no accommodation provided, meaning the couple was again apart.

"I reminded (my boss) that I was due to be demobilised early in January, I was newly married and had not experienced a Christmas at home for four years," Eric said of the time. "The Department was sympathetic and offered to grant me leave and to fly me home for Christmas."

Your Great Grandad Eric was working in Boulder, cycling the 6.5km to Kalgoorlie every day from the first family home at 67 Ward Street, Lamington, when the couple's first child, Walter John Foreman, arrived in 1948 – "We rode our bikes for transport, with a baby seat attached when Wally was old enough to use it," recalled Great Grandma Norma.

But even that year had its challenges.

"The year 1948 had its pleasant surprises and sadness," Eric said.

"Our son, Walter John, was born on 5 January 1948. What a lusty bundle of charm he was – he could yell as loudly as any of them, as we were to discover, due mainly to a difference of opinion between our doctor and clinic sister regarding feeding formula.

"Later in the year – 9 November – Norma's father (Jack Regan) passed away at the age of 58 years. We named Wally after Norma's twin brother, who was reported missing, presumed lost, off Bundaberg, Queensland. Norma's mother never quite got over this tragedy, so Norma and I with Wally decided to move back to her house at 9 Brockman Street, Kalgoorlie, for company."

The family was split again two years later when Eric was transferred and promoted to Clerk of Courts of Bruce Rock and, again, accommodation was not provided, meaning your Great Grandma Norma, five-months pregnant at the time, was forced to remain in Kalgoorlie until Eric found a house. In November 1950, your great grandma loaded your two-year-old grandad and your newborn Great Aunt Sandy into the family's first car – a second-hand Hillman 10 – and drove the 380km to Bruce Rock.

The family was finally reunited and would not be separated through life again.

Family is important, Charlotte, always remember that.

If you're fortunate to be born into a loving one – which you were – they will never leave your side. And family was among the highest of priorities for your grandad in his later life. His work and his passion for that work was also of great importance to him and the two would occasionally conflict as he, like all of us, tried to find that elusive idyll of work-life balance.

However, there were particular moments of the week, month and year that the balance was unequivocal: Christmas Day was always a family day and work was not permitted to interfere; Boxing Day was a similarly celebration, but with friends, and the barbecue at the Foreman house in Duncraig was rarely missed; the Easter holiday period was always a 10-day family holiday to Canal Rocks Beach Resort and, later, Coral Bay; every Friday was dinner with your nana for the "weekly download"; every Sunday was family dinner at Zeno's Café at Hillarys Boat Harbor.

When written down like that, it seems unfathomable that your grandad dedicated the amount of time he did to work. But he did.

Those first years of your great grandparents' marriage and the early stages of your grandad's life would seem far from ideal for any young family, but it was the heartbreak of being constantly together-then-apart and the decision to leave the independence of the first family home after such a short time to support your great grandma's grieving mother that impressed on your grandad the importance of family.

Those days – particularly the proceeding decade in Bruce Rock – also instilled in him the work ethic of his dad and gave him a living example that strong family ties and the pursuit of a career would not always be easy to manage, but they could coexist. Your Great Grandad Eric was living proof of that.

When one worked in 1950 regional Western Australia as a Clerk of Courts, one was not simply a Clerk of Courts. Your great grandad was Clerk of Courts, District Registrar and the official representative for eight other government departments, as well as being handed the title of Manager of the Commonwealth Savings Bank, despite knowing "absolutely nothing of bank procedures".

He was involved with the Church, secretary of the Bruce Rock Agricultural Society, secretary – followed by president – of the Bruce Rock Tennis Club and was foundation secretary of the Freemason Nunagin Lodge.

Your Great Grandma Norma was only slightly less involved, being active in the Hospital Auxiliary, Red Cross, playing as the church organist and on the P&C Committee.

Kay Djukic (nee Anderson), a school friend and classmate of your grandad's, described the Bruce Rock community as having an ability to "absorb" newcomers, as if they were a vital part of the town's existence. It was a community that fostered engagement and made for a happy, healthy and engrossing life – a feeling that was not confined to the Foremans and was probably best described by Robert Kilminster in the book, *Bruce Rock: A Century of Memories*.

"The enjoyment comes from the recall of a childhood that was in so many ways wonderful – the freedom we had, the safety of family, the variety of experience and the wide open spaces," Kilminster wrote.

"The tears for a way of life that has gone forever."

That feeling of belonging was not lost on your grandad.

"He had a pretty good life up there and he enjoyed everything that came his way," your Great Grandad Eric said. "I think Bruce Rock had an influence on Wally, in particular, and Sandra. He enjoyed school, was a reasonably top scholar and he was quite popular. It was a pretty fair and easy life, to be honest."

Good teachers make for good students.

For your grandad, that good teacher was a man who finished national service and a posting in Collie and on the last weekend of March 1958 left behind an All Australian baseball career to make the "eight-hour trip" in a ring-pull Renault to arrive in Bruce Rock as teacher of the 52-student fifth grade class.

His name was Colin Smith and he was never forgotten by your grandad.

"I've always felt that the accessibility of sporting facilities and sports clubs and programs was very important in the direction my life took, but there were other influences," your grandad said in his 2001 interview with Liam Bartlett.

"I happened to have a school teacher in around about Grade 5 in Bruce Rock, his named was Colin Smith and I haven't seen him for 40 years. He was a former state baseballer and was heavily involved in sport in the town and he really encouraged me.

"We used to have a general knowledge quiz at the end of class each Friday and it used to deteriorate into a sports quiz between the teacher and Wally and I often look back now and wonder what the rest of the class actually thought. I'll never forget it."

It was a moment in his life that had such an impact on your grandad that he later replicated the quizzes with his second son – your uncle – Mark over our family dinners at Zeno's Café. Your Uncle Mark inherited your grandad's passion for sport and had a remarkable ability to memorise statistics and facts. The two would go toe-to-toe, with neither gaining the upper-hand at any stage.

The train rocked side to side. A few passengers glanced in our direction, probably equal parts impressed and confused.

Impressed, because your Uncle Mark, just six-years-old, was rattling off answers to maths questions his 14-year-old brother – me – was firing at him. Confused, because we were speaking English.

It was a family holiday to Europe that was currently swaying its way through Paris.

"Twelve times three," I said.

"Thirty-six."

I looked to your nana. I needed guidance: I might have been eight years older, but I had no idea about maths and was being easily shown-up by a kid in the second grade. It is one of my favourite memories. It happened because of your grandad.

Those family quizzes were a little piece of 1950s Bruce Rock that your grandad dragged us into. It was no different to the way he and Colin Smith forged a special bond through their mutual love of sport and often dragged the class along for the ride.

"At school, the teacher used to love getting him up in front of the class to talk sport," Kay Djukic, a classmate of your grandad's said.

"If there had been a cricket match on, he would be able to tell you exactly what happened: he was a born natural. It'd be ball-for-ball, dropping names. I remember Sandy (your great aunty) saying he would sit there for hours on end listening to the cricket. Everyone knew that sport would be his end-goal, even as kids. It was in his blood.

"He was cheeky, though, and he got away with hell. I remember one particular time when our parents were playing tennis: we were hiding from the boys in dad's car and Wally and Bryan Kilminster mixed up this bucket of mud – and I mean mud – and tipped it through the driver's side window all over the seat. We were in the back seat, I got up and thought, 'We're going to get killed'. I was yelling that I was going to tell on them and they said, 'If you do, we'll get you at school on Monday'.

"Mum asked how it happened and I said we were just playing and the bucket got caught on the window when I was running past. She said, 'When you get home, you've got your father to deal with', and I copped it from dad and got a hell of a belting that night. They were cloth seats, too.

"So, on Monday for show-and-tell, they asked what everyone had to tell and I thought they were going to get me afterwards anyway, so I stood up and said, 'Wally Foreman and Bryan Kilminster put mud in my parents' car while they were at tennis'. They got called up to the front of the class and asked why they did it and they just said it was an accident.

"They took one look at Wally and he got sent back to his seat. I don't know what it was about him, but he never got in trouble for anything."

Your grandad might not have seen Colin Smith for 40 years, but he had spoken to him. Once – about 18 months before the interview with Liam Bartlett in 2001. It was a time when your grandad had become weary to the point of exhaustion with continuous and unrelenting battles at the WA Institute of Sport.

In moments of stress, it's easy to get caught up in the thoughts of simpler times. Undoubtedly, a pang of nostalgia for his Bruce Rock days led him to pick up the phone and dial the number of one of the people who had forever set him on the path he found himself on at the time.

There's an eerily ironic twist to the tale, too.

I needed to find Colin to interview for this book, but, as you can imagine, with no-one having any idea where he was or how to get in touch with him, calling every "Smith" in the phonebook was not really an option. I asked two of your grandad's colleagues from his time at the ABC – the late Eoin Cameron and Geoff Hutchison – if they could help me locate Colin by announcing it on their highly-rating radio shows. They kindly did and within 24 hours we had found him.

He could have been anywhere in the state. Anywhere in the world. Instead, he was living a few streets away from us in the same suburb. And he remembered your grandad very well.

"It was the middle of the day and I had my wife, my daughter and Nick (son-in-law and professional golfer Nick O'Hern) sitting there when the phone rang," Smith recalled of the moment your grandad reached out to his childhood teacher.

"My daughter came back and said, 'Dad it's for you', I asked who it was and she said, 'He just said you'd know him'. I picked up the phone and he said, 'Colin, it's Wally Foreman', and we talked for two hours. Just talked and talked. We were both nostalgic. We both loved Bruce Rock and each other's company: he was always ready to laugh and he was very quick.

"Any teacher would love to have that sort of person in their class. When Wally called, it was like he'd just walked around the corner and said, 'Hi, Mr Smith', all over again. As a teacher, you remember certain students and Wally was one of those."

The large cohort of Mr Smith's class was comprised of children from all over the region, from Ardath, Belka and Korbel to Muntadgin and halfway to Narembeen.

The class had its typical characters: the standout students, the avid sports followers, those who weren't interested in sport at all and, of course, the disruptive members, one of whom was a good friend of your grandad's. But your grandad's loyalty for his mate never waned, despite warnings that he was not the ideal character to spend time with.

"Let's be honest about it, he never gave us any problems," your Great Grandad Eric recalled of your grandad.

"He threw stones on people's rooves and things like that and we'd read the riot act to him and would say, 'How would you like it if people ganged up and bombed our place?', and more-or-less made an example of it. I can remember one incident when they stoned the house of a little old lady. Well, she wasn't a little old lady, she was actually quite a hefty lady, but she was a most inoffensive type of lady.

"Whether it was stones on the roof, or they belted the cat or something, I don't remember, but I do remember I said to Wally, 'Son, there's only one thing you can do to sort this out: go and see the lady, tell her you didn't mean to do any damage and that you won't do any damage again'. In other words, apologise. Well, he did it. That's the thing that counted in my view. He was man enough to admit it.

"I think there's something inside a boy and a man that pulls him up at the last moment. If he listens to that voice, or that instinct, there's nothing wrong with him. If he doesn't listen to it, he's going to go off the straight and narrow."

The antics of your grandad and his classmates were typical of most childhood pranks, but as mentioned, family was important to your grandad and it was the cause of probably his closest encounter with anything that could be labelled trouble. It occurred around your Great Aunty Sandy when a school bully learnt a simple lesson: sibling rivalry was quickly discarded if anyone made the mistake of messing with a Foreman.

"I remember one day, outside the school yard someone was picking on Sandy and Sandy was crying and Wally stormed over there," Djukic said. "I don't know what he said to him, but he came back and said, 'I fixed him'. As little as he was, he was never frightened of anybody."

Confrontation rarely frightened your grandad – you'll learn that through later chapters in his life – and, while always walking the line of parental guidance, that high value on family was a point of pride to Great Grandad Eric.

"They got along really fine; Wally was the protector," Eric said. "I know that, at times, Sandra in particular would take her troubles to Wally, which is a good thing. If she didn't get the satisfaction with Wal, she'd come to me or her mother.

"Wally was a guardian angel to Sandra, particularly at school. I know that for a fact, because I remember one of the mothers telling me Wally had threatened their child. The kid had a few words with Sandra and called her a few nasty names and Wally said he would bash the living daylights out of them."

As for the pranks, they were not confined to little old ladies. Colin Smith was on the receiving end of them as often as he was invited to the Foreman dinner table for an evening meal. That might sound confusing, given the education environment your generation (and mine) would have grown up in. But, like everything, times have changed.

The friendship between Smith and your grandad was likely struck in the way it was due to the limited generation gap. Smith was just 19 when he was posted to Bruce Rock, with less than a decade's age difference between himself, your grandad and the other children in that class.

"One day, they set me up," Smith said. "I used to have this beautiful, big wooden swivel chair that my mother gave me and I took it everywhere I went.

"It was in underneath the school desk and I remember looking at it and thinking, 'That's a bit weird, because I didn't leave it like that'. I pulled it out and there was a snake curled up on the seat. It scared the living daylights out of me. The school bus had run over it and they set it up on there. I never found out who it was, but I have a feeling Wally had something to do with it."

The thing about sportspeople, though, is their abilities are rarely confined to the sporting arena and that applied to the baseballer in Smith.

"That didn't help when we misbehaved in class," recalled your grandad's football friend from The Vacant Block, Trevor Riley, who is now Chief Justice of the Northern Territory.

"He would be able to grab the piece of chalk and ping you off at the back of the room with no trouble at all. He was a good teacher. You remember some and you don't remember others, but he's one we all remember."

Some lessons are not covered by a syllabus. Acceptance is one of them. Acceptance of differences. Acceptance of people.

The impact of war is endless: it infects every aspect of life and in the 1950s, it altered the fabric of even the most remote country towns. That class of 52 students in Bruce Rock offered more than good humour and education; it offered a lesson on the diversity of post-war Australia and regional Western Australia.

Of all the people interviewed for this chapter of your grandad's life, none said racism was an issue – at least, not among the children – and most labelled the acceptance of and by their peers among their favourite memories. That is not to say that everyone got on well and Bruce Rock was a mecca of peace.

It would be disrespectful to the challenges faced by many, particularly the Aboriginal people of the time, to suggest otherwise. Bruce Rock was governed by the same laws as the country in which it resided and under the Aborigines Act 1905, racial segregation was widespread. Indigenous people were not permitted to live in the town centre, they were placed under a 6pm curfew and were forced to live on reservations (parcels of Crown Land set aside for Aborigines).

There were, of course, those who pushed back against the currents of fear and hate and Bruce Rock benefitted from their courage. It was written in *Bruce Rock: A Century of Memories* that the 6pm curfew, for example, was banned in the town around the 1940s as a result of Rosie Mabel Gidgup – with help from Justice of the Peace Stan Farrall – standing up to a police officer who attempted to enforce the law.

The thing about racism and prejudice, though, is that it's taught. When a child is born into the world, they have no perception of skin colour or ethnic background, no preconceived ideas on how to react to those issues. That perception and any attitudes towards it is taught to that child throughout its life.

So, with the clean slate of childhood, equality reigned with Bruce Rock's children. Those who disagreed, argued or fought, did so because of an objection to a person, not the person's race or colour. Proud indigenous families called the town home and several were among the circle of your grandad's friends, particularly the family of James Richard "Jimmy" Gidgup – a talented footballer.

"We first knew each other as kids in Bruce Rock," your grandad said in his eulogy for Jimmy in 2004. "Our families were friends, initially through dad's work as the Clerk of Courts.

"The Gidgups were a well-respected family in the town and my dad (Eric Foreman) was recalling earlier this week how he depended on them for Aboriginal matters. In a town as small as ours, kids of all ages, shapes and sizes played together after school. One of my lasting memories of those days is that everybody wanted to be in Jim's team, because if you were in Jim's team, you were almost certain to be in the winning team.

"I saw him play very little senior football, but one game I did see him play was his very first League game. I was a devout West Perth supporter and my boyhood idol was Mel Whinnen. Jim decided to play for South Fremantle ... but his first game was against West Perth and he played on Mel Whinnen. I went to that game with divided loyalties and I was even more confused when I left.

"Jim played probably the game of his life, given the opposition. South Fremantle won and, if my memory serves me correctly, Jim got Sandover Medal votes. He certainly beat Mel that day and I remember dad making the almost blasphemous comment on the way home to the effect that if Jimmy was going to stay in Perth, we might actually have to follow Souths."

The effects of war diversified the population of Western Australia and, while World War II might have been fought on fields a world away, its far-reaching impact was a reminder of just how small that world could be at times. Even Bruce Rock and the wheatbelt played a role in the aftermath. The Northam Army Camp was converted to the Northam Accommodation Centre, which received refugees and "displaced people" from mostly Warsaw Pact nations, which had found themselves occupied by the Red Army, despite not officially being recognised as members of the Soviet Union.

The Northam camp would assess the skills of the migrants and disperse them throughout the state as required for work. Some faced the disheartening reality that their qualifications were not recognised in Australia and had to accept what work they could. The result for your grandad was a class rollcall that contained as many complex surnames of Ks, Js and Zs as it did the typical "Williams", "Wood" and "Gibson".

"The thing with those refugees, or whatever you want to call them, was that they suffered something that most West Australians at that point had never suffered and that was starvation," your grandad's friend Bryan Kilminster said.

"We've never, ever suffered – except for the 29, 32 depression – what those people suffered, particularly during the war. They saw Australia as a place of plenty: they'd seen Australian soldiers as fit, lean and healthy. We'd never had a war in our country, we had a democracy where you could say what you like and wouldn't have to worry about being put up against a wall and shot.

"Most of those farms out east of Merredin were settled by Italian people who were given their four, five thousand acre blocks, an axe and away they went."

It was an important time for your grandad to live through.

He always accepted people for who they were, not where they came from or how much power they held. Spending a decade of his most formative years in the environment of post-war Bruce Rock helped guide his moral compass and beliefs later in life, first as a journalist and then as the man on the frontline in defence of Western Australia's athletes, who were often the victim of national injustice and perceived prejudice.

The inclusive nature of Bruce Rock made that acceptance possible and there was no doubting the role that sport played in achieving that.

"You grew up with the mentality that you played sport with each other, regardless of what colour they were or where they were from," Ray Williams said.

"You were like brothers."

One sport sat above all others for your grandad.

Sport was aplenty in Bruce Rock and that was largely due to the work of individuals who brought their passions to the town. Colin Smith, for example, introduced basketball. None, however, held a candle to the devotion your grandad carried for tennis and he later injected that love through the airwaves in calls of Davis Cups and Australian Opens alike.

Tennis had already existed in Bruce Rock when the Foremans arrived, but the belief was that it was not for young people – or, at least, that there was no need to entice younger people to play it. The damage that belief was inflicting on tennis in the region was significant. Membership numbers were falling with each retiree and a refusal to invest in the next generation meant they were not being replenished.

That was until renowned state representatives, passionate coaches and – later in life – effective administrators Alan and Mary Hicks arrived in town in 1956 in their cream-coloured VW Beetle, reacquainting themselves with their friends from Kalgoorlie, your great grandparents Eric and Norma Foreman.

"The first person to knock on our door was Norma, with one of her sponge cakes," Mary said. "The Foremans were the making of us enjoying our lives in Bruce Rock. She was the friend to everyone in town – the teachers, or anyone new – and she always had people around for meals."

Alan added: "They were models to be followed in Bruce Rock. Everyone loved the Foremans."

That sentiment peaked in the nine months leading up to 22 March 1959, when talk of a pregnant Norma Foreman spread around the town like wildfire with the excitement of the impending arrival of another Foreman. Your Great Aunty Jill later took great pride in reminding everyone at your grandad's memorial "that I was the only one to be born there (in Bruce Rock), despite all Wally's claims to be a Bruce Rock boy".

"That was big news," Mary Hicks said. "Something like that, when Norma Foreman is pregnant and there's another Foreman on the way, that's big news. I was a bit annoyed, because she had to pull out of badminton."

Badminton might have been on the decline, but Mary and Alan Hicks ensured tennis was not and the pair had a simple philosophy when it came to the sport they loved: share the passion with anyone who wanted to embrace it, regardless of age.

"The club was going down and down, the committee was getting older and older, because there were no new players coming through," Mary said.

"So, we suggested that maybe we should start a juniors program. There was one man who was very against it, because we did it on a Sunday morning when he thought the kids should be going to church. Quite a lot of kids used to turn up – 40 to 60 at least – and the parents got excited and it flourished again."

There was a long-running joke regarding the early days of the Western Australian Institute of Sport that the one-and-a-half members on staff did not refer to the part-time secretary, but instead referred to the short stature of the full-time director, your grandad. As with any good joke, the humour laid in the truth of it.

Your grandad was never tall or well-built for his age, especially as a young country boy. That limitation as an eight-year-old in Bruce Rock meant that, despite his abundance of enthusiasm, he was not immediately able to join the Hicks' burgeoning tennis clinic for juniors.

"He was so small, you couldn't really tell his age," Mary said.

There are some people in this world who are so determined to achieve a goal that nothing can get in their way. Many people would probably label your grandad as president of that club. And when it came to joining the Hicks' tennis program, your grandad held a pair of aces up his sleeve: the Foreman family was gatekeeper of the tennis club key and few people in the world were as dogmatic and stubborn as your grandad.

"All through my life, there were a series of people (who steered me down the path I took)," your grandad later said in an interview.

"Alan started a coaching clinic on Saturday mornings for the Police and Citizens Youth Club, of which I was not a member, but we had the key to the tennis club at our house. I knew what time Alan would be coming – or, 'Mr Hicks', as he was then – to pick up the key. I used to stand in the drive and hit the ball against the kitchen wall so that he had to walk through my rally to get the key.

"After about four weeks of that, he eventually gave in and said, 'Why don't you come down and join the squad'."

It was a moment Alan remembered well.

"One day, it was towards the end of the season, it just came out and I said, 'Wal, how about you come along to tennis next week? Next year, you'll be old enough to be in the class'," Alan said. "His eyes lit up and the following week he was down there before anyone else. Everybody loved him."

Tennis underwent a revolution under Alan and Mary.

The old weatherboard and iron clubhouse with eight bitumen courts at the east side of the building was replaced by a new brick building, with an asbestos cantilever roof that extended to provide a social area. Lights were erected on the exhibition courts, which were resurfaced with WalkTop and re-fenced, giving Bruce Rock some of the best facilities for the sport in the region.

Alan and Mary also secured the first State Hardcourt Championships for the town to replace the annual Easter Tennis Tournament, which, as another of your grandad's childhood friends Phil Perry recalled "attracted some of the state's tennis celebrities, most of whom were billeted out with the locals". Bruce Rock embraced the occasion, with banners hoisted along Johnson Street to welcome visitors. Alan Hicks would remarkably make two trips a day down to Perth – a total of about 1000km – to ferry the city-based players up to the event.

"There were hundreds of kids from all round the eastern wheatbelt coming to their clinics," your grandad recounted of the time. "They did so much for tennis, but those little things throughout my life did so much for me."

And it was amidst this fervour that an echo of the future came to your grandad.

"The kids made the most of the facilities and continued to play tennis after the adults had finished," Phil Perry said. "Wally Foreman, more often than the rest of us, used to mount the umpire's chair and give running commentary of the play as he saw it".

Work swept the Foremans into Bruce Rock, carrying their energy on the winds of an easterly from Kalgoorlie. A decade later, it again picked up the then-family-of-five and continued their journey west.

Your Great Grandad Eric had been appointed as Registrar of Trade Associations in a contentious and peculiar promotion: it was a position he had neither sought, nor applied for. And it was non-appealable. However, 50 years on and despite three passengers of that car ride having passed away, the Foremans' bonds to Bruce Rock have continued.

"I had the honour of meeting Wally personally, along with his father Eric, in Bruce Rock for the official opening of our refurbished swimming pool (in 2002)," long-serving Shire President Stephen Strange said.

"When Wally introduced me to Eric, I said, 'It is a pleasure to meet you Mr Foreman'. His quick-as-a-flash reply was, 'We have met before'. I said I didn't think we had, but he told me to go home and check my birth certificate.

"When Karen I got home that evening, we retrieved the certificate and there it was: Eric's signature as Clerk of Courts all those years ago."

The memories that tie your grandad and the family to Bruce Rock are the kind that grow stronger and more frequent with time. Life does not begin with reminiscing. That comes later. Your grandad was no exception to that rule.

His friend Ray Williams could almost pinpoint the moment nostalgia took a firm hold within your grandad: when the group lost Jimmy Gidgup in 2004. The memories were already leaking out of your grandad, but that moment – losing one of the gang – acted like a floodgate to the thoughts of friends, fun and farms, the peace and quiet of country life that contrasted the hectic existence he was living and the safety of certainty that only the past can offer.

Your grandad was working with ABC Radio at the time and the on-air recollection of stories became more prevalent and the pull of Bruce Rock – or the past – became stronger. He even made the trip up to the town on a whim but found only empty houses, as his spur of the moment decision did not involve enquiring whether anyone would be around to receive him and using a mobile phone to check was out of the question.

Williams that evening returned to his house on the Merredin-Bruce Rock Road to find piping crudely arranged on the gravel near the back door. The makeshift note read: "Wally was here".

"You know, sometimes I think people know when they're going to die," Williams said. "I don't know what it is.

"Another friend of mine called me up and was asking me all these things about cricket and I said, 'You alright, Bob?', and he said, 'Nah, I'm not really. I'm just putting a few memoirs together'.

"About a month later, he died."

The Windsor Hotel. South Perth, 2 October 2004.
What a night.

It was the 50-year anniversary of that special group of Bruce Rock Primary School's Infants Class of 1954 and they gathered in a defiant stand against time, which had gradually dragged their lives apart and to all corners of the country. Class members Kay Djukic, Patti Lock, Bryan Kilminster and your grandad had met in a coffee shop months before and begun the unenviable task of tracking down members of the class. It often involved the arduous process of trial and error; dialling every number under a surname in the phone book.

The efforts resulted in a memorable night arranged to reconnect a memorable class and, as such, the invitation read: "Since this reunion will involve a great deal of reacquainting, story-telling and reminiscing, it has been agreed by the convenors to exclude partners/spouses in this instance". The majority of the class turned up, including its Grade 5 teacher, Colin Smith.

That reunion was an important moment for your grandad and I wish I understood it the way I do now. He needed to be dropped off – of course, as well as a "great deal of reacquainting", the invitations neglected to mention the great deal of red wine that would also be involved – and asked me for a lift. I complained, but I eventually obliged.

I don't remember many details of the car ride, except that he argued that I was being unsafe when I did 70km/h through an intersection that was marked 70km/h – your grandad was the world's worst backseat driver. But I do remember how excited your grandad was as he told me about his expectations for the night and some of the stories behind the characters who would be there. Hindsight and life experience can only be gained with time, but, again, I wish I understood the context for him of that night. It would have meant the world to him if I'd shown interest.

The group was not able to return to a past they all felt so strongly for, but, for a night, it was like they could drag the past to them. And your grandad was going to make sure the people he felt needed to be there, were there.

"I wasn't travelling well financially," Ray Williams said.

"I don't know, Kay must have told Wally I wasn't going. Wally called me up and said, 'I'll pay your accommodation and everything' and I said, 'No, you won't be doing that, Wal, but if you want me there that badly I'll come down and leave at midnight and drive home'.

"Wal said there was one other thing: I had to bring Wimpy (Lindsay Moroney) with me, which I did."

In Colin Smith's case, not even a battle with a heart condition could keep him away.

"The reunion was one of the happiest times I've ever had, mostly because everyone seemed happy to see me," Smith said.

"I was the only teacher they invited and I'm sure Wally had something to do with that, because he'd been trying to find me, but he said he asked all the students and the only one they wanted was me. That's wonderful if it's true, but I don't know.

"I was still pretty crook at that stage, too, and my wife didn't want me to go, but I said, 'Jan, I don't care if I have to catch an ambulance, I'm going'. There was something in the class and Wally was a class leader."

"What was it about you and dad?," I had asked Smith during the interview. I mean, the age gap wasn't significant, but the teacher was still 19 to your grandad's 11 when they met. That is a significant difference at that age.

"I've looked back on it and I've often thought of Wally," Smith replied. "I've had the same conversation with my wife when she asks, 'Why did you and Wally get on so well?' I honestly don't know. I walked into that class in 1958 and Wally went, 'That's my teacher'."

Like most good nights, the 2004 reunion extended well beyond the night.

But this is a biography of a man who has passed away and those joyous memories now carry with them a pang of sadness upon the realisation that they cannot be relived. The Infants Class of 1954 was far greater than your grandad and he himself would quickly denounce any suggestions otherwise. However, as this chapter began, Bruce Rock and Wally Foreman are synonymous and when the latter was lost two years after that reunion, he took a piece of the former with him.

"Wally and I were actually trying to get another reunion going for 2008 to commemorate the year of our 60th birthdays," Kay Djukic said.

"He had his heart attack on the Tuesday, I'd spoken to him the day before and we were going to meet on Wednesday afternoon for coffee and see if we could get some things together. I got a phone call from Bo (Ray Williams) on the Tuesday afternoon and he said, 'How are you?' and I said, 'Good, how are you?' and he said, 'You haven't heard, have you?'

"I couldn't believe it; even now, it makes me shiver. Everyone kept saying, 'When are you getting the reunion together for our 60th?', and I just said I couldn't do it. I was going to do it with Wally and I just couldn't go through with it. I was only up in Bruce Rock a month ago and Bryan and Bo asked me if I was going to organise another one, but I don't know.

"Wally was such a big part of our lives and he wouldn't be there. Dianne Kilminster has gone and Lindsay Moroney, too. There might come a day when we do it, but I just can't."

Now, Bryan Kilminster has gone, as well. He passed away in 2015. I was fortunate that I got to spend time with him before he passed away, having interviewed him for this book. It meant I could pass on a gift to his family that we had in such abundance with your grandad: the audio recording, so that they will forever have his voice. You met him, too, as I mentioned at in the introduction to this book, and there is a beautiful photo of he and Ray Williams holding you in the Bruce Rock Club bar, undoubtedly with their close mate – your grandad – smiling down upon them.

There was a reason your grandad was so driven to see the 2004 reunion come to fruition and perhaps it was the same urge that drove others seeking a follow-up: time keeps moving forward and the longer it goes, the more it leaves in its wake and the more it can take from us.

"You just wish you had more time," Ray Williams said. "We always have time to go to somebody's funeral, or to see them when they're sick."

Kilminster added: "We stood a little bit taller when we said we were Wally's mates."

He paused.

"Why wouldn't we be proud?"

Chapter 2

Family and Friends Matter

IT WAS HIDEOUS. WHO IN their right mind would have ever considered attractive a garage door painted in three horizontal panels of black, purple and turquoise?

It was late January 1960 and a car jammed with people and belongings pulled up to No. 67 Nanson Street, Wembley, and it did not take long for a voice, as opinionated as it was small, to take issue with the move from Bruce Rock: "I'm *not* going to live in *that* house".

It was your grandad. He loved the country and, therefore, hated the city. Well, at first – and was determined to let the rest of the family know it. Your great grandparents had earlier left the three children in Bruce Rock for a couple of days as they identified Floreat Park as their desired location and found the nearby rental property in Wembley to put a roof over the family while construction was underway.

The Nanson Street property was a typical post-war era house of brick and tile construction, leadlight doors and windows, a small front porch and a lock-up garage with double timber doors.

"Wal took one look at the ghastly garage door and flatly refused to get out of the car," your Great Aunty Sandy recalled.

"Wally didn't even bother to look at the rest of the house. I assume, now that I'm older and wiser, the performance he gave was more to express his great disappointment at having to leave his friends in Bruce Rock and his nervousness at starting at a new school. I know I was terrified at the prospect."

Your great aunty and grandad were not alone in their feelings for the move.

"Wally liked the country far more than the city, but so did I. We were 'like father, like son' there," your Great Grandad Eric said. "I don't think Norma wanted to come down, either, but when she saw it was my promotion, a brand new job and I was going to jump three or four grades – which would have taken five or so years for a grade like that – she could see, financially, we were far better off."

The tantrum ran its course and the Foremans soon settled into an area that would become pivotal for your grandad. Despite his early reservations, he was now based in the same area as several people who would remain close friends and prove important throughout his career and for the rest of his life.

The area also had echoes of Bruce Rock. Kathleen Perkins, a close friend of your great grandparents from the country town, moved two streets away a year after the family's arrival, while Bruce Rock's former doctor Keith Stewart and his wife Nan were close by in City Beach. There was a back-lane that acted as a thoroughfare for the neighbourhood's children, rekindling the memories of the games on the Vacant Block and a shopping precinct was a short walk down the road.

It was Nan Stewart who later that year sat beside your Great Grandma Norma on a then-undeveloped plot of land on the corner of Thurles Avenue and The Boulevard for the sale of several blocks. Somewhere in between the animated and ongoing discussion from the pair of renowned talkers and the auctioneer asking your great grandma, "Madam, is that hand raised as a bid, or is it part of your conversation?", the Foremans secured the title for No.3 Glenties Road, Floreat.

Your great grandad used to call it "Gentiles Road" and it became the family's home until the children began following their own paths in life. You've probably heard by now the many labels people will use to describe your dad – me – and undoubtedly somewhere near the top of the list will be, "cheap". I prefer "thrifty". Either way, I got the trait from your grandad, who got it from your great grandad.

The Glenties Road house was a good example: your great grandparents received the clothes hoist and letterbox for free, having permitted the builder to use the property as a display home for certain periods.

See: thrifty.

"Smart alec".

They were the words your grandad used to describe himself, scribbled on an A4 piece of paper that he used for a speech. But the Bruce Rock prankster was about to meet his match. Your grandad was enrolled for his final year of junior school at Wembley Primary, walking the short distance to Grantham Street with little sister Sandy in tow, and it was there that he first came across an infectiously rebellious George Young.

Young was a special talent in a lot of ways, both as an athlete and as a person. He went on to become a skilled footballer for St Kilda in the Victorian Football League and an inductee to the Western Australian Football Hall of Fame, but he also became one of the closest and most loyal friends your grandad would ever have. He has since been a close friend of all the Foremans.

Young was one year younger than your grandad but, as it had done in the country, sport built bridges for friendships across all ages and the pair got to know each other through school football and cricket. The families became close and the duo became inseparable, considering each other closer to brothers than friends.

The one-year age difference placed an early fork in the path of the friendship, with your grandad moving on to Perth Modern School and missing by one year the opening of what would become the area's catchment school, Churchlands Senior High School, which drafted in Young. However, the pair had linked up through the Subiaco Cricket Club outside school and became even closer one day in 1961.

"Wally and I shared in a 100-run partnership in the Under 14s Grand Final in 1961 on Subiaco Oval, when they had a turf wicket there," Young recalled.

"Wal would have been 13, I was 12 and that partnership won us the grand final. We were playing a team called the Subiaco Police Boys, who were a lot bigger, a lot stronger and a lot more aggressive than what we were. Wal actually went to school with a few of them, because they all lived in that Shenton Park area and went to Perth Modern School.

"There was a lot of rivalry there, because Wally had started his cricket with Subi and had stayed with our club, which made him the odd one out and playing against his mates from school. There was quite a bit of banter.

"I remember we both made our 50s within an over of each other and our coach called us in and we had to retire, because we needed to give the other guys a bat. One thing I do remember as well is, as we walked off, our coach was there waiting for us with a small bottle of Coca-Cola as a reward.

"That was the first time we had a partnership and I suppose you could say we then had a partnership for life."

Would it be any surprise if I told you that weekend sport became an institution for the Foreman family?

Your grandad joined the Wembley Football Club, the Floreat Park Cricket Club – and, later, the Subiaco Cricket Club – and the Reabold Tennis Club. Your great grandparents spent the days taxiing their children from one sport and venue to another, while always getting involved in whatever way they could, be it the official roles of umpiring or scoring, or simply fetching the balls or handing out drinks.

"He was a very keen cricketer: he wouldn't have missed it for quids and we always enjoyed going to watch him play," your Great Grandad Eric said.

"His character was very good. He occasionally got a bit sour when he was given out, but he didn't think he was. I got him out of that habit very early in the piece by saying, 'Look, one of these days, you might be an umpire and you put yourself in that bloke's position. He's the one that counts, not you'.

"He'd have a bit to say on the field, though. I don't think Wally was ever short of a word."

The religion of sport was well balanced by the religion of faith and your great grandad ensured Sundays always began at St Nicholas Anglican Church in Floreat. It was a poignant location: it later became the place where your nana and grandad got married.

The Foreman household was also strict on etiquette and table-manners and that never changed for your grandad, who brought the same expectations when he and your nana had their own family: your Uncle Mark and me. Why is that worth noting?

The Sunday roast was a tradition of your great grandparents, but during the winter months, somehow that etiquette was permitted to bend and the meal was eaten in front of the television while watching Channel 7's *World of Football*. Such was the power of sport to the Foremans. I can recall countless times being scolded by your grandad as I attempted to juggle a plate of dinner while fumbling in a rush for the remote control, ultimately failing to switch off the TV in a vain attempt to pretend I hadn't been watching it before he walked in the door from work. The two exceptions when I was growing up for having the TV on while eating were sport and the news. At the time, I had no interest in either.

So, it is only worth noting because, all these years later, I write these sentences with a wry smile of understanding.

Your grandad's passion might have been sport, but his love was for his family and friends. The move to the city allowed the extended Foreman family to reconnect and a tradition began that Christmas as your great grandad's brother Ernie, his wife Iris and their children John and Romney came together.

The tradition was the typical Christmas lunch, but of course included sport. Cricket, to be precise. And it carried on for the better part of half a century to the point where your Uncle Mark – born in 1992 – and I – born in 1984 – were involved.

"At one of the first Christmases we had at their place at Brandon

Street, South Perth, John strummed a tune on a musical tea chest and Romney played 'Mack the Knife' on the piano," your Great Aunty Sandy said.

"They became our idols. As we all continued to grow up, marry and add children to the clan, we were still alternating Christmases between the family homes in South Perth, Floreat, Thornlie, Booragoon and Bull Creek and each Christmas included a cricket match: 'The Foremans v The Rest of the World'."

The Rest of the World consisted of anyone who was not a direct descendent of Ernie or Eric, or who carried the Foreman name. The game included everyone from the youngest child to the oldest grandparent and came equipped with dubious rules and even more dubious umpiring decisions.

"In his adult years, Wally led the match as chief organiser and captain of the Foreman team, umpire and scorer," your Great Aunty Sandy continued. "I'm not sure how he got away with this, but he was deadly serious and we all toed the line."

The shared Christmases were eventually abandoned as the family grew too great for one house to accommodate. The match, however, remained. It was relocated to "The Beach Shack": your great grandparents' holiday spot at Point Peron.

And a shack it was. It was a wood and asbestos prefab building that sat on stilts, with dated – even for the time – lino covering the floor and an electric hot water system that needed to be switched on to provide hot showers, then switched back off, and that would insist on giving the operator an electric shock each time. The beds felt like they had slinkies for springs and if the sea breeze decided not to blow, it felt like the mouth of Hell on a summer's day. It was also home to hairy spiders the size of an adult palm.

But it was also fun. Lots of fun. And it's a shame the venue was abandoned long before you were born. Its trimmings might not have been flash, but they didn't need to be, as it overlooked a large oval with an artificial cricket pitch in the middle, making the shack – or, cottage, as your great grandma preferred – the ideal Players Pavilion for The Foreman v The Rest of the World match. Tall trees lined the northern boundary, what seemed like hundreds of cars were parked along the west and the row of shacks on the southern edge made the ground feel like a stadium. It was perfect.

The Beach Shack was also homebase for a fishing trip that I would take with your grandad and great grandad every Easter Friday until I grew too old for it, but not old enough to recognise its importance. The fact the fishing tradition continued for maybe the eight or so years that it did was a testament to your grandad's love for family, because a sailor he was not and he was overcome with seasickness most years.

It was during those fishing trips that I also came to the realisation that, while your grandad could be courageous in the face of many adversaries, he could be selective in the application of that courage. I always remember the time we were pulling in herring within minutes of a cast. Then, they stopped biting.

Suddenly, an all-engulfing shadow approaching the boat. A manta ray, so big that its wings were visible from both sides of the little tinny, swam beneath and, as we all peered over the edge to marvel at the beast, the sunglasses atop your grandad's head slipped off and sunk straight to the seabed. Your grandad then struggled to accept the refusal of his 12-year-old son to jump from the boat, swim to the bottom and fetch the glasses.

"Right up until the time he passed away, I know Wally yearned for more of the good old days, especially the Foreman get-togethers and the eternal cricket match," your Great Aunty Sandy said. "It was his favourite tradition and one that truly embellished what family meant to him."

For all that it lacked in comparison, the city had one great advantage over the country: proximity. That was the case for family, but also for sport. Your grandad found himself within driving distance – often even walking distance – of the heroes, the games and the sports that he used to hear broadcast.

West Perth was the club of choice – the passion began at the top with your Great Grandad Eric and filtered through – and the family could not have timed its run better, arriving in Perth the same year its beloved Cardinals ended the season on top of the table, before clinching the Western Australian National Football League premiership for the first time in almost a decade. For your grandad, it meant Peter Medhurst had gone from being a persona of his imagination as a 10-year-old on a vacant block in Bruce Rock, to plying his trade right in front of his eyes.

"We regularly went to the matches at Leederville Oval on Saturday afternoons and sat on the grassy bank," your Great Aunty Sandy said.

"Mum would pack the thermos and afternoon tea basket. Wal was allowed to take one mate and a footy to kick around. I was usually content to just play with our little sister Jill or step and stride along the bench seats around the oval. Mel Whinnen, Bill Dempsey and Blue Foley were all names I remember being talked about on the way home in the car."

Which friend would join him at Leederville Oval soon became a difficult choice as your grandad's friendship group expanded with the graduation to high school. It was at Perth Modern School that the Wembley boys merged with the Floreat alumni to form a group of friends that would stand the test of time.

It brought your grandad together with Phillip and Sam Gannon, the latter of whom went on to become a talented Australian cricketer. There was Craig Thompson and Barry Morrison, as well as Steve "Nugget" Heal, who the Foreman family was happy to embrace after his father, Stan Heal, had spent more than a combined two decades as a player and coach for West Perth.

The group of friends was so close that you have met several of them, despite your grandad no longer being around. The family's Glenties Road house had been built and the group of friends became regular callers, relaxing and engaging with the entire family, or spending time in your grandad's room – the first time your grandad and great aunties had their own space – and dodging the open-plan wardrobe (read: floor-strewn clothes) to listen to sport on the radio or music on the turntable.

It was loaded with vinyl records from artists that your grandad would become renowned for later in life: The Kinks, Herman's Hermits, The Rolling Stones, Gene Pitney, Johnny Cash, Patsy Cline, The Seekers and John Denver. They were the same artists who received extra airtime through the covers that unheralded performer Walter John Foreman would belt into the shampoo bottle mid-shower.

Your grandad hooked into the sporting influence of Perth Mod's Senior Sports Master Eric Strauss and played what he could for the school. His small frame ruled him out of football and he struggled to break into the First XI cricket team, but he excelled in the games he had enjoyed in Bruce Rock, representing the Modernians in First XI hockey and captaining the school tennis team.

However, as was the case in the country, the size of the dog was noted as often as the size of the fight.

"Wally Foreman – Made up for his size with vigour and determination and initiated many forward moves," school captain Douglas Kagi wrote of the hockey team in the November 1965 edition of school publication, *The Sphinx*, while the tennis coach wrote with tongue-in-cheek: "Wally Foreman (capt.): Reliable service – solid ground strokes and great will to win – very solid, the form horse of the team, volleys well for such a giant, quieter on the court this year."

Proximity and passion: two crucial ingredients for the success of sport. They were accentuated for your grandad in the family's second year in the city, when Perth hosted the spectacle that was the 1962 British Empire and Commonwealth Games.

Such an opportunity comes around for a city rarely. In fact, Perth has not hosted an event as diverse and of that magnitude since. Beatty Park Swimming Pool hosted the aquatics, the Lake Monger Velodrome – which no longer exists – hosted the cycling, while Floreat's Perry Lakes Stadium hosted the ceremonies, athletics and boxing. Perry Lakes was just a short walk from the Foremans' Glenties Road house and your grandad, 14-years-old at the time, was going to do whatever he had to in order to be involved.

That turned out to be selling ice creams out of a Streets cart. The job was as uninspiring as they come, but the location was not: your grandad's Streets cart was positioned a short distance from the stadium's iconic scoreboard with a relatively unobstructed view over the arena. That scoreboard still stands and by the time you read this, I undoubtedly would have dragged you along to see it.

I wouldn't expect you to understand the gravitas of a decaying monument of the past, but that scoreboard is the last standing feature of a stadium that meant a lot to our family. The rest of it was torn down and replaced by houses. But those houses stand on the site where your grandad met your nana and I spent many weekends exploring the catacombs of abandoned rooms, while your nana coached athletics. A highlight of those weekends was your grandad and I making our way to the stormwater outlet of the nearby lake and feeding bread to the turtles. It sounds mundane, but I hope you go for a wander around that lake some time and imagine where it all began for you.

The athletics at those Commonwealth Games had been good to Australia, which topped the medal tally with 12 gold, 12 silver and 13 bronze. One of those silvers came on Day 3 through Charles "Chilla" Porter, high jump silver medallist from Melbourne's 1956 Olympic Games and a man who would later work alongside the intently-watching ice cream boy as a Chairman of the Western Australian Institute of Sport.

The mercury was rising in a crescendo of festivities when on Day 10 – the final day of the Games – the excitement surrounding hometown pole vaulter Trevor Bickle, as he began a late surge to eventually claim gold with a leap of 14ft 5in, became too much for your grandad.

"The pole vault that day went for nearly six hours and it was really hot: easterly in the morning and a south-wester in the afternoon," Bickle said, 60 years on.

"I was about middle of the field, but I was feeling good, the track was nice and, as the heights progressed, I was improving. In the last two hours, it was really on and it looked like I might have been in medal contention.

"The story from Wally himself goes that he went and stood under the scoreboard, which was immediately adjacent to the pole vault run-up, and he just didn't move for about an hour and a half. All of a sudden, he remembered he had to take his money and stock back to the station and by the time he got back, the ice creams were milk."

It was a moment that undoubtedly filled your grandad with dread: imagine being a 14-year-old, attempting to manufacture a legitimate reason as to why Streets' entire stock of ice creams had become unsellable. However, it was also a moment that linked him with Bickle through good humour from that point on.

"In that era, there were so many functions that we attended together and he would tell that story," Bickle said.

"Wally and I had a good relationship and it all started because of that moment. I've heard from other athletes that he used to tell the story even when I wasn't there, but the ice cream bag got bigger every time he told it. When Wally passed on, it was really the end of an era for track and field being out there to be read about or heard about. I mean, if it's not Steven Hooker (2008 Olympic pole vault champion), it's nobody anymore.

"Wally was never like that; he would talk about everybody."

There are moments in our lives that shape the way we look at the world and dictate that which we are passionate about. They usually happen without us knowing it.

A colleague of mine when I was still working at *The Sunday Times* used to say to me: "You'd cover two flies racing up a wall if you could". And I probably would have if the two flies were West Australian. I got that passion from your grandad.

He was exposed to a diverse range of people and sports from an early age in Bruce Rock, he learnt to embrace that diversity through an almost unbreakable bond to the ABC's broadcasts, he was encouraged to get involved with whatever he could through his socially active parents, spurred on by the talents and achievements of his friends and the culture of his high school and inspired by seeing first-hand one of the world's largest sporting events through a hometown British Empire and Commonwealth Games.

So, when 1962 came around and at just 14-years-old, the trait that Trevor Bickle recalled in a far older version of your grandad – "Wally was never like that, he would talk about everybody" – was one that was already engrained. And it had been noted by his close friends.

"My early memories of Wally were that he was an effervescent, happy person, and he was sports mad. When I say 'sports mad', I mean unbelievably sports mad. All sports," Sam Gannon said.

"His dream was always to become a sports journalist. As a young person, I remember talking to him about it. He would study it and he would be an absolute fountain of knowledge of all things sport and of all sports. Olympic Games, Commonwealth Games, tennis, football, hockey, cricket; everything."

It is probably not until we analyse a life in its entirety that we realise how many twists and turns fate placed in its path to lead to that life and this was another important time in the building of your grandad's life. He was self-assessing enough that he had come to a realisation: he was not as talented as his friends at either football or cricket and, while he was better than most at tennis, he lacked that extra edge that would allow him to pursue the sport as a career.

It brought journalism and broadcasting into the fray as more than just reading material to hone his knowledge and entertain his evenings and weekends. The media began to loom as an opportunity to be involved in the world he was obsessed with and he recorded on a small tape recorder his first piece of commentary as a 15-year-old, describing a junior football match.

"It was around about that time that I was starting to think that I'm obviously not going to be a league footballer or a Davis Cup tennis player, and perhaps sports journalism or sports broadcasting started to emerge as an option," your grandad told *The West Magazine* later in life.

"I recorded (the commentary) on a tape recorder and played it back at the barbecue afterwards, which was very embarrassing, but it was probably an indication of my interests.

"But I think that playing a wide range of sports was important in terms of my journalistic and broadcasting career and what I'm doing now, because it did give me a very good working knowledge and understanding of all the sports from the point of view of rules and strategies and tactics."

However, as Gannon admitted himself, neither he nor your grandad were "the greatest students". The difference between your grandad and his talented sporting mates, though, was that the direct route to his dream required him to be. He needed good marks in leaving; good enough to help him stand out among the hundreds of hopeful candidates who applied for a cadetship placement at *The West Australian* every year.

He didn't get them: "I messed up".

The group of Perth Modern School and Churchlands High School mates had grown inseparable, with the age brackets of sport ensuring Sam Gannon – one year older – and George Young – one year younger – would spend at least one year in the same cricket and football teams as your grandad.

School days were ended at either the football field, in the cricket nets, or by meeting at the trolley bus terminus at the bottom of Oceanic Drive and riding to City Beach for a surf, returning with the wind in their backs. That group began to blossom with sporting talent: footballers such as Young, Graham Bushell and

Steve Heal, and Gannon through cricket.

Your grandad's dream, though, seemed out of reach. He graduated from Perth Modern School in 1965, but did so without the required marks to obtain the cadetship he so wanted with *The West Australian* and having attained only two subjects in his Leaving Certificate: English and History. His application for the 1966 cadet intake was his first of an eventual three and it was his first rejection.

It was at a Church of England Youth Club earlier that year where as a 17-year-old your grandad had set his sights on a girl two years his junior, Lee Hunt, and manipulated the scooting of a barn dance to arrive by her side. The pair "lived in each other's pockets" and remained together for several years, attending church, playing squash and singing along to the Gene Pitney records of your grandad's collection in the early days and driving across the country together in the latter stages of the relationship.

It was to Hunt that your grandad confided his bitter disappointment at his first cadetship rejection.

"He was shattered, because that's all he wanted to do. He was so determined to get in," Hunt said.

Your grandad's selfless nature was part of the reason he endeared himself to so many and, while he was hurting at being knocked back from *The West*, he remained focused on his dream and being positive for his friends.

"He was unbelievably supportive and excited when his friends started doing well, George Young especially," said Gannon, who achieved his first Sheffield Shield selection in 1966.

"He followed diligently my cricket career and was very supportive. He was proud of the likes of George and Steve Heal and he knew everyone in town. In the winter months, in the afternoons, we would go and watch Nugget (Heal), Bushy (Bushell) and George playing footy at Subiaco.

"It was business as usual and he just got on with it."

Proceed with caution here.

Your grandad was in his late-teens and entering early adulthood at this stage, Charlotte. His life has some poignant lessons to teach you, but during this time, he also had some bad habits. Learn from the lessons. Don't pick up the bad habits.

For all your grandad's disappointment, his dream of entering the media was never considered lost, it was simply deferred. That meant he needed a job, if not for spending-money at the hotels that were about to become well-frequented, then for something to occupy him during the day until it was time to head to those hotels.

The Floreat branch of the R&I Bank was hiring and your grandad found his first full-time work and, although he did not see out the year there, his employment coincided with two crucial moments in history: the introduction of decimal currency to Australia on 14 February 1966 and; the opening of the Floreat Hotel on the same day.

The Floreat Hotel, which was abutted against the city-side of the Floreat Forum until it was covered over by the two-storey carpark that now occupies the space, was a hive of activity across its three bars – front, lounge and saloon – as it catered for the western-most customers who previously had to travel to the Wembley Hotel for a drink. It was close to Floreat Cricket Club, close to home and it also was one of the only hotels in Perth at the time that had an 11pm liquor license.

Those advantages made "The Floreat" the perfect homebase for your grandad and his mates and it remained that way for much of their young-adult lives.

"Wally would always boast that he carried the very first float bag from the Floreat branch of the R&I Bank to the Floreat Hotel," Gannon said, unsure of whether the story was fact or fiction.

"So, he used to claim that he helped start the Floreat Hotel. When we first went there, we were underage because the drinking age was 21, so it cost you more, because you'd have to buy a squash and a beer. You'd put the squash in front and the beer behind. That way, if the place was raided (by police), it just looked like you were drinking squash."

Your grandad teamed up with Gannon's younger brother Phil and friend Craig Thompson in playing fourth-grade cricket for Floreat. This was for a couple of reasons: they were not skilled and/or dedicated enough to join their more talented mates in the higher grades and, as Sam declared, "fourth-grade cricket for them was all about filling in the afternoon until it was time to go to The Floreat".

The first year out of high school came and went and 1967 brought another failed application for a cadetship at *The West Australian*, but as with the first rejection, your grandad regrouped and moved on.

He had done his time at the R&I Bank and followed your Great Grandad Eric's footsteps into the Crown Law Department, holding a position fondly referred to as "Rat Room Filing Clerk" – officially a C-IV government employee – at the Local Court on the corner of Roe and Beaufort Streets.

It was a position also once held by Fred Miller, a short and affable character raised as a choir boy in a respectable Catholic household with four sisters. Then he met your grandad on one of those afternoons at The Floreat Hotel. Who corrupted who is an easy determination to make, but the pair quickly struck up a lifelong friendship.

You never heard your grandad on the radio – at least, not live – but part of his on-air appeal was his ability to relate to and respect people from all walks. Many credit that to his country upbringing. However, if there was one job that would ensure a person remained grounded, it was that of the Rat Room Filing Clerk.

"We both had the same job, but at different times – weren't there at the same time and didn't know each other – but the job was referred to as the Rat Room Filing Clerk," Miller said.

"All the old files were put in a depository in a back room – the Rat Room. The Rat Room was all the way down in this old 1880s building, with dim lights, with the files in old cardboard boxes that were placed up on shelves. They'd have summonses and bench warrants in, with all the boxes dated on the front.

"It was the Rat Room Filing Clerk's job to fill any requests for documents in those boxes. We'd have a hook on a stick and have to pull the box down and, of course, all the rat shit and dust would come tumbling down and you'd have rat shit all through your hair.

"The lawyers all had good looking sheilas to help them, because they got the best attention. There's the Counter Clerk out the front with this row of 30 good looking women wanting summonses issued, or whatever and he'd sit there with that job, then we'd come out all covered in rat shit. I remember Wal and I had independently come to the quick realisation it was going to be difficult to pick up a girl as a Rat Room Filing Clerk."

The humour of the role would not have been lost on your grandad, either, because as well as his ability to relate to people, he was also known for his self-deprecating wit. When your grandad passed away, one of his former colleague at ABC Radio, Glenn Mitchell, noted: "The punchlines to many of his jokes was himself; he was the human punchline".

And he often was, usually through his own failings or those around him that impacted him. Rat droppings tumbling off a shelf and through his hair would have been right up his alley. Your grandad never had to look far for material, though.

There was a band of friends in later life that he named the Duncraig Domestic Dyslexics and that he described as: "A group of people who have distinguished themselves through appalling performances around the house". Your grandad would have been secretary, president and chairman of that group and its antics became folklore upon his return to the ABC from 2001.

They often involved stories of failings so horrendous they walked a fine line between hilarity and concern, such as the time your grandad sprinkled dynamic lifter – a foul smelling fertiliser – on plastic indoor plants. It was bad enough he used it on indoor plants, but plastic indoor plants? "They didn't grow, either," he exclaimed to Liam Bartlett when quizzed on air about the incident.

Even back in the 1960s, those domestic follies were the source of great humour for your grandad's friends.

"The family would occasionally go on holidays and would leave Wally in the Glenties Road home on his own," George Young said.

"We'd always go around there and have parties or whatever, but you'd be looking for a stubby holder in the kitchen and you'd open up the cupboard and inside is a saucepan, a fry pan, cereals, bowls and what-have-you and every one of them had a note attached to it from Wally's mum on what they were to be used for."

They were raucous times for the close group. Friends mattered. Family mattered. More than that, people mattered to your grandad and he loved spending time with them. He took the view of, "You're a mate, until you prove otherwise", as opposed to requiring someone to first earn that bond. And if a person was keen for a beer at The Floreat, they were almost instantly ordained as a pseudo brother or sister.

Your grandad formed friendships quickly and, often, for life.

He and his friends were enjoying a carefree, sheltered suburban life and the pursuit of their dreams to an extent that most 20-year-olds still enjoy today: with a loose knowledge that the future existed, but without the life experience to comprehend exactly what that meant. However, there was one major difference between 20-year-olds then and 20-year-olds today.

And that sheltered life was about to be shattered.

Chapter 3

Make the Most of the Hand You're Dealt

Two wooden barrels sat side by side. They were suspended on a spindle between lacquered and polished vertical arms that allowed them to spin freely. Their appearance, however, was deceiving and the corporate, professional look concealed their true nature.

On 15 March 1968, as your grandad continued to be showered by rat droppings at the Local Court, those barrels spun and the total of 365 numbered marbles rattled within. Each marble – 181 in one barrel and 184 in the other – represented a birthday and, on that Friday, the marble representing 5 January 1948 was drawn.

Your grandad had been balloted into National Service. And despite the enormous number of fellow draftees, there was a sense that he was going alone. Only one other member of the friendship group had his number called, however, as a university student, that person was among those permitted an academic deferral until his course was complete, by which time the practice of conscription had ceased.

Public support for the Vietnam War at the time had begun to wane, with a vein of anti-conscription sentiment running across the nation, spearheaded by groups such as Save Our Sons and Youth Campaign Against Conscription. Then-leader of the Federal Opposition, Labor's Arthur Calwell, referred to the Birthday Ballot as a "lottery of death" and the Australian Labor Party suspended the practice when the Whitlam Government was elected in 1972. There were, of course, supporters of the war and conscription, as well as those who were indifferent to it all.

Your grandad was closer to the latter and, while he would have naturally been fearful, he would have felt a duty to defend the process and the Australian government out of loyalty to his country's leaders. I can say that with some degree of certainty due to a conversation I had with him when I was about the same age as he would have been when conscripted.

The topic came up over dinner and he asked me what I would do if my government asked me to go to war. I said I would go, because I trusted that those asking me had determined it was the best course of action for our country. I also commented at the time on the irony of priorities in such countries as the US, which allowed 18-year-olds to be sent to die, three years before they were legally permitted to consume alcohol. Your grandad agreed with me and told me he thought it was a mature statement.

I remember that conversation because of how proud I felt from the praise, but Charlotte I hope you never have to experience war and make that decision, just as I'm fortunate enough to have not had to. Your grandad probably wouldn't have been as proud in that conversation today: my answer wouldn't have been the same.

However, the difference in answers between then and now highlights the thought process of a 20-year-old when it comes to war: the loose understanding of what the future may hold rarely includes a comprehension of death and finality and there are far more pressing issues for most 20-year-olds than the world of geopolitics.

"We went off to war with some trepidation, tempered with the prospect of adventure and excitement," said one of your grandad's closest friends from his army days, 2Lt Bob Lewis.

"There was also an element of needing to be tested, to prove to ourselves the meaning of courage and mateship. Infantrymen knew they would be at the sharp end and were reminded that, 'the strongest steel is forged in the hottest flame'."

It should be mentioned that life was not completely carefree for your grandad and his friendship group, as they were forced to deal with the loss of good mate Neil Bennett to a motorcycle accident before their 20th birthdays. However, regardless of the motivating factors, your grandad attended as ordered his local national service office in the two-week registration window of

January 1968 and submitted his details to the Department of Labour and National Service (DLNS).

He had come full-circle with his namesake.

World War II ticked into its 1005th day.

The Australian depot ship *Kuttabul* was torpedoed and sunk by Japanese submarine *M-24* during an attack on Sydney Harbour. Its target had been the heavy cruiser warship *USS Chicago*; instead, it sunk the converted ferry and killed 21 sailors. And further up the coast, about 1300km away, a twin-engine Anson plunged into the waters off Bargara, Queensland, killing its three occupants.

It was 1 June 1942. It was a Monday and cold – even for balmy Queensland – when a routine training flight went horribly wrong. On board AW902 was Flt Sgt Ronald Campbell Davies, LAC Clifford James Lucas and LAC Walter James Regan.

And, in a remarkable twist of fate, a Wireless Air Gunner named Eric George Foreman was elsewhere in the country when he heard the transmission of the crash on his radio. Its significance was not lost on him: he had heard firsthand his then-girlfriend's twin brother, Walter James Regan, pronounced lost.

Nine days later, on 10 June 1942, the RAAF officially abandoned the search for AW902. The bodies of the three crew members were never recovered, with the official Air Force report stating, "It is advised that hope of finding the bodies of the three airmen comprising the crew of Anson Aircraft AW902 when it crashed into the sea on 1st June, 1942, has been abandoned". It was a report from Bundaberg's No.8 Service Flying Training School to the Headquarters at Wagga Wagga.

There was a theory that was never proven that suggested AW902 had accidentally discovered the location of the Japanese warship escorting the submarines to Australia. The Japanese through June launched attacks from Sydney to Newcastle and the suggestion of the rumour was AW902 stumbled upon the staging vessel and was shot down before the crew could alert HQ. However, as mentioned, no evidence supporting the rumour has been uncovered.

Eric George Foreman – your great grandad – ended his service with the close of the war and made his way home to Kalgoorlie, marrying Norma Lyle Regan within a month of his return on 31 October 1945. The couple welcomed their first child, a boy, less than three years later on 5 January 1948. As you know by now, that child was your grandad, Walter John Foreman.

"Wally was given the name of 'Walter John', after mum's twin brother, who had recently been lost in the war," your Great Aunty Jill said at the memorial service for your grandad.

"Whilst mum and dad and mum's parents thought this was the most wonderful choice of name, Wally probably took 50 of his 58 years to appreciate that. The Wally Walpamur ads in the 1980s didn't help and the Where's Wally books in the 1990s didn't help his cause either.

"However, it was when he visited the special memorial built in Kings Park to honour the 50 years since World War II ended and saw our Uncle Wally's name there, that I think he fully appreciated the significance of his name."

This remarkable tale unfolded thanks to a lady named Barbara Paramor, who, like me, embarked on a journey to learn the story of her dad. Barbara's father was Flt Sgt Davies and her journey led, first, to the establishment in 2007 of a memorial plaque in Bargara dedicated to the three crew members and, secondly, a mission to advise the families of the other crew members that the memorial had been founded.

Only when she contacted your great grandad was it revealed that he had heard about the crash as he manned the radio at that precise time. Walter Regan and Walter Foreman had never met, but on 1 May 1968, your grandad shared Regan's experience of service in Australia's armed forces. Your grandad was issued the service number of 5716043 and sent to Puckapunyal, Victoria, for the initial 10-week recruit training.

A person's life starts well before they are born.

It was a conflicting time for the Foreman household.

Your Great Grandad Eric was – and forever remained – proud of his only son's service to the Australian armed forces. However, your Great Grandma Norma wrote very little about the conscription in her life story, despite the fact that it must have reignited memories of her twin brother and the time spent apart from her husband. Then, there were the girls – your great aunties – who had to watch their big brother be sent away from home for the first time.

"I distinctly remember the day he got the letter saying he was called up," Great Aunty Jill said. "He was crying and Mum was crying. Dad was stoic and I was terrified, having never seen anything like this in the family before."

Your grandad, by his own admission, was fearful of the idea of being sent to Vietnam. A large part of those concerns was the fear of the unknown that haunted the entire experience. He had never lived away from home, let alone been in the army or considered being involved in a war.

Those fears slowly began to ease as his time in service progressed and, after viewing the military infomercial "National Service Officer" during basic training, he applied to be posted to the Officer Training Unit at Scheyville, New South Wales. It was no easy application, as only a select few volunteers from each intake were accepted for officer training after undergoing intelligence, leadership and physical testing.

"When Wally was at Puckapunyal, he found a phone box and called me one day and said, 'I'm going to apply for Officer's Training'," Sam Gannon said. "He used to have to go on these marches through the bush for 10km where they'd jog and walk, jog and walk, jog and walk. He said, 'Mate, I can't lift the pack, let alone carry it'."

Your grandad's application to join the Officer Training Unit was accepted and in July 1968 he was dispatched to Scheyville, an area about 55km north of Sydney previously used as an internment camp for "German aliens" following the First World War. Your grandad's attendance at Scheyville was a lofty achievement. Few were selected for the training; fewer actually graduated.

The Officer Training Unit at Scheyville existed out of necessity and operated as such. The National Service Act was passed in 1964 and allowed the national service scheme to be re-established, swelling the numbers of those enlisted in Australia's armed forces and adding to the expansion of the Royal Australian Regiment to nine battalions.

The increased number of those enlisted men undergoing training due to Australia's military commitment in Vietnam led to a requirement for greater numbers of junior officers to oversee that training and command platoons on active service. And they were needed quickly.

Scheyville was the result: an intense and condensed proving ground that jammed the usual 52-week course of a Portsea syllabus into 22 weeks. Its testing was rigorous and demanding and could not be understated.

"It was a terrifying experience for most, if that's the right word," said your grandad's close friend and fellow Scheyville graduate Bob Lewis. "It was typical military where the green machine tried very hard to break the spirit to prove a candidate's unsuitability for the task ahead. Precisely why one needed a highly developed sense of humour and a degree of mental and physical toughness."

Days were long – 14 hours – with leave permitted strictly between 7am Saturday and 11pm Sunday and only on weekends where training was not scheduled. There was never an attempt to soften the expectations for cadets as to the challenges they would face. Official military publications stated, "From the precise moment when … the first cadet of a new intake touches OTU soil, he begins a period of mental and physical stress generally not hitherto experienced".

The demands of the Officer Training Unit were such that only the best were accepted to Scheyville. More than 100 officers-in-waiting – including your grandad and, elsewhere amidst the room of intake 3/68, future Victoria Premier Jeff Kennett – were told they were around the top one per cent of all army recruits. They needed to be, because, mentally, program was taxing. Physically, it was exhausting.

Cadets were told they were entering a specialised "pipeline" system that was costing the Australian taxpayers millions of dollars – a point made to emphasise the importance of seizing the opportunity – but the benefits through the skills equipped to those who graduated were invaluable. Hopeful officers could make the choice to embark on the training, but once they commenced, they were not permitted to review their decision for a period of 30 days.

Of course, the first 30 days were the most gruelling. It was a deliberate strategy that empowered cadets as they witnessed first-hand what they were capable of, providing an unparalleled motivation to continue. The timing of your grandad's arrival meant his 22-weeks of officer training ran from the bitter chill of the colder months to the blistering heat of summer, with the torturously long route marches through the Blue Mountains taking place regardless of either.

Your grandad, as he always did, embraced the challenges the training presented, mainly through the camaraderie that was built among a group enduring the same physically exhausting tests as each other, much the same as the camaraderie built through sport. And, while he would not have known it at the time, his mind was being trained in a way that would prove of great benefit to him in later life.

Your grandad at times seemed to have a superhuman ability.

It was related to his memory: he was able to learn within an hour the names and numbers of two teams of footballers, simply by writing them in their positions on a blank A4 piece of paper, alternating between red and blue ink for the corresponding teams. It was a skill that must be honed by all sports broadcasters pursuing excellence in a call, but your grandad seemed particularly gifted at it.

He would repetitiously mutter those names and numbers back to himself once the page had been filled and seemed to almost immediately absorb the information. He needed to be that quick, too, given he was often calling football for the ABC around his fulltime job at the Western Australian Institute of Sport, meaning he had drastically reduced preparation time compared to his broadcasting colleagues.

However, what your grandad was doing was not exhibiting a superhuman ability; he was employing a skill he had learnt at Scheyville. It was a process called "Training By The Numbers". As detailed by another Scheyville graduate, Dr Michael Hewitt-Gleeson, it was a technique of "breaking down complex tasks into small, bite-sized memes, then converting them into strong cognitive patterns using practice, repetition and rehearsals, then gradually building them back up again into smooth, robust skills".

Time taken to learn is rarely time wasted. You never know when a skill will come in handy.

Summer at Scheyville brought scorching heat.

It also brought the season of cricket and, amidst a heavy syllabus in its final month, a weekend off for your grandad fortuitously coincided with Western Australia's first interstate match of the 1968-69 Sheffield Shield season, bringing east close friend Sam Gannon and teammates such as John Inverarity, Rod Marsh and well-performing English Test recruit Tony Lock to play New South Wales. The brief time off presented your grandad with a window of opportunity to reconnect with his sporting passion, his love for his home state and his mates, as he attended the weekend of 16-17 November.

The gruelling training of Scheyville was approaching an end and your grandad yearned to graduate and move on. The intense nature of the Officer Training Unit resulted in a high failure rate of about 30 per cent, so when it came time for cadets to select their corps preferences, your grandad gravitated towards those with the greatest number of vacancies, such as Service and Ordinance.

However, the primary goal of Scheyville's Officer Training Unit was to produce infantry officers and that was where 2Lt Walter John Foreman, OTU Graduate 783 of intake 3/68, was sent, placed in command of 1 Platoon A Company 3rd Battalion of The Royal Australian Regiment (3RAR), garrisoned at South Australia's Woodside Barracks.

"It was during the final exercises that one of the instructors, Captain Goddard, came to me and he said, 'Would you be interested in changing your selection?'," your grandad said.

"I said all I wanted to do was graduate and I would go wherever I had the best chance of graduating. He thought I was suited to infantry, which was always the prime core of graduates, because what they were trying to do was to turn out infantry officers. So I actually saw that as a bit of a feather in my cap, I guess. There were only four of us that graduated to infantry battalions, two went to 3RAR (your grandad and his friend Bob Lewis) and two went to 1RAR and one of those two was Jeff Kennett (who went on to become Premier of Victoria)."

The turn of the year came and brought with it a period of leave between the completion of officers training and meeting up with 3RAR at Woodside and a January birthday meant your grandad had the opportunity to celebrate his 21st with family and friends back at the Glenties Road house. The amount of relationships, close friends and family he had already developed meant that multiple celebrations were required. Most importantly, it allowed the family to temporarily reunite.

Many would have considered your grandad a born leader, given the way he later steered Western Australia's peak elite sporting body for almost two decades. Your Great Grandad Eric did not subscribe to that thinking and it wasn't until Scheyville that he saw a change in your grandad.

"He was never a born leader, although, when he got into the army, that's when he showed his leadership qualities," Eric Foreman said.

"It was the making of him. When Wally first went into the army, he could see another side of – not legal – but problems that he'd never faced in Bruce Rock before."

The brief break was over quickly. The army had taken your grandad from Puckapunyal, Victoria, to Scheyville, New South Wales, and he again departed. His next stop was Woodside, South Australia, and 3RAR.

He was dispatched to a proud battalion.

3RAR was highly-decorated and respected with the nickname "Old Faithful", having notably been awarded a US Presidential Unit Citation for its efforts in the Korean War. The citation specifically was awarded for the battalion's extraordinary gallantry at Kapyong on 24 April 1951 when it was strategically placed to halt the advance of North Korean and Chinese troops aggressively pursuing and American and South Korean retreat – a mission it was successful in.

The battalion was later dispatched to Malaya to counter Communist Terrorists activities in the late 1950s and was again called upon in the region to assist Australia's Commonwealth counterpart upon the 1963 formation of Malaysia, which led to the Indonesia-Malaysia Confrontation. The battalion was moved to South Australia's Woodside Barracks at the end of its involvement in Malaysia and it was there that it received a new platoon commander – your grandad – in early 1969.

3RAR had returned to Australia at full-strength, but having needed to be reinforced by Task Force HQ after its first of two Tours in Vietnam resulted in 24 men KIA and 93 wounded. The returned complement was immediately sent on leave, with most members discharged at the completion of their service, or dispatched to other units. A number of soldiers remained with the battalion, but it was essentially reformed through new intakes of National Servicemen and postings from other units.

Your grandad arrived at a time when there were very few troops on the ground for 3RAR. His command of 1 Platoon A Company was a result of that group being the first of regiment to be rebuilt and raised, reforming in preparation for another deployment.

One of those returnees was a private named Morey Grafton: a fellow West Australian from Doubleview who, like the majority of your grandad's mates, became a lifelong friend, despite a first meeting that could have had him seriously dealt with by his superior.

"I'd been there three days, maybe, and there was talk of 'The Phantom'," Grafton said.

"This was the platoon commander, who only a couple of guys had seen. I remember rushing up to the window one day after some of the guys said, 'There he is', and it was like the typical adventure stories, where all I saw was a foot disappearing into a hut. The next day, we got up in the morning and this little bloke came to the door and told us we had about five minutes to get in our rec outfits – sports gear, basically – and to meet him out the front.

"I don't know what it was, because I'm not a quick thinker, but this little bloke was standing there and I just assumed small stature, small rank. He's got us out standing there and took us off for a run. We stopped and he started doing some static exercises – star-jumps and those sorts of things – and I didn't like that, because he started with us and then suddenly stopped and was walking up and down the line.

"I thought this was bloody outrageous. I was about to say something when he came past, but I restrained myself and thought it wasn't worth it. I held my tongue and it wasn't until I got back to the camp and there was a sergeant waiting there and the little bloke said, 'Take them and do something with them', and the sergeant said, 'Ok, Mr Foreman'.

"I thought, 'Shit, that was a good move keeping my mouth

shut': it wasn't some little Lance Corporal it was my Lieutenant. That was the first time I met him."

Your grandad was able to relate to people from all walks of life and that was a trait he needed to embrace at Woodside, while putting into practice all the skills gleaned from Scheyville, because the situation he found himself in was undoubtedly intimidating. He was barely 21-years-old, he had never seen combat and had spent more than six months bouncing from basic training to officer training alongside fellow youthful cadets in a National Service intake.

At Woodside, he found himself commanding a platoon comprising some members who had recently returned from a conflict zone attracting global critical attention. It was a platoon made up from a mix of career soldiers and National Servicemen, some of whom had seen and experienced the type of action that many dreaded and that left several with lasting physical and emotional scars. Your grandad had, of course, trained for that exact situation, but training and reality are often vastly different experiences.

Complicating the situation from an incoming commander's perspective was that many of the servicemen – such as Grafton – had only a few months remaining of their two-year National Service commitment. 3RAR's Second Tour of Vietnam was not scheduled to commence for another two years and, having lived through the experiences they had in the First Tour, there was a natural attrition of motivation for army life and its strict regimes in the knowledge that they were effectively training just to go home.

It was a delicate situation that required handling in a sensitive way. It required doing what was needed to be done – not always what was expected from a commander – to ensure 1 Platoon A Company was operating efficiently.

A round of one-on-one interviews had introduced him to Grafton on a more personal level, along with another West Australian, Pte Kevin Harrison – an Albany native who had grown up south of Perth. The trio shared few acquaintances, but the home-state link meant they quickly developed an understanding of each other.

Grafton told his commander he had "had a gutful of trudging through bush and cleaning my rifle" and simply wanted to see out his remaining five months of service. Harrison had contracted malaria while serving in Vietnam – an illness that was symptomatic of severe health problems he suffered later in life – and was still recovering from its effects, but had already "divorced myself from the army – I'd had enough".

So, your grandad arranged for Grafton to fill a vacant job behind the bar in the Officers Mess and made Harrison his batman – a personal assistant of sorts – in a position that permitted a more relaxed approach to army life.

"I always thought he was very smart in the way he learnt to handle the returned, as well as the new ones," Harrison said. "He was very conscientious when in uniform and with the military, but once he was out of it and away (from Woodside) he was a totally different person. Just a larrikin and very popular. Wally always liked a lot of attention."

It was a win-win-win situation for the three, particularly with your grandad having strategically placed Grafton behind the bar.

"Wal was very popular with everyone: the whole platoon loved him, the junior officers loved him," Grafton said.

"The senior officers, well they just thought they needed to watch that Mr Foreman and were always looking over at him. We had a good time. For me, there was no closing time until he left the bar and very rarely was he not the last person to leave. Several times I had to lead him back to his room.

"It meant nothing to me at all (that Wally hadn't been away to Vietnam) and Harro would say the same. It was a bit of an issue for your old man, though. I think he felt a bit awkward about it. He didn't need to, though, because it's just the way things are; people do different things."

A friendship that likely broke several regulations developed and the trio made the most of a life that was far more flexible than that which was required in the conflict zones of Vietnam and the strict training environment of Scheyville. Weekends were generally their own, as were evenings, with the exceptions the times when prolonged marches had been scheduled through the picturesque surrounds of the Adelaide Hills.

Sport, once again, had a role to play.

Inter-battalion football was played at the Woodside Barracks and the taller Harrison was ruck to your grandad's rover, but that combination further developed off-base. The pair joined nearby club Hahndorf, about 12km from the barracks, and competed in the newly established Hills Football League, joining midway through the 1969 season for about 10 games.

The names "Harrison" and "Foreman" were rather unique on the Hahndorf team sheets, with the club based in a town that has deep German roots dating back to the 1800s. The football field was a ground of equality and, with rank a non-issue, Harrison took as much delight in barking orders to your grandad as your grandad did to Harrison.

The unflappable loyalty and dedication of West Australians to their own – an us-against-the-east mentality that only West Australians fully comprehend – had the trio also make the 30km trip to watch Norwood Football Club play a scratch match against Subiaco, cheering on your grandad's friends Steve Heal and George Young in a game that marked a significant 1969 pre-season for the latter. The 2013 WA Football Hall of Fame induction biography of Young detailed the role played by his breakout performances in the scratch matches, leading to him playing all but one league game that season.

As another mate previously recounted, "Wally made friends wherever he went", and a trip to the Norwood Football Club bathrooms – after frequenting the Norwood Football Club bar – led to what was undoubtedly a conversation of the highest intellect with a man who turned out to be Norwood's president. Your affable grandad had gleaned three season memberships, gratis, and the trio's weekends were set.

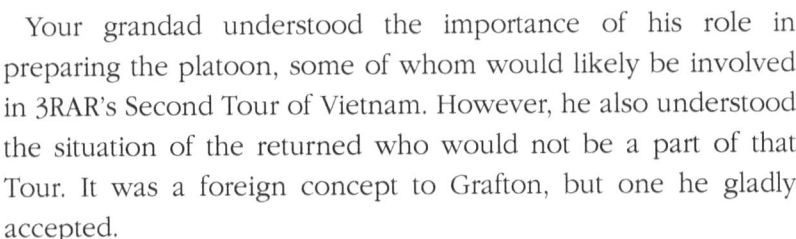

Your grandad understood the importance of his role in preparing the platoon, some of whom would likely be involved in 3RAR's Second Tour of Vietnam. However, he also understood the situation of the returned who would not be a part of that Tour. It was a foreign concept to Grafton, but one he gladly accepted.

"Your old man wasn't the perfect officer: for starters, he got to know me and he treated me as a mate," Grafton said.

"I would always make a point of calling him 'Mr Foreman' or 'Sir', but the senior officers came to know after a while that on weekends and on time down, Mr Foreman would likely be with his Private Grafton down at some bar. I was going to say we weren't always in a bar and also went to the football, but when we were at the football, we were in a bar.

"We spent most of the five months together in a bar of some description. It's a wonder I remember anything at all about that time. It was the start of our friendship. He was always there for you, we never had any arguments and I always just found him solid: if I ever needed anyone, he was always there. There were no ups and downs, with Wal.

"I always felt quite comfortable that he would look after me. He quite surprised me one time – I'd only just known him then – when one night I was behind the bar and trying to spear a keg, making a bit of a stuff-up of it. A captain happened to have a go at me, belittling my efforts. Your old man turned around and bloody snapped at him, put him right in his place, but your old man was several ranks below him.

"He definitely didn't say what a lieutenant should be saying to a captain, but he told him what he thought of him and told him to pull his head in, which the captain did."

A fearless and uncompromising loyalty to mates was a theme that repeatedly stood out in your grandad's life. He stood by them, no matter what, and his first reaction to any situation involving a friend was to always back them, even to his own detriment. That was the case when batman Harrison, mentally sapped from the experience of Vietnam and physically exhausted from the sickness that plagued his body, came unstuck.

Grafton was on-hand, working the bar job your grandad had secured for him, as the situation unfolded in the Officers Mess.

"Harro was always going to sleep. Any chance he got," Grafton said.

"The senior officers always had an eye on Mr Foreman, because Wal tended to be a bit loud: his laughter was always a bit louder than it should be, he was pushing and shoving and carrying on a bit more boisterously than he should be.

"Anyway, one day, the CO – a Colonel – said, 'Your batman, Mr Foreman, what's he like?', and Wal says, 'Oh, he's good, sir. He's from WA, he works hard and he does a good job'. The Colonel says, 'That's good. Well, you might want to go and wake him up, because he's sleeping on your bed now'."

It was a moment Harrison recalled clearly – "He got into strife and it was because of me. I was caught sleeping in the officers' quarters when I was supposed to be out doing a parade" – but it was difficult for your grandad to discipline a private with whom he had been partying in Adelaide the night before.

I don't want to paint the wrong picture of your grandad, but it's equally important to explain his ability to perform a task, while man-managing a group in such a way that even the most unmotivated soldiers wanted to follow his lead. And Harrison and Grafton often covered for him as much as he did for them, with the latter often having to make the suggestion, "Let's move on, Wal".

The behaviour of 2Lt Foreman had occasionally drawn the ire of his superiors, which he documented in a letter home to his mum – your Great Grandma Norma. The age-old saying of, "Never let the facts interfere with a good story", applied to one particular note, as he explained he had been "getting into a spot of bother" with a young private named "Legs Grafton".

The nickname "Legs" had been borne from a game of backyard

cricket, referring to Grafton's vulnerability to LBW dismissals. Your great grandma explained that if Legs was "a troublemaker, then it's best you keep away from him", oblivious to the reality, having never met the unassuming and inoffensive Grafton.

"I thought, 'Mrs Foreman, if only you knew'," Grafton said.

"Excuse me, sir, may I be excused," 2Lt Foreman asked the Mess President.

"No, Mr Foreman."

Your Great Grandma Norma might not have been aware of your grandad's involvement in the shenanigans of Woodside, but the senior officers of the base certainly were. And they seized on the opportunity to respond in kind.

It was the officers' Dining-In Night – a formal dinner designed to foster camaraderie within the group of officers on base. Officers were required to wear their dress suits and finery, while the Mess was transformed into a fine-dining experience, with silver cutlery and crystal glassware. But camaraderie often requires humour and the formalities disguised the jovial aspects of the night. Etiquette was required to be followed and rules were swiftly enforced by the President of the Mess Committee when transgressed.

Broken etiquette was punished with fines, but exactly what those rules were was up to the discretion of the Mess President: anything from the more obvious, such as a late arrival to the dinner, to the more obscure, such as haggling over imposed fines. The Mess President had the ultimate say at all times throughout proceedings and one rule above many others was that only he could give permission for diners to leave the table.

"It's very flash and something to behold, really," your grandad's friend and Woodside Pte Morey Grafton said.

"That night, he was at the bar and I said, 'Wal' – and there was no-one else around otherwise I wouldn't have said 'Wal' – I said: 'You need to go in. Go and get dressed, do what you need to do, because the Dining-In night is only half an hour away'. No, he stayed and had a few more beers. Then a few more beers.

"There's a few rules you must obey at a Dining-In night: once you're seated and the evening has started, there's the Mess President, who all requests must be made to – which I think was a Major, from memory – and Wal had decided after a short time, which didn't surprise me, that he needed to have a leak.

"I was serving and I didn't realise at the time, but he had been asking the Mess President, 'Excuse me, sir, can I be excused', to which the Mess President kept saying, 'No, Mr Foreman'. Wal kept getting more uncomfortable, but kept drinking, of course. Again, 'Excuse me, sir, may I be excused?', and, 'No, Mr Foreman'.

"I don't know how long this went on for, but he'd had a belly full, because he'd been drinking at the bar and he'd been drinking at the table. After a while, I came around serving glasses of wine or whatever and he said, 'Legs, can you get me an empty bottle?'.

"I thought, 'Oh, sh-t'. I had to keep going, topping up glasses and I don't know how long it took before I was back, maybe 10min at most, and I offered him the bottle. He shook his head and said, 'Don't worry about it'."

The dark dress pants hid the evidence, but Grafton understood exactly what had happened.

"I swear I'm not making that up. Sometimes I think about this story and I think, 'Am I making this up?'," he said, recalling a story verified by Bob Lewis, who was seated next to your grandad on the night. "It's funny: the Mess President knew who he was dealing with. He knew that was Mr Foreman."

The year passed and Grafton and Kevin Harrison bid farewell to their mate and superior as their service time expired, with a promise to reunite once they all returned to Western Australia. They kept that promise to each other for the rest of their lives.

It was May 1970, mere days before your grandad was scheduled to end his National Service commitment.

It was a Friday and he was sitting in one of the hotels of Adelaide's Rundle Street, as were most members of 3RAR, enjoying some well-deserved leave and refreshments after a week of tactical training in the scrub of the Adelaide Hills. It was a challenging exercise, as expected, in preparation for the battalion's return to Vietnam.

Alongside your grandad was friend and fellow 2Lt Bob Lewis. The pair spoke and enjoyed each other's company as only close mates can. In fact, they were so close that in the years that followed, your grandad was asked by Lewis to be best man at his wedding, a duty which he happily undertook.

Suddenly, word passed through the ranks of the soldiers that there was a demonstration against the war in nearby King William Street, just 100m from where your grandad and Lewis were. Both men joined the large number of soldiers who wandered down the road to see what was happening.

"We very quickly became incensed at the sight of enemy flags and chanting, long-haired demonstrators trying to convince us and like-minded people that Ho Chi Minh was a hero, that the war was a travesty and military personnel involved were traitors to Australian values," Lewis said.

"Bolstered somewhat by extended doses of bravery pills obtained over the bar and our relief at being free again in the civilian world, we started in on the demonstration to get rid of the provocative flags they were carrying and which we'd been trained to recognise and attack over many months."

Mayhem ensued and amidst the chaos, most of the enemy flags vanished, engulfed in flames on the sidewalks. And more than a few physical altercations broke out. Your grandad and Lewis returned to the latter's home in Belair, only to see themselves and their fellow servicemen on the evening news, incensing Lewis' mother.

"I was unrepentant. I left home in an alcoholic huff never to return," Lewis said. "Wally, who was on with one of my sisters and an 'angel' with no sin, stayed."

Lewis probably wished he had also remained; he was arrested

upon returning to the Woodside base in the early hours of Saturday morning and charged with Conduct Unbecoming. He fronted a furious commanding officer and was confined to barracks, along with a number of other soldiers.

"I do recall Wally wandering about the battalion lines in the week that followed with a smile of innocence, frequently enquiring as to our welfare and wondering what had happened to have caused all the fuss," Lewis said.

"Butter would not have melted in his mouth – and that's not in the derogatory sense. He was an active part of the history of those times, but he was also Teflon-coated. Wally glided through the drama with exquisite indifference."

Mark Dapin wrote in *The Nasho's War: Australia's National Servicemen in Vietnam* that "towards the end of his two years, a man's military service often seemed to fade away", with a former servicemen commenting to the author, "There was not a lot happening. It was pretty bloody boring, just waiting out my time".

It was a similar situation for your grandad, whose close companions Morey Grafton and Kevin Harrison had left for home while he had a further six months to serve, knowing he would not be a part of 3RAR's return to Vietnam in 1971. Serving out his time though was a relative luxury compared to having to go into combat.

Taking up the position of platoon commander of 3RAR's 1 Platoon A Company might have left your grandad feeling awkward at times, but the alternative could have changed the course of his future in far worse ways and our entire family is fortunate that he did not have to serve overseas. You might not have been around to read this book if he had been so dispatched and I might not have been around to write it.

The conflict of Vietnam impacted an entire generation of young Australians, with 63,740 men drafted into service. More than 500 did not return and many of those who did, brought back with them more than they expected. More than they could cope with. The impact was devastating in an era that was not yet aware of Post-Traumatic Stress Disorder, let alone how to understand and treat it.

The impact of the Vietnam war zone was conveyed by a friend of your grandad's, who served in a different corps and whom I've deliberately not named. Almost 50-years on, the anguish it had inflicted was still evident.

"I'd just walked out of a bloody jungle, they chucked me on a plane back here and said, 'There you go, now get back to city life'," he said.

"You get back from having the shit shot out of you, blokes trying to nail you every night and sleeping in a bloody hole with a rifle, then they tell you to get back to work. Looking back, it was crazy. I was like a caged lion. I didn't have any sense of responsibility: the drinking; the women.

"Nowadays, I think they've wised up a bit and guys coming back from Iraq and combat areas, they follow them up with counselling and things like that. There wasn't a thing – not a thing at all – when we got back. I remember saying to my mum one day after I'd been out drinking and wiped myself off, all I wanted to do was head out into the bush somewhere and live in the bush for a few months.

"We weren't superheroes able to deal with these things – we were just kids."

Official support for returnees was left wanting and the public displays of protest groups would have undoubtedly left some servicemen feeling lost. As an example, your Great Grandad Eric had been awarded the Caterpillar Badge for surviving a war-time parachute escape from his bomber, during which he sustained head trauma on landing and, as a result, suffered from severe headaches for the rest of his life. His reward? The government generously subsidised his Panadol purchases, making the packet of paracetamol tablets slightly cheaper than their shelf-price of $2.

It was a time when family and friends were crucial for those suffering the effects of Vietnam and Harrison said your grandad was one friend who remained with him throughout his life.

"I was 49 and I'd been a director of over 60 companies, I was an executive of a hotel chain, I was chairman of the Tourism Commission and a whole stack of things," Harrison said of his life after the army.

"Then I got hit – they say it could have been Agent Orange – and I had a heart attack, I got cancer, I got Crohn's Disease and I really got crook. Before all these were diagnosed, it used to be funny in a way: I'd be out to breakfasts with the Premier or launching something and I'd just fall asleep.

"Through it all, Wally always came and saw me (in hospital) and I thought that was the sign of a true friendship. Even though we'd drifted apart with our different lives, he was still there to see if there was anything he could do.

"That's a real credit to the person."

Harrison was not alone in the respect he forever held for your grandad. After extensive searching, one of his closest friends from his army days, Bob Lewis, was located and when advised of the project of compiling this book, was eager to support it. All for a man he likened to a "comet flying through history and singeing us all".

"He made great friends of great people because of his irrepressible character and personality," Lewis said.

"I've bumped into blokes like Rod Marsh, Dennis Lillee and Sam Gannon, to name just a few, from time to time, and still hear these legends in their own lifetime speak of him in awe. Not only should you be so proud of him but you should aspire to be so well loved and respected.

"Do not be overawed by your father's achievements. Seek only to add to them."

This was a challenging chapter to write. Not for the stories that were told, but for the stories that were not. Most of the anecdotes recounted around this time were humorous in nature and my questions about anything deeper were often deflected. As one of your grandad's mates said: "You do tend to remember the good and funny times. You hardly ever talk about the tough times."

Your grandad understood the tough times. Not through first-hand experience, but through the empathy that made him the person he was. He saw in Grafton and Harrison and soldiers like them a fatigue and wounds that could not be healed by the regimented routines of the army, but instead needed the type of genuine, light-hearted, long-lasting mateship, camaraderie and comic relief that was found in the life of almost every 20-year-old in that era.

Every 20-year-old, that is, before they are plucked from paradise and dropped into hell. Your grandad understood. And he never took for granted his good fortune at not being sent to Vietnam himself.

The calendar turned to May 1970. Your grandad's time as a national serviceman came to a close. He ended his commitment as a man far more equipped to deal with life than the boy who entered and he had a new, steely resolve: "I'd wasted a few years up until then, I'd readily admit."

But while the army had been a significant moment for your grandad and it had taught him skills and introduced him to several people with whom he remained close for the rest of his life, it also interrupted the pursuit of his dream to enter the world of sport and sports media. His discharge in 1970 allowed that pursuit to continue.

This time, there would be no rejection letter.

Chapter 4

Never Give In, Never Give In (Never, Never, Never)

To say your grandad was responsible for Western Australia winning nine Sheffield Shield and six one-day domestic cricket titles would probably be overreaching. Well, undoubtedly overreaching.

But we'll come back to that in a moment.

Your grandad left for national service as a 20-year-old kid, but returned home a vastly more experienced man and the position of platoon commander with 1 Platoon A Company held him in good stead upon his resumption of civilian life. Sports journalism and broadcasting remained the dream and your grandad still looked at *The West Australian* newspaper as the place to achieve it. However, the timing of his discharge from the army meant he missed the 1970 cadetship application window and had to wait until the following year to lodge his third and final request.

It meant a year of filling the time and, back around his close mates, that became easy. George Young the year before had been convinced by his brother Robbie to take his Wembley amateur-honed skills to Subiaco Football Club and, after performing well in scratch matches, including the clash against Norwood witnessed by your grandad during his time at Woodside, he was amidst a successful 1970 WANFL season, in which he played every league game. Young went on to represent Western Australia in the state tour of Victoria and Tasmania and again stood out in a showing that would prove pivotal in the coming years.

Young was joined in the Subiaco ranks by other friends of your grandad's such as Dennis Blair, Graham Bushell and Steve Heal. The entourage, combined with the passionate dedication to the Maroons of girlfriend Lee Hunt, meant your grandad's allegiances – historically with West Perth – became equally shared with Subiaco. Sam Gannon had built to 14 Sheffield Shield appearances for Western Australia in the time your grandad had been serving and was continuing his battle with some of the state's most iconic names in pace bowling – Dennis Lillee, Bob Massie and Ian Brayshaw – as he pushed for selection 15.

It meant that there was plenty of sport to watch and catch up on. The venue for the latter, of course, was The Floreat Hotel over a beer, but the mix of First Grade cricketers for Subiaco and the rise of Subiaco football's next generation of soon-to-be drought-breaking champions meant The Floreat was now accompanied as a regular haunt by "The Shents" – The Shenton Park Hotel – on the corner of Nicholson and Derby Roads in Shenton Park.

The on-again, off-again relationship with Hunt was back on with your grandad having returned home and the pair loaded up the latter's second car purchase, a pale blue Ford Capri, and drove across the country.

"Licence number UAP-188," Hunt recalled with a clarity that seemed amazing until bettering herself by further recounting the numbers of the Prince Skyline it replaced, "UPD-207".

Hunt had spent some time living in Sydney while your grandad was completing national service and the pair made the drive to New South Wales, stopping into Adelaide to see some army mates along the way. Your grandad had a lot of idiosyncrasies, but one of the more prominent was his taste in music.

As his son, I dealt with it often. My first words were "Jolene, Jolene", as I sang duet with Dolly Parton in the back of his car and I remember the challenges and trade-offs for tape-deck time that had to be made when I got older: "You can play it for half an hour", he would say of my then-penchant for punk bands such as Unwritten Law, the likes of which he never quite embraced.

And, then, there were the bedtime ballads. I began singing to you "Forty Shades of Green" by Johnny Cash. It was your favourite and could soothe you in one line. I would then move onto Gordon Lightfoot's "Cotton Jenny" and "Morningtown Ride" by The Seekers. I got all of those from your grandad, substituting traditional nursery rhymes for Country and Western.

There was always one song that I remembered in full, because your grandad later sung it to your Uncle Mark and it started, "Telephone to glory, oh what joy divine".

"When he came out of national service, we drove to Sydney," Hunt said. "We were driving across the Nullarbor and your father kept singing 'Royal Telephone'. I said, 'If you sing that song one more time, I'm seriously going to get out'. He loved it, but he didn't just sing it once: it was over and over."

The relationship that had begun at a church dance and grew to your grandad walking the short distance to Hunt's house and escorting her to weekend netball, church or to just spend time together, began to wind down after the trip east. Hunt had previously met someone in Sydney, before later marrying. However, the pair remained friends and never missed a phone call for each other's birthday.

It was the end of a relationship, but not a friendship.

Your grandad, having been mostly out of the loop for two years, introduced what would become a tradition that lasted his entire life: the New Year's Eve celebration. It began in its early years with a booking at the Contacio International Motor Hotel, which was at 156 West Coast Highway, slightly north of – and not to be confused with – the current Contacio Bar.

The old hotel boasted 46 air-conditioned rooms and about 20 of your grandad's friends and their partners would fill the room's bathtub with ice and drinks, before heading poolside to usher in the New Year alongside several groups doing the same.

"From there, we just kept on doing New Year's Eve and it would be us, the Bushells, the Blairs, the Youngs, Sam Gannon used to come from time to time, and we kept that going nearly up to the day your dad died," Steve Heal recalled. "He really valued his old friends and he was the one that made sure that group always got together."

The New Year's venue changed, but the tradition lasted, as did the one that would usually precede it; the Christmas beer with army mates Morey Grafton and Kevin Harrison, along with artillery serviceman Stuart McKeown, a friend of Grafton's and third-grade player for Subiaco, who was instantly absorbed into the Floreat Hotel group of mates.

"We would occasionally not get served at the bar, thanks to your father, who could belch very loudly," Grafton said. "I remember one occasion; my cousin was serving at the bar. She said something like, 'That rude prick, he's not getting another beer and neither are you'."

The 1970-71 summer brought with it another cricket season, which gave your grandad the opportunity to return to the action himself, instead of watching from the grass banks. He had joined George Young in playing Fourth Grade for Subiaco Cricket Club in the 1965-66 season – the year the club moved from Subiaco Oval to Rosalie Park – and had been guided by club Life Member and father figure at the time John Dickens.

Your grandad returned to the club, but found time had forced an even greater divide between his talents and the skills of his higher-grade friends, so he embarked on his first foray into sports administration as club secretary. It would have been an uneventful position not worth a mention in a biography, if not for the fact that it was a position held by your grandad and your grandad never did anything by halves.

Which brings us back to the nine Sheffield Shield and six domestic one-day titles.

The Subiaco Cricket Club was starved for success as the 1960s turned into the 70s. It had won six premierships in less than two decades from 1930, but failed to add to that through the 20 years that followed and had managed just two appearances in the decider.

It was a painful shift in fortunes for the club that had produced Western Australia's first Test representative, Jack Rutherford – another Bruce Rock boy. The club produced its second national representative, left-arm quick Jim Hubble, a decade later. Yet, despite these successful products and the recruitment of former Test bowler Des Hoar as First Grade coach, Subiaco was unable to break the drought.

How your grandad came to hold the position of secretary at the club is an issue of debate. The more tactful of his friends, such as George Young, claimed "Wally felt like he had to participate in some capacity, so he volunteered as Club Secretary". The blunter Kim Hughes put it as simple as "he happened to go to a meeting and no other prick wanted to do the job, so they said, 'You're it, Foreman'."

Either way, in 1971, he was secretary at Subiaco Cricket Club, sitting on the committee alongside Hughes' father and club president, Stan.

The Hughes family was one of many that became involved with Subiaco when it imported promising cricket talent from local sub-district club Floreat Park, which fielded teams from Second Grade down, but had no First Grade side, meaning its best players, such as Hughes, Sam Gannon and Terry Alderman, were required to shift clubs to play at the highest district level.

The move reunited the younger Hughes with your grandad, who had coached the former in Under 14s, making it a miracle that he eventually went on to captain Australia. The Geraldton products of the Hughes family also found the country link with the Foremans and had become friendly through mutual membership at the Reabold Tennis Club.

Cricket gave the hotels of Perth another income injection from your grandad and his friends, who would wander to The Shents after trainings and usually end up at The Floreat to make the most of the 11pm liquor licence. Gobbles Nightclub would then follow and, as Hughes recalled, the nights "after a while became about trying to get home".

Army mate Morey Grafton had become a regular among the group of friends, complementing your effervescent grandad – "We got on very well: Wal liked to talk, I liked to listen; he liked the spotlight, I liked the shadows" – and nights out became a full-time arrangement.

Irony weaved its way through a large portion of this book for me. When I was in Year 4, I delivered to your nana and grandad a stern letter from school advising that their son – me – had been walking around singing a ghastly recital of Old MacDonald Had a Farm, changing the words and tune to, "Old MacDonald sitting on a fence, picking his bum with a monkey wrench".

The lyrics made no sense and your grandad found no humour in them at all. How he kept from laughing is beyond me, though. Thursday night at The Shenton Park Hotel was also Entertainment Night and that entertainment would often feature a performance from the Subiaco Cricket Club players reciting "the dirty version" of Old MacDonald Had a Farm.

The group was led through crescendo by your grandad.

"The bulls are bulling here and the ducks are ducking there," recalled Kim Hughes, refraining from using the precise adjectives of the bulls and ducks' actions.

Hughes was in his second season with Subiaco when your grandad took the reins as secretary, having joined the club in the 1969-70 campaign. The talent pool was there, but the results were not, which led your grandad to pick up the phone at the end of another failed campaign and place a call to a man who had only recently arrived in Western Australia: Daryl Foster, a devoted Victorian Grade cricketer with a penchant for coaching.

Foster had moved to Perth to complete the highly-regarded Physical Education degree at the University of WA – the only institution in the country at the time to offer more than a diploma in the field.

"In my first year here, I promised my darling wife that if she was willing to come to Perth and relocate with three children that I wouldn't get involved in cricket anymore," Foster said.

"Well, the end of the story is that I did. I went down to pre-season training at Rosalie Park and met Wally and met George Young and all the other people who were a part of the club in that year. My first memory of the season was that there was this little blonde-haired guy over in the nets, being thrown full-tosses and he was smashing them away.

"I said to your dad, 'Who's that?' and he said, 'Oh, that's a young cricketer named Kim Hughes and that's his coach'. I never knew, at that moment, that I was looking at a future Australian captain."

The recruitment of Foster paid immediate dividends for Subiaco, which went on to win the premiership and club championship and end its barren run. The significance of the moment had been made apparent to Foster in the lead-up to the decider against University, as he was excitedly told that the club had not won a final in 17 years, immediately placing a larger weight of expectation on the captain-coach's shoulders as he headed into a match against an opponent captained by John Inverarity and with Ric Charlesworth in its ranks.

Crucial to the club's success was the enticement of Jim Hubble back to Subiaco. It was a move often credited to Foster, but one which the former coach credited equally to your grandad. However, if the results of the drought-breaking season could be attributed at least in part to the presence of Foster, then it was also a success that might have never happened.

Oblivious to the promise Foster had made to his wife that cricket would be absent from their lives in Western Australia, your grandad almost undid his good work in enticing the coach back to the game he was destined to immerse himself in.

"At the same time as Wally was talking to me to come to Subi, my wife Leonie was in hospital having Jamie," Foster said.

"Jamie was born in September 1971, our fourth child and only Sandgroper, and Leonie received a card from Wally, saying,

'Welcome to the new skipper'. The only problem was; that was the first Leonie knew of my association with Subiaco. She had a little bit of trouble with labour at the time, so I delayed telling her, but had told Wally that Jamie was born.

"He sent the card as a good bloke, but that let on what was going on."

Foster and your grandad developed through the Subiaco Cricket Club a close friendship that spanned a successful era for both men and it was the former who, a little more than a decade later, first advised your grandad of a job going at some place called the Western Australian Institute of Sport.

Foster finished his Physical Education degree in 1972 and returned to Melbourne, before again heading west in 1974 to take up a position at the secondary teachers college. The head of the department was respected WA cricket figure Len Pavy, who at the same time held the position at the Western Australian Cricket Association of State Senior Squad Coordinator and was due to take long-service leave.

Pavy requested that Foster take over coaching duties of the state's First XI side, "just for a year".

"Twenty years later, it all finished," Foster said. "If I hadn't of got the opportunity at Subi, there's no way known I would have gone on to coach WA."

It would have been Western Australian cricket's loss, as Foster went on to devote decades of service to the state through positions ranging from Chairman of Selectors, Game Development Committee Chairman and Board Member, while having sat on the board of Cricket Australia.

And, as coach, he steered WA to nine Sheffield Shield and six domestic one-day titles.

I began my journalism career in 2007, shortly after your grandad passed away. Contrary to what the timing would suggest, it wasn't some misguided venture in search of him.

I had previously flagged interest in it, but your grandad had shot down the suggestion, much to the disappointment of your nana, who scolded him with: "He finally has an idea of what he wants to do and you dismiss it". However, after his death, your nana said, "There's nothing holding you back from journalism anymore".

Then-editor of *The Sunday Times* Brett McCarthy was good enough to meet with me and helped form a blueprint for my career. That led to my enrolment in journalism at university, a few bits-and-pieces jobs, then fulltime employment at *The Sunday Times* a couple of years later. I enjoyed the job thoroughly and I miss certain aspects of it, however, it ultimately wasn't for me.

The path I embarked on and the idea of the media as a career, while pursued out of my own free-will, undoubtedly first sprouted from your grandad's involvement in it. Your grandad was working for the Government in the Crown Law Department and, while he made the most of the jobs he had throughout his younger life, he had found himself in those positions because he was unable to secure the job he dreamed of and had followed in his father's footsteps.

Working for the government for the length of time he did was a point of pride for your Great Grandad Eric Foreman and his promotion after 49 years and seven months' service to Chief Electoral Officer was a result of his determination to one day be a department head.

But that was your great grandad's dream, not that of his son. And, in the winter of 1971, your grandad began for the third and final time his application to join *The West Australian* cadetship program.

The process began during an application window that ran from September to December, requiring aspiring cadets to complete and submit their responses to a form that asked who they were and, more importantly, who their father and family was.

It was a highly-competitive program that attracted hundreds of submissions, which were vetted and whittled down for the second round of the process. Those who were not dismissed during the vetting process went on to face-to-face interviews in the lead-up to Christmas at Newspaper House at 125 St Georges Terrace. It was an intimidating moment for the majority of candidates, with tertiary qualifications a rarity and most fresh out of school, having to sit directly across a boardroom table from about six senior news executives, who proceeded to grill applicants on their knowledge of Perth and current affairs.

It was described as a "highly imperfect process" by 1970 cadet and former editor of *The West Australian* Paul Murray. Not for the intent of the aforementioned stages, but for the deep vein of nepotism that ran through them. An applicant's family connections and background, their appearance (if they were female) and their sporting ability (if they were male) held significant weight in decision-making. Decades of experience and overhauls by editors have since reshaped the process.

The third and final stage was for successful applicants to be notified in early January: a time that allowed unsuccessful candidates to commence tertiary studies without waiting in hope. Your grandad had gathered together his application, complete with a glowing reference from Subiaco Cricket Club President Stan Hughes, who held the respected position in society of a primary school headmaster and, importantly in that time of the process, was the father of a trailblazing 17-year-old cricketer named Kim, who was tearing through First Grade ranks.

There was nothing remarkable when the name "Wally Foreman" was received in the first and second applications in the mid-1960s: your grandad had been just like the other hundreds of graduated high school students looking for a job. Nothing had set him apart.

That was not the case in 1971.

Those responsible for the vetting process found themselves looking at the application of a soon-to-be 24-year-old – six to seven years older than the majority of the applicants. The reference was impressive, as was the position his father – your Great Grandad Eric Foreman – held, but it was the experience that drew the spotlight: National Service; Scheyville Officer

Training Unit; Woodside Barracks and platoon commander of 1 Platoon A Company for the decorated 3RAR; a Second Lieutenant and a C-XXI Government employee.

And he wanted to be a cadet?

It was a crossroad of irony. The Lottery of Death that had left your grandad frustrated as it tore him away from the desperate pursuit of his dream had, in fact, been the moment that resulted in him finally achieving it. Your grandad made it through the vetting process. He sat the interview. And, in early January, the greatest birthday present to that point in his life arrived via notification that he had been selected as one of 17 successful applicants for *The West Australian*'s 1972 cadetship intake.

The role that your grandad's army experience played in that selection cannot be understated as it was a talking point around the newsroom before he had even started. The army had taken your grandad from an indiscernible teenage applicant and turned him into, as Paul Murray recalled, "a very unusual model for a *West* cadet" that could not be ignored.

Rejecting the cadetship offer would not have even registered as an option, but it did represent a significant drop in salary back to the days of the Rat Room.

"I remember when he told me he'd got this cadetship; I told him he was mad," said Fred Miller, the man who had shared the experience of the Rat Room Filing Clerk at the Local Courts.

"He'd finally got out of the Rat Room and had got a promotion to a C-XXI. I said, 'You're crazy: here you are with this long line of good looking sheilas to talk to all day and you're going to take a cadetship'. Anyway, he didn't take my advice, went and did it and the rest is history."

Miller's reservations were purely economical and he joined with the entourage of friends in celebrating the moment. The group of Floreat Hotel mates had always had each other's backs and revelled in everyone's success, but up until that moment, your grandad had to find joy in the success of others.

George Young began receiving interest from VFL clubs, Steve Heal and Graham Bushell were playing League football, Sam

Gannon was a regular among First Class ranks and would go on to represent his country and Kim Hughes was catching the eye of the cricket world. And, finally, your grandad would be a journalist.

"He was like a dog with two dicks, when he got that cadetship," Sam Gannon said. "Typical Wally, he enjoyed every minute of (working at the bank and courts) and he gave it 110 per cent, gave it his all and worked his ass off, but the underlying fact was that he wanted to get into sports journalism.

"That was what he wanted and he wasn't going to rest until he did it."

And it was just the beginning.

Chapter 5

Always Follow Your Dreams

COMMOTION INTERRUPTED THE ADRENALINE-FILLED, ORGANISED chaos of the hall. It was the police. They had locked the doors and were closing in, rounding everyone up like cattle. There was no escape.

It was 1972 and a wave of panic came over your grandad as he stood frozen alongside close friends George Young and Dennis Baker – Subiaco Football Club teammates – as the WA Police located and raided the regular, yet illegal, gambling ring.

How the trio came to be a part of that particular gambling operation was a combination of the harmless rogue element inside them and your grandad's experience with some of the more colourful members of his new employer, *The West Australian*. The Subiaco Cricket Club had moved to Rosalie Park a handful of years earlier, making The Shenton Park Hotel the most suitable venue for post-training drinks and debrief.

The Subiaco Cricket group was well known at the hotel. They shared the Rosalie changerooms with the local rugby team that was filled with English expats and supporters, leading to the cricketers learning a hymnbook of chants, the type that are synonymous with English football and which both groups would then belt out in unison and full voice at The Shenton Park Hotel until the 10pm closing time, at which point they would take their songs to The Floreat Hotel.

However, the Shenton Park Hotel also held secrets. The cricketers were of course not the only patrons at the venue on a Thursday night and, somewhere among the crowd, two figures would slowly spread word of an alternative venue; one that shifted with the spontaneity of a gypsy caravan to avoid authorities and that thrived on secrecy and games of chance. An eclectic mix of up to 200 people from all walks of life would wait for the whispers that revealed a location, before abandoning the

Hotel and converging on the new location.

It is often said that the house always wins. That is usually a mantra directed at gamblers, but on this night in 1972, it was a timely reminder for the group of Subiaco cricketers. The gambling rings offered a particular drawcard for poor sportsmen and the fiscally frugal grandad: the offer of free beer to anyone investing in a game of crown and anchor. It seemed like an immediate win against the house.

The problem was, the "house" was a den of illegal activity and winning was always considered temporary. The crowd in the Cambridge Street hall in Leederville, directly opposite the current JB O'Reilly's pub, came to a stand-still. Undercover police had infiltrated the operation and observed its activities until sufficient evidence had been gathered. Then, they locked the doors.

Panic rushed like a wave over your grandad. He had fought tooth and nail to realise his dream of joining the media. It had taken years and the gruelling trials of Scheyville and the army to even get an interview for a cadetship. Now, he was staring down the barrel of immediate dismissal.

The arrests would be made, charges laid and – the nail in the coffin for your grandad – the details, including the name of young cadet Wally Foreman, would be provided to *The West's* late-night police roundsman for publication the next day. There was an irony in all of that, though: that young cadet had just been posted to assist with the police rounds.

"Wally had just started with *The West Australian* at the time and he was shitting himself," George Young said.

"We all handed in our names and addresses and they picked 20 blokes at random. We all had our names taken. In those days, police reports were filed immediately and they were in the paper the next day. At 9-o'clock, Wally frantically went into *The West Australian* office so that when the police report came in – 'Club Raided' – with all the names of those apprehended, he could try and get them out.

"I said to Wally: 'Well, gee, if you wouldn't mind, could you see if you could get my name out? I don't think the Subiaco Footy

Club would be too pleased if I was out until all hours at an illegal gambling joint'. He said, 'No worries'.

"Low and behold, the next day the newspaper report came out and there was 'George Young', but there was no Wally Foreman in there. He got his own name out, but he couldn't get anyone else's out, he reckoned."

The event was – years later – undoubtedly humorous, but it equally spoke to the rebellious streak that ran through your grandad; the one that occasionally tested the boundary of harmless fun and what lay beyond it. It was also another example of your grandad's ability to endear himself to those around him, because the removal of names from the paper of record of those involved in police matters was no small feat.

Police roundsman Cyril Ayris spoke of the era of reporting to ABC Local Radio's Geoff Hutchison in 2012, describing "a very different newsroom in those days to the newsrooms of today". Receiving a parking ticket was usually sufficient cause to be named and shamed, unless, Ayris explained, the parking ticket was received in Kings Park, in which case the report was usually seen as a badge of honour, given the late-night activities the recipient was likely involved in to receive such a ticket.

It was all considered the news of the day. There was also the moral obligation to do what was considered appropriate and not what was easy. *The West* would frequently receive calls from friends and family of those set to be named, lobbying for the exclusion of those names, at which point Editor in Chief Fred Morony would point to his own drunk driving offence that had been published and respond: "Thank you and goodbye".

So, while it is possible to look back now on the anecdote and laugh, it was a sufficiently serious incident at the time to have your grandad, at the lowest peg of the editorial hierarchy, extremely concerned about his future at the newspaper.

That was your grandad, though: he was as comfortable among those staff wielding power as he was among fellow cadets and beer-swilling gamblers.

Your granadad was part of a 17-cadet intake group – a large number for a group of cadets – that was spread across *The West Australian*, the *Daily News* and the *Weekend News*. The group also included a young teaching graduate, Geraldine Doogue, who went on to forge a respected reputation with the ABC, where she continued to work at the time of writing this book.

Those who were considered as having the most potential, such as your grandad and Doogue, were reserved for *The West Australian*, although with that came the almost 150-years (at the time) of history and tradition. The cadets who went to the *Daily News* and the *Weekend News* often found themselves with a freedom to write and extrapolate far greater than that of their colleagues at *The West*, who in a way had their creativity shackled by the responsibilities of the paper of record. However, creativity holds little importance in news writing – it just takes up space and interferes with facts.

Cadets were assessed throughout a strict, orthodox 12-week training program and, under the tutelage of Jim Dunbar, they attended daily shorthand classes that ran for the first-half of every day, before they were introduced and briefed by members of industries that they would come in regular contact with, from those involved in the fire, police and ambulance services, to lawyers and members of government. Lectures and writing tasks interspersed the week, while cadets were encouraged to develop and pitch story ideas, which the group would workshop before Dunbar took it to the Chief of Staff.

The intake was an eclectic mix of aspiring journalists – some with degrees, some fresh out of high school and others, such as your grandad, with more unique backgrounds – and once their training was complete, they were farmed out to the different rounds of the papers based on their perceived ability and maturity.

Doogue, who was classed as a fourth-year cadet due to her university degree, was immediately assigned to the courts round.

Your grandad was graded lower as a third-year cadet due to his lack of tertiary qualifications, but his potential as a journalist and his understanding of people and the way society operated was quickly apparent and had him placed on the police rounds. It meant the pair avoided the usual mundane tasks assigned to cadets, such as compiling the weather and shipping news and it was a significant post for your grandad.

The police round was a respected round that demanded a high level of responsibility and could, at any moment, require its reporters to cover high-profile and high-impact stories that demanded acute accuracy. It was also a placemen that had your grandad taken under the wing of the esteemed Cyril Ayris, a stylish and respectful man, whose stories regularly provided the paper with its front-page splash and whose life was so intriguing in itself that it required he write his own biography to go with the 20-or-so he had written about others.

Ayris was a self-described "refugee from war-torn England, who stumbled into newspaper work" and went on to record a 25-year career with *The West Australian*, beginning in the accounts department. He was a hard-working, principled man and a guide as perfect a fit for your grandad as the round was for a cadet coming from a background of working in the courts and regularly dealing with police and law.

The newsroom of *The West Australian* – like any newsroom, for those who do not spend their days in one – was an impressive hive of activity; an open-plan expanse of desks and people, who moved to the soundtrack of typewriters, the rumbling of printing presses and what seemed like a hundred blended conversations. Chaotic is not the right word, though it might have given that impression. A newsroom more closely resembles a living organism.

The definition of the word "awesome" has been hijacked and watered down over the generations, but when awesome is used here to describe the sight of a newsroom in full operation – particularly to uninitiated eyes, such as the cadet intake of *The West Australian* in 1972 – it is used in its traditional, awe-inspiring sense. A few offices – a rarity in any newsroom – framed in timber and opaque glass, branched off to the right from the entry hall and were reserved only for the most senior reporters.

A line of sub-editors – the problem solvers and artists of the news world, who make oversized or misshapen pegs fit in the available holes and correct errors along the way – ran along the back of the room, with a horseshoe-shaped cobbling of desks nearby to house the hierarchy of the office, from the editors and deputy editors to the copy takers. The layout was such that the line of sports desks connected to the sub-editors in an L-shape, hugging the four-person groupings of general news reporters in the centre.

It was among that central group that your grandad found himself positioned, directly opposite sports writers Alan East and Colin Hopkins in one of the closest seats possible to the sports department without being one of its writers and within easy conversation distance of larger-than-life journalists Geoff Christian and Ken Casellas. There was plenty to discuss.

Besides the ongoing news of the current sporting world, Christian had also taken a year off work in 1960 to assist West Perth Football Club coach Arthur Olliver in preparing his group for what would be the drought-breaking premiership season – as witnessed by your 12-year-old Cardinals faithful grandad in his family's first year in Perth.

The arrival of this new cadet Wally Foreman was also intriguing and cause of some initial confusion for Christian and Casellas, who recognised the name, but certainly not the face. It was an almost unfathomable occurrence of coincidence that just four years before your grandad arrived in 1972, a senior sports writer named Wally Foreman retired from *The West Australian* in 1968.

More freakish was the parallels between the two Wally Foremans: both attended Perth Modern School, both had spent time in Kalgoorlie, both had held positions with the state government before embarking on a career in the media and, of course, both became journalists at *The West Australian*.

"We knew Walter Victor Foreman – WV Foreman – very well, then all of a sudden after he retired, we found out there was this new bloke coming to work at *The West* named Wally Foreman," Casellas said. "We thought, 'He can't come back; he's too bloody old'.

"We quickly got to know this new Wally, because he was always cheery, always smiling and he was a dapper young fellow when he first started there. He had this great urge to squeeze into the sports department, but there were no spots. That was his entire ambition in life; to be involved in sport."

Wally Foreman – the 1972 version – got to know Geoff Christian and Ken Casellas as quickly as they did him and a mutually beneficial friendship was soon struck.

Your grandad was assigned to the night police rounds, which had his days begin between 5-6pm and end once the last of three rolling deadlines had passed shortly after midnight. Your grandad's job as the police roundsman involved late-night drives, doing the rounds of town to see if there had been any crimes, fires, or emergencies on which he would be required to report.

The timing was perfect for Christian and Casellas, whose days began a few hours before your grandad's and an unofficial role of their new cadet mate was to chauffeur the pair to the Latin Quarter, cabaret lounge Il Trovatore on James Street, or various other nightclubs around Perth. The venues might not have been the most savoury, but it was another invaluable opportunity to rub shoulders with the sports team that your grandad so wished to join and network with their contacts along the way.

"We'd ring up Waldo and say, 'Come on Waldo', and he'd come and pick us up from the Latin Quarter, or wherever we were," Casellas said.

"The most memorable moment in Wally's time of chauffeuring us around was one day when we came into work and he said, 'You know what happened last night: I had a drink with you blokes at the Latin Quarter, it got late and, all of a sudden, I got woken up by a policeman knocking on the window of the car'.

"He'd parked his car in the middle of Murray Street in Perth and was blocking the traffic."

Casellas and Christian were two of Perth's most authoritative voices in sport at that time and remain among the most respected sports journalists the state has produced. Christian ruled with an iron fist and was protective of his football round, ensuring he reviewed all stories that went to print. He had worked his way into the sports department from General News and had held the Chief Football Writer mantle since 1957.

Christian was also an accomplished runner, holding the state 100 and 220 yard titles, and only narrowly missed selection for the 1956 Olympic Games in Melbourne when he finished fourth in the latter at the national selection trials. Only his decision to take 1960 off work to assist West Perth prevented his tenure as Chief Football Writer reaching the 30-year mark and he retired in 1987, before passing away 11 years later.

Casellas, fondly known as "Mouse", began with *The West Australian* as a cadet in 1954, specialising in football and trotting, before heading to London, where for Sydney's *Daily Mirror* he covered two Wimbledon tennis championships, two English Derbies, Commonwealth boxing bouts and the 1960 Olympic Games in Rome.

He returned to Perth in 1961 and began forging a revered reputation in racing coverage, becoming the doyen of trotting reporting through *The West Australian,* his commentary commitments across radio and his involvement in TV. Casellas' status as a preeminent reporter was further strengthened the year your grandad arrived as a cadet at *The West* in 1972, as he succeeded Jack Lee as the paper's Chief Cricket Writer and held the position until his retirement in 1999.

It was lofty company for your grandad to keep and was particularly important, given the duo held senior positions in the department he aimed to one-day join. However, there was the other side to Casellas and Christian; the side that involved knocking on backdoors and staring at bulky bouncers through peepholes, trudging up darkened staircases and having seats reserved in the corners of some of Perth's shadiest night spots.

That is not a comment on that lifestyle and the men's careers are testament to their ability to balance it with work, but for a young, impressionable cadet such as your grandad, who had a penchant for walking the line that his idol Johnny Cash often sang about, the balance was not always as easily managed.

The Ford Capris sped through the winding course, snaking its way through suburbia as its driver attempted to push its small engine to its limits. The driver was your grandad and he was returning home after a night of drinking. His speed was reckless; him driving in the state he was in was sheer idiocy.

Yet somehow – as he had done his whole life, from cheeky primary school student, to carefree cadet – he got away with all facets of his life intact.

"He was a silly little man," your grandad's army friend Morey Grafton said.

"He was working at *The West Australian* and had bought himself a little Falcon sports car, not a particularly big motor, but it looked the part. He'd had a few beers and he was going through Perry Lakes – that road that runs right through the middle – and in those days, there used to be a big, fat tree, with branches that came right to the ground.

"You could park a car under there and you couldn't see it and, this night, he didn't see the cops until he was right upon it. He thought, 'Shit, what do I do, I've been drinking and I can't get caught drink driving in my job'. It wouldn't have been good to get caught running from the cops either, mind you, but he was just around the corner from home, so he decided to put his foot down and head for home.

"He got to Glenties Road and his folks weren't there, so it meant he could go straight down the driveway, through the carport and around the back. He said he peered out the window and would see a cop car driving past every now and then. It gave him a fright and he might have given up drinking for a bit after that.

"That actually gave him a fright. He knew he'd done the wrong thing."

It should be mentioned that this was a time of greater tolerance for – and far less education around – offences such as drunk driving. It doesn't excuse your grandad's actions, but there wasn't the same understanding of consequences then as there is now. Even the illegal gambling dens were tolerated, in a way, until they went the way of the dinosaurs with the 1980s application for a casino at Burswood. However, those that dodged the police bullet were generally far more important, renowned or connected than a newspaper cadet.

Your grandad survived both the gambling den raid and flee from police and built on his early positive impressions to begin turning heads at *The West*. The only issue was one of staffing and, despite his knowledge, enthusiasm and potential, there simply was not a vacant position on the sports desk and there was little prospect of one arising in the foreseeable future, given the young age and talent of those in the department.

As the saying goes, though: there is more than one way to skin a cat.

December 1972 became a month of celebration for the Foreman family. Your Great Aunty Sandy married Lew Shaw, a country boy from Beverley, on 9 December and your grandad was groomsman, employing his car's recently proven getaway skills to whisk the married couple away after the reception. Then, on Christmas Eve, your grandad received a phone call from *The West Australian*.

The potential seen in him had him earmarked for the coveted 18-month posting as Melbourne correspondent after just a year as a cadet reporter. He had not been first on the list of candidates, but had benefited from others declining the offer of the position. It would once again mean time away from the family he loved, but this time it would provide an opportunity to embrace his passion: sport.

This was an issue, though, that proved difficult to confirm for this book. I found little evidence that the Melbourne staffer prior to your grandad's appointment was required to cover much sport at all. Today, the position is almost completely sport-focused.

I was told by a senior figure from *The West* that your grandad, determined to cover sport, convinced the editor that the Melbourne correspondent could also provide far more appropriate coverage of the VFL, with a West Australian-focus, while doing the same with opportunities such as Test cricket, Davis Cup tennis and the national hockey championships. We had plenty of West Australian sportspeople proving successful in all those sports, after all.

As I mentioned, the Melbourne posting for *The West Australian* today is completely sport-focused and if it is true that your grandad was the one who convinced the editor that the role should be that way, journalist friends and colleagues of mine such as Steve Butler, Shayne Hope and Craig O'Donoghue, who spent time in the country's mecca of sport during my time in the media, held a position inspired your grandad.

Because, in late 1972, your grandad accepted the Melbourne posting. He prepared for life in the east once more. And to hell with what had come prior: his role was going to focus on sport.

Your grandad arrived in Melbourne in early 1973 and was relishing the opportunity, given the freedom and scope of news coverage. The position was also based out of the renowned *Herald and Weekly Times (HWT)* offices at the corner of Exhibition and Flinders Streets in the heart of Melbourne and he sat alongside some of the country's most revered journalists.

The office itself was a building to behold. The looming five-storey monolith that spanned almost a block encapsulated the stereotypical appearance of the media industry. A newspaper boy standing on the corner shouting "extra, extra" would have been the only thing missing to make it a scene ripped straight from a cliché Hollywood cityscape.

The simple straight-line carvings of the Exhibition and Flinders faces were accentuated by the Ionic pilasters that scaled its sides from their first-floor bases. Spherical lights reached out with cast-iron arms from below every one of those bases and illuminated the sidewalks, while drawing eyes upwards to the roof, past the dozen windows that ran horizontally along the length.

It was there that sat the features that made the building the icon of media, power and power of the media that it was. The crown was punctuated with the jewels of a large "Herald Sun" neon sign, with each letter two tall metres of bold, bright white and bookended by two radio towers that punched into the sky like raised arms of victory, spreading the gospel of radio station 3DB, which was housed within the building, alongside the *Herald*, the *Sun News-Pictorial*, the *Weekly Times* and the numerous outlets from around the country that were represented by their correspondents.

It was an impressive and intimidating vision that looked as though it could have been lifted from the industrial streets of America and dropped onto one of the most frequented corners of Melbourne. It felt flooded with history and that history was appropriate, given your grandad was for 18 months to represent an outlet that remains Australia's second oldest surviving newspaper, behind only the *Sydney Morning Herald*.

Your grandad found himself an apartment on the first floor of a dark red-brick block of flats in South Yarra and embarked on his role as Melbourne correspondent.

It was a demanding position that required him to match timezones with Western Australia for filing purposes, while still operating in the Victorian timezone for news gathering, but at least he had the company of the other correspondents. The *Daily News* and *The West Australian* both had representatives in Melbourne and they were based in the aisle referred to as Interstate Alley; a corridor which branched off from the main, open-plan newsroom.

It housed correspondents from every major newspaper around the country. *The West Australian* office sat next to the *Brisbane Courier Mail* and opposite South Australia's *The Advertiser* and *The News*. An *AAP* office was nearby and the domains of the *Sydney Morning Herald* and *Sydney Sun* sat at the opposite end.

The 1970s were a far different world to that of the technology-flooded one in which we live today. Undoubtedly, by the time I finish writing this biography, almost everything about it will be redundant: the recorder I used for interviews, the laptop-tablet hybrid I wrote it on, maybe even the notepad I scribbled notes in and, almost-certainly, the writer himself.

But, back then, the technology of the era meant there was no instantaneous sharing of stories at the click of the button and it was up to each correspondent to wire the information back to their outlets. Your grandad's task was to seek out and produce his own stories, while collating the news of the day from the *Herald* and sending it all back for publication in *The West*.

It required stories to be written onto perforated tape, which was fed into a telex machine and transmitted back to Perth. It was a time-sensitive task that required all race results, sports results, stock market details and the likes to be fed into the ever-hungry machine. So, not too dissimilar from the internet after all.

"They'd be wanting to get onto the Cranbourne dogs or something, so they'd be ringing you and saying, 'Get those bloody dogs on the wire. Get them on the wire, now," said former editor of *The West Australian* and former Melbourne correspondent Paul Murray.

"So you'd have to go and chase the sports department at the *Sun* and ask them for the dog results, take them back, give them to the teleprinter operator, who would key them in and then you'd feed them into the machine. It was all-go, all the time."

Of course, work also had its perks and for your grandad there were few greater than that which was afforded to the Melbourne correspondents on their first day of the job. A correspondent was instructed to make their way to the foyer of the *HWT* building, where they were met by "the MCG man" and presented with a

Gold Pass for the historic, mecca of Australian sport.

This was a ground that hosted the 1956 Olympic Games, regularly housed names such as "Lillee" and "Thompson", who were bowling to equally impressive names such as "Gavaskar", and it was home of the ever-strengthening VFL.

Your grandad had unfettered access.

Your grandad loved his mates and despite the thrill of his new position, would have undoubtedly felt pangs of homesickness. That all changed ahead of the 1973 VFL season when one of his best mates, George Young, committed to St Kilda. Your grandad could barely be happier: he held an exciting position at work, he finally had a role that allowed him to write sport and he now had the opportunity to write those stories about his best mate.

And Young's VFL debut on 7 April for St Kilda was certainly one to write home about. The half-forward had barely touched down in Melbourne, with cricket commitments having delayed his trip east until mid-March, but played the MCG like he had grown up on the hallowed turf, booting 4.2 with 20 possessions to top the goalkickers list in a 33-point win over Melbourne, captivating almost 45,000 fans.

The following week did not go to plan, however, and Young sustained a bad knee injury, snapping a knee ligament that sidelined him until Round 13 in the middle of June. It was certainly not the way Young had hoped his VFL career would begin – aside from the outstanding debut match – but it suddenly presented him and your grandad with an opportunity to catch up on lost time.

Young partially credited your grandad for his arrival at St Kilda – "I was probably 85 per cent committed, but Wally brought that other 15 per cent, knowing that I wasn't going to be totally alone and that one of my best friends was living over there" – but the loss of football and its match payments through injury meant he was required to find a job to supplement his income.

Mondays had previously been a day off for both young men and they would play golf – "the only sport Wally could beat me at" – before attending the evening training session at the football club. That looked set to end with Young's requirement to find additional work, but the pair had other ideas and, despite your grandad having a very demanding full-time job already, he joined his mate at a second place of work.

"I got a part-time job working for an electrical retailer on Kings Street in the heart of the city, Stanmore Appliance Centre, because the owner was a St Kilda supporter and good enough to give me a job," Young said.

"Because Wally had Mondays off, I got him a job there helping out packing toasters and transporting them off to clients who wanted them posted out. We used to work together every Monday and that would have gone on for four or five months. Wal and I would always sneak off at lunch time to the local bar and knock down about six middies, then come back.

"It was a double storey retail outlet and we used to also sneak upstairs, because there was a phone up there and we used to ring back to Perth and find out what was going on with all the district scores and everything."

It was a sign of how close the two friends were, as was your grandad becoming a pseudo-son to Ian and Joan Crook, the lovely couple who Young had been billeted to, but who did not realise at the time the "buy one, get one free" requirement of the Young-Foreman friendship.

However, they accepted your grandad with open arms and regularly accounted for an extra mouth to feed at the dinner table.

The Crooks were not the only ones to come to the realisation they had got more than they bargained for in the Young deal. St Kilda topped that list and the club found itself welcoming your grandad into the fold.

Young appeared at his first training session for St Kilda with his sidekick and, after being introduced to the president and iconic coach Allan Jeans, your grandad was handed a membership to the St Kilda Football Club by secretary Ian Drake.

Jeans, who ended his Hall of Fame coaching career as a four-time premiership coach across St Kilda and Hawthorn, was a father-figure at the club and immediately connected with your grandad – "he loved Wal; just took such a liking to him," said Young – as he could see this ever-present journalist was likely to make his football player's life in Melbourne easier. The friendship extended from the coach to one of the most senior and important players at the club, Kevin "Cowboy" Neale, who was a member of Jeans' 1966 Premiership-winning side and a man who went on to record 256 game and 301 goals with the club.

Your grandad's acceptance by a figure as revered as Jeans, as well as the club's go-to-man in front of goals, Neale, opened doors to an inner-sanctum usually reserved only for players and staff. He became an unofficial, unlisted member of St Kilda and found himself running onto Moorabbin Oval for Monday night trainings alongside players he idolised, assisting and taking part in drills and weights sessions.

If your grandad is in Heaven now, then he was certainly on Cloud Nine then and, as his acceptance grew among the group, so too did his confidence.

"He'd be kicking the ball around with us, then we used to have a gym session, where we'd go through one-minute rounds of punching a medicine ball," Young said.

"We had to work in pairs and, if we were ever one short, Allan Jeans would get Wally and he's there holding the punching bag for Cowboy Neale, or one of the other greats of St Kilda. There's a great story and I was privileged to witness it: when you're doing three one-minute rounds hitting the bags, well the bags can't hit you back, so you've got the gloves on and you've got to encourage your partner, 'Hit the damn thing, hit it harder, I can't feel the bloody thing'.

"Well, Wally's confidence has started to soar and he's told this bloke, Jimmy O'Dea: 'For God sakes, hit the damned thing will you, Jimmy'. Jim was one of the roughest, toughest blokes going around and he's just rocked back and given it one of the biggest left jabs of all time. Wally went flying and was spread-eagled across the gymnasium, holding this bag and on his back. With that, Allan Jeans has given him a right-old serve: 'For God sakes, Wally. Stand up and hold your ground'.

"It was one of the funniest things I've seen at a Monday night training."

Young returned from injury to VFL football against Fitzroy at Junction Oval on Saturday 30 June in front of 13,500 people. He again stamped his mark on the game and played like he invented it, bettering his four goals on debut to post 5.2 in a tally that was matched only by Neale (5.1) and which helped St Kilda record a 60-point win and further strengthen the club's case for finals.

It was a tremendous day for football and, apparently, a tremendous day for skiing, because instead of being at Junction Oval for his mate's illustrious return, your grandad had sought to make the most of his day off – *The West Australian* did not have a Sunday paper to write for – and was on the slopes of Mt Buller with former girlfriend Lee Hunt, not expecting such a return from his close mate.

Never one to be outdone, your grandad wrote the story anyway, with the headline blaring, "Young returns in blaze of glory", and described the "scintillating" skills of Young, who was so good his impact was felt 250km away on top of a mountain.

Young's sincerity was ongoing and effortless as he spoke about his "little mate", whose loyalty and love, he said, was again exemplified through that article. Your grandad, in turn, would have told anyone who would listen that Young was among the greatest players to have ever played the game.

St Kilda spent the next nine matches teetering on the border of finals, until ending the season in fifth and snaring the last berth. The club played Essendon on Sunday 8 September in an elimination final at Waverly Park and, as if improving exponentially, Young kicked 6.2 to again top the goalkickers list and lead the Saints to a 67-point win.

The semifinal did not go as well, for either Young or the Saints, with the former managing just one major and the latter falling by 40 points to Richmond at the MCG in front of an imposing 86,000 people. The exit did mean, though, that Young and your grandad were able to take in the awe of the Richmond-Carlton grand final a fortnight later, along with their Floreat Hotel mate Fred Miller, who had stopped in on his drive back west from a job in Canberra.

George and Peta Young forever remained a part of your grandad's life and were a constant support for your nana after we lost your grandad. That support is a legacy of the close friendships your grandad forged and reflects the sincerity and depth of those relationships. Life for our family after your grandad's death would have been far less manageable without them.

Yet, if it was not for that sincerity and depth, the relationship between the Youngs and the Foremans could have ended promptly on Christmas Eve of 1973, when your grandad's passion for friends almost cost his mate a wedding.

"He didn't come back for our wedding, but he told us where to have it. That's absolutely true," Peta Young said, before George explained further: "On the day we were coming back to Perth for our wedding, Wally drove us to the airport. It was Wally's idea that, if he wasn't going to the wedding, then we were going to have a few drinks.

"We went to Tullamarine – the plane was delayed, so we had a few more drinks – then we went into the international bar, which was a little bit more comfortable. We thought, 'Shit, this is good. We haven't heard our plane called'.

"After about three hours, I said to Peta that she better go down and check on our plane, which she did, and came back to tell us our plane left two hours ago and that they don't announce domestic departures in the international section."

It was devastating news for the bride-to-be – "We'd missed the plane home for our wedding. I burst into tears" – but not so for the two mates who, after briefly consoling Peta, continued their farewell celebrations.

"Wally thought it was the greatest thing of all time, because he'd pinched another four or five hours with us," George said.

The friendship continued past the football season and, once the newly-married Youngs returned to Melbourne, your grandad again integrated himself into George's life, this time befriending the Carlton Cricket Club fraternity.

Young kept himself fit and busy through the off-season by playing A Grade with a side that boasted some lofty names, such as Keith Stackpole, Paul Hibbert and Johnny Scholes and whenever the group got together after training or a match for a few beers and a debrief, there was your grandad.

"He was just a part of the deal," Young said.

"That was only in a short period of time and he had long-standing friendships with a lot of those guys, whether they were St Kilda footballers or Carlton cricketers. Even 20 years on, quite often there'd be comments on various trips I'd make over there, 'How's the little fella going?'"

There was something else beginning to gain momentum as 1974 rolled on and the friendship with the St Kilda fraternity had, by chance, opened another door for your grandad. A young Claremont rover named Bruce Duperouzel had agreed to join the Saints for the 1974 season, playing alongside Young in a career that ended with him having represented St Kilda in 139 games and appearing for Footscray 25 times.

Duperouzel had also represented Western Australia in Sheffield Shield cricket alongside another close friend of your grandad's, Sam Gannon, during the summer of 1971-72. The connection between your grandad and Duperouzel was not strong, but it was strong enough to introduce him to one more degree of separation, which played a defining role in his career.

Duperouzel was a close friend of a young ABC Radio broadcaster named Drew Morphett, who was based in Perth alongside tyro Dennis Cometti and working under George Grljusich out of the Adelaide Terrace offices. Through those mutual acquaintances, your grandad and Morphett saw each other regularly whenever the latter was in Melbourne and the former was back in Perth.

On more than one occasion, your grandad had used the opportunity to express to Morphett how interested he was in joining the ABC. He longed to work in a pure-sports role and had decided that broadcasting was his passion. Morphett towards the end of 1974 took up a position with ABC documentary unit *Sportsnight*. It was a position he had been considering when he bumped into your grandad and alerted him to the opportunity that was likely to become vacant back in Perth.

The latter's time as the Melbourne correspondent for *The West Australian* was coming to an end, but it had provided him with invaluable experience covering sport, arming him with a CV that could potentially secure the job. Morphett recalled that your grandad's "ears pricked up, because he'd always wanted to get into broadcasting" and, with the advice that an attractive position with the ABC was up for grabs, a seemingly never-ending stream of job applications from one Wally Foreman began flooding into Grljusich's in-tray.

According to the in-depth thesis on *The West Australian*'s sports department by David Marsh, there were 16 sportswriters with the paper at the beginning of the 1970s. Ken Casellas was only in his 30s and owned the cricket and racing rounds, while Geoff Christian was the same age and entrenched as the football writer. Neither were going anywhere anytime soon and the prospect of a vacancy opening up with the paper seemed slim. If your grandad wanted to work in sport, he was going to have to leave *The West*.

Your grandad returned to Perth and towards the end of 1974 was asked to attend an interview with Grljusich at the ABC's Sound

Broadcasting and Television Studios at 187 Adelaide Terrace – a building that was impressive at the time, having opened in 1960 as Western Australia welcomed television to the state.

Your grandad's heart would have undoubtedly skipped a beat when he entered the foyer to be greeted by a familiar face. It was that of *The West* sportswriter Alan East: a man who carried far more impressive credentials at the time and whom your grandad had sat opposite during his first year with the paper.

It was not surprising that there were a number of candidates for the job, given the ABC held a revered reputation and its sports department was viewed as the best of the best: "The elite," said East. It was a competitive position that was on offer and getting an interview was only half the battle for your grandad. However, he had one advantage over his better credentialed counterparts: he was young, which meant he was relatively green and, in turn, cheap – a factor that remains highly important to the public broadcaster.

"I'd been in sport at *The West* for a couple of years," East said.

"It was all very secretive: George contacted both of us independently and told us to come down and have an interview. So, unbeknown to each other, we ended up in the foyer of the ABC together. I said, 'What are you doing here?' and he said, 'The same as you, probably'.

"I went in there first and George grilled me pretty heavily, went through it all – especially money – and because I was a bit ahead of Wally in terms of salary, I said to George that I wasn't interested, because it was a really basic, cadet wage. I came out and said to Wally: 'You're it'."

Your grandad got the job. He began with the ABC at the start of 1975 and remained there – in one capacity or other – for 31 years.

"Now I can throw out this bloody folder of all your letters," Grljusich said.

Chapter 6

Dreams Can Come True

A 27-YEAR WAIT TO ACHIEVE a dream: one would have thought that was enough time to adequately prepare for the moment. Or at least not drop the c-word to a state-wide audience. Twice. And a third time years later, for good measure.

Your grandad arrived at ABC Radio, Perth, working underneath one of the most respected broadcasters at the time, George Grljusich, and alongside the man considered guru-in-waiting, Dennis Cometti. The expectations on the standard of delivery from the strong sports department were high, however, the workload was not as demanding.

There were commentary commitments or a required attendance at live sport during the days, followed by the production of highlights for the evening, but interspersed was ample time for the department staff to get better acquainted. That resulted in a close friendship between your grandad and Cometti, who recalled the period as "some of the funniest times of my life". The camaraderie was undoubtedly helped by your grandad's devotion to his beloved Cardinals, as Cometti had played 40 league games for West Perth.

Both men had a supreme base of sporting knowledge across a wide range of sports and spent hours on end throwing quiz questions at each other in the office. They were entrenched in the life they had always longed for and often made the most of it. "Hard living, hard drinking", was how Cometti explained it in one of his books, in a description that drew the ire of your modest Great Grandad Eric.

Thankfully, your grandad had learnt lessons from previous indiscretions at *The West* and had now taken to leaving his car at home, with former Sports Department Secretary Jillian Mellet recalling that she often received a call at the office early in the morning that went something like, 'Jill, it's me. Not feeling too good. Can you come and get me?'"

Life was comfortable. Sometimes too comfortable.

"One day, we were doing the footy and your dad – and we've all done things on air that, in retrospect, we wished we hadn't – but he had to call a 'punt kick'," Cometti recalled, as he went on to suggestively nod as to what word was broadcast in place of "punt".

"Your dad was cool, he just continued on, but we all looked at each other like, 'Did that just happen?'. We didn't get the giggles that time, because it's fair to say that it was best to pretend it hadn't happened, but we've got back to work on Monday and the general manager has called him in.

"Wal's come back into the office and it was like, 'What did he say?', because it wasn't as if anybody tried to do that. Wal said: 'He doesn't want me to do it again'. So, all week, your dad's going, 'I must not say it again, I must not say it again', and, of course, you know what happens. And we all laughed that time.

"He got it in his head and we're all taking the mickey. Certainly, in the first place, I don't think there were any complaints, because it was just a slip of the tongue. The following week, he'd looked for help and, of course, there was none, because we were all cowering and laughing. He had to carry on and battle through it.

"I shouldn't even be talking like this, because you can induce this sort of thing."

It was a quick lesson for your grandad that he was now working for the national broadcaster and his calls were going around the state. Live. To this day, your grandad's close friend Sam Gannon recalled the moment with even greater clarity than Cometti.

"I vividly remember Wally's first game he commentated," Gannon said, naming the 1975 WANFL Round 1 clash between Claremont and Subiaco at the Claremont Showgrounds.

"He'd spent all day and all night studying the players, going down to training to put faces to names and numbers. In the opening 15min stretch that he had – I thought I'd stay home and listen to it, rather than go and watch it – he described a passage of play. It started so well: 'He's taken a towering mark at centre-half forward, now he's back on his mark'.

"But then Wally says: 'He moves in and elects to use the c--t pick'. That was his first call. He thought it was the end of the line for him."

Try as he might, your grandad was never able to live up to the advice of the general manager, Arthur Povah, to "never let it happen again", because the remarkable aspect of the tale is that it was not until writing this biography that it was realised the error actually occurred on three occasions: twice alongside Cometti and again later when he was moonlighting in the late 1990s with ABC TV on weekends, broadcasting the WAFL alongside Glenn Mitchell.

They were almost identical circumstances, amidst a similar passage of play and attracting the same reaction from the commentary team, who struggled to hold their composure as your grandad scrambled to recover.

"It was 1998, East Fremantle Oval. I can still remember it," Mitchell said.

"The ball went out of bounds on the full at the golf course-end. It was Lane Spencer, the Claremont fullback, and he went to kick the ball back in and your dad's said, 'And he loads up with a massive spiral c--t'.

"I do not know how it happened, but I'm on one side, Bucky (Gary Buckenara) is on the other. Bucky's ripped his headset off and all you can see is his shoulders bobbing up and down from under the desk, because he's laughing so much. I'm shaking my head and your dad was just getting redder and redder in the face, because he knew that if he laughed or anything, it would have confirmed to people what they thought they heard.

"It was one of the funniest moments. Bucky and I put our headsets back on and looked at each other and there were just tears rolling down our faces."

There was no-one who judged your grandad harder than himself and, funny as they are in retrospect, those moments would have hung over him for much of his life. This was part of what drove his enormous work-ethic: he had inherited that trait from his father, your Great Grandad Eric, because he saw first-hand how much one person could achieve and he would never allow himself to partially commit.

He expected 100 per cent effort and performance, or nothing. And it was rarely nothing.

The 2006 AFL Grand Final – your grandad's first AFL grand final broadcast – was a special moment for him, but he felt he underperformed due to calling the incorrect player name a couple of times. He corrected himself immediately and, to the average listener, the moments would have passed without much notice.

However, your grandad could not let it go: it was not the perfect call he had wanted and prepared for. If he was upset over a couple of cases of mistaken identity, you can imagine the impact the moments early in his career would have had on him. The third slip at least occurred when he had already established his credentials, but the first two came as he was intensely trying to prove he deserved to be there.

And there were high expectations of someone in his position.

The Australian Broadcasting Commission was – as it remains – a highly-respected broadcaster. Its reputation was built upon high standards and a history of excellence.

Sports broadcasting at the time your grandad entered it, especially in Western Australia, was coming into its identity in a new era, but that was not viewed as an excuse for its commentators to become cavaliers of the microphone.

There was a clear standard to which broadcasters were expected to hold themselves and there were particular structures for sports to be broadcast. For example, with tennis, a commentator was to announce the toss of the serve before it happened, to ensure they were on top of the action, before calling the striking of the ball and the proceeding action of the point. That structure was still apparent in your grandad's later career, when he called the tongue-twisting 2003 Australian Open quarterfinal between South Africa's Wayne Ferreira and Spain's Juan Carlos Ferrero – a call Dennis Cometti likened to "a sobriety test".

The teachings were so well-engrained in the commentators of the day that they became engrained in the listeners as well, as recalled three decades on by Geoff Hutchison, a former work experience student with your grandad at the ABC in the 70s, who then became a colleague at the NINE Network, before the pair reconnected back at the ABC in early 2006.

"I remember hearing some radio commentary of his – and I know he died before the cricket season started, so it must have been something I'd heard previously – but it was: 'Good morning everyone and welcome to the descriptions of play of the third day of the Sheffield Shield match between Western Australia and…', Hutchison said, as he trailed off, but not before recalling without error the precise and orchestrated delivery of the words.

"I used to mimic that as a kid, because I would always hear him say that and, if ever I was going to become a sports commentator, I knew that was going to be the very introduction – 'Good morning everyone and welcome to the descriptions of play' – that I would use.

"Very formal and never knockabout. They might knockabout later in the day, or when something jokey happened, but never in the introduction. There was a way you did it and that was how you did it. I remember now, because I heard it all the time as a kid.

"It was a great attention to everything that needed to be said."

The standards would have been unsurprising for your grandad, who had spent his formative years in Bruce Rock glued to the broadcasts of commentators such as Jim Fitzmaurice, who at the time of your grandad's arrival had only recently left the Perth office. Fitzmaurice was highly-valued by the ABC and was promoted to Program Director upon Ron Halcombe's retirement in 1968, before being moved to Sydney shortly after.

George Grljusich took over from Fitzmaurice as Supervisor of Perth's Sporting Department. Talented 20-year-old Sydneysider

Drew Morphett arrived in 1969 and Cometti, who had begun his career at radio 6KY, before moving to Melbourne and back to Perth to work for 6PR, was implored in 1972 by Fitzmaurice to apply for an opening in the Perth department. Morphett's departure a couple of years later created the opening for your grandad to join the team.

The ESPN biography, *Those Guys Have All The Fun*, describes a small, American cable television network that dreamed big, with no real blueprint to follow, resulting in sports broadcasting's version of the wild west. The sports department of ABC Perth in the mid-1970s shared similar traits.

And the Perth trio was as capable of being the cowboys as it was the posse that would steer the station into a brave new world.

It was for the most part an enjoyable environment for your grandad and Dennis Cometti, especially under the calm and fatherly guidance of State Manager Arthur Povah; another Perth Modern School graduate, a hard-working man who had climbed from basement to ceiling of the hierarchy and a man who had great affection for the members of the sports department.

Your grandad and Cometti spent days on end in each other's company, calling almost every ball of the Sheffield Shield and sitting alongside one another in the football commentary box, becoming firm mates along the way. The pair conducted themselves with the utmost professionalism, but even amidst the strict suggestions on how to call every sport and with a hard-nosed boss like Grljusich, the two friends were simply enjoying themselves.

"I don't want to incorrectly claim anything, but it felt like we were best mates," Cometti said.

"Now, whether we were or not, I don't know, but he certainly was one of my best two or three friends at the time and the fact that we kept in touch was testament to that. We certainly had a real liking for each other and all those things that broadcasters shouldn't do – getting the giggles on air and all that sort of stuff – we did, because we had a good time.

"It sounds almost unprofessional and strange these days, because, while things like it exist, I don't think they exist to the same extent and I don't think the tolerance is there from the listeners or the organisations."

It was an enjoyable job for much of the time, but the relationship between Grljusich and Cometti and the environment that the former had the potential to create as a result of external stresses was not always positive.

Grljusich was as entrenched at the ABC in 1975 as Geoff Christian and Ken Casellas were at *The West Australian*. He had been with the broadcaster since beginning as a 21-year-old in 1960 and impressed most who came across him, or heard his broadcasting ability. He was meticulous in his preparation and outstanding at his job; it was other factors that proved detrimental. Grljusich's title was in 1976 changed from Supervisor of Sport to Chief Broadcaster as a result of budget cuts and restructures across Australia.

That might sound inconsequential and I do not presume to know how Grljusich would have felt about the change, but it certainly had the potential to bruise his ego, particularly given his relationship with Cometti at the time.

Cometti had been identified as one of the country's brightest prospects in broadcasting and that reputation alone had caused some unrest in Grljusich. As detailed in the latter's biography, *George!*, the relationship then began to deteriorate further when Cometti was recommended and pushed by ABC Perth management to play a role in Test cricket broadcasts. The result was Cometti joining revered Test caller Alan McGilvray for the 1973-74 Ashes series and, after performing well, he held the role in international cricket for 12 years.

It would have been unlikely that there were any external beliefs that Cometti's rise must result in Grljusich's fall, but it was just another piece of straw placed on the back of the tenuous relationship. The Test cricket move for Cometti also meant the younger broadcaster was no longer under his manger's jurisdiction for large periods of the year. It also marked the first instance that Cometti had been chosen ahead of Grljusich and the pecking order of the Perth office was beginning to destabilise.

It was a build-up of events that, as individual occurrences, might have had very little impact on the pair's relationship, but as a whole they were a breeding ground for disharmony. They had the potential to generate a feeling of insecurity within Grljusich and those feelings were compounded by his life outside work. Financial strains had a tendency to arise as a result of his penchant for a pun, while his challenges in his personal life meant the boss was not always an easy person to get along with.

The difficult environment that could occasionally result also put strains on staff and eventually drove commentator Drew Morphett back to Melbourne, creating the opening for your grandad to join the ABC Perth team. It was an environment of excitement, tension, fun, drama and occasional unease. And it was the environment your grandad entered in 1975.

Grljusich, however, was not locked in a state of tyrannical dictator. He was also capable of having a laugh, especially by testing his young team's abilities to adapt on the fly. One such time occurred when your grandad was attempting to read the news bulletin live on air, only to have his boss set fire to the bottom of the script, resulting in him having to read faster and faster, before ending with, "That's all we have in sport", and a pile of ashes on the desk.

The group also welcomed the company of a 15-year-old Kalamunda High School student named Geoff Hutchison, who looked at the trio like they were superheroes. Hutchison had written to your grandad's predecessor, Morphett, enquiring what he needed to do in order to one day sit behind the microphone. Hutchison, who has since gone from aspiring broadcaster to one of the most respected and talented in his field, shared a life-long connection with your grandad, reuniting at the NINE Network and again on the latter's return to the ABC.

But he always remembered that first meeting.

"Dennis was the man about town: it was like Dennis was Batman and your dad was Robin. Dennis was the most impressive and your dad was the kindest," Hutchison said.

"On a couple of occasions I wrote to him. I went for a couple of cadetships with them, but I was only 16 or something stupid, but he knew me and he knew I was keen. Those were the moments I remember and it was just brilliant; I could have had a ham and cheese sandwich for lunch, but it would have been the best sandwich, because the whole day was just brilliant."

It was an emotion that was often the same as that felt by the sports broadcasters, however, the reality was that the "brilliant" times were shared mostly between just Cometti and your grandad.

"We should have had the best job in the world and, I can't speak for your father, but my relationship with George was shaky at best," Cometti said.

"We probably did need a bit of bringing into line from time to time, but when the job needed to be done, Drew Morphett, your dad and myself, we could all broadcast and that's been proven since, but George never wanted to relinquish control. Really, it wasn't a system based on any sort of ability, it was a system based on seniority: if you were there the longest, you got the job.

"I think your dad was more considerate of George than I was and I remember we went to George's wedding and one of the most vivid memories I have of your dad is that George got up to make a speech on behalf of he and the bride and he thanked his friends, thanked Ken Casellas first, me second and Wally third.

"I didn't care and expressed that, but your dad was softening before my eyes. He had more compassion for George than I did and, in hindsight, I respect that."

Cometti and Grljusich were – and remained – highly-respected executers of their craft and both were strong personalities. That your grandad was able to maintain such a strong and mutually-respected relationship with both men concurrently, given the deteriorating rapport between them, spoke to his ability to relate to people.

That was evident in not only Cometti's comments, but also Grljusich's, who at his 30-year function said: "It's not really been my own work. It's been with the fact that the ABC has been able to have world-class people working for it, both as broadcasters and experts.

"And my greatest solace since I became sports editor is that we were able to attract people like Dennis Cometti, Ian Brayshaw and Wally Foreman, whose knowledge of sports is as comprehensive and impressive as that of any person I have encountered in more than 33 years of sports broadcasting anywhere in the world."

Ken Casellas was a close friend of Grljusich's and knew your grandad well from *The West* and later when they worked alongside each other during football broadcasts for the ABC.

"It was considered an outstandingly strong sports team," Casellas said.

"You had to know George to understand George. Things weren't particularly personal with George; George would (be difficult to) you, not because he didn't personally like you, but mainly because he'd just lost $500 on the last favourite in Melbourne and he'd take out his frustrations on people.

"But George wouldn't tolerate people who weren't any good and not only did he tolerate Wally, but he thought Wally was a wonderful talent. Wally was a breath of fresh air, even in the early days when he was working with Cometti and George at the ABC, because there was always this undercurrent of rivalry between George and Cometti, whereas Wally was always smiling."

Your grandad had always connected with people, but it was not until he began working in broadcast media that the opportunity was presented for people to connect to him.

Dennis Cometti and George Grljusich might not have enjoyed the strongest personal relationship, but professionally they were exceptional at their jobs and the pair introduced a concept in 1982 that would become a mainstay of the department and one of the strongest connections between listener and broadcaster. It was talkback radio for sport and launched with the two-hour program *Saturday Morning Sportstalk*. Your grandad had left the ABC for the NINE Network at the time *Sportstalk* was introduced, but the program played an important role in his return to the ABC in 2001 in transforming his relationship with the listener from disconnected broadcaster, to real person.

The broadcasting styles between your grandad and Grljusich, especially on talkback radio, were chalk-and-cheese. The latter enjoyed an adversarial relationship with callers and would frequently challenge their view or opinion with an unrelenting barrage of his own opinions and views until the caller either submitted or had their call terminated. In the words of the Grljusich biography: "His rudeness in cutting off a caller with his trademark line, 'OK, mate, you've had your say', became legendary".

Your grandad, in stark contrast, enjoyed the company of callers and all they brought, including opposing points of view. He never hesitated in delivering his own opinion, but he equally welcomed those of others and considered that an issue was never an issue because it was one-sided, but was instead made up of opposing views and fact likely laid somewhere in the middle. In the words of Mick Colliss' poem, *The Legend from Bruce Rock*: "Totally unbiased and guided by the facts. To callers he was entertaining, engaging and relaxed".

Of course, the beauty of individuals and an entertainment medium is that there is no correct or incorrect style and both worked well for broadcaster and listener. And the one aspect that must not be lost in any tales of personalities and clashes is that Grljusich was very good at his job. Exceptional, even.

Grljusich "had a point of view about everything", as was written about him in his biography, but it was not simply an opinion built out of being contrary: it was one formed from arduous research that allowed him to debate and argue in such a way that he could rarely be denied. That research began at 4am every Saturday and consisted of dissecting every morsel of sports news for six hours before *Sportstalk* began.

Your grandad knew as a journalist the importance of being informed, but the immediacy of radio is far less forgiving than print and, while the latter is more permanent, it offers more time for preparation. Your grandad saw in Grljusich the power of an opinion and belief, and saw how that power was founded on a dedication to being informed and prepared.

Your grandad learnt a significant amount from Grljusich and, although he recalled the teachings as "do as I say, not as I do", they cannot be understated, because in less than 10 years after joining the ABC team, he was to become the inaugural director of the Western Australian Institute of Sport. One does not become an inaugural director of one of the first state institutes in the country without having well-formed, well-argued opinions and beliefs.

There was also another side-effect of the relationship with the boss.

Grljusich was a head-strong man. He could be stubborn and dogmatic. Occasionally, those traits resulted in clashes with others, but had he not had those characteristics engrained in him, these words you are currently reading might have never been written. And you, Charlotte, might have never been born.

The ABC hit budget strains in the mid-1970s, coinciding with your grandad's arrival in 1975. The Commission introduced a Federal Programme Unit, which, as the biography on Grljusich detailed "centralised decision-making in the eastern states. Amateur sport was bypassed". This was in direct contrast to the environment that Grljusich had been raised in.

The introduction of television and the opening of ABW Channel Two on 7 May 1960 resulted in the Perth sports department being required to generate four hours of television content for Saturday's *Sportsview* program and a further two hours for the Sunday edition. Amateur sport was the beneficiary of that time, with little else on offer in Western Australia. So, when the order to bypass amateur sport came through to Perth and the time was filled by videotape sent from the eastern states, Grljusich's stubborn streak would not allow him to relent.

He refused to overlook local sport. In the summer of 1979, Grljusich handed your grandad an assignment: he was ordered to interview one of the state's most promising track and field athletes.

Her name was Lynette Young and she became your nana.

Chapter 7

The Legend from Rivervale

LYNETTE MAY YOUNG WAS TOUGH, resilient and hard-working. She had to be: she was the youngest and only daughter of May and Les Young, entering the world on 5 March 1957, and gender was never an obstacle in the roughhousing of her two brothers Les (jnr) and Steve.

You never met your nana's parents – they passed away before you were born – but May would have been your Great Nana and Les (snr) would have been your Great Grampie. The family was as blue-collar as they come, growing up on Acton Avenue in Rivervale, with your Great Grampie Les a train driver who would regularly make "tuckerbox" trips that took him away from home for two days at a time along the regional railways. It required him to pack a large metal box each time, from which the nickname of the trips was derived.

Your Great Nana May was a devoted and loving mother to her three children. Money was tight and, when your great uncles Steve and Les and your nana had moved into high school, your great nana took up work for retailer David Jones during the day, but always ensured she was home in time to greet the children once the school day was done.

Your great grampie was an authoritative and imposing figure, who could at times be oppressive, but he was balanced in the household by your Great Nana May, who was a kind, caring and beautiful example to follow. Her stoicism and independence was later shown after the children graduated high school and she put herself through art school to explore her passion and extraordinary talent of drawing and painting.

The Youngs, like the majority of households in the area, kept chickens in order to source their own eggs and supply the centrepiece for the Sunday Roast, with the self-sufficiency helping to save money on food. A large rooster named Ginger was trained by your great grampie to be wild and aggressive, mostly in order to protect the chickens. Mostly.

The ageing of Ginger and his eventual demise was the only time the Sunday Roast was not eaten by the three children, who instead wept as their rooster disappeared, one forkful at a time. The tuckerbox trips would also yield rabbit, which your great grampie would shoot once the train had made its regional stop, bringing it home to be skinned and cooked, although it was an unacceptable dinner for your young nana at the time, who instead chose to go hungry, having not been able to shake the images of Bugs Bunny from her mind.

Both meals were prepared by your great nana over a wood stove that was fired up, regardless of how hot the summer was. Washing was a similar experience, with the absence of supplied hot water to the wash house requiring a wood fire to bring to boil the liquid held in a large copper vessel, which the clothes would then be washed in. The regime changed very little even when the Youngs replaced the copper with a washing machine, as there was still no hot water piping to the wash house, requiring your great nana to manually heat the water.

An electric hot water system at least provided hot showers in the main house, but the financial situation meant your great grampie strictly monitored usage. And it was not to be used for washing dishes – that was a job for the kettle.

Sunday was the most dreaded day for your nana and her brothers, as it was bath day and the running of fresh, hot water for each person was not allowed; the water was to be reused for all and, given their father always had the luxury of bathing first, it was not an enjoyable experience. In fact, you would have to question the point of the exercise at all, given the state of the water being used for the purpose of cleaning.

Your nana has never slept well and her light-sleeping as a child meant she often laid awake, listening for the clip-clop of the Clydesdale-drawn milk cart that wound its way through the streets for the early-morning delivery. And while luxuries such as a refrigerator and television came along later, they were not always a part of the household. People in those times had to keep perishables from spoiling by buying blocks of ice to bring home.

It was the only life the family knew and they were never left wanting, because, as your nana recalled: "We didn't know we were missing out, because we never had it to begin with. You don't know what you don't know."

The Young children made their own fun, building tents and cubbies in the backyard as they launched tree nuts at each other in war games that often resulted in the only girl having to play the "bad guy" and being hung from the back fence. Hanged, might be more accurate because that was the nature of some of the more vicious games. The brave "allies" would quickly scatter, though, when their father arrived home from work.

The two Young brothers were polar-opposites: your Great Uncle Les was the introvert, quiet and unassuming; your Great Uncle Steve was the extrovert, four years older, a lover of sport and ready to tackle any challenge. It meant Les was often the one dragged into "playing schools" or with dolls when his little sister had enough of being the fielder or bowler in backyard cricket.

There was never a thought to ask for a lift to school and your nana used to make the short march to Tranby Primary School from six-years-old. A lengthier trek came later in the day, as she made her way to Kooyong Road to see best friend Viv Uren, before the pair headed to the swings at the nearby Wilson Park.

It was an active childhood for your nana and her teenage years were no different, as she filled in the spare time of the summer holidays by working for a dry cleaner. The pay of 20c and hour was minimal, even by 1970s standards, but your nana was too respectful to ever question it. Money was to be earned, not questioned, and it was twice the rate of her 10c a week pocket money.

She had learnt the hard way the importance of treating money with respect, having earlier in life made the poor choice of exchanging her entire weekly allowance for a bag of lollies, attracting an "absolute belting" from your great grampie, before she was forced to share the lollies with the family. The dry cleaning job was exchanged for a role with Myer in the Better Jewellery section and all pay cheques were usually spent on buying Christmas presents for the other members of the family.

If you go to the front door of our house, Charlotte, you'll see the beautifully crafted, German-made wooden temperature, barometer and hygrometer instrument that adorns the entry wall. That was a present from your nana to her father – your great grampie – and was paid for with her first pay cheque from Myer as a 15-year-old. It sits on the wall because the house we live in used to be your great nana and grampie's house after they had moved out of Rivervale.

Family always remain connected in one way or another.

Your nana's family was far from poverty-stricken, but life was certainly devoid of some of the luxuries of the wealthier communities and it meant there was little that the children could truly take ownership of.

The status of working-class had forged your nana into a strong character, but she longed to belong to something. Something that was hers. That opportunity arrived when she was 12-years-old and her Uncle Arthur phoned to advise he was looking after the local Canning Districts Athletics Club in the regular coach's absence and invited your nana to attend the sessions at McCallum Park, Victoria Park.

It was exactly what your nana was looking for, despite the club members being far from welcoming. The cliques ensured any newcomer was made to feel isolated, but they underestimated your nana's tenacity. She vowed to always embrace new faces to ensure they were never made to feel as she had. Your nana continued her involvement with Canning Districts, but had not invested in it as a dream until six years later.

She had begun working full-time as a clerk with the Community Recreation Council, now known as the Department of Sport and Recreation, as a 16-year-old, having left high school after her fourth year. Your nana was a much-loved employee. Her role as clerk, among other tasks, involved putting together the afternoon tea cart. The staff were required to chip-in money for biscuits, but regularly consumed more than the funds covered, leading to the young clerk selflessly using her own money to buy more biscuits for the office, unbeknown to anyone.

The sporting body had changed its name to Youth Sport and Recreation within a couple of years and moved from its James Street base in the city to Perry Lakes Stadium, when your nana found herself among other women of the organisation being handed a project. They were asked by the secretary of the director to write down one goal: their life's ambition.

Your stunned nana had never thought about the issue, so she felt possessed as her hand took on a life of its own and began scribbling words on the paper in front of her. She watched the ink with intrigue before digesting the message: "I want to run for Australia".

It was a lofty goal. To that point, the then-18-year-old was in Division 14 and "ran like a bag of spuds". Genetics was also against her: she did not know it at the time, but her body consisted of 75 per cent slow-twitch fibres, meaning talent alone would never have her run fast.

However, your nana never considered "talent alone" as an answer for anything. She was raised on hard work. So, having committed herself to running for her country, she set about overcoming her lack of natural talent and worked harder than ever before. The dividends were immediate and in 1975, the same year she jotted down her goal, she won her first national title, streaming home in 60.7sec – almost a second ahead of second place – to capture the 400m hurdles at Lang Park in Brisbane.

It was the first time she had travelled for athletics and, of course, she paid for it herself. In fact, your nana paid the costs to attend every one of the eight national championships she competed and was even advised in a letter to "make your way to Sydney" when she was selected in her first Australia team.

The hard training continued and focus was shifted towards specialising in the 400m hurdles. Your nana was taken under the wing of three-time Olympic champion Shirley Strickland, training alongside the likes of Beth Nail and Raelene Boyle and finished second in the following two national titles, before she began to emerge as a potential world-beater.

The cheapest national championships that your nana ever attended came in 1978-79, simply because she did not have to travel far: Perry Lakes Stadium, Perth, Western Australia. Having won the 1975 titles with a 60.7sec run, the sprinter had gradually clawed back her times and in late March, she blitzed her rivals to set a personal best of 57.56sec and claim the crown in front of her home crowd.

It was a performance that had the country talking, with the 1980 World Championships on the horizon. Your nana achieved her goal of running for Australia within four years of setting herself the task when she was selected for the World Cup in Montreal, Canada. The achievement even had the local media buzzing. Your nana was busy working away at her desk a few days later in the Youth Sport and Recreation offices at Perry Lakes Stadium when she received a phone call.

On the other end of the line was an ABC journalist named Wally Foreman.

Your grandad used to say he thought he would do your nana a favour and marry her, that way she could change her name from Lyn Young so it no longer sounded "like something off a Chinese Takeaway menu". The irony was that your nana cringed when the Youth Sport and Recreation secretary advised that someone named "Wally" was on the phone for her.

Your grandad had been assigned her story and needed an interview. He told your nana he intended to come to her office at Perry Lakes Stadium.

"I usually do my interviews over the telephone, but let's just say the telephone was out of order when it came to the interview with Lyn," your grandad later told WA Newspapers in 1980.

Your nana was embarrassed: she was only a 22-year-old clerk and was not high enough up the pecking order to allow a journalist to interrupt the office. She also was – and forever remained – too modest to believe the attention was warranted. Your grandad was persistent, though, and while she relented, she took the dogmatic broadcaster out to the carpark to do the interview.

The pair had met briefly once before. Your nana had dated a footballer named Wayne Nicholson, who had several connections to your grandad: Nicholson's boss was your Great Grandad Eric; he had played football for Bruce Rock; and your grandad had even coached him in cricket at one stage. So, when Nicholson took his then-girlfriend to a hotel for a drink and saw your grandad perched at the bar, the pair was introduced.

It made for easy conversation and, once the interview was complete, your grandad continued the questioning: "Are you still going out with Nicko?"

No, she was not, he was informed, before he followed up with an invitation to lunch. Despite some initial resistance, a lunch date was secured. However, your nana was preparing to go on a month-long holiday overseas with a friend, so told him it would either have to be before she left, or he would have to wait. Anyone who knew your grandad would tell you how little he enjoyed waiting.

"He said he'd come and pick me up for lunch, but I wouldn't let him do that, so we planned to meet outside London Court," your nana said when explaining her first date with your grandad.

"I got there early and I couldn't see him, so I ducked into the shoe shop that was on the corner and kept a lookout for him, because there was a pair of shoes I was interested in. I came out and he was waiting, but I thought, 'I can't yell out Wally', because I couldn't quite come to terms with his name, so I went 'psst'.

"I was so green. I didn't know anything about the airs-and-graces; I was just dragged up through life. Between the interview and meeting him there, though, I'd had my hair permed and it was not good. I hadn't gone out for three days and I had a big blind pimple that I couldn't cover up. It was April and my hair was stuck under a beanie and he didn't recognise me.

"Anyway, he liked the shoes, so I bought the shoes and we went to a fine-dining hotel."

The Perry Lakes interview – or, interrogation, as it seemed to your nana at the time – resumed at the hotel.

"He was asking me about my boyfriends and stuff like that, so I asked him: 'What about you, are you going out with anyone?' and he just goes: 'Oh, I live with someone'," your nana said. "I almost spat my food out. He'd given me the third degree and here he was living with someone."

Your nana had an easy escape from the awkward moment: she was flying out two days later for the holiday and would not return for a month, in which time she felt confident the situation would dissipate. It did not.

She instead returned to an angry father, who insisted she immediately return the calls of a very persistent Wally Foreman, who had not stopped phoning for weeks. It left your nana frustrated: she had clearly told the keen suitor that she would be out of the country and those frustrations only grew as she placed a call to the ABC Sports Department on the hour, every hour, from 9am to 12pm before finally reaching your grandad.

"Gee, that's a good job you've got," she exclaimed.

Your grandad had a favour to ask: the Bruce Rock Lions Club had invited him to present the inaugural Sportstar of the Year Award at his childhood town and the previously arranged special guest, 1968 Olympic 100m butterfly gold medallist Lyn McClements, had cancelled, as she was stuck on a plane returning from America.

"I've just got back myself," your nana argued, initially refusing. However, she was quickly realising how futile denying your grandad was and relented, again, and joined him on the trip to Bruce Rock. The three to four hour drive each way created ample opportunity for conversation and the pair began to grow closer.

The event itself was enjoyable. Your grandad interviewed your nana on stage, before the latter took the opportunity to catch up with friends she had met through Nicholson, hitting the dance floor with your grandad's childhood friend Ray Williams. Williams and your nana often sat in the car, watching the football as rain pelted the players, with the former's playing days cut short after a car accident required him to use a wheelchair for the rest of his life.

The night wound down and your grandad drove his guest to the motel, before cheekily advising of where his room was and saying, "I hope your electric blanket doesn't work". And he was not far away when your nana woke the next morning.

Your nana could see only a silhouette pacing up and down the front of the motel, as its movement caused the stream of morning sunlight to flicker. Your grandad was the opposite of your nana: he fell asleep as soon as his head hit the pillow and he was an early riser. By the time your nana awoke that morning, he had already done a lap around the town and was eager to again spend time with the girl he was falling in love with.

The pair loaded the car and began the return to Perth, stopping in via Beverley to visit your grandad's sister – Great Aunty Sandy – whose offer of eggs was politely accepted from your inwardly-cringing nana, as she was then introduced to the featherless chickens that had laid them. The journey home resumed, but not before your grandad got lost.

"Well, he said he got lost," your nana said. "He was a hard man to say 'no' to," your nana said.

The relationship had begun to take hold for your nana, but it had gripped your grandad from the moment he was sent by George Grljusich to do that interview at Perry Lakes. And that moment was vividly recalled by Sports Department secretary Jillian Mellet.

"I remember like it was yesterday when your dad was sent down to the Perry Lakes track in Floreat Park to interview a young lady who was being touted as the next great track and field athlete. Her name was Lyn Young," Mellet said.

"Heading out for an interview was nothing out of the ordinary, but the change in this young man when he returned to the office was remarkable. He was smitten and I do believe he knew from that moment that Lyn was going to be with him on his life journey.

"I do think it was love at first sight and I remember so well that he made a comment that Lyn 'had a fabulous backside'."

Mellet was not the only colleague to recall the change in your grandad. Dennis Cometti said at his friend's memorial service, "Wal the romantic; Leigh Matthews becoming a Wiggle would have surprised me less". But, away from the audience, he remembered fondly the same moment.

"He liked the girls – and they liked him – but none as much as your mum," Cometti said. "He was a smitten kid when he came back. Suddenly, he put the brakes on and he was a different fellow. He wasn't worse or better, he was just more subdued."

Your grandad had made no secret of the new love in his life, remarking to close mate Sam Gannon: "Gee, mate, I think I've found something pretty good". And Morey Grafton, the former private who served under your grandad in the army, equally noted a change in his former housemate's behaviour.

"It was tiring, living with Wally and I did at one stage suggest he put a 'Welcome' mat outside his bedroom window, but as far as I'm concerned, your old man was different when he met Lyn," Grafton said. "That was the first time he was smitten and you could tell his attitude to her was different".

However, it was his comment to Gannon that was most poignant. The two were living just streets away from each other, after your grandad had moved out of the City Beach house he shared with Grafton and in with his girlfriend in Karrinyup. It was a reminder to your grandad that he was not currently in a position to pursue your nana. And the latter made it very clear she would not be pursued.

"After Bruce Rock, he asked me out, but it was then that I asked if he was still living with his girlfriend," your nana said. "I told him I wasn't going to go out with him, because I wouldn't like that to happen to me."

Your grandad moved out of the Karrinyup house and returned to the family home on Glenties Road, Floreat, and began the pursuit of his new love interest with trademark vigour. Your grandad's trait of demanding something be done right if it was to be done at all meant he was fully invested in chasing your nana and the pair saw each other on an almost daily basis.

Your nana's life as an athlete meant she was usually too tired at the end of a work day to go out, yet her lunch breaks had to be devoted to training and the placement of the Youth Sport and Recreation offices at Perry Lakes made for ideal access to the stadium. Your grandad overcame that challenge by attending the stadium during lunch and laying the hurdles around the track, much to amusement of coach Shirley Strickland.

It was a new and welcomed level of interest for your nana, too, although she recalled: "He was so happy when I switched from hurdles to 800m".

The devotion even extended to weekends. The underfunding of track and field resulted in the sport having to place caveats on athletes competing at carnivals, one of which required a club to provide a certain number of officials for allocation to events over the course of the day for that club's athletes to be eligible to compete.

That caveat resulted in your grandad rushing to Perry Lakes and manning the stopwatch for your nana's races, hunched on the steps of the timing stand adjacent to the finish line. Your nana then climbed the steps and took his place once she had finished her race so he could return to work.

It was a whirlwind love that had been sweeping up their lives for eight months when on 5 January 1980 the pair sat at El Sombreros Restaurant, overlooking Matilda Bay to celebrate your grandad's 32nd birthday.

Well, they *had* sat together. Then, your nana was left on her own. Waiting. Your grandad had gone to the bathroom, but had taken so long that your nana began contemplating where the relationship was going. He finally returned and your nana's question was answered as he produced a Georg Jensen ring that she had commented on during a previous date.

"Is it now? Is this happening now?" your nana stammered in disbelief, before saying yes. Several times.

The ring box had bulged from your grandad's coat to the extent that he was not able to keep it on him and had to store it in the car while he built the courage to ask the biggest question of his life, hence the long wait while he retrieved it. There was one more surprise, as your grandad asked his new bride-to-be to dance.

"But you don't dance," she replied.

Such was the devotion to the girl of his dreams that your grandad had secretly taken dance lessons at Arthur Murray Dance Studios during the lunchbreaks when he was not on hurdles duty. The discretion of the lessons was tested when he ran into long-time friend George Young – no relation to your nana – during one of those breaks and the latter insisted they go to lunch together, oblivious to his mate's actual plans. Your grandad apologised and said he couldn't as he was meeting his father.

"Oh, I haven't seen Eccles (Eric Foreman) in ages. I'll come along," George Young said, before being rebuffed for a second time and sent on his way. It was a beautiful gesture and a small symbol of the love your nana and grandad shared.

Lyn Young became Lyn Foreman on 20 April 1980 at St Nicholas' Anglican Church in Floreat Park – just 11 months after properly meeting the relentless journalist from the ABC, who was impossible to say "no" to. The venue was, of course, your grandad's family church throughout his childhood, but St Nicholas' Church, when consecrated, was also dedicated to sportsmen and women.

The current of sport flowed throughout the day: Rev Keith Wheeler, a friend of your nana's and a national middle distance champion from the 1960s, presided over the ceremony; Sam

Gannon was the best man, with army mate Morey Grafton completing the bridal party; and Subiaco footballer Brian Doogue provided the music, strumming "Never Ending Song of Love", by Delaney & Bonnie.

The service was completed and the group left the church, returning to El Sombrero Restaurant for a reception that featured two speeches – the best man's and the groom's – but might as well have heard from every attendee.

"Wally made the longest speech of all time," friend Steve Heal said.

In fact, it went for 45 minutes. Someone timed it. And when it finally ended, Fred Miller yelled out, "Half time", before everyone bolted out of their seats for the nearest bathroom. Such was the duration of the groom's address that the run-sheet was thrown into chaos and the cutting of the cake was completely overlooked, despite the pre-prepared and staged photos suggesting otherwise.

"The days after that, he would wake up in a panic and say he'd had a dream that his speech went for too long," your nana said. "He'd ask me and I'd say, 'Everyone thought it was great', which it was; it's just that it went for 45 minutes."

If something is going to be done, it must be done thoroughly. That 45-minute speech was aptly timed: it was a preamble to the 26 years of unconditional love your nana and grandad went on to spend together. Your Uncle Mark and I were fortunate enough to be raised in a household that was emotionally as solid as a rock, built on a foundation of mutual love and respect from our parents towards each other.

There were challenges, of course, but that respect was never lost. It was also never hidden and came across regularly in later life when your grandad was on air and recounted stories that inevitably ended with him as the punchline, while describing the advice from your nana that he had chosen to ignore. It came come across as he recounted passionately the stories about your nana and her running career.

And his devotion to your nana and our family was exemplified through such times as our Easter holiday, when we would take a 10-day family trip to Canal Rocks, Yallingup, with Bryan and Steph Cousins and their children, despite him having to then travel back to Perth and back down to Yallingup to call the football on the weekend.

There's a common question that's asked whenever anyone gets married – "How do you know when it's the right person?" – and it's usually responded to with an equally-common answer: "You just know". It's true. You just know. I knew for your mum and your grandad knew for your nana. The stories mentioned here are a small number of examples from a lifetime of love that they shared. It was passionate and lively; it was beautiful and real.

And it was timeless. Much like the 45-minute speech that started it all.

Chapter 8

Sometimes the Grass is Greener

THERE ARE MOMENTS IN EVERYONE'S lives when we do what we think we *should* do and not what we *want* to do. We are all prone to moments of believing the grass will be greener elsewhere and your grandad was no different. In the winter of 1980, he made a professional decision that he always regretted: he left the ABC for STW Channel 9.

Many people have claimed since his passing that your grandad did not have a hint of ego. That is partly correct: he rarely gave any hints of it, but he had a healthy ego. It is impossible to exist in the media without one.

Your grandad's former cadet colleague at *The West Australian* and respected ABC broadcaster Geraldine Doogue described journalism as a mixture of being nosey and a gossip: journalists needed to be nosey enough to find a story, enough of a gossip to want to tell it, but – importantly – also hold a self-belief that they had the right to tell that story. A healthy ego is a prerequisite to entering the media, then the media grows it further.

I remember a time that I experienced that ego first-hand: your grandad had just called a WAFL game for ABC TV at, I think, Leederville Oval. It was the early 1990s and I was younger than 10-years-old. He and I were walking down a corridor, when two young boys of about my age came up and asked him for his autograph. He signed the books and we walked away, but not before I asked him, "Why did they want *your* autograph?", with an emphasis on "your".

His response was something along the lines of: "Because what I do matters to some people". This was more than two decades ago, so I'm paraphrasing the conversation, but the unforgettable aspect was the genuinely offended tone in his response. Class and status were always a consideration of your grandad's, even though it might not have been overly apparent to others and he probably wasn't conscious of it, either.

Your nana, having been raised in a blue-collar life, would buy your Uncle Mark and me nice clothes for Christmas – that's what she always received – only to be told by your grandad that kids don't get clothes for Christmas because they were "no fun". When our family home was being built in Turner Close, Duncraig, your nana insisted there be a tree for the kids to climb – that's what she had done growning up– only to be told, "Don't be silly", and palms were planted instead.

And there was always class-difference veiled in humour when your grandad would refer to your nana as having attended Reform School – his name for Belmont High School – where he claimed she had studied "Lock Picking 101" and "Car Jacking". None of it was ever said with any malice, but the perception of class-difference was there, nonetheless.

"He would always say he got me out of the gutter and gave me a chance at life, but I would always say, 'And I taught you how to treat people right'," your nana said.

And so came a moment in 1980 when your grandad had to make a career decision and the choice he made was one based on money and status, as opposed to passion for the job.

Your grandad was alongside George Grljusich and Dennis Cometti – considered at the time as the two most talented broadcasters in the state and among the most talented in the country – and he loved it.

He later told *The West Australian*, "That was a fantastic experience ... and they are some of the fondest memories of my working life".

But the talent of his colleagues also meant your grandad was always third-fiddle. Perhaps claiming ego was a factor is unfair and ambition is more accurate, because your grandad was always ambitious in every facet of his life, but for as long as he was third-fiddle – Robin to Cometti's Batman, as Geoff Hutchison mentioned – there was only so far that ambition would allow him to grow at the ABC.

There was also the undeniable issue of wages and, again, when playing third-fiddle to the great Grljusich and lauded Cometti, there was little chance of those growing. And there was the Moscow Olympics; the one time your grandad and Cometti clashed.

Cometti specialised in a lot of sports: he had played league football and broadcast it brilliantly and his CV glowed with years' experience covering Test cricket. However, he was not considered a specialist of Olympic sports, which your grandad had devoted much of his career focusing on. Even before Lyn Young became Lyn Foreman, he had been reporting on the exploits of Western Australia's track and field athletes.

His TV reports showed him on several occasions standing on the north-west balcony that overlooked the Perry Lakes track, wearing the same red, with black and white trim Le Coq Sportif windcheater that covered what was likely an unironed business shirt, with only the oversized collar protruding. He had documented the difficulties of WA's athletes and the additional challenges they had to overcome in order to take on the world. He had been doing it so well that when the 1980 Moscow Olympic Games approached, Grljusich was preparing to put his name forward to attend.

It was a defining moment for your grandad: he was never going to overtake Cometti or Grljusich in the pecking order of football or cricket, but maybe he could make his mark in other sports. However, the state of the relationship between Grljusich and Cometti led the latter to believe he had been deliberately overlooked, instead of your grandad's selection being a reward for work produced.

The fallout was decisive: an infuriated Cometti, feeling his professional progression was being stymied by his boss, confronted Grljusich, who promptly ended both men's hopes of travelling for the Games and instead went himself.

"I did the wrong thing and I didn't understand the ramifications of it," Cometti said.

"I felt George was doing me over, because your dad was going and I wasn't. Now, I wasn't an Olympic caller by any stretch, but I really had my nose put out of joint when George said I wasn't going, because my rationale was that I'd done the Test cricket for almost 10 years as a senior broadcaster.

"I apologised to your dad several times since, because he really copped it from me going after George. George liked your dad and respected him as a broadcaster – he certainly liked your dad more than he liked me – but that's not a reflection on why he made the decision. I reacted, because I thought he was shafting me and that cost your dad, because neither of us went. George went.

"That was the only time Wal and I clashed, but it did linger with me, because I regretted that I cost him that trip."

The sincerity of Cometti's regret over the incident was undeniable, but it was what he closed on in recounting the incident that perhaps gave insight into what happened next: "Things had worked out well for him later, of course, but at the time, we never knew where our next feed was coming from". The next Olympic Games was not for four years, by which time, your grandad could have easily been left further behind the guru and the tyro.

So, when the position arose of Sports Editor at STW Channel 9 to work under notable Sports Director Bruce Walker and it was offered to your grandad, he accepted. In doing so, he left a job in which he had covered the pinnacle of one of his most loved sports in Davis Cup tennis, Test cricket, the Esanda World Hockey tournament, countless Australian Rules Football matches and a plethora of smaller, yet global sports.

Your grandad began at Channel 9 on 17 November 1980, telling *WA Newspapers* that he believed the future of sports telecasting lay with commercial television, "particularly because of the problems the ABC faces in securing rights for major sporting events". The truth was that your grandad was likely toeing the company line.

It was certainly correct that the ABC was finding it increasingly difficult to compete financially for rights – it had lost coverage of the Olympics (television), Test cricket and Wimbledon in the years preceding his move – but that was not the overriding concern for him at the time and he was unable to completely conceal those feelings, admitting he felt frustrated "to a certain degree" at his junior position on the ABC sports desk.

"I felt that if I was to develop my career, I had to make a move and I'm grateful for the chance Nine have given me and I'm looking forward to the new challenge," he said.

It would have been difficult to judge the decision as a poor one at the time: Channel 9 was a respected broadcaster and had the year before, in 1979, topped the ratings and was consistently "trouncing" its rival news broadcasts, as recalled by anchor Russell Goodrick. Your grandad's position also came with considerable profile, as it involved taking over the sports presenting from Bruce Walker, who had moved into the Director role.

The ratings were a shot in the arm for morale in the newsroom, but the environment could also be an interesting place to work for reasons that weren't always positive. Channel 9 was owned and operated by a group of about four Perth businessmen, the most notable of those being Laurie Kiernan, whose family had gained a strong financial position through freight and transport operations.

Kiernan worked as the broadcaster's Managing Director and, as one former employee recalled, was believed to sign staff pay cheques out of his own pocket when the finances were not going well. The group, along with General Manager David Aspinall, was referred to as The Gang of Four: "They could be your best buddies, or they could be merciless," one former staff member recalled.

Some of those merciless moments came at the end of a financial year, when "management would always get a bit toey about the profits, so they'd go around and have a purge and sack 10 or 15 people". Those who found themselves without a job only had to wait a couple of weeks, before being re-hired in the new financial year.

Brian Rogers was Deputy News Editor at the time your grandad began and it marked a reunion of sorts for the pair, who first crossed paths when the former was a cadet with *The Daily News*, dealing with then-Counter Clerk at the Fremantle Courts Wally Foreman. He recalled the environment as "a funny place to work" and "different", which certainly would have been the experience for your grandad, whose newsroom experience was that of *The West* and *ABC*.

"They were going around the newsroom one Friday and your old man rang a guy in the field and said, 'Mate, don't come back. They're sacking people'. So he didn't, but then he came back in on Monday and they sacked him on Monday," Rogers said.

Your grandad also found himself at the mercy of a different audience to that which had grown to know him through the public broadcaster. It was one that did not necessarily invest as much interest in in-depth news, analysis and stories, but instead was satisfied by bite-sized entertainment packages. They were the sorts of packages that sponsors lapped up as well; sponsors such as Walpamur Paints, which became a hit with a marketing campaign based around the mischievous antics of a monkey named Wally Walpamur.

The monkey and the name made for an easy connection for the audience and became the bane of your grandad's existence. A morning swim at City Beach often resulted in a barrage of "Oh, look, it's Wally Walpamur" and "Hey, have you seen the monkey's wife; she's got blonde hair" directed at your grandad, who would submerge himself and attempt to swim away.

"He hated that bloody monkey," your nana said.

However, this was your grandad and he was rarely a person to let a situation get him down and, much as he endeavoured to enjoy the trials of the Rat Room after several knockbacks from *The West Australian* for a cadetship, he was equally determined to make the most of his time at Channel 9. Or, at the very least, have a laugh along the way.

The latter was the reputation he quickly forged.

The environment of Nine was as far removed as possible from the ABC studios and your grandad invoked the mischievous spirit of his Walpamur namesake on a regular basis.

It was up to your grandad, as host of sport and the last segment of the news, to throw to the weather and that presented several opportunities for an in-house laugh that went completely unnoticed by the home viewer, be it referring to friend and weatherman Steve Curtis as Pod, or testing his colleague's ability to hold his nerve while live on air.

"Wally used to call me Pod on air – 'Coming up next, Pod with the weather' – but 'Pod' was actually short for Tri- Pod. If only the viewers knew, but nobody ever asked," Curtis said.

"Back then, I had the hots for a reporter named Jennie-Anne Jones and I sent her anonymous red roses to the newsroom once. When I got in there, they were on her desk and I had a wry smile to myself knowing she wouldn't have a clue it was me. Well, that night on the news desk, just as Wally was to say 'Pod is next with the weather', he brings out said red roses on camera and asks me if I know anything about them.

"My face went redder than the roses. Then there was the night I was on camera doing weather – it was an above-waist shot – and I see your dad start to crawl across the floor under the camera shot. The next thing I know, he's hurled a glass of cold water into my crotch. I kept going and prayed the director wouldn't take a wide shot.

"I sure do miss those days – and Wal."

The consistent thread of loyalty and your grandad's desire to help whoever he could, whenever he could, again came to the fore when he caught wind of a Golden West Network reporter who had a passion for sport, but was struggling to see a career pathway that would lead him back up to the city.

Your grandad resolved to helping lay that path and soon had a young Geoff Hutchison driving up to Perth on the weekends to work for Channel 9, before returning to his GWN post by Monday. He had remembered the name of the Kalamunda High School student who had completed a day of work experience with him, Dennis Cometti and George Grljusich at the ABC and was determined to help if he could.

It was not long before Hutchison was a full-time employee of Nine and assisting your grandad in his one-man crusade to provide coverage to all athletes, regardless of whether they kicked a football or held a bat.

"I'd trail after him on the hockey field, because he was single-handedly making hockey important, and he'd introduce me to Richard Aggiss, David Bell and Richard Charlesworth," Hutchison said.

"I remember Steve Ovett and Sebastian Coe were competing in the 800m World Titles and he spent time with Steve Ovett and I thought it was fantastic that he actually knew one of these runners. It was an interesting sign of the times that squash was a regular part of the bulletins, including the amazing feats of Jahangir Khan.

"Australia of course had some good squash players, including WA's Dean Williams, who was the up-and-comer, and Wal would be really keen on Dean Williams and, 'Could he ever beat Jahangir Khan?'. Today, we wouldn't care, but we cared about those things then, like there was this little bloc of a certain kind of sports that mattered and it was very West Australian.

"When those other characters were around, they didn't care as much about getting things right."

Hutchison and your grandad formed a bond that spanned their careers from that moment on. Hutchison left for overseas opportunities, before he returned to Australia on the east coast and their paths rarely coincided again, until he was approached in 2006 while working on the *730 Report* about a position with 720 ABC Local Radio WA to host its *Mornings* program.

Hutchison himself would hose down suggestions that he and your grandad were best mates, but they certainly held a mutual respect for each other and, when that job offer came, there was only one person the former wanted to call for guidance.

"Wal had integrity: he liked everyone, thanked everyone and liked being in the company of an editor as much as a soundo and would joke with them and would be very comfortable with them on that level, whereas the further up the chain you got the more people tended to treat other people like shit," Hutchison said.

The interaction with Hutchison – the boy who began as a work experience student at the ABC, became a casual worker on sport at Nine, before forging a respected career and coming full-circle to the ABC in Perth – was another example of your grandad's devotion to helping those he felt deserved it.

It would be a disservice to Hutchison's dedication, achievements and talent to suggest your grandad was the catalyst for that career, but the friendship showed why some people considered your grandad as being far more than just a sports reporter or administrator.

Your grandad certainly made the most of his time at Channel 9, however, the laughs and enjoyable moments were the exception to the norm and there was no escaping the regret he felt over leaving an experience he thoroughly enjoyed at the ABC. As your nana recalled: "He was a bit disillusioned. He got more money, but in the end, he liked the professionalism of the ABC".

There was also a nagging frustration of a promise that never came to fruition, one that might have altered the entire experience for him had he been able to pursue it.

"When he was there, he was always funny, always bubbly and he was just a great person to work with," newsreader Russell Goodrick said. "But I know – because he confided in me one day – that he was terribly unhappy that he had been promised that, if he joined Channel 9, he would get his own program, his own sports show. It dragged on and on with promises that it would happen, but it never happened and he was really upset by that."

Goodrick ended by saying, "But sometimes those negatives can turn into positives". He was referring to your grandad's resignation from Nine and eventual stewardship of the Western Australian Institute of Sport from burgeoning promise into world-leading institute. However, his disillusionment began leading to action of a different nature.

Your grandad had experienced the challenges faced by certain sections of athletes through the stories he compiled for the ABC and the new life he was leading with your nana, who was among those working harder than their professional counterparts, yet receiving less – or, no – government funding and assistance. Not only was your grandad becoming disenfranchised with his position within sport at Nine, he was becoming disenfranchised with the position of sport in general in Western Australia.

The system was broken, it needed to be fixed and he believed the people charged with fixing it were failing in their jobs. Your grandad began to express that disharmony to whoever would listen.

In 1981, someone did.

Your grandad had held the position of Sports Editor of Channel 9 for three years when he returned home in late 1983 and told your nana they had something to discuss: he had been offered a job back at the ABC, which would have him looking after the sports department. It was an opportunity to return to the broadcaster he loved in a position of higher influence.

The only catch was that it was in Adelaide.

"I wasn't happy about leaving WA, but I knew he wasn't happy (at Nine)," your nana said. "We sat there talking and it went from light to us sitting in the dark.

"In the end, I said, 'Alright, so you want someone to make a decision' – because he was umming and ah-ing – so I said, 'We won't go'. So, ok, he's happy with that. He picks the phone up and by the end of the conversation, we were going to Adelaide."

Your grandad left Perth at the start of January – Day 1 of his job with ABC Adelaide was 9 January 1984 – with your nana following a few months later. She was undergoing surgery for endometriosis and could not make the trip any sooner. It was worth the wait, if I do say so myself, because towards the end of the month, she called your grandad to tell him she was pregnant with their first child – me. It was news that thrilled your grandad, because they had been trying for a child for some time.

Your pregnant nana joined her husband on her birthday, 5 March, in their new home in Hawthorn, a suburb a short drive south out of the Adelaide CBD. Buddy, the budgie, had also made the trip east. Your grandparents made the most of their time in South Australia and ensured any days off were never short of a drive to the wine region, or catching up with army mate Bob Lewis. "He was such a doer; he was like a fart in a bottle," your nana said. It was during one of those moments of action that his life significantly changed course.

It involved a dinner with a friend from an earlier time, one who had found himself in the position he was in partly through the influence of your grandad: it was former Subiaco Cricket Club coach turned Western Australia mentor Daryl Foster. WA had travelled to the state to take on South Australia in the one-day domestic final on Sunday 4 March. Unfortunately, the visitors were trumped by eight runs, but it was a dinner in the lead-up to that match that impacted your grandad.

"We had a state team tour in Adelaide and I went to dinner with your dad," Foster said. "At that stage, I was on the Western Australian Sports Council and I knew this job was coming up. Your dad wanted to get back to Perth, it was pretty obvious, and I just said it was an ideal job for him, because they needed someone with PR skills, as well as someone with a sporting background."

The job Foster mentioned was around the State Government's search for someone to lead a new body being formed. It was being referred to as the Western Australian Institute of Sport. Western Australia had swung from almost a decade of Liberal governance to Labor and the previous party's reluctance to invest in the development of sport and sports infrastructure had been replaced with the ardent approach of the Burke Ministry.

The system that your grandad had identified as broken was being reviewed.

The news was not entirely surprising to your grandad.

The disillusionment of his position at Nine had spurred him to begin championing a need for change in Western Australia's administration of sport. Lotto had been introduced to WA in 1979 and three years later, the Liberal government created the Sports/Culture Instant Lottery, which allocated a per centage of proceeds to the Treasury accounts of the Minister of Cultural Affairs and the Minister for Sport to distribute to groups within the community.

The challenge for the distribution of those funds was that there was an inefficient model being operated in WA, which had a focus overly weighted on recreation and participation funding, while the elite end received nothing. The reason was due to the ever-expanding powers of the Department of Community Recreation – the latest in a long-line of incarnations of what is today the Department of Sport and Recreation – and the almost redundant existence of the WA Sports Federation within that model, while there was no official body representing elite athletes.

Those deficiencies began to grow more significant and apparent after respected University of Western Australia academic John Bloomfield was commissioned in 1973 by the Whitlam Government to produce a white paper that laid the groundwork for the establishment of the Australian Institute of Sport in 1981. In 1978, Bloomfield produced a follow-up paper that focused specifically on Western Australia's sporting system and, while it included the recommendation that a State Institute of Sport be constructed, it also recommended sport in the state be administered by a Department of Youth, Sport and Recreation.

Your grandad held concerns for both the existing model and the model Bloomfield was suggesting be adopted and began writing letter after letter to ministers on both sides of government, outlining the inefficiencies and changes he believed needed to be made.

The Liberals appeared disinterested in making the groundbreaking changes that were being discussed, given they were significant and would require the realignment of government departments, as well as the creation of a new state institute. It was the last thing an incumbent government needed to undertake in the lead-up to an election.

However, the Labor opposition seemed far more open to suggestions. Pivotal to that reception was a man named David Hatt; a talented hockey player, who as a 13-year-old from Narrogin had first met a relentless Bruce Rock representative named Wally Foreman at Country Week Tennis in the late 1950s. More importantly, Hatt was at that time a Labor Party activist and advisor to Shadow Minister for Sport, Keith Wilson. Wilson had charged Hatt with the task of developing Labor's sports policy to take into the next election and the latter was determined to produce a solid, considered and advanced framework.

The official history of the era records Professor Bloomfield as again being the architect of change for sport, this time in his home state of WA, and without a doubt he was pivotal. Bloomfield chaired the production of a third report once Labor took power and on 30 November 1983 handed over a document titled *A Report to the Hon. Keith Wilson MLA of the Sports Development Working Party*.

It made a raft of recommendations, including the empowerment of the WA Sports Federation, the establishment of a powerful advisory group named the WA Sports Council and the development of the Western Australian Institute of Sport to "complement the

Australian Institute of Sport" and to "cater for the development of talented young sportsmen and sportswomen of this state".

It was a solid framework that had Bloomfield rightfully credited with much of the vision that steered WA sport in a more productive direction, particularly given his earlier productions of the 1973 and 1978 reports. However, that document was produced in 1983. It also included Hatt in its acknowledgements.

Hatt had read the numerous letters your grandad had written on the direction of sport, so two years before Bloomfield's recommendations were made to the Burke Government, he and your grandad met on numerous occasions to discuss and prepare the policy that Labor would take into the election. That vision was formed across 1981 and 1982 and, crucially, it included the diluting of power of the Department for Youth, Sport and Recreation and the establishment of the Western Australian Institute of Sport (WAIS).

Your grandad's vision for WAIS differed to that of Bloomfield in that it was to be completely independent incorporated body. Bloomfield's proposal to the government within the White Paper had it operating under a board that was a sub-committee of another body, the WA Sports Council – of which the professor was Chair – and that would have the institute employ only a program co-ordinator to act out the directions of the Sports Council through the WAIS Board.

The involvement in the planning ignited your grandad's desire to influence sport in a more significant way than discussing it through the media, however, the fact was that Labor was not in government. The policy was formed, but lay dormant awaiting the election. A year later, your grandad accepted the position with the ABC in Adelaide and forgot all about WA Labor and WAIS.

So, when Foster – a member of that powerful Sports Council group that had been formed under the recommendations of Bloomfield once Labor took office – over that dinner in South Australia mentioned that the Burke Ministry was intending to establish WAIS, the concept was not foreign.

It was the fact that action was being taken by a government that your grandad found intriguing.

Your grandad's interest was piqued, but he thought nothing more of the job Foster mentioned: he had only recently joined the ABC in South Australia and, while he was strongly engaged in the process of developing Labor's sports policy, he had not considered that his involvement would amount to something greater than the behind-the-scenes contribution. After all, he was a journalist and broadcaster, not a sports administrator and he did not even have a university degree.

Labor, however, thought otherwise.

The Burke Ministry also brought with it an admirable trait of action over rhetoric and, once a decision was made, it seldom took long for it to be put into effect. The party won government in 1983 and David Hatt implored Minister Wilson to act on the policy that had been formed. Wilson did and established a board to oversee the formation of WAIS. It included some lofty names: Bruce Elliott was the inaugural chairman, water polo great Tom Hoad was a member, as was Ric Charlesworth and Hatt, along with Professor John Bloomfield.

The applications for the inaugural directorship of WAIS came flooding in. Leading the list of candidates were two men: an East Perth footballer named Gary Martin and a squash player named Nigel Champion. Both had strong credentials. Neither were your grandad.

Moving into office resulted in Labor's inheritance of bundles of correspondence from the previous government on every matter imaginable, but there was one bundle in particular that stood out.

"Wally was publicly critical of the way in which the money was being distributed and he made this comment along the lines of, 'Here we are, subsidising the performances of people spinning discs (Frisbee) on the Esplanade, while our swimmers and athletes can't get a scholarship or assistance from the government'," Hatt said of the moment he began trawling through your grandad's file from the Liberals.

"The Labor Party came to Government in 1983, I was the advisor to the Sports Minister, Keith Wilson, and we got all this correspondence, which included a whole bunch of letters from Wally Foreman. It was the 'flying disc' thing that actually caught my attention.

"When 1983 happened, I said to Keith Wilson that we had to do it. We had to establish an institute of sport and we needed Wally Foreman."

The ideal candidate was in front of them: your grandad had shown a propensity to fight for his beliefs, had shown an ability to form well-considered strategies and, importantly, had shown an ability to attract publicity. That was crucial for a fledgling body that would be unable to survive on government funding alone. The problem was, your grandad had not applied for the job.

Either he had not known about it, or he did not believe he was a suitable candidate. Hatt and Labor disagreed on the latter and set about ensuring the former was not the case.

"Gary Martin and Nigel Champion were both good candidates, but the guy we needed to get out there and fight for money was Wally, who also had a better concept of how the institute should work," Hatt said.

"I said, 'Keith, We've got to invite Wally'. He never applied for it. We invited him to apply as part of the process. He did and he came across for an interview. I was convinced, so was Keith. UWA was not and they weren't impressed – they were pushing Nigel Champion – but we needed someone with a profile."

Your grandad never believed he had a chance. He had attended the interview while your nana had caught the train to Melbourne to stay with a friend and take in the national athletics championships. She had used the time to gather her thoughts and returned to Adelaide with a renewed determination to "give it a good go" in their new home.

She declared as much to her husband as she disembarked at the station and was met with a hug, only to hear words similar to those she had been told barely months before: "We've got a decision to make".

It was a difficult decision.

Your grandad was torn between what he felt was a selfish ambition to be more involved in the administration of sport and his obligation to an ABC that had only recently been good enough to welcome him back. It had been just three months since he accepted the Adelaide job and your nana reminded him of as much.

The indecisive conversation that led them to Adelaide in the first place seemed to play on repeat and it was again left to your nana to make the decision.

"I said he couldn't leave, it wouldn't look very good as he'd only been there three months, but it was always something he'd wanted to do; he wanted to be in a position where he could affect the future of sport, not just talk about it," your nana said.

"We tossed it up and he couldn't decide. I said, 'Look, as much as I would like to go home and have our child in Perth, I don't think we can. You can't leave the ABC again'. So he picks up the phone and by the end of the conversation, we were going back to Perth."

On the other end of the line was David Hatt, who had his No.1 candidate advising him that he could not accept the position.

"I asked him what he was doing and he said the same thing he was back in WA," Hatt said.

"Richard Charlesworth was involved at this point as a Board Member and keen on Wally coming back as well and the Minister was very good in that he took my advice at the time and not that of the UWA people.

"Wally said to me, 'I can't see myself jumping over Dennis or George', and I said to him, 'Forget about that. Come back and do the WAIS job. We'll give you the funds, we'll provide the right environment, you'll have to start at UWA, but we'll find a home for WAIS as soon as we possibly can'.

"I said, 'This is your passion, mate. Come back and do it'. He said ok."

At the heart of the decision was a feeling that had been steadily growing stronger in your grandad. He had spoken to the *Sunday Independent* in 1981 for a story that focused on his move from the ABC to Channel 9. However, that was also around the time he was growing disenfranchised with his role and he uttered words that meant little to the journalist at the time, but resonated when Hatt made the offer.

He had said: "I want to be a decision maker. I'm ambitious enough to want to go all the way in this business".

The boxes had only just been unpacked, but they were being packed up again. Your grandad was to be announced as the inaugural director of the Western Australian Institute of Sport. The ministerial notes of 30 April declared he would commence at WAIS in "early June", in time for the institute's official opening in July.

Your nana, who had enjoyed her train journey to Melbourne, demanded that if she was going to be shipped around the country pregnant, then she wanted to at least see and enjoy the country and the return trip to Perth must be made via train. So the Foremans boarded the Indian Pacific, with Buddy the budgie swaying gently on his totem in the pet hold.

They sat, waiting for the train to pull out of the station. Your grandad turned to your nana: "So, what do we do now?"

Your grandad always cherished and took pride in his rural roots.

He was born in Kalgoorlie, where he is pictured left as a two-year-old by the family car, which was packed and moved the Foremans to Bruce Rock.

Even school was a hit for your grandad in the country, especially Grade 5 under teacher Colin Smith. He is top, second from right, as a 10-year-old in 1958 with members of that class as part of the production of Origin of a Roast Pig.

However, all good things come to an end and the family farewelled Bruce Rock, pictured above, and headed for Perth.

Sport always played a big role in your grandad's life, be it as a member of Wembley's 1960 Grand Final football team (front row, second from left), at Country Tennis Week at Kings Park, or just surfing the local breaks with cousin John Foreman.

Your grandad felt like he wasted much of his youth, until he was drafted into National Service as a 21-year-old.

The regimented lifestyle and guidance of the army had your grandad first go through Officer's Training at Scheyville, NSW, and obtain the rank of 2Lt, before leading 3RAR (top) based out of South Australia's Woodside Barracks.

It was the discipline and qualifications he needed to finally enter the media.

Fun times, friends and a beer were always important to your grandad, whether that was in the army (top, L-R: Bob Lewis, Morey Grafton, Wally Foreman, Kevin Harrison) or with the Floreat Hotel regulars and other mates, pictured below.

It took your grandad three applications and two rejections before he was finally accepted into *The West Australian*'s cadetship program in 1972 (left).

It marked the beginning of a life in the media that only ended with his passing.

He moved from *The West* to the ABC, where he worked with renowned and respected figures George Grljusich and Dennis Cometti, pictured above, second from right and far right, respectively.

He went on to also work for *The Sunday Times*, the NINE Network, Radio 6PR, Network TEN and Channel SEVEN.

The joke was that he owned a jacket for every outlet except SBS; the humour was in the truth of it.

Your grandad used to joke that your nana was lucky when in 1980 she went from Lyn Young to Lyn Foreman, meaning her name no longer sounded like something off a Chinese menu. Given your grandad was a 32-year-old journalist, marrying a 23-year-old athlete, most people understood who the lucky one was.

PART TWO

Chapter 9

The Western Australian Institute of Sport

MICK AITKEN HAD BEEN SITTING in his boss's office at the Sports Council in Manchester talking about golf courses. He knew little of the Western Australian Government, little of the state's sporting infrastructure and he had never met your grandad.

That was the start of 1984. By 1987, he was wishing it was 1984 again, because he suddenly found himself in Rome among a delegation representing Perth's bid for the 1991 World Championships in Athletics and being told, in no uncertain terms from the most unsavoury of sources, that it was "not a good thing to be involved in this bid".

It was the panicked message being passed on from one of the members of the IAAF selection panel. He had been stopped outside his room in the hallway of the hotel the group was staying at and given the very clear warning. Your grandad and Aitken were stunned. And how would West Australian icon Herb Elliot, patron of the bid, react?

It was a moment of clarity for your grandad that opened his eyes to the true nature of international sport and the covert deals that secure events for host cities. As I write this chapter, soccer's world governing body FIFA is undergoing mass investigation that has involved several arrests for alleged corruption around the way in which the sport is run and into whose pockets money has allegedly flowed. Most major international bodies have had similar allegations levelled against them at some stage and athletics is no different.

As a silver lining, the Rome moment was also one that reflected the rapid development and growth in significance of a fledgling body called the Western Australian Institute of Sport. It was also another example of the ongoing investment of WA Labor Government. Your grandad and WAIS were important pieces of the Burke Government's plans for sport in WA, but they were only a couple of pieces nonetheless.

Aitken, a specialist in sporting facilities development and financing, was another of those pieces, as was the WA Sports Federation, at which he was the Executive Director. Aitken had fallen in love with Perth as a 13-year-old watching the 1962 British Empire and Commonwealth Games on a tiny black and white TV from his home in the UK. Not Australia, but Perth.

"I was in awe of the beauty and rawness of the place," Aitken said. "I wanted to go to Perth from that very day".

He got the opportunity when the Burke Government's investment in WA sport led to the creation of the first Executive Director position at the WA Sports Federation. Aitken had previously been to Perth on a familiarisation tour for work in 1981, but Australia's struggling economy meant employment opportunities were non-existent.

However, a friendship struck with then-Director General of the Department of Sport and Recreation John Graham led to him being made aware of the position at WASF three years later, which led to a phone call from Australia that interrupted his conversation about golf courses.

"Calls from Australia in 1981 were few and far between for anyone, let alone little old Mick," he said.

It was a senator named Jack Evans, a recent President of the WA Sports Federation, who offered Mick the position. He arrived in Perth on 24 June 1984 and began work immediately, coinciding almost precisely with your grandad's beginnings at WAIS.

I'm going into detail about Aitken for a couple of reasons: firstly, his role in helping establish WA's sports system was crucial and I at least want to recognise that contribution where appropriate here; but, also, because he was an extremely important man in your grandad's life and was one of his closest friends. They were allies in several political and sporting battles across their tenures at WAIS and WASF and they were close outside of work.

They were recalled by others as being as "thick as thieves" – where one went, the other was by his side – and that included in death; Aitken was one of the pallbearers who carried your grandad's coffin.

"It was an incredibly tense time – intense and tense – and euphoric at times, but we were comrades at arms, your dad and I, and it was by virtue of the complexities of life that we both went into it at the same time," Aitken said.

Mick Aitken was heavily involved in the development of the Perth Superdrome – the state's first wet and dry, multipurpose stadium – and, for this part of the story, played an important role in helping the State Government establish EventsCorp.

Part of the reasoning behind the construction of the Superdrome was to allow Perth to bid for and host international and national events. Aitken's experience with the UK Sports Council had him foresee the requirement of another entity: an events arm of the government that would be capable of facilitating and managing such bids.

Among the first of those bids made was the 1991 World Swimming Championships, for which Aitken operated as the Secretary during the bidding phase, before becoming Event Director upon securing the titles with the help of renowned Olympic water polo coach and WASF President Tom Hoad. It was a proud moment for Perth and one that filled it with a sudden sense of pride that had been lost in the years of apathy that followed the 1962 British Empire and Commonwealth Games.

Suddenly, Perth began to again dream of having the world's sights upon it and, having secured the swimming, a bid was mounted to secure the IAAF World Championships in Athletics for the same year. It was an ambitious bid, to say the least, but confidence was high. The proposed venue of Perry Lakes Stadium would have been 30-years-old by the time the championships arrived and was in dire need of refurbishment.

However, your grandad and Aitken – already close friends by this stage – were buoyed by the excitement of the swimming success. They were confident they could secure the titles and became Chairman and Secretary of Perth's bid, respectively, making the shortlist alongside the internationally renowned cities of Los Angeles, Berlin and Tokyo. They were invited to Rome for the final stages of the bidding process, held around one of the IAAF's council meetings.

The proposed venue and the competition made for imposing challenges, but Perth had a trump card to play: Western Australian athletics icon Herb Elliott.

"Three of the great cities of the world and then little old Perth, but it was a masterstroke of Wally's to get Herb Elliot involved as the patron, because, if you know the history of the sport, it was in Rome in 1960 where Herb achieved immortality, in sporting terms, when he won the gold medal," Aitken said. "The connection between Herb and Rome was strong."

And that made Perth's bid strong. That might sound like an overstatement of the runner's presence, but this was a man who was never beaten in 42 races between 1957 and 1961 in either the 1500m or mile distances and whose world record 1500m win at the 1960 Olympic Games was achieved in such a fashion that his time would have secured gold at Games into the mid-90s.

Elliott's presence held weight and had put Perth on the verge of achieving what had initially appeared impossible. However, that was publicly and what your grandad, Aitken and Elliott quickly learnt was that there was another side to bidding for international events. A side that did not necessarily reflect public perception.

I must say for legal reasons that any perceptions of untoward activity were only alleged and nobody was accused or convicted of any wrongdoing. This story is one recounted by primary sources, supported by media reports of the time, so should be understood as their opinions and perceptions of what occurred, not necessarily as fact.

The International Association of Athletics Federations was run by an Italian man named Primo Nebiolo, who was a polarising figure and who passed away in 1999. He helped athletics achieve a great surge in fortunes and oversaw its emergence from amateur ranks and growth from a budget of about $50,000 to $40-million at the time of his death. That number would be far higher now.

However, as the *New York Times* reported, "He was a figure of great ego and ambition who expected to be treated regally and drew criticism as an intractable autocrat". The paper also quoted former US Olympic Committee president Dr LeRoy Walker as saying: "He probably has an ego metabolism that takes more feeding than others. He is the president and wants to be treated that way. He likes being exalted beyond all others".

Nebiolo had been implicated, but never charged, in several controversial matters during his time at the head of track and field. And, prior to his life in athletics, renowned British journalist David Walsh in his account of the Lance Armstrong-doping affair Seven Deadly Sins named Nebiolo as being implicit in supporting the blood-doping regime of Italian sports doctor Francesco Conconi.

While Nebiolo was greeting the Perth delegates in 1987 as president of the IAAF, he was also the president of the Italian Athletics Federation. At the World Championships of that year, in that city of Rome, an Italian long jump bronze medallist was stripped of his placing after investigations showed Italian officials "rigged the measurement". Nebiolo was never implicated in the matter, but resigned from his position two years later. He was also connected to cost-overrun investigations surrounding the refurbishments of the Olympic Stadium, in Rome for the 1990 soccer world cup.

He exuded personality traits of stubbornness and narcissism and the *New York Times* quoted Nebiolo as having said of his oft perceived arrogance: "I believe that all big men in life want to get some position for themselves. If you don't have ambitions in a position where you don't receive money, why are you doing this? You do this surely for ambition."

The IAAF was beginning to emerge as a major powerbroker in world sport, dealing in large sums of money, as opposed to its meagre $50,000 budget for track and field internationally. It attracted global cities to bidding processes for its events. Events such as the world championships and cities such as Perth. But for whatever reason – legitimate or otherwise – your grandad and his friends were not wanted in Rome.

"We'd mounted this bid ... in the belief that having got the World Swimming Championships, anything was possible and it was an era that was just awakening to the fact that events mattered and could make a difference to all sorts of aspects of life in the cities that held them," Aitken said.

"We rolled up into this fabulous hotel in Rome, where the decision was to be made and we were all based for a few days. The IAAF membership was all huddled in a group and we saw the look on their faces when we walked in with Herb. We could see that we were clearly not wanted."

If the gazes on arrival were not enough to send a message to the Perth delegates that they were not wanted, the warning conveyed by that member of the IAAF inner circle certainly did. It also sent another message: there was sufficient belief within the IAAF inner-sanctum that the Perth bid was strong enough that it required a warning shot fired across its bow.

If there was one thing your grandad loved, it was a good verbal stoush with a hint of tactical manoeuvring and the challenges to the Perth bid simply served to motivate him further.

It was a dangerous game, given he had no way of knowing whether those verbal warnings could have turned into something more. And what your grandad decided to do was another move of pure naivety mixed with bold defiance and politicking by the Perth group.

The delegates had heard that International Olympic Committee president Juan Antonio Samaranch was also in Rome. The Perth bidding group swiftly organised a dinner, utilising its most valuable negotiating weapon, Herb Elliott, as a drawcard and inviting Samaranch. A displeased IAAF arranged a conflicting dinner in response, to attempt to keep distance between the Perth group and the powerful Samaranch, but it failed to discourage the IOC boss. Instead, Nebiolo and the IAAF members briefly attended the Perth dinner, before departing with Samaranch in tow.

There were perceptions among the Perth group that the formalities in Rome for the shortlisted candidates were just that – formalities. They believed it was a known fact that the decision had already been made and that Tokyo had secured the championships before the shortlisted delegations ever arrived in Rome. It was known behind closed doors, they said, and it was displayed in clear view, when Tokyo was announced as the winning bid with the unveiling of a beautifully crafted poster of the city that read "Tokyo 91" that appeared to fit perfectly onto its custom-made easel.

So, when Perth swaggered in with its Olympic icon and began hosting dinners with the IOC president, that balance of power and possibly pre-arranged plans were suddenly being destabilised. The dinner invitation caused controversy within the IOC and IAAF ranks, but in the end it was agreed that Samaranch, the IOC Members and Nebiolo would attend the event for a short while, before leaving for another function.

"We set the head table up so that Herb was sitting in the middle, Nebiolo was on one side of him and Samaranch was on the other," Aitken said.

"I was at the door welcoming people with Herb and what happens is Nebiolo came in, saw the seating arrangements and just moved it all, with the back of his right arm, and he says, 'I am the president and I sit here (next to Samaranch)'. Neither Herb, nor Samaranch were there at the time, but I saw it."

The dinner ended without further incident and the time for the presentation of the final bids arrived the next day.

A twist of irony took place which actually worked in Perth's favour. Out of the four bidding cities, all produced a proposal video, but only Perth's worked during the presentations. Maybe it was Karma. Maybe, despite all the theories and suggested evidence, there was nothing untoward in the bidding process after all.

"We did a very good presentation, as you can imagine with your dad and Herb, and we all trooped out and went to the unveiling of the winner," Aitken recalled.

As many already suspected, Tokyo won the bid.

"I'll never forget," Aitken said. "In the aftermath, the IAAF people all filed past us and there was one guy there from the old East Germany, his name was Georg Wieczisk, and as he walked passed us, Georg just said: 'Last night, Perth had the votes'. He repeated it and then left."

The report in *The West Australian* by David Marsh read: "Voting on the successful applicant – which also included West Berlin and Los Angeles – was held by IAAF delegates by a secret ballot.

"The IAAF would not release details of the voting. The Australian delegates were certain that considerable behind-the-scenes wheeling and dealing by the Tokyo delegation gave that city the right to host the world's No.1 track and field meeting."

Your grandad reaffirmed his suspicions.

"Dealing with the International Athletics Federation was like dealing with the New York Yacht Club," your grandad said. "We believe that Perth had numerous attributes that would have made the championships an enormous success here. We made an extraordinary impression on those associated with the IAAF. For that reason, Perth is well placed to submit a bid for the next championships."

And even the inoffensive Herb Elliott added: "I'm very disappointed, both for the athletes of the world and particularly for the athletes of Australia."

Aitken again preferred not to be drawn on what he believed could have taken place in Rome in 1987, but he still managed to find some humour in the situation.

"You might well argue that it's just as well, because trying to stage the World Championships at Perry Lakes might have been something that not even Wally could manage," he said, wryly.

"If your dad had ever written a book – which I'm sure he would have done – this would have been a chapter, because the experience in that hotel, with the IAAF and the players in that game there, was something else. The most important commodity you can bring to life in any relationship is trust and Wally and I trusted each other implicitly and we were a great team.

"It was a fantastic bid that almost pulled off the impossible."

David Hatt hung up the phone. He had convinced his No.1 man – your grandad – to accept the inaugural directorship of the Western Australian Institute of Sport. It was early 1984 and the first required piece to address an ailing WA sports system had fallen in place. Next, he needed to address the issue of the government's Department for Youth, Sport and Recreation.

Hatt was no slouch when it came to sport: not only did he have the intellect and nous to administer it, he had the passion, talent and work ethic to play it.

Hatt's country upbringing in Narrogin had him turn to similar sports to your grandad and he was among the first Australians to be offered a tennis scholarship in the US collegiate system and thrived in hockey, playing for, coaching and managing Western Australia's state team in a career that secured nine national titles, before later representing his country at Masters level and assisting close friend and then-head coach Ric Charlesworth in managing the Australian men's side.

His administration career took in roles as president of Hockey Australia, Chief Executive of the Fremantle Dockers, a position as commissioner with the Australian Sports Commission and a decade long tenure as deputy chairman of the Western Australian Institute of Sport. It was that latter role that had him work closely with your grandad, but which came to an end when the State Liberal's took Government in the early 90s.

Hatt, a year older than your grandad, left the country to study at Teachers College in 1962 and quickly became involved with the Labor Party as an activist. His interests in sport and understanding of both administration and policy led to the Minister for Sport Rev Keith Wilson requesting he write Labor's sports policy for the then-shadow government, led by Brian Burke, to take into the next election. That was when he involved your grandad in the planning phase of that policy and Hatt then left teaching when Labor took government in 1983 to take up the role of Chief Policy Advisory to Wilson.

To say Hatt was solely responsible for implementing the changes to WA sport that involved your grandad would be disrespectful to the others who invested significant time and energy and who put their reputations on the line. People such as Wilson, Professor John Bloomfield, well-respected former president of WASF Tom Hoad, your grandad and Mick Aitken and even former Premier Brian Burke, who admittedly later in life probably was not too concerned about his reputation regarding sporting decisions.

But Hatt was the man who got the right people together, who planned the right moves and who had access to, and the ear of, the right people to turn those plans into actions. Hatt was the man who guaranteed your grandad complete autonomy and independence if he was to accept the position at WAIS and who then worked feverishly behind the scenes to keep that promise.

That promise focused on two bodies of concern, the University of WA and the Department for Youth, Sport and Recreation, both of which believed they had a right to ownership over "this sexy new thing in sport", as current WAIS director Steve Lawrence described the early perception of the institute. There was certainly a case to be argued for WAIS's independence from the government, which centred on the inability of public sector rules to adequately handle the realities of high performance sport.

That battle could have been won by the allies of independence, however, Hatt took a much larger view of the situation and, instead of fighting a micro-level debate with the department, he was preparing to launch a counterpunch that would ensure

WAIS's independence would be secure far into the future. That counterpunch focused on the department itself and Hatt's belief that it had grown disproportionately powerful, while concentrating too much on recreation and leaving elite sport lagging.

Balancing the department's influence, role and significance was all a part of the original plan that David Hatt had developed with your grandad for sport in the state.

The Department for Youth, Sport and Recreation needed to exist; even WAIS needed it to exist. Hatt had worked with inaugural WAIS Chairman Bruce Elliott to develop a constitution and establish the Institute as an incorporated body, which meant it could receive government funding, but that funding had to be channelled through a government agency, a la the Department for Youth, Sport and Recreation.

However, the department had also gained a position of significant power and had "become above public comment or analysis", as Mick Aitken recalled. It had the appearance of doing whatever it wanted, whenever it wanted, without being particularly beholden to the government of the day. It largely got away with those behaviours simply because high performance sport had not progressed beyond a peripheral issue.

Hatt and your grandad shared the view that intervention was required because of the Department's apathy towards elite and high performance sport. The solution, under a policy that was developed with the help of your grandad and strengthened by Professor John Bloomfield's report to the Minister for Sport in 1983, was two-fold: establish a Western Australian Institute of Sport; and empower the WA Sports Federation.

WAIS was to look after high performance athletes and sport, while WASF was to be the peak body leading and representing all the state's sporting associations and assist government in policy and event matters. WASF prior to 1983 had existed as an organisation staffed primarily of volunteers and composed of delegates of the major sports, but did little other than hold an annual dinner to elect the WA Sportsperson of the Year.

That needed to change and the body was required to lift itself from insignificance. Hatt and Bloomfield recommended those changes be achieved by WASF receiving a sudden, ongoing and dramatic increase in its funding from the State Government.

They were actions that aligned with the recommendations of Bloomfield's 1983 report and the injection of cash allowed for the creation of WASF's first Executive Director position, which was filled by a person capable of contributing to policy and events: Mick Aitken. The moves did not sit well with the Department for Youth, Sport and Recreation and resulted in an environment of tension. It had Aitken feel as though he had landed in the middle of a political warzone from the moment he was collected from the airport by the Department's director John Graham.

"He told me the government had put a bit of money into the Sports Federation, but that it wouldn't last and I'd be better trying to find something else," Aitken said.

"I arrived in a very dynamic environment. It was just after Brian Burke's government had come in, unbeknownst to me. What was clear was there was a government agenda that did not trust the Department of Sport and Recreation and all it stood for: its smugness, its complacency, its arrogance and its inability or unwillingness to do anything serious about high performance sport.

"I came over thinking I'd gone from one comfortable job to another, to find out I was in this maelstrom of intrigue and subterfuge behind the scenes that caused a lot of tension, but a lot of creative tension, too, because it was an astonishing time for WA sport that I happened to find myself parachuted into as one of the key players.

"I don't say that with a sense of arrogance, but the government wanted to set up a seat of power that was alternative to the old guard and that alternative was the Sports Federation and the WA Institute of Sport. That's how your dad and I found ourselves in a headlong charge, not just to improve sport, but to take on the bureaucracy.

"And we had the government's full, if tacit, support."

I always thought this book was going to be an enormous body of work, but it rapidly grew to a scale that I could never have fathomed and that is simply because of the links and trails throughout a life that held such significance to not only our family, but this state.

Like Mick Aitken, I don't say that with a sense of arrogance, but I thought, for example, your grandad's appointment as inaugural director of WAIS would account for a paragraph as a short statement of fact in a story. It instead accounts for several thousands of words.

Perhaps I've overwritten it, but it became clear that your grandad's appointment as inaugural director of WAIS was so much more complex than a simple job appointment. His appointment was a part of a larger plan for sport in WA, riddled with backstories of events and people that make this feel as much a history of sport in the state as it is a history of your grandad and it was an appointment made in conjunction with the hiring of Aitken.

And your grandad's appointment was not simply because of his vision for sport and his ability to attract media coverage and build a profile for WAIS, but it was because of his tenacity, ability and willingness to fight for WAIS against whoever he was required to fight against, including governments and their departments. It was all of that, because it was going to be a long fight and your grandad needed allies, who were again put in place by David Hatt through the formation of the now-defunct WA Sports Council.

It was another recommendation made by John Bloomfield in his 1983 report, but it was also one that your grandad and Hatt and formulated for Labor's policy in the late 70s. The council comprised of representatives from key bodies – WAIS, WASF and the Department for Youth, Sport and Recreation – and individuals, chaired by the respected Bloomfield. It carried the power of review and comment over any policy recommendation made by the Department for Youth, Sport and Recreation to the

Minister for Sport. The group's influence also allowed it to advise the government on funding for sport.

"The first time I met your dad was at a meeting of the WA Sports Council," Aitken said.

"I'd just arrived at this point and your dad breezed in and I thought, 'Crikey, I want to get to know this bloke'; he was always opinionated, in the nicest sense of the word. He wanted to speak his mind. Wally had a philosophy on sport that you could love or hate, but there was no denying that he knew what he wanted and why he wanted it and I think I was drawn to his sureness of direction that was needed and his magnificently articulate way of presenting his case to friend and foe alike.

"I had to become street-smart to learn the tricks of survival and to get to know people in the state. Your dad was instrumental in helping me understand that and linking me into the players who were supportive.

"The support of your dad – and there were others: John Bloomfield, Daryl Foster, Bruce Elliott, Tom Hoad – was enormously influential in me working out who I needed to work alongside in order to survive. He was a phenomenal help and we were friends from very early on."

Aitken's friendship with your grandad developed rapidly and included the ongoing company of David Hatt. The Subiaco Hotel was a haunt every Friday afternoon and the new model for WA sport had the two constantly working together, including on the previously mentioned bids for swimming and athletics meets, as well as travelling to the 1986 Commonwealth Games in Edinburgh. Although, the closeness of the friendship was tested by hotel management in Edinburgh with the arrangement of just one bed in the room.

"Wally looked at me and said, 'Is there something you're not telling me, Mick?'," Aitken said. "Wally took his work and his view on life seriously, but he didn't take himself seriously. You could always take the piss out of Wally and he'd happily soak it up, before giving it back, times-10".

That was no throwaway line from Aitken, either. This was a time when WAIS was under threat of takeover, under enormous pressure to justify its existence and your grandad was facing intra and interstate scrutiny from all angles. Yet, he always made time for humour.

"Wally, one day, says to me we were going to perform a bit of a trick on Mick and he needed my help," David Hatt said.

"He said we were going to go to a meeting of the World Swimming Organising Committee, which Tom Hoad organised, because he was the chair of it, and we're going to tell Mick that the pool's short. This is a week before the World Swimming Championships were supposed to start; it had the water in it and the whole shooting match.

"We told Mick we'd had it measured by an engineer from the University of WA and it had come up 49.7m. Mick absolutely shat himself and Wally's trying to keep a straight face, Tom's looking stern and I'm trying not to laugh. Mick's absolutely lost it: here's the pinnacle of his achievements, he'd got the championships here, the athletes were already arriving and the pool was too short.

"We kept it up for hours and he was like a ghost, but eventually, because he was so upset, we had to tell him. He was going to kill Wally."

It was a moment of humour in a trying time.

The Department for Youth, Sport and Recreation underwent another name change to the Department for Sport and Recreation and Aitken needed the alliance with your grandad as much as your grandad needed him. That was especially the case given WASF's initial home was in the bowels of Perry Lakes Stadium: the same location as the Department.

It was a frosty relationship and Aitken's presence was barely acknowledged by Department staff, with the exception of Brian Cook, who later became an administrator at the West Coast Eagles and Geelong Cats football clubs.

"Brian said to me one day: 'Mick, you must have known what you were coming over to, that you'd been brought over to create shit about everything?'," Aitken said. "I didn't have the faintest idea until I arrived that June morning and John Graham spelt it out for me in the car."

The threat from the Department was very real and for evidence of that your grandad and Aitken needed only to have watched in the subsequent years as the country's first state institute in South Australia began to unravel.

The South Australian Sports Institute (SASI) was established in 1982 and its inaugural director, Michael Nunan, was of great support to your grandad as WAIS attempted to find its feet. Nunan, like almost every person I interviewed who was involved in sports administration from that era, was physical education-trained.

He had been strongly advocating for the South Australian government to be mindful of its obligations to sport, not just the arts, and to complement its devotion to volunteers and recreation with a balance of elite sport. The result was Nunan being sent around the world on a government-funded tour to examine sports institutes and, upon his return, he wrote a report outlining his proposal for a State Sports Institute that resulted in him being named the inaugural director of the country's first state institute: SASI.

The cornerstone of Nunan's report – and an issue your grandad was very vocal about – was that whatever model was to be established, the result had to be an independent institute that sat outside the jurisdiction of government. The reason was simple: sports institutes could not be hamstrung by the employment policies of governments when they needed to hire, fire and rapidly distribute money to elite athletes and coaches.

It was the model that was established in South Australia and one which operated very successfully for 10 years. Then the government fell apart.

South Australia's State Bank dropped about $4-billion as it collapsed in 1991, which caused Premier John Bannon to resign and led to the defeat of the South Australian State Labor Party in 1993. The result was a government that became paranoid about anything "loosely attached to it" and it set about clawing back control over independent bodies that received government funding.

SASI fell into that category. The government achieved its goal and, to this day, SASI exists as a division of the Office for Recreation and Sport.

"And that's why it's basically useless," Nunan said.

"I resigned before that happened, because I didn't want to be a part of going back into government. If there's a legacy to Wally's administration, it's that he was able to win the battles on not just a sports front, but also a political front and what he built was so successful that it was able to remain independent.

"What we've got in South Australia is the direct opposite and we've lost the focus. When you're dealing with elite sport, your athletes come and go, your coaches come and go, there's standards that are set, you want people with good sporting and managerial knowledge and then you have to set standards and criteria for those people.

"Then you have to set standards and criteria for individual sports and how you're going to interact with them. It was something that was best decided by sport, not governments or politicians."

The threat from the Department for Sport and Recreation always lingered in the background and your grandad felt its looming presence right up to the time of his resignation.

As Aitken recalled: "Your dad and I were always fighting for the survival of our respective organisations. The only way we would survive was if we won, because if we didn't win, they'd wipe us out. They wanted to wipe us out, or at least return the status quo to what it had been."

However, the empowerment of WASF and the arrival of Aitken turned that organisation from "a pimple on the backside of government" into a crucial ally that allowed your grandad to survive the most dangerous days of WAIS's inception, while the rebalancing of power by David Hatt ensured any play from the Department was far less intimidating than it would have been had the "status quo" remained.

"They became, really, irrelevant in terms of the direction the state was taking in its ambition to become a powerhouse in sport and a producer of talent in sport, through vehicles to present the best that sport had to offer," Aitken said. "They became a recreational organisation, which they had essentially always been, but because they had largely ignored high performance, we had changed the way government funded sport."

Your grandad and Aitken played a major role in that change in direction; they were the ones on the frontline, implementing visions and fighting the public and boardroom battles. But they were put in place by the man who had given them the ability to fight and win. Hatt remained a close friend of your grandad's throughout his and both men remained modest and proud of what their contributions helped the state achieve.

"Me, Mick and Wally, we had a productive time and we did fundamentally change sport in Western Australia," Hatt said.

"Mick and Wally just clicked, which helped, because we had all these initiatives that needed energy, like the WA Institute of Sport in its first years, and we funded the WA Sports Federation so they could do a different job to what they were doing. The Institute could have fallen in a heap, the Department could have fought and said, 'We're going to take this', but none of that happened.

"We were Wally's two greatest allies. The Labor Party in those days was a very ancient organisation and anything seen as elitist, sporting or otherwise, was viewed as everyone needing to have the same; a lot of the old socialist ideas were strong. It took me a long time to get it accepted into our policy and accepted by the Labor Party itself that we needed an institute of sport, so that when we went to the election, it was actually a part of our policy.

"John Bloomfield helped considerably with that. People say hurtful things about Brian Burke, but he was the one who Keith Wilson and I convinced; give us the money, give us the credibility, give us the people like Wally and Mick. We could not have done any of it without Brian Burke. Whenever we had problems, Wally and Mick would come to me and I would go to Brian."

It was a sentiment that was shared by your grandad and Aitken.

"I know the (Burke) Government has been hugely discredited in many ways since, but I – as well as your dad – never missed an opportunity to say what a fantastic job they did for sport in WA and I still passionately believe that, to this day," Aitken said.

"Every day, going into work, we faced lots of challenges and I don't know how history will present it, but I imagine that period of time – from 84 through to the early 90s – was as innovative, invigorating and exciting a period of time as there's been in WA sporting history and it was a privilege to have been a part of that. There were so many times I was absolutely exhilarated to be working, but there were lots of scary moments where we weren't sure whether what we wanted to do was achievable, or whether it would backfire on us.

"We had a Minister for Sport at the time, Keith Wilson, and after Keith left, we had Graham Edwards, both with whom we had a good relationship. I think it's fair to say Graham never wholly trusted either of us or our motives, but he could have done, because we were absolutely committed to that government.

"Not in a political sense – Wally and I never discussed politics, although I think Wally probably had more Liberal leanings – but I loved that government for what they did for sport and I would have done anything for them and was loyal to that government. I know Wally felt exactly the same.

"My friendship with Wally was just a way of life. It was life. It was something to enjoy and look forward to. There are only a few relationships in your life that are as fundamental to your life as they are to the other person's and that was your dad and I.

"He taught me the need to tackle problems head on and, I think conversely, I probably helped temper some of your dad's natural tendencies to want to address things as soon as possible. Your dad wanted to get from A to B as quickly as possible and he taught me the ability to see where B was and the need to get there as quickly as possible, while I taught him that sometimes consensus helps to move things forward quicker.

"What your dad did to me, I'd never come across before and I've never come across since. He had this sureness of the destiny and the road in which sport had to travel down and he had the armoury through intellect and how articulate he was that allowed him to convey and drive that destiny.

"I'd come from a sheltered system, where you talked quietly and if there was a problem that couldn't be resolved, you'd shelve it. Your dad would never shelve a problem; it had to be sorted. We would sit and have endless conversations, his feet would be drumming on the floor, his hand would be running through his hair and you knew that was Wally at his agitated best, wanting to get on and fight that bloody world, 'Right here and now, Mick, come on we've got to do it'.

"He taught me to be a fighter, Glen; to fight for my ideals and my beliefs."

Your grandad was good at a lot of things, Charlotte, but chasing money was not necessarily one of them. He was among the first to admit that he struggled to manage even his personal finances. However, when it came to seeking corporate support for the institute, he had great success and understood the importance of it, given the more money brought in from the corporate sector, the more WAIS was able to support the athletes.

It took a lot of his energy to achieve those results and the support of a man named Peter Conroy – whose marketing company Peter J Conroy and Associates was far more skilled in the area than your grandad – was crucial in securing eight foundation sponsors: Coca Cola Bottlers Perth; Kentucky Fried Chicken-Hungry Jacks; Medibank Private; Parry Corporation; Prestige Toyota; The Swan Brewery; Town & Country WA; Woodside Petroleum. It was an important and impressive group and each pledged $20,000 a year for the first three years of WAIS's existence, helping the institute achieve a Year 1 budget of $518,000.

It might not sound like a lot of money for a state institute by today's standards, but it was a significant total in 1984-85 and one that helped WAIS and your grandad support 225 athletes in 22 sports, with 48 of those receiving individual scholarships.

It wasn't that your grandad was not capable of chasing the dollars, it simply wasn't his passion. His passion was around the practical aspects of building a world-class body that was capable of supporting athletes. He was a people person, not a numbers man. In saying that, it was those interpersonal skills that resulted in a high satisfaction rate from the sponsors and had most remain involved for some time with WAIS.

Steve Lawrence, one of WAIS's first employees and its executive director after your grandad, recalled your grandad as a man who "whenever he met someone, it was always a firm handshake, look them directly in the eyes", while Bruce Elliott, the inaugural chairman of WAIS, said it was a strength of your grandad's in the way he made the sponsors feel appreciated and a part of the journey, by involving them in the lives of the athletes they were helping.

His connections in the media and the freedom given to him by David Hatt and the Board to get WAIS as much traction as possible also meant the sponsors were receiving good exposure for their dollars, which was made easier by the synergies with some of the partners attracted by Conroy. Partners such as Town & Country Bank not only forged lengthy relationships with WAIS, but also a friendship with your grandad.

There was a limit to what could be achieved simply through putting pieces in place to create a space of independence for WAIS and your grandad.

If WAIS failed to create a significant identity, or failed to make itself significant, there would have been little incentive for corporate sponsorships, which would have resulted in insufficient funds and, in turn, a hasty collapse of the Institute as an independent body. It would have been pounced on for absorption by the Department for Sport and Recreation or would have lost power to the University of WA.

However, while identity and independence was an easy issue to be vocal about in the face of the government, it was a precarious issue for your grandad to balance. That was especially the case with the University of WA.

Your grandad wanted to give elite athletes in Western Australia a home with WAIS, yet WAIS itself did not have a home in 1984: its administration base, including your grandad's office, was housed within the walls of the University of WA's Department of Human Movement and Recreation Studies building. It permitted WAIS access to sports science equipment and the expertise of one of the most advanced schools of its kind in the southern hemisphere.

The relationship had been established during the planning stages of WAIS: the government needed a place to put its new creation and the highly-lauded UWA seemed as appropriate a place as any. As a result, the University had several representatives on the inaugural WAIS Board, including in the role of chairman, Dr Bruce Elliott. There was also Daryl Foster, Associate Professor Brian Blanksby and Professor John Bloomfield.

The goodwill of the University towards WAIS in those early years cannot be understated. Prof Blanksby, the head of the Physical Education School at the time, was joined by Elliott on the UWA oval in the early 1980s when the pair was asked by David Hatt how the University would feel about WAIS occupying some of its space. It was a question followed in later years by the further goodwill of Prof Bloomfield, who when questioned by Premier Brian Burke where a State Sports Centre (the Superdrome) could and should sit, had replied glibly, "The University has plenty of land".

WAIS could have been left homeless had UWA not agreed that it would be a good opportunity for both the Institute and the University to form a relationship. Your grandad was provided a small office on the first floor and the University also agreed to share its expertise in sports science and make available its expensive equipment to WAIS athletes and staffers, bucking the usually conservative approach of most institutions of the time.

That expertise was invaluable.

UWA was a national leader in the area of sports science and physical education and its graduates were being picked up for positions within government departments across Australia. It was also the first university in the southern hemisphere to house a physical education department.

Your grandad had been pushing the elite sport barrow within Western Australia for several years, but the establishment of the Australian Institute of Sport in 1981 meant other states and their governments were also beginning to awaken to the need to support the top-end athletes. Blanksby had been asked to write a paper for the Victorian Government to assist it in developing its sport system and the University department's staffers were regularly providing consultations around Australia and internationally on the topic.

The University also agreed to share administration resource, Mrs Maureen Roberts, who became WAIS's first employee following the appointment of your grandad and whose time was supposed to be an even 50-50 split between the parties – an agreement that always ended up weighted in your grandad's favour.

"But we didn't care," Prof Blanksby said. "As long as everyone could cope with the workload."

Your grandad was grateful for UWA's involvement, but it was not always an easy relationship for him to manage. As David Hatt recalled: "Living at UWA was difficult; Wally wasn't an academic and never pretended to be."

Your grandad's vision for elite sport in WA required independence and he achieved that with the government, yet there he was within the walls of the University, with a feeling that the architect of the national institute could peer over his shoulder at will, while he was answerable to a Board that at one point had slightly less than 50 per cent of its members UWA staffers.

It was uncomfortable at best. Untenable at worst.

"It was a pretty difficult position for your dad, because I was on the board, Elliott was on the board, Bloomfield was on the board, Foster was on the board," Blanksby admitted. "I would like to think I didn't make life too hard for him, but who knows."

Even Prof Bloomfield could see the challenging situation that was created for your grandad. However, he himself was in a similar position.

"I think he might have felt a bit threatened by it – I'm sure he would have – but Wally was a particular type of bloke," Bloomfield said.

"He was able to push that aside a bit and keep moving down the track he thought was particularly important. I don't think those things worried him; they might of, I don't know. I'd say we had a good relationship. He didn't agree with some of the things that I thought were important, but Wally didn't care about that – he just kept going.

"I was in the unfortunate position of being Chairman of the AIS at the time and was trying to continue moving things along. The problem was that I was seen to be the 'AIS man' and I wasn't the 'state man'. That created a few problems for me and I felt the people here were fairly unjust, because I'd done a huge amount to get it set up.

"I was just as keen in having a WAIS as I was an AIS. But these are the sort of things that happen to you and nothing in this world ever goes perfectly; you're going to get clobbered every now and then."

The larger and quicker WAIS grew, the more issues arose between it and the University. Among the first to emerge was your grandad's desire to hire Lawrence as a full-time WAIS employee. Blanksby had recommended him for the position as WAIS's sports scientist, but had intended for that position to be contracted for the University to fill and oversee.

"The problem was that I then needed to negotiate with the Department access to the resources, because we didn't have any, and that's when the debates began to evolve over quality of equipment and access," Lawrence said.

That access quickly brought the issue of independence to a head.

"I think you've picked the only time that we had a raised voice together," Blanksby said when asked about an incident regarding "the changing of the locks".

Lawrence had one day found himself unable to access his work lab, following an altercation between your grandad and Blanksby. The latter had PHD students requiring access to a lactate measuring machine, while your grandad had athletes needing to use the same machine.

"I was saying, 'They're our bloody labs and if I want to use them, then I'll use them', and he's saying, 'I've got a group of athletes out here that have got to be able to have freedom to come in on their time'," Blanksby said.

"I wondered how I was going to change it, so I said to the chief technician Rod Ronaldson, 'Go and change the locks. Just go and do it now'. It was only a matter of a couple of hours that it took and then I got another phone call from Wally and we had it out again, this time over the locks.

"What was good was – and we laughed about it afterwards – Wally went to the government and said he needed money for another lactate machine, because I'd kicked him out of the lab. Within a week, we had another lactate machine, so it was worth it in the end. I can be a stubborn bastard as well, at times."

The professional relationship between your grandad and the group of UWA staffers who worked in close proximity to him was at times strained, but it is important to remember that most productive working partnerships are – the shared passion for a cause can at times lead to friction. The input of Blanksby, Bloomfield and Elliott at the board level ensured your grandad was held to account.

Any strains in the relationship came from the fact that both bodies were playing such significant roles in WA sport and needed their own space and, while that issue needed to be addressed, the respect for the work of each other was never lost in comparatively-trivial debates over equipment access.

"A few minutes with Wally would make you think, 'Gee, this guy almost sounds interested in what I'm doing'," Blanksby said.

"And, if he wasn't, then he was a damn good actor. You came out of a meeting with Wally thinking, 'Yeah, we can do that. That can happen'. Whereas, some blokes you have a meeting with and you feel like slashing your wrists. What's the saying: Wally was the sort of person who would sell you something worth $10 for $20 and make you walk away feeling like the winner."

Chapter 10

There's Always Another Way

THE HISTORY OF THE AUSTRALIAN Institute of Sport requires a book to itself. In fact, there are several.

But it's also important to touch on a few points here, because perhaps the most confronting situation for your grandad in the arrangement with UWA was his proximity to Professor John Bloomfield – the man credited with providing the blueprint for the Canberra palace and who had played such a deep and public role in the development of sport across Australia and within WA.

A strive for independence by WAIS was always going to be challenging with Bloomfield holding such a close association with the Institute, not because of his intentions or actions, but for the fact he was the Australian Institute of Sport's foundation Deputy Chairman and later Chairman, as well as later becoming the co-chair of the Australian Sports Commission. In a way, the interests complemented each other, but as WAIS grew to a scale that challenged the AIS, they at the very least created perceptions of conflicting interests.

There were suggestions by many that your grandad and Bloomfield were polar opposites in philosophy and often clashed in pursuit of those goals. That was not necessarily the case. The situation was far more complicated than that: your grandad would have agreed with some of Bloomfield's recommendations and approaches, but there were other conflicting barriers placed in front of the pair that weren't necessarily the fault of either man.

The fact they collided was more to do with poor governance at the federal level than differences in personalities.

Australia won one silver medal and four bronze medals at the 1976 Olympic Games in Montreal. It was more than embarrassing; it was a catalyst for change.

The Federal Government had three years earlier commissioned Prof John Bloomfield to prepare a report on how to best support Australia's suffering recreation system and the result was the white paper *The Role, Scope and Development of Recreation in Australia*. The AIS was eventually established as a result of that report.

Its history states that Bloomfield's report was based on "studies of sports institutes in Europe and their success in developing elite athletes" and that "Bloomfield suggested to the Federal Government that it should establish a national institute of sport similar to those operating in European countries". That explanation is perhaps too simplistic for such a complex history.

Bloomfield's brief from the Federal Government upon commissioning for the white paper did not include elite athletes or elite sport. The professor was intelligent enough to encompass elements of high performance sport within his paper. For example, he wrote that a national system needed to be established so that "sporting representatives of our nation may have the opportunity to compete at the international level without suffering materially".

However, that rationale was based on recreation and participation goals, because he understood the importance of elite athletes as role models capable of inspiring generations into an active lifestyle. In writing in favour of athlete scholarships, Bloomfield said: "The pursuit of excellence in sport ... must be fostered in the same manner as in other fields of human endeavour, for example, music and the performing arts.

"The second reason is that Australian athletes have always been fine ambassadors abroad, whether they were winning or losing. The writer feels that young people such as Shane Gould have done this country great service in the field of international relations. The third reason is related to the image that healthy young sportsmen and sportswomen can create for our youth. They are heroes in this society and should be supported if they are constructive and desirable young citizens who can influence children and youth in positive directions."

High performance sport was never intended to be the focus of the Bloomfield report. Instead, he had been requested to identify weaknesses in the Australian recreation and fitness culture which were leading to greater societal problems, such as health issues, then examine existing systems around the world and propose recommendations on how the nation could implement its own solution.

That, in itself, was enough to put your grandad's philosophy for sport at odds with some of the report's concepts. Your grandad's belief that there was too much focus on recreation and participation and a neglect of high performance athletes within Australia and WA was central to his work with David Hatt in establishing Labor's sports policy. He believed there was so much funding being caught up in recreational red tape and being used so inefficiently by governments, clubs and associations that some needed to be redirected to elite sport.

Your grandad might not have understood at the time, but Bloomfield himself battled a similar dilemma. He pushed for several years in the late 1970s, for example, to drop the "youth" from the Department of Youth, Sport and Recreation at state level, because he believed it clouded the importance of sport with the importance of youth. To illustrate Bloomfield's reputation as being ahead of his time, that same government agency is today named the Department of Sport and Recreation.

Bloomfield at that point in time had also had considerably more experience than your grandad with governments. He knew that sometimes a bit of give needed to be relented to receive some take. Therefore, some of your grandad's objections might have been aligned to Bloomfield's own beliefs, but the latter had chosen to pick his battles.

"You see, sport was seen to be a very amateur thing," Bloomfield said.

"It was fine that if someone like your dad had some money and they could invest it in a better coach and that would help. But in many respects, sport was 'the gentleman's pastime'. The average young Aussie, even after the Second World War, didn't get much of an opportunity (to play sport at a high-performance level). If you went to a fancy private school in Sydney, there was a pretty good chance that if you had any talent at all you'd end up in the Australian Rugby Union team, but that was it.

"As time went on, I was changing my attitude to what it (the system) should be. Bob Ellicott said to me, 'John, we can't be supporting all these causes, we don't have the money, so we'll pick out a few sports'. Somehow, you have to work it so that you're giving a fair bit of rope to the Minister, but you're also getting to do some of the things you want to do."

The blending of elite sport with recreation would have been manageable between Bloomfield's system and your grandad's involvement as the two men would not necessarily have needed to come in contact with each other. It was what the Federal Government did next that created conflict.

Bloomfield wrote that a national recreation system needed to be established which "should focus its attention on encouraging every Australian to make an informed decision about the level of fitness he requires in order to achieve maximum enjoyment and satisfaction from life". At the top of that national hierarchy, Bloomfield proposed the Federal Government establish a National Institute of Sport and Recreation.

That was the area of Bloomfield's report that the AIS latched onto as the blueprint for its construction, but that proposed National Institute of Sport and Recreation was recommended almost solely based on the requirement for administration around the proposed recreation model. It was also intended to be an education and training base, but Bloomfield himself noted: "Such a centre would not offer long-term courses for 'all comers', but rather would organise short-term coaching courses of a more technical nature for leading coaches from each State".

The National Institute was supposed to be a hub for sports science research and, as a training base, the recommendations only referred to teams converging for their final sessions before international meets such as Olympic Games. Even that, though, was based around the fact that his proposal specified that those teams be funded by the Federal Government.

And there was another crucial element that Bloomfield believed was important in ensuring the success of the system and that was Recommendation No.10: "It is recommended that the Australian Government encourage the State Governments to form Departments of Recreation if they have not already done so."

So, firstly, Bloomfield's system was focusing on the reparation of an ineffective recreation and participation network. Secondly, it required state hubs to operate efficiently.

Those recommendations were supported by the 1974-75 follow-up Coles Report, produced by University of Queensland academic Dr Allan Coles, which was designed to establish the feasibility and rationale of a national institute, having examined European models. That report's recommendations clearly stated: "That a National Institute of Sport be established in Canberra with branches located in the states".

Within Bloomfield's recreation model, everything was fine: Western Australia already had a government department looking after recreation and participation and had done so since the state established the Community Recreation Council in 1972, as a result of recommendations by Bloomfield. In fact, it effectively had two: the Department for Youth, Sport and Recreation and the WA Sports Federation.

It did not have a Western Australian Institute of Sport, designed to look after and manage high performance athletes. And not a single state in Australia had such an institute at that time. So, when the Federal Government decided to pick up Prof Bloomfield's report after almost 10 years of doing nothing with it and dump his recommendations onto the country's high performance sports system, presumably believing the model was transferrable, it set the system up for collapse and failure. And it put your grandad on a collision course with that failing system.

There were big problems with that decision: participation and recreation can be managed by government, but high performance sport cannot; the states had supporting departments of recreation, but they did not have supporting hubs of high performance; the model called on the empowerment of clubs and associations to boost participation levels in their sports, but high performance sport and your grandad looked at the inefficiency and self-gratification of clubs and associations as the biggest contributing factor to the failings of our athletes at the international level.

A focus on grassroots and participation is crucial to the sustainability of success in elite support, because that will be from where the next generation of athletes emerge, but that was not the focus of Bloomfield's report. He was commissioned and delivered the report before the Montreal debacle ever happened and it was seven-years-old by the time Minister for Home Affairs and Environment Bob Ellicott decided to do anything with it. Even the Coles Report had aged five years.

Details have a habit of getting murky when that amount of time lapses and for a multitude of reasons Bloomfield's recommendations for participation and recreation had been combined with Coles' to encapsulate high performance sport. Yet, in contradiction to both recommendations, it was combined in a centralised model.

That model was not Bloomfield's original plan, yet it claimed his report as its foundations and the professor's ownership of it was emphasised further by his roles on the AIS Board. It morphed into a model that was in direct contrast to your grandad's vision – and, ironically, the vision outlined in Bloomfield's reports as well – of what would be in Australian sport's best interests. The intended vision had the AIS positioned as a service provider and a support base for a state institute network, but what eventuated was a body that perceived itself as being at the top of the food chain.

Bloomfield wrote in his 2003 book *Australia's Sporting Success – The Inside Story*: "In late September 1974 the Federal Minister for Tourism and Recreation had appointed a committee to report on the feasibility of establishing a national Institute of Sport, which had been previously recommended in the 1973 Bloomfield Report … Many of the recommendations related to support services for elite sport, and this was in contrast to the high performance-oriented Australian Institute of Sport model which was eventually set in place by the Fraser Government in 1981.

"Unfortunately, the Coles Report was not tabled in Parliament before the Whitlam Government's dismissal; thus, its recommendations could not be implemented and it was pigeonholed by the incoming Fraser Government."

The alterations made by the Federal Government to the vision for Australian sport suddenly had Prof Bloomfield in a position that would require his constant interaction with your grandad and set up the AIS as an opponent to state institutes in certain situations.

"To be quite blunt about it, it was about (Wally) being treated in one quarter like a bit of a servant boy and having somebody breathing down his neck," Prof Brian Blanksby said. "I think he just felt he was being swamped by a point of view that he did not see – and he was proven correct – was going to work and the only solution was to expand."

The Federal Government undoubtedly took the actions it did believing they were the best it could manage with the resources it had, but it had two models developed for recreation and a national institute supported by state hubs, then effectively discarded the key recommendations, centralised the system and implemented it for sport across the board.

Bloomfield and Cole's recommendations for state hubs were crucial given Australia's land mass, as one body was totally insufficient, especially when based in Canberra, but when the government implemented the model for high performance sport, it failed to establish that network. States were left to develop their own plans for the support of elite athletes, but when they did, the AIS conveyed a sense of superiority and made the states feel like subservient satellites designed to feed big brother.

All roads, in its plan, were supposed to lead to Canberra, despite Canberra having initially left the states to fend for themselves. Bloomfield himself wrote in his *Australia's Sporting Success* book on the centralised action by the government that concerns had been raised early by states and that decentralisation "had also been discussed, but it was not possible to act on it until the budget built up as the institute grew".

He continued: "In fact the writer had discussed a decentralisation policy in early 1980 with the Minister and his staff and Bob Ellicott presented a possible future plan to the Recreation Minister's Council in Darwin in mid-1980. This proved to be a popular recommendation, but unfortunately, because of other pressing items and some personnel changes, it did not eventuate until 1983. By then, South Australia had already established its own state institute, while Western Australia was planning one."

Bloomfield regretted the Federal Government's centralised approach, but when interviewed for this book admitted that, given the state of high performance sport in the country, receiving something by way of investment from the government was better than nothing.

"I thought it was better to have that (a national institute) than nothing and then, from there, if it worked, then you can move out to the states," he said.

"It didn't really worry me, because I thought we could get going in Canberra and move on from there. You can't do much in a situation like that; you've just got to wait your turn and for the right pollies to pop up and be interested. The institutes really aren't that different (from the proposed system), it's just a matter of which way you work it."

However, regardless of the way Australia's system ended up, the Federal Government's initial approach impacted the states and, in turn, your grandad's relationship with some of those around him.

"Wally's relationship with UWA and John Bloomfield was difficult at times: I used to describe them as oil and water," David Hatt said.

"They were never going to mix, they were different people and probably different philosophies. Wally saw that they should be, not on top, but on tap, which is how he used to put it. We used their undoubted expertise, but we were in charge of WAIS."

Tensions between WAIS and the AIS further flared around athlete-relocation programs, which was never in the initial proposal of Professor John Bloomfield either, other than the recommendation that the national centre operate as a convergence base for teams prior to a major international meet.

Both the Bloomfield and Coles reports were based on examinations of the European system, with the latter having sent a task force to the continent. There was a focus on one of Europe's leading sports bodies, the French National Institute of Sport, which had been operating since 1936 and undergone a renovation to house 580 full-time scholarship holders two years before Australia opened the doors to the AIS.

It was another square-peg-round-hole problem: Australia is 12 times the size of France and the model was simply not going to work due to geographical challenges. An athlete could relocate to a central institute within Europe and still be driving distance from their home and support network, but that was not always possible in Australia.

Even Coles, the author of the report, had foreseen that issue. That was why the original model proposed had considered approaches such as West Germany's 50 institutes and included the establishment of elite training hubs around the country. However, the damage was done.

What Prof Bloomfield proposed and what was put in place as a result was of undoubted significance. He and his staff at UWA were also ahead of their time in what they contributed to elite sport through sports science developments and understandings and their implementations into training and competition practices. But his work was initially supposed to address an issue of a different nature.

And even when that work drifted from recreation into high performance, some of his key recommendations – and those of Dr Allan Coles – were discarded.

"John would say that they didn't have different philosophies," inaugural WAIS Chairman and UWA staffer Bruce Elliott said.

"In all honesty, I think the real problem – and I use that word guardedly – was that John, at that stage, was the Deputy Chairman of the AIS and effectively running it, because the chairman at the time was basically a high-flyer who wasn't going to be able to do the day-to-day operations. I had this almost-argument with John a number of times, but I don't think he ever actually impeded WAIS or anything WAIS tried to do, but he always appeared that he had a bias towards the AIS.

"I think that's all it was: it was the hat that he was wearing then. I mean, it was his paper that actually established the place, so he can't say he didn't play a role in its establishment, but he didn't play much of a role in its growth beyond that actual paper. He said to me that he's always been in favour of state institutes.

"It was more about what he didn't do, than what he did do and I can't recall that many arguments or conflicts between Wally and John."

The AIS opened in 1981, right around the time your grandad began writing letters to the State Government, petitioning it to take action to fix a neglected high performance system. And years after he and David Hatt had already formed their recommendation for the establishment of the Western Australian Institute of Sport.

The need for WAIS's independence had been flagged in the planning stages, but it had become an issue of urgency within just two years.

An overarching mantra was attached to WAIS in its infancy: "WAIS will never be a bricks and mortar structure". The idea was that it would be housed within the school of Physical Education at UWA, which would also feed services into it, or it could later link in similar relationships to other service providers. That was one way to interpret the mantra. In a way, it was a very clear statement. However, in another way, it was rather ambiguous and I am not convinced that either was accidental.

WAIS has been housed within its own dedicated bricks and

mortar structure since the mid-90s when it moved into a building constructed to the side of Challenge Stadium and today has a new, multi-million dollar state-of-the-art facility on the eastern side, overlooking McGillivray Oval. However, the twisting of semantics means that it could still be argued that WAIS remains a support service to athletes and is not a bricks and mortar structure.

It is impossible to know what the intended definition of that statement was, given we can never ask your grandad. Either way, those semantics were important in juggling the relationship with the University, because, despite how challenging it could be for your grandad at times, UWA had provided so much to WAIS and held significant sway in its direction. So much sway that it was ironically responsible for losing any control it might have had.

Beyond everything that WAIS owes UWA, the state itself is equally indebted to the University for the role it played in establishing not only support for elite athletes, but also Western Australia's newest – at the time – international multi-purpose sports facility. Your grandad and David Hatt had spent countless hours developing the sports policy that the Burke Government took into the election in the early 1980s and which resulted in the establishment of WAIS, but it also identified the need for high quality facilities.

The centralised approach towards elite sport of the federal government through the Australian Institute of Sport left the states requiring a solution to overcome the issues that had been created. The WA Sports Council was formed as a significant group that carried great weight in any recommendations it made.

Your grandad's close friend Mick Aitken had begun his working life as a sports teacher, studying at the highly-regarded Loughborough University, and later joined the Sports Council in Manchester, finding his niche in a facilities planning and investment role. However, even Aitken felt challenged when one of the first tasks handed to him upon his arrival in Perth as Executive Director of the WA Sports Federation in June 1984 was to develop a brief on the top-end sports infrastructure WA required to return to some level of significance.

Saying, "some level of significance", is not being harsh either: nothing had happened in Western Australia to that point since the 1962 British Empire and Commonwealth Games, at which your 12-year-old grandad sold ice creams. Harsh would be to point out that nothing significant has happened since then, either. By the time this story has been published, the state's new stadium still won't have been completed, despite it being almost two decades since the discussion of its requirement first began.

And until that stadium is constructed, Western Australia will not be in a position to host an event close to the size of a Commonwealth Games. That highlights why your grandad was so passionate about fixing a broken system: our sporting infrastructure is in such a state that it will be almost 60 years before it is in a position to bid for an event it held in 1962.

That was also the damning assessment Aitken made to the media upon his arrival, which led to Prof John Bloomfield meeting with him as chairman of the WA Sports Council and requesting he produce a report into what WA needed in terms of elite sports infrastructure.

Bloomfield was an intelligent man and when he told Aitken, "I'll get Daryl Foster to give you a bit of a hand", it was a strategic move of insurance for the project as much as it was support for Aitken. Foster had no experience in facilities development, but he was a well-liked, respected and relatively quiet man with few opponents and his presence alongside Aitken meant whatever the latter developed would not be dismissed without review.

What was developed was an argument that WA required a large, multi-purpose sports centre with wet and dry facilities. It needed to be, as Aitken stated, an indoor arena with a swimming facility complementing it and one that could house a reasonable indoor competition in a variety of sports. And it would put Perth on the map as having the largest multipurpose sports centre in the southern hemisphere.

The WA Sports Council held significant weight in its recommendations and, within days of submitting his report to Prof Bloomfield and before he had even had any official reply,

Aitken picked up a copy of *The Sunday Times* and read a bold headline of: "$20M Sports Super Centre for WA". That $20-million "super centre" was the State Sports Centre, which became the Superdrome, which evolved into Challenge Stadium and fulfilled its objective in returning Perth to some level of significance in its capabilities to host elite sport competitions.

"Honestly, Glen, it was the most incredible thing," Aitken said.

"John Bloomfield had taken this idea to Keith Wilson and Brian Burke and they said, 'Yep, we'll build it'. If I said I'd been there six weeks, I'd be exaggerating and it was more like a month and there I was, the bloke who'd provided the brief for what would become the Superdrome and Challenge Stadium; the biggest indoor multipurpose sports centre in the southern hemisphere.

"Euphoric and validated, probably best describes how I was feeling and it was the clearest sign that the Sports Federation was going to be taken seriously. I'm under no illusion that it was absolutely the power, authority and influence of John Bloomfield that made it happen, though."

The speed of that announcement was no accident, either.

It was yet another example of the influence of the WA Sports Council. As iconic coach, doctor and former Federal Minister Ric Charlesworth recalled: "Burkey (Premier Brian Burke) was so much in control that they just did what they wanted; the other mob were in disarray".

The WA sports fraternity was also supported by a well-balanced Sports Minister in Rev Keith Wheeler, who was spoken of highly by everyone who had been involved with him. Prof Bloomfield recalled him as "a man of great integrity", who was "one of the two best state Ministers of Sport Australia has produced", due to his philosophy that it was the government's job to be a catalyst, not a manager of sport.

The plans for the Superdrome had been picked up by your grandad and the WAIS Board, given the view that the facility could house the ever-expanding institute, and taken to the Minister and Premier.

"I remember going to the meeting with then-Premier Burke to get the Superdrome, Challenge Stadium," WAIS's inaugural Chairman Bruce Elliott said.

"That's when, all of a sudden, WAIS was formulated as a proper institute. It came about very rapidly and it's hard to know whether that's a plus or a minus, in some ways. Brian Burke approached that the way he approached many things: there was a proposal brought to him by the WAIS Board and Wally – it was Tom Hoad, David Hatt and Daryl Foster, your dad and I at the meeting – and, effectively, we had the money for the Superdrome at that first meeting.

"He said: 'Yes, this sounds like a good idea, it's something the state needs'. That approach might have caused him a bit of grief later, but in that case it was a good thing for WAIS. I think, more than anything, Brian thought it was the right thing for Western Australian sport and ... if we wanted to be competitive across this country, then we needed to establish that.

"It was then that WAIS, as a bricks and mortar organisation, was established."

It was a proactive approach that also sat well with Hoad.

"We got a decision in five minutes from Burkey," he said.

"These days, you've got to go from EventsCorp with a recommendation, to the Department with a recommendation, back to the Government with a recommendation and every Tom, Dick and Harry has a say about it and, in most cases, don't end up doing anything.

"There were mistakes made by some of those people and I'm not debating that in the slightest, but from a sporting perspective, shit, things got done and it was never a big deal. They were nice times to be involved in."

The concept and approval was just half of the challenge, with the other half being where to put the facility. Again, Prof Bloomfield and the University of Western Australia were defining in a moment of history for WA sport and the former was recognised in that role with the naming honour of the John Bloomfield Lecture Theatre within the stadium.

The land that Challenge Stadium and WAIS have always resided on, regardless of where on that land the buildings sat, were the property of the University. Prof Bloomfield arranged for it to be given to the government to allow for the building of an elite training and competition centre that would be capable of hosting national and international events.

"They were huge drivers for what was created," Steve Lawrence said of the University's contribution to WAIS and WA sport.

And Bloomfield and the University also became allies of your grandad, WAIS and the government's objective of ensuring the Department for Sport and Recreation understood where it sat in the hierarchy of sport in the state.

"John Bloomfield was making a point to John Graham, the head of Sport and Rec at the time, that they were not key players in this at all: they had no part in it, they didn't know about it until it was announced," Aitken said of one particular meeting of the WA Sports Council.

"We met to discuss the brief around the facility (the Superdrome), with it already having been a fait accompli, and when we all met, John Graham brought in a sheet of paper and said, 'Before we get started, I'd just like to hand this around'. It basically said that they knew the government had devoted $20-million to build the high performance centre, but they were of the mind that perhaps it might be better use of the money if we were to build 20 facilities for a million each and spread them around the state, so that there was a multiplicity of sports centres for local use.

"John Bloomfield just looked at him and said, 'John, we're not here to discuss whether or not we're doing one or 20; the decision has been made and we are building the State Sports Centre. End of discussion'. It was all done terribly politely – there was no fist shaking, or banging on the table – but the power had shifted irrevocably."

This chapter opened by stating that UWA's power was so significant it ironically led to it losing all hope of control over WAIS. That was because it perhaps underestimated the significance of the proximity to WAIS in relation to its ability to affect the Institute's direction. When it handed over the land to a plan that included the relocation of WAIS, it lost its impact on that direction.

"The one thing I really wish hadn't happened was that they left and went out to Challenge," Prof Brian Blanksby said.

However, it had been a deal-sealer for your grandad in accepting the WAIS job. He had been assured that WAIS would break from UWA as soon as possible.

"That was really important (the move to Challenge Stadium)," David Hatt said.

"One of the things we had in the back of our mind when planning the stadium was that it would provide a home for WAIS. We never advertised that, but it was in my mind and it was in Wally's mind, because we always knew that we couldn't stay at UWA because of differences in ideas, personalities and whatever.

"We wanted to be independent and more than anything else, we wanted our own individual identity. We got that with the move and we grew. I am still grateful – always was and still am today – to UWA for taking us in and John Bloomfield, because whether people liked him or they didn't, a lot of his ideas underpinned the establishment of WAIS."

And it was a view that was unanimously accepted with the benefit of hindsight.

"Good facilities don't develop good programs; good facilities only help the good people develop better programs," Prof Blanksby said.

"The key thing is to get the right person and WAIS had the right person. He was really strong, motivated and passionate. If he'd been hamstrung within the university sector, with all those people around him who thought they knew more about sport than anyone did – even though he knew more than all of us – then it's sad to say, but the move had to happen."

The statement that WAIS would never be a bricks and mortar structure is as true today, with it sitting in its multi-million-dollar standalone building, as it was when it was housed by the University of WA.

It simply depends on how you read and interpret the words.

Chapter 11

'Good Facilities Only Help the Good People'

INDEPENDENCE NEVER COMES EASY AND often must be fought for. The Western Australian Institute of Sport was no exception to that. Those fights had to happen and your grandad had to learn from them, because the first decade of WAIS brought some of the biggest battles of his life.

The initial years of living with UWA might not have always been pleasant for your grandad, but they were important for WAIS, because, as inaugural WAIS Chairman Bruce Elliott said: "I think if we were in a building, we might have come under a bit of criticism, because we wouldn't have known what to put in it".

WAIS had ironed out its basic kinks. Your grandad had been directed by the Board to sort out the sports, the programs, the athletes within those sports and programs and how professional coaches would sit within that system. The debates had been had over whether to assist financially strong sports, or just focus on those included in Commonwealth and Olympic Games schedules and the funding sources had been secured on multi-year contracts.

There were still plenty of mistakes made, including from a facilities perspective the expensive installation of an insufficient gymnastics floor at the Superdrome that was causing injuries and had to be removed and replaced. But, overall, the worst of the teething pains had been endured. And relationships had been maintained; WAIS and the University of WA preserved their partnership within memorandums of understanding, which still exist today.

WAIS had grown in staffing numbers, with the appointment of Administrative Secretary Barbara Wilmot and national hockey representative Craig Davies, who was in the role of Sports Program Co-Ordinator. The pair joined your grandad and Sports Science Co-Ordinator Steve Lawrence.

Wilmot was a friend of your grandad's. She had known him since their teenage years through his first major girlfriend, Lee Hunt. The roving life of a Lt Colonel's wife had taken her from New Guinea and the Middle East, to London and the eastern states and she returned unemployed before your grandad, in need of a new secretary, fortuitously bumped into her one day in 1986.

Wilmot recalled of WAIS an environment that was as exciting as it was demanding, from the Institute's struggles to approve finance for an athlete's running shoes, to its offering of fully-financed scholarships. She also fondly recounted a trait that your grandad held with him for life: his love for the written word. Wilmot still carried with her the handwritten note your grandad wrote for her when she resigned from WAIS and presented it at the interview for this book.

She was not alone: Mick Aitken had a similar note from your grandad.

"He was always a writer, your dad," Aitken said. "He believed that the written word is indelible and as such it carries weight for all time."

No matter how busy and big WAIS got, how much red tape built up, what was being argued about or how much money was required, it was always the people – the athletes, coaches and those around them – who were your grandad's focus.

Swimming was one of the only sports I was ever even partially good at. I was carrying a few too many kilos at the time, so maybe it helped me float better than others.

My high school swim team held its after-school training at Challenge Stadium in an arrangement undoubtedly organised by your grandad, given the school I went to was 30min drive north and there were plenty of pools closer. But whenever we finished training, I headed up to WAIS for a lift home. Your grandad was invariably always deep in conversation with an athlete or coach who had wandered in.

I say, "wandered in", because of one important fact: his door was always open. I don't mean that metaphorically. Barbara Wilmot recalled the same welcoming presence from a director who ended up taking on more work than he probably needed to as a result – "All the athletes would come in and want to see him, they wouldn't necessarily go to Steve or Craig first, so he would take things on" – but it never bothered him.

Your grandad showed that care for everyone involved with WAIS, especially the athletes and staff. And he showed it for his family as well. He held himself to the same expectations when dealing with everyone and he expected those expectations to be returned.

"Glen, you can't be coming up here with a towel wrapped around you and no shoes on," he said to me after the first training session finished. "How do you think it looks: the athletes and coaches aren't allowed to do it. My son can't be allowed to, either."

Still, I got free access to the fridge full of Coca-Cola.

Craig Davies was a high school teacher and national hockey representative with one of his eventual-three Olympic Games under his belt by the time your grandad called and asked if he would join WAIS in 1986.

Davies had two years earlier applied for the WAIS Director position, but had not heard anything back. His resume had been kept on file and when your grandad was in search of a program co-ordinator, Davies finally heard from the Institute. Your grandad's offer to Davies was the first of what would become a regular display of understanding for the life of high performance athletes.

He adjusted the staff contract and offered the hockey player six weeks of paid annual leave with flexible in-work hours for two reasons: to allow Davies to continue representing his country; and to help him support his young family, which had just expanded. The national hockey team travelled up to 16 weeks a year and, as a teacher, Davies was only receiving two weeks' paid leave.

As Davies' wife Jenny recalled: "We were living off our savings from one pay cheque to the next. The opportunity to have six weeks leave with pay; it allowed me to be a mum".

Your grandad's gesture not only helped the Davies family, but also helped Australian hockey hold onto a man whose international career went on to span 15 years and 193 games and included the national captaincy from 1987 to 1990. The decision to join your grandad at WAIS was an easy one to make and Davies remained with the Institute until his resignation following the Sydney Olympics.

Almost everyone I have come across speaks highly of your grandad, with the usual explanation given as to why, "it was because of who he was". It was important to try and capture that – "who he was" – within these pages so that you could understand that side of him, but the great difficulty was how to quantify it in stories; how to show "who he was".

That was because your grandad did not show his kindness through grand displays; he did so simply through his daily life. He prioritised people over policy and he always supported people at times of their greatest need.

A photo was taken at the 2006 WAIS Annual Dinner of your grandad with Craig Davies on stage. Both men were clearly emotional.

It was taken during Davies' induction into the Hall of Champions and the pair was emotional because of the journey they had been through together. Neither of them knew on the night, but it was also the last time they would see each other. Your grandad passed away less than a week later, but for much of their lives, it was Davies who was closer to bidding farewell to the world.

Peak physical fitness and a solid work-rate was the hallmark of Davies' career, so when he began losing fitness for no apparent reason in 1995, there was an immediate concern. Initial scans showed no abnormalities, but the doctor was concerned enough with the symptoms that he recommended Davies to a specialist.

Further tests revealed cardiomyopathy; a condition where heart cells are damaged and killed off, causing other cells to become larger in a bid to compensate and resulting in an oversized heart that is not as effective. It was a serious and life-threatening condition that required immediate action. I can still remember your grandad telling me, with tears in his eyes, that "Craig has a problem with his heart". It was an April diagnosis that required constant hospital stays through to December and an implanted defibrillator.

A worsening of his condition had Davies placed on the transplant list at the end of 1995, before his heart rhythm stabilised in early 1996, allowing him to return to work and winding down one of the most terrifying periods for the family. And it resulted in changes at WAIS.

"I remember calling Wally on a Friday night; I had to go into hospital the next day and I didn't know what the outcome would be," Davies said. "Wally was extremely supportive and it resulted in him going to have a check as well, but he also put in place medical insurance and income protection for everyone and that was instigated by my condition and organised by Sam Gannon. There was never any talk of when I was coming back to work and that meant a great deal to me."

It was the Davies family that was going through the worst, but your grandad's actions were those of a person who actually cared. He did not go through a box-checking exercise, make some anonymous phoneline available, put in place a couple of self-help sessions or roll out the latest training course from the Human Resources manual; he actually cared. And it meant a lot to the Davies family.

"The children were only seven and nine and I was working," Jenny Davies said.

"I wanted to maintain that work for my sanity as well; it allowed me to go into a world at times where all this wasn't on my mind. I just knew that we never needed to worry about the impact of it all on Craig's career, because Wally was so supportive and I owe him a huge amount for that.

"He'd often ring up, but I'd be at the hospital and my parents would be here looking after the children, and so he formed a relationship with them as well. It was that personal relationship and not just support from afar. He was wonderful and I don't think we could have asked for anything more."

Your grandad's priority above all else in life was people. He cared for them, beyond what was expected in whatever role he held. That was the case for staff, it was the case for athletes and it was the case for family and those values would have crumbled if he had not truly believed in them, because the pressures in his life were immense.

Particularly in the early days of the Institute.

In addition to managing the new and demanding beast that was WAIS, your grandad was also a husband to your nana and a new father to me. Those parenting demands doubled in 1992 when your Uncle Mark was born.

As my daughter, you can probably imagine that I was not the easiest baby to manage around directing a fledgling institute. I had a range of issues, from clinical to behavioural, and all had me testing your grandad like no UWA, AIS or government conflict ever could.

"I remember your old man telling me you had such bad reflux that he used to have to get you out of the house and drive you down to the beach," said Brian Rogers, a former colleague of your grandad's from Channel 9. "He said you were bawling so much, he'd just lock the car and go for a walk. I'm sure he loved you dearly, but, you know as a dad, sometimes you've just got to walk away."

The support that your grandad showed the Davies family and his emotional investment in that situation also unwittingly gave him the experience to deal with my diagnosis of a blood condition in the same year.

Your nana, grandad and I used to have a game we would play in the morning while I was getting ready for school: count the bruises on my body. It started as a bit of a laugh, with each leg easily surpassing 20 bumps on a daily basis. I was too young to be concerned, but your nana and grandad weren't and those concerns heightened when I had no answer to their questions of how the bruises got there.

They had initially thought they were the typical bumps of an 11 to 12-year-old, but the sheer number made my legs appear more blue than skin-colour and I was booked into the GP for a check-up, whose concerns echoed those of your nana and grandad, referring me to a specialist. I was not told of the worst-case scenario, but it would have sent tremors through your nana and grandad: leukaemia.

The situation was made more challenging for your grandad by the fact your nana was preparing to travel overseas for work and departed the day of my first test. So, your grandad was left juggling a full-time job, looking after your two-year-old uncle Mark and the weight of having to take his oldest son for a leukaemia test. It must have been hell for him, but he never showed it.

The test involved a bone-marrow extraction, which was the most excruciating moment of my life, and required a doctor literally punching a thick syringe into a bone in my pelvis. I still remember your grandad holding my hand tightly and stroking my hair as I laid on the hospital gurney, unaware of the pain the doctor was about to inflict – out of necessity, of course.

I was ultimately one of the lucky ones. The results were negative for leukaemia and my ordeal largely ended there. I was diagnosed with immune thrombocytopenic purpura (ITP), which meant my antibodies were attacking my platelets – my good guys were attacking my good guys – and it was resulting in my blood not clotting as expected.

It meant I could not play contact sports and I had to look like a goof when surfing with my mates as I had to wear a helmet in even the smallest of conditions, I had to undergo courses of steroid treatments or short-term hospital stays which caused me to gain a lot of weight, my glands to swell and immense muscular and headache pain, and it hung around for about 10 years longer than it does in most cases. But it was not the life or death diagnosis that the other kids in Ward 3B at Princess Margaret Hospital had to deal with.

"That was a huge shock for Wally. A huge shock," Craig Davies said of the concern around my test, followed by the diagnosis.

"In some ways, we were able to compare notes in having to see doctors and specialists. I can vividly recall when your count would start going up (the steroids would assist by causing my platelet count to increase), how thrilled and relieved he was. It stretched him. And then you add all the WAIS stuff in on top of that."

If the pressures of your grandad's personal life were compounded by the demands to build WAIS's profile, he never showed it. On the contrary, he looked at that requirement as a way to capitalise on his connections within the media and continue a role in it. Your nana remembered him being "in his element".

Your grandad was excited by the challenge that WAIS offered and loved it, but he also left a role that he had longed for as a broadcaster and commentator in the media. The requirement to build WAIS's profile allowed him to do both and he joined the Network Ten commentary team at the 1984 Olympic Games in Los Angeles, where he had sat in the press tribune alongside Drew Morphett, the man whose position he had filled at the ABC in the mid-1970s, to call Australia's first gold medal of the Games.

"I was working for ABC and Wal was working for Channel TEN; there were two Australian broadcasters – one radio network and one TV network – and we were the two," Morphett said.

"He did all sorts of sports, bouncing from one to another, but the one I was doing was cycling. I was broadcasting on my own and he was working with Dick Ploog and we called Australia's first gold medal at the games, which was the cycling team pursuit. The competition had been absolutely dominated by the

United States and, subsequently, it was proved that they cheated, but they'd won the individual pursuit, the road race – men and women – but they'd blood doped.

"They had never won a cycling gold medal for about 100 years before that, then won everything except the team pursuit, which we won. That's nearly one of the broadcasting highlights of my life and I reckon if you asked Wally, he'd probably say the same. It's one thing to call a footy game of Carlton and Collingwood, or the Eagles and Dockers, whatever, but when you're overseas and it's your country verse another, you win a gold and you hear Advance Australia Fair, the hairs on the back of my neck still stand up when I think about it to this day.

"We were high-fiving each other, Wally and me, like we won the medal."

There was a running joke that your grandad had a sports coat from every media outlet in Australia except SBS and the humour is in the truth of it. Over his career, he worked for every major media outlet WA had available at the time. He added radio station 882 6PR to his resume following the LA Games, hosting a three-hour sports talk-back program designed to go head-to-head with that of the ABC, which was manned by his former colleagues and friends Dennis Cometti and George Grljusich.

It was a program that was put together swiftly and your grandad called upon the help of Peter Sweeney, one of the more colourful characters in your grandad's life – as anyone who has come across "Sweens" will attest – and who had worked as a journalist with the *Sunday Independent* before becoming the media liaison officer with the Western Australian Trotting Association.

"One day, the phone rang; Wal said he had been asked to present a Saturday morning sports show for 6PR," Sweeney said.

"I asked what that had to do with me and he said, 'I want you to be the producer'. I said I'd think about it, but he said, 'No time, we start Saturday. The ABC are starting a sports show next month and we have to be first'. And for the next 18 months, Wal, myself and Ric Rodgers – Mr Golden Tonsils, who manned the board – produced and presented Saturday Morning Sportstalk.

"We like to think we put up a quality three-hour show every week and the ratings suggested the listeners thought we did. Wal wasn't into the neddies (horse racing), but our first interview was with trotting trainer-reinsman Barry Perkins, who a night earlier sat behind Preux Chevalier when they won the Miracle Mile in Sydney.

"Horses, especially races, gave me the funniest memories of my professional times with Wal. You see, in those days, Radio 6PR was not only the talkback station in Perth, but the TAB station. It was written into the deal that every race covered by TAB in WA had to be played on air. So that meant the Dapto dogs, the Grafton gallops and the trots from Terang.

"Wal hated that. Sometimes it was five minutes before Golden Tonsils Ric got back to Wal. Wal was meticulous with his research into his subjects and his introductions were always written out in longhand.

"One day, he was introducing a sportsman and the intro was seemingly going to go longer than the interview. Ric warned him, '10 seconds, nine, eight', which was the warning that we had to cross to the course. Wal took no notice until Ric cut him off in the manner many of us got cut days after birth. Wal ripped the headset from his ears, flung it into a wall, which then got Wal's size-whatever shoes.

"It was hilarious and I hit the floor doubled over in laughter."

Your grandad was succeeding in building the profile of both himself and WAIS in the media and that proved a double-edge sword, that media focus flipped in late 1984 and early 1985 requiring him to justify the dual roles and refute any conflicts of interest to both *The Daily News* and *The Western Mail*.

"The two jobs are compatible," he said. "It is necessary for the Institute to maintain a high profile and my appearances are one way to achieve this."

It was a synergy that drew no ire internally, though, as your grandad had made his media strategy very clear to the WAIS Board, before advising that his $32,000 a year salary was far less than what he was earning in the media positions he had left to join the Institute.

"It was a two-way street: WAIS grew his profile and he, in turn, grew the profile of WAIS," said inaugural WAIS Chairman Bruce Elliott.

Even in the 1980s, there was only 24 hours in a day.

Your grandad was juggling being a husband, a father, working Monday to Friday with the Institute and, throughout his career, working weekends on talkback or football broadcasting – or, often, both. Your nana plays it down, of course, but she was an unbelievable support throughout your grandad's career and he would not have been able to achieve any of it without her.

In addition to your grandad's work, your nana was always working at least part-time herself and the pair was equally as defining in each other's career. Your nana was making a return to running after giving birth to me and was in inspiring form, having switched to the 800m – a distance she now knows, due to the advancement of sports science, that she should have run all along – and she was closing in on Seoul and her first Olympic selection.

However, as she entered the home straight I in the selection trials, she felt a "crunch" in her ankle and with 50m to go, she felt another. Your nana had partially ruptured her Achilles tendon, but to highlight how tough, how gutsy and how good your nana was, the time of 2:01.30 in which she crossed the finish line was still quick enough to qualify for the Games. The injury was too significant, though, and your nana retired after surgeries were unable to correct the problem in time for the Olympics.

Your grandad's solution was simple: coach. Your nana was exhausted after the rollercoaster ride of her career, which included three national titles and qualifying for the final of the 1980 World Championships, in which she finished seventh, meaning only six women in the world at the time were better than her.

Your nana's personal best of 56.85 in the 400m hurdles still has her ranked just outside the top 10 of Australia's all time results and it is poetic that one of the women who sit above her, fourth-placed Lauren Poetschka, was among the first athletes your nana coached. Not bad for a woman who likened her running talent to that of a "bag of spuds".

It was a taxing life and your nana also had the requirement of looking after me; all she wanted to do was relax for a while, but your grandad would have none of it.

"You can't take time off, otherwise no one will know who you are when you come back," he had told her. Your forever-modest nana quipped back that no one knew who she was at the peak of her career, but within a week of retiring from running, your nana was coaching.

She received a $10,000 scholarship from WAIS to pursue the trade which morphed into a fulltime position when the Institute expanded its track and field program under Tudor Bidder. Along with Poetschka, among the first of your nana's charges was Commonwealth Games silver medallist and Olympic distance runner Sarah Jamieson.

Your nana was a hell of a runner and remains one of Australia's most experienced, most respected, best credentialed and most consistently successful athletics coaches. Make sure you remind her of how good she is. They were an unbelievable team, your nana and your grandad, and they loved and respected each other as much as two people can.

"Those early days of WAIS, Lyn would come in with the kids," WAIS Administrative Secretary Barbara Wilmot said.

"She was always very supportive of what he was doing with WAIS and fighting for the athletes. She kept Wally on the straight and narrow: he would say he was going out for drinks, but Lyn had told him he had to be home at a certain time.

"When I saw Lyn, she was this sweet, young girl and I thought, 'How can she have such a hold on him?', but she did in her quiet way, because he didn't want to get Lyn upset. He would do the right thing by Lyn, always, and I loved seeing that."

Our family never went without and your Uncle Mark and I were spoilt in a lot of ways and that was because of how successful your grandad and nana were at their jobs. We were fortunate enough to see much of the world, with your grandad at times taking a lower pay from a broadcaster in order to include a few extra flights and nights' accommodation, or by tagging a family holiday onto the end of an event that had included at least one of your nana or grandad to be there already.

The trade-off was that your uncle and I would either go to a family friend's house after school, or be minded by a babysitter until your grandad's busy day and nana's evening training sessions finished. That would usually be about 7pm. And, in one instance, I even went to school in Beverley while staying with your Great Aunty Sandy on the farm, as your nana and grandad had to attend the same Olympic Games in their different roles.

All of that, however, might explain why you probably now see me as a grumpy, antisocial old man, who wants nothing more than to stay home with his family. Certain moments were like living in a madhouse with your grandad – your nana laughed when she recalled my birth and your grandad whisking off to a meeting in the morning when he realised that labour "might take a while", before returning in time for my arrival – but I always remember him being there.

He was always there when I or your uncle had sport and always there to help with school work – although he struggled with the maths problems – and every Saturday morning, before he had to work, he would take me, Josh and Clint – my two friends who lived in the same street – to Trigg Beach. That meant a lot to all of us and was the reason Josh and his wife Hayley bought you a beach set – a bucket, spade and sand moulds – for your first birthday.

Your grandad always made time for family holidays, even if it meant he had to drive down to our Easter destination of Canal Rocks Beach Resort in Yallingup, only to return to Perth for the weekend of football commentating, before driving back down again at the end of the match. And Christmas was one of the most important times of your grandad's year. It was always family time, without exception.

It takes a lot of devoted, loving people to make life work.

"He loved it. He wanted to contribute to something," your nana said.

"He had this idea of what sport needed. It was like being a developing athlete: he had nothing to lose and everything to gain. He was always the first at work and the last to leave, because he didn't think it was fair on the others if he wasn't there when they were, but we always had ways of spending time together: Fridays was always just us; Saturday was always with friends; Sunday was always the family.

"He had Sportstalk on Saturday and he called the WAFL on Saturday afternoons and there was usually something on Sundays, as well, but he did it because he liked it, he liked doing it. He was like a fart in a bottle. Even when he was home, he would really wear me out, because he always had to be doing something.

"If I just wanted to chill out and he came home, I'd have to get up and do something to make it look like I wasn't sitting down. It's not that it was how he made me feel, it's that when someone is going a million-miles-an-hour around you, it kick-starts you. I enjoyed when he worked Saturday, because I would use that time to visit my parents, so we had a routine and it worked."

And while it was hectic and at times challenging for more than just your grandad, it was mostly fun, or at least working towards fun. It was the passion for what he was doing that had the special man your grandad was enjoy every minute of life's madness.

"It was away from the airwaves that I had my funniest times with Wal," your grandad's 6PR producer and friend Peter Sweeney said.

"The funniest one was on Graham Bushell, from Ardath, a pimple-sized whatever up near Bruce Rock. I told Graham I was from a cigarette company and we wanted to reshoot commercials for the cigarette Ardath and what better place to do it than Ardath the town. It took a while, but he swallowed the bait and he nearly had the bags packed.

"Every time we would set something up, Wal would ring. Most of the times he came out of WAIS board meetings and ask: 'How did you go? What did he say?' and most of the times I hadn't even had a chance to contact the bloke, so Wal would go back into the meeting and then ring again 10 minutes later.

"When the result was achieved, he would cry with laughter. He was like a little lad locked in a lolly shop on a long weekend. Wal: he knew how to have a good time and few, if any, knew their sport as well as he did.

"I don't miss how he started every *Sportstalk* show – with a visit to the bathroom, where he would spend a considerable amount of time before exiting and proclaiming, 'I wouldn't go in there for a while' – but I, like many, many others, miss him."

It was WAIS's big move. Even more significant, it was the grand opening of the Superdrome.

There was to be a great unveiling: busts of the 14 foundation members of a new, illustrious group named the WA Hall of Champions, were to line the foyer of the largest multipurpose wet and dry sports facility in the southern hemisphere. And there was a problem: the athletes the busts were honouring wanted nothing to do with them.

The WA Hall of Champions is both an intangible salute to our state's best athletes, as well as a tangible collection of captured moments that reflect their achievements. It is – at the time of writing this – housed at Challenge Stadium in Mount Claremont and features images and plaques of more than 120 inductees, with the busts of the foundation members lining either side of the arena's foyer.

It is a significant moment for an athlete to be honoured by induction into the elite group and it is largely because of your grandad that the opportunity exists to be recognised in such a way. The history of the Hall of Champions credits its inception to a group known as the Sportswriters Association of WA, which in 1983 took its brainchild to the government to be developed fully. It was officially inaugurated by Minister for Sport the Hon. Keith Wilson two years later.

The full history involves your grandad – of course.

The Sportswriters Association of WA was created in 1982 by your grandad and Allan East, one of the men he had previously worked with at *The West Australian* and who at that point was editor of *The Western Mail*. East had received a letter from some people over east advising they were starting an Australian Sportswriters Association group and wanted to open branches in each state. East elected himself president, your grandad elected himself vice president and the Sportswriters Association of WA was born.

One of its first and most successful functions was a lunch in the lead-up to Brisbane's 1982 Commonwealth Games hosted at the Inglewood Sports Association and for every Western Australian who had won a gold medal at the Games. It was a prestigious event that made the evening news on every station and, sponsored by Qantas and Ampol, it secured athletes such as Dixie Willis, who was living in Brisbane at the time, and Herb Elliott.

It was also an event that made it clear to East and your grandad that WA should have a way of adequately recognising the achievements of its athletes and the idea of a Hall of Champions began to develop, with the support of respected journalist Geoff Christian.

Creating an air of significance around WAIS was a complex challenge for your grandad and he engaged the media on any issue he could to ensure its profile steadily built. But in the Hall of Champions he had an initiative that presented a win-win-win opportunity: the athletes would receive the recognition they deserved; the Sportswriters would have a place to house the Hall, which until that point had proven one of the more challenging issues; and WAIS would have a ready-made annual event that gave it the significance of publicly reflecting on its commitment to elite athletes.

It would also create the requirement of a function around inductions to the Hall of Champions, adding another significant piece to the profile puzzle your grandad was building. The result of that function was the highly successful WAIS Annual Dinner. So, your grandad seized the opportunity and WAIS took ownership of the WA Hall of Champions, garnering support from the Hon. Keith Wilson and David Hatt, who became a member of the selection committee.

It was inaugurated at the WAIS Annual Dinner in 1985 and given a physical home within the Superdrome from 1987. The inauguration, as it turned out, was the easy part. The Hall's importance of place in WA sport was highlighted by it being identified as an opportunity to also raise the profile of the opening of the new stadium that would house it.

Busts of the 14 foundation members were created and were to be unveiled at the grand opening. But, there was a problem.

"Shirly De La Hunty couldn't even recognise her own bust," David Hatt said.

"We paid a fair amount of money for those things and they were commissioned as at least part of the opening of the major sports centre. It was terrible: Herb Elliott came in, had a look at his bust, and said, 'That's not me, mate'. Shirly said, 'You are not putting that bust of me looking like that in the foyer'.

"All this collection of great athletes didn't want to have anything to do with them and then we had the guy who actually did the job, he refused to change them, because he said it was his artistic work and it did look like them. Eventually, they were changed and they're still there today.

"The Hall of Champions, Wally was very interested in and wanted to do. We needed a system of awards to honour our athletes. We had a WAIS athlete of the year and all that, but he believed we had a wider role to play in celebrating our elite athletes and our dinner now is the only time in the year when the whole sporting family comes together."

WAIS had been through its own growing pains in establishing its identity and the issue of the unrecognisable busts was the first of the pains that went with the Institute leaving the University of WA for its new home at the Superdrome.

WAIS had grown to the point where your grandad believed it needed its own "shop front", as Steve Lawrence recalled, and while its place at the University created a perceived segregation from the athletes it was designed to support, the Superdrome was a more appropriate home. However, your grandad was always striving for more success and better results. He was a hard man to please.

Your grandad praised the WA government for its investment in the state's athletes and could not help but give a sly nudge to Canberra at the opening of the facility, telling *National Nine News* it was "the best among all of the state institutes and I think it's as good, if not better, than what the AIS has got".

The problem was, the Superdrome was not built solely for WAIS and also needed to turn a profit to remain viable. It was a situation that put WAIS frequently at odds with stadium management, which at that point in time your grandad quipped was a recycling centre for Brownlow Medallists, with AFL Hall of Fame inductee Ross Glendinning being succeeded by three-time Essendon Best and Fairest winner Graham Moss in the roll of Marketing Manager for the Sports Centre Trust.

Moss eventually took over as General Manager of the stadium and it was a credit to the respect each man had for the other that he and your grandad remained close friends, with Moss a pallbearer at your grandad's funeral. They had first met when Moss was the inaugural general manager of the West Coast Eagles and was in search of a training venue for the AFL team, following WAFL club Subiaco's refusal to allow access to Subiaco Oval.

Your grandad and Moss began working on a solution to have the Eagles based out of the Superdrome, with McGillivray Oval to host two playing fields; one to replicate Subiaco Oval and the other to cater for conditions similar to Victoria's "mud heaps" of Moorabbin, Western Oval and Windy Hill.

"Our close friendship really developed over a conflict of interest," Moss said.

"WAIS came to the Superdrome, which was built in John Bloomfield's vision of an elite training venue for sports and the public was barely allowed in the joint. When we first started there, the public was only allowed in to swim after the first session in the morning which was about 9-o'clock, until about three or four, when WAIS had total access to all the lanes.

"In the main arena, the netballers were training, the Wildcats were training and WAIS was running programs out of there. They were paying us nothing, basically; there was some sort of general hire of the Superdrome that covered everything. If it added up to more than $50,000 a year, I'd be surprised, whereas I could have one concert or one exhibition in there and I'd make $50,000 in a weekend.

"So, something like a craft show would come along, or a Persian Rug Clearance Sale, and I'd get this call from Wally: 'Mossy, stitches and craft show? What the hell is going on?'. It was that sort of constant juggle of managing our objectives that had us develop a respect for each other and a really strong friendship and relationship.

"I don't know if that relationship could have worked between anyone else"

The friendship survived the hoard of stitches and craft shows and continued beyond both men's tenures at the venue, with Moss, your grandad and Glendinning ensuring they caught up semi-regularly for an annual lunch. Although, your grandad did like to push the boundaries of any relationship as far as they could go.

The Superdrome housed both WAIS and the WA Sports Federation in its first four years of opening, bringing Mick Aitken and your grandad even closer together with a shared office, before WASF moved into the dedicated Sports House of John Bloomfield's recommendations in 1992. The Federation's departure from the stadium freed up some larger office spaces and Moss thought he would take the opportunity to finally move out of his small room on the ground floor.

"Nope; Wally had grabbed them already, expanded his empire and put partitions in and everything," Moss said, laughing as he remembered the moment.

"So, when they built their new facility there (in 1996), tacked onto the Superdrome, I thought, 'Ok, well Wally's got this brand new $10 million facility there, or whatever it was, so I'll go up there now'. Nope; he was happy to give up the office bit above me, but I said I needed the conference room as well and he said no.

"He had this beautiful new building, but he still wasn't prepared to give away that space. He would do anything to enhance the lot for the athletes and coaches. He always put them first and if that meant having a fight with government over funding, or me over a room, then so be it."

The athletes and the coaches: they were the reason behind everything your grandad did with WAIS and, as Moss said, he was going to push everyone around him as far as he could to help achieve the best possible result for them.

When your grandad passed away, heptathlete Kylie Wheeler spoke at his memorial service on behalf of the athletes that he had helped throughout life.

Wheeler had a special connection with our family, as she was one of your nana's athletes. Her dad had passed away when she was 13-years-old, with her mum raising her and her brother Jono, who lives with a disability. Wheeler's mum felt sport was an important way for her daughter to develop away from the challenges she might have faced at home and so enrolled her in little athletics at Kingsway Athletics Club.

Wheeler shared with your nana the trait of modesty and, despite strong results and having regularly represented WA at junior levels, refused to believe she was "any good". Wheeler had taken a year off from athletics for her Year 12 studies as she targeted a result in her TEE that would allow her to study medicine and returned to running in 1998.

It was a World Junior Championships year and your nana told her, "let's have a crack", and Wheeler qualified to represent her country in the 400m hurdles. It was going to cost her $2000 to run for Australia and was a total beyond the recently-graduated, teenage Wheeler.

"Your mum was amazing and, I suspect with your dad's help and using his networks, they found the extra money and the Carbine Club put it in", Wheeler said. "That was beyond what they needed to do. Mum would have been able to pay, but they felt they didn't want to have to ask that of mum. It wasn't a job for your dad; it was what he wanted to do and it was his passion."

The relationship continued that way from the moment your nana began coaching Wheeler and an endless game developed of the athlete attempting to sneak envelopes of money as payment for coaching into your nana's bag, before your nana would attempt to sneak it back. The money was set aside by Wheeler's mum in the event her daughter was unsuccessful in passing it on and, in 2008 when your nana was overlooked for a coaching position with the Australian team, Wheeler's mum repaid the favour from a decade prior and covered the costs of the coach to join the athlete at the Beijing Olympics.

Your grandad had passed away by then and Wheeler retired a year later as a two-time Olympian, a Commonwealth Games silver medallist and a four-time national champion, but the relationship that continued between our families was a legacy of the commitment your grandad made for the athletes of this state.

"It all goes back to his job, but that it was more than that," Wheeler said.

"I felt enveloped by your family which was lovely and I'd do it all again. He did have a special interest in me because of your mum, but to me, I always felt he would work hard to the end for any athlete. So many people would owe their careers and their success to him and what he was able to do. There's plenty of people out there who would have an interest, but it's whether they would go that extra distance."

Your grandad's constant drive for the athletes and for better results had him find symmetry with those athletes.

Working in high performance sport is a challenging life, be it as an athlete or administrator. It is a profession that has no ceiling for success. Just as talented bands do not pack up their instruments after one successful song and call it a day, so too must athletes and those around them constantly strive for the next level of success.

Justin Langer, one of Western Australia's most respected athletes and a man I was fortunate enough to work with, had five pillars he instructed the state cricket team to live by during his time as coach: work hard; celebrate success; respect the past; speak honestly; look after your mates. He ensured "celebrate success" was in those values because of how debilitating on athletes the effects can be of the endless demand for personal best performances.

It is certainly not an environment for everyone and most roles within high performance have a limited shelf-life before people need to get out for the sake of their own wellbeing, because happiness in high performance is usually a synonym for complacency. Your grandad was always striving to ensure that message was being heard, especially amidst the euphoric and oft-blinding fog of success and he made that point to *National Nine News'* former reporter Dixie Marshall following Sydney's successful bid for the 2000 Olympic Games when discussing the funding injection it would result in.

"I think Perth has to stir itself out of its apathy, because I think it's been very apathetic towards the Sydney bid until today," he said. Your grandad was forever wary the hard work of establishing WA's elite sports system was not looked upon as "job done" and that was an ongoing challenge, especially in dealing with governments.

"I think your dad really brought me back to earth with how far there was left to go," said Graham Edwards, Minister for Sport from 1987.

"Funds started to dry up and money started to get tight and I think that was a frustration of your dad's, because he wanted to grow WAIS and grow it fast. While I thought we were doing a good job, Wally had done an interview with *The Sunday Times*, where he basically said that WAIS was broke, needed money and needed resources.

"He did it quite nicely, although I remember he and I had a discussion about it. Your dad was always appreciative of what the Burke Government had done, but he was always impatient about what needed to be done. He was always straight-up-and-down; I don't think he ever played politics as some people did, like trying to play Labor and Liberal off against each other. He was balanced and you could always see where he was going.

"He just wanted to get there in a big hurry. I think that was reflective of the neglect – he was very critical of previous governments, very critical of the decision to boycott the Olympics in Moscow – and I think that was something Brian (Burke) had an opinion on."

Your grandad remained involved in high performance sport for as long as he did for a combination of three reasons: his passion and love for sport; his passion and love for people; and his loyalty to those people and the mission to help them become better. He never relented in that mission for those people and with that passion, regardless of who his beliefs put offside.

He told *The West Australian* in 1984 upon first taking the position of director that "every four years the public and politicians jumped on (the athletes') bag and had great expectations for them and made great demands in an Olympic or Commonwealth Games year", before saying that "Australians have ridden on the backs of their sporting champions for so long ... I don't think we can go along ignoring the high performers in sport".

His resignation from WAIS in 2001 ended a 17-year tenure in charge of the institute and with WA having gone from being inadequate in its support for its athletes, to being recognised as having among the best services for elite sportspeople in the country. And it was because your grandad always – from start to end – refused to accept that what had been done for athletes and coaches was all that could be done for them.

"Every day and every week just brought another challenge," your grandad told *The West Magazine* in 2001. "You'd sort of scale one little hill and you could see another one down the road."

Chapter 12

When Two Worlds Collide

Life alongside the Australian Institute of Sport was not always unpleasant, but it was always likely to be.

The problem went back to the establishment of the AIS as a standalone centre, without the state support network that had been recommended in several reports. It led to the states having to develop their own path and that ultimately led to rivalry.

There were attempts to overcome those challenges, such as the AIS decentralising programs into states – the hockey program, for example, was based in Perth a year before WAIS had even opened – but even those moves were problematic due to the lack of consultation. The AIS hockey squad was initially set up as a development program, which led to the younger players receiving large amounts of resources with significant financial investment, while the senior players who were actually representing Australia received little to no support.

Craig Davies, a member of the squad at the time, said he "looked upon that situation pretty negatively" and that your grandad "recognised that (imbalance) as well". Your grandad did recognise it and told *The Canberra Times* in 1989 when the AIS was considering disbanding its hockey unit.

"It's a ludicrous situation that the development squad has two fulltime coaches earning more than $100,000 combined, while the national coach receives only $15,000 and is expected to carry on part-time," he said.

"The AIS has created a comfort zone for men's hockey: there's a certainty of getting into the Australian team for the scholarship holders, while the other kids go back to the states without fire in their bellies, knowing they've got no chance. The results of the Australian men's team have not been up to scratch and we ought to consider the needs of the Australian players in the light of the last two Olympic tournaments."

They were issues that were symptomatic of a system plagued with uncertainty: it was uncharted territory for all involved, nobody knew what their role should be, so everybody created their own identity and plan that they were then determined to defend when challenged. That went for the state institutes as well as the AIS.

"The AIS I think has lost its way at times by not being sure whether it's a university or whether it's in actual fact a service provider," WAIS Chairman at the time Bruce Elliott said.

"The AIS was new and we had so many arguments with them. Some of my most bitter memories in sport in this country are of your dad and I battling with – I won't say who – a number of people within the AIS as to their philosophy on sport development and our philosophy; a la gymnastics and a la cycling."

Were the states independent institutes, or did they fit under a structure headed by the AIS?

That was the primary difference in philosophy that had no answer, because of the lack of foundation work in the AIS's establishment. It began to pose interesting situations even from within WAIS, which had Professor John Bloomfield sitting on its board as well as the board of the AIS, while fellow WAIS Board Member Tom Hoad had the view of Canberra having "far too much influence from a bunch of bureaucrats who don't have any practical experience".

The issue of "badging" became a topic of fierce debate that raged between the states and Canberra. The states had invested heavily into athletes that had largely been neglected prior to the establishment of the AIS – and even after its establishment – therefore they felt they were entitled to be represented by those athletes at meets, particularly international meets. That meant the athlete was to wear WAIS – or whatever state the athlete belonged to – tracksuits and branding.

However, the states were often finding themselves in a position where they had funded an athlete to attend a meet, only to see images of that athlete wearing an AIS tracksuit due to the ongoing perception that the Canberra institute held some sort of ownership over athletes on an international stage.

"We were fighting to be recognised for what we did for our athletes, even when they moved across to the AIS and it took a while to get past that," inaugural Queensland Academy of Sport director Wilma Shakespear said.

"I remember sitting through so many meetings when this bloody badging bit had come up and I'm thinking, 'Oh, for goodness sakes'. We knew where we needed to go, but we needed Canberra to give us recognition and to come with us. For a while there, there was this idea that we'd all become AIS outlets, but that had Buckley's hope."

The sense of superiority that was emanating out of the AIS did little to foster a positive working relationship with the states and the results and events around South Australia's cycling program stood as another example of that. Cycling had not been among the foundation sports of the Australian Institute of Sport, which left Mike Nunan's South Australian Sports Institute pouring resources into a program in Adelaide.

It gave SASI and its state allies some valuable currency after Australia won the team pursuit gold medal at the Los Angeles Olympics in 1984.

"The classic story goes that Nunan walked in, put the gold medals on the table in Canberra and said, 'Where are yours?'," Shakespear said.

The system evolved over the years to a point of sophistication and success and the states now have a far more collaborative relationship with the AIS and vice-versa, but that has only come about because of the battles your grandad fought with his state counterparts.

For much of the time, it was only he and Mike Nunan attempting to stand their ground against unwanted, or ineffective influences from Canberra. And if they needed any reminding, there were moments that highlighted exactly who the pair was fighting for and that steeled the resolve.

A WA female swimmer had been sent to Canberra and put through what was termed a "Hell Week", which consisted of 10 x 400m swims every day. WAIS Board Member at the time Brian Blanksby said the athletes were not permitted access to sports doctors or support and were told to "tough it out".

"This kid, it stuffed her," Blanksby said. "She was sent home for 'repairs' and she never swam again. So there were issues like that and the rivalry grew."

Blanksby's role as WAIS Board Member and his being on staff at UWA alongside Bloomfield had him with your grandad as a regular attendee of the meetings on the issues of the AIS, which stemmed from the national institute attempting to fit the states into its own model, while having no right to do so or having contributed little in establishing the states at the start.

"We thought that was stupid, but in time it probably turned out to be the best thing they could have done, because it meant they had seven states against them," Blanksby said. "Nobody wanted to send their athletes to Canberra, so they all set up their own institutes."

There is truth in Blanksby's statement that, ultimately, Australia developed a highly successful network to support elite sport, but the way in which it went about it was more akin to a civil war targeting revolution than the cohesive rollout of a strategy. It would be fair to say that the resulting system was a convenient by-product rather than intended.

The system that was put in place was ineffective and at times required young athletes – children – to leave home and head east if they wanted to be successful in their sport. It was always a mission statement of your grandad's in establishing WAIS that an athlete should not be forced to leave their home state to receive the support they deserved.

"I've toured the world from a biomechanics perspective and I've worked in the US institute system," WAIS Chairman at the time Bruce Elliott said.

"The only thing I know is that you need a system that works for your country. The arguments with the AIS and those in the east, really, almost all revolved around letting West Australians of a variety of ages succeed within Western Australia. There are times when they may have to leave Western Australia – and we accept that – but you must be allowed to develop your skills in your state."

It was an ideology shared by SASI director Nunan, who was attempting to ensure an athlete was "successful for a career, not successful at 18 and then on the scrapheap by 20".

"The thing that stood out in my mind was that whenever we would be at an institute meeting – which was basically the AIS, Wally and myself – it was the AIS versus Wally and myself," Nunan said, who despite the challenging times also remembered your grandad fondly as "just enjoyable to be with", particularly in the social settings around meetings that often involved red wine.

"It was the Western Australia-South Australia coalition and it was two guys who were really passionate about sport, arguing with administrators and primarily public servants, not necessarily people who had any sort of passion or knowledge of sport. It wasn't a hard alliance, but we shared certain principals: you had to, without fear or favour, recognise talent and you had to actually provide for that talent in the best circumstances for the person to develop."

Your grandad and Nunan began gaining allies as the other state institutes began coming online, with Tasmania following WAIS in 1985 and Victoria in 1990. Shakespear joined the posse when QAS opened in 1991 and formed a feisty duo with your grandad that was fondly referred to by the other directors as the "W and W Show", referring to the tenacious tag-team debating style the pair employed against opponents.

Those opponents were often AIS representatives who made the mistake of believing they were ahead of the states.

"We were up at a meeting in Darwin and the AIS was there with this overenthusiastic guy who started to tell us all how we should do talent ID," Shakespear said.

"Wal and I had been doing talent ID, really in there and working at it, for quite a while and here is this guy, talking to the lot of us as if we have no idea. We really put the questions back to him – we asked him what his background was, how many athletes he'd produced, asking him for hard data – and the others thought it was so funny that they just let us go.

"Our colleagues said afterwards, 'That was the W and W Working Over that he got'. It was really difficult to find somebody like that, fresh out, who had not bothered to do the homework and understand the effort and work that others had put in."

The rapid development of talent ID was a significant achievement by the states, yet it was just one of several accomplishments they achieved as a result of the national go-it-alone model.

WAIS had retained its independence, it had moved into one of the most impressive sports facilities in the southern hemisphere and it had a highly skilled sports scientist on staff in Steve Lawrence who, with the close links of UWA's expertise, was helping WAIS pioneer the trade in Australia. The Institute also began to bring in international coaches who were better credentialed and experienced than those being employed anywhere in Australia, including at the AIS.

It was made possible to attract those coaches largely due to eventual funding that came from the national system, which matched states dollar-for-dollar on investments made in the "Super Seven" programs, which was a group of the most notable Olympic sports, such as athletics, swimming and gymnastics. WAIS seized the opportunity under the motto of "Part-time coaches produce part-time athletes" and the institute's staffing numbers began exploding, almost doubling the initial four people – your grandad, Steve Lawrence, Craig Davies and Barbara Wilmot – within its first year of moving to the Superdrome.

WAIS suddenly had a staffing list that included inaugural coaches Liz Chetkovich in gymnastics and Gerry Stachewicz in swimming and soon boasted international names such as Tudor Bidder, brought over from the UK to head up track and field, head gymnastics coach Andrei Rodionenko, who had been lured from Russia, the French Canadian cycling specialist Martin Barras, Krzysztof Lepianka from Poland as its canoeing coach and Stephan Muhlenberg from East Germany heading up the rowing program.

"We engaged a lot of people from a wide variety of backgrounds, so what you had was the best people in the world coming to WAIS," Lawrence said. "There was no doubt that Wally created an opportunity for that to occur. The Australian sports system was starting to become really known and we had a lot of good things to sell."

WAIS had also played an active role in bidding for international events and, as the institute's first Olympic cycle wound it closer to the 1988 Seoul Olympics, WAIS had also developed enough of an identity to declare its mission for national representation: "10 per cent of the team, from 10 per cent of the population". The statement flared the badging issue again in attempting to classify which athletes were Western Australian, but that meant little to the politicians, who loved nothing more than an easily referenced slogan to sell to the media.

"Athletes can now 'touch' international sport – we've made their dreams a reality, they can see what they need to do to achieve international success," your grandad later told *The West Australian*.

Your grandad had created an institute within a couple of years that was making significant progress and doing it at a pace that both permitted and justified its independence, within WA and nationally. And he did it by building it around talented people, who became loyal allies.

"There's no doubt he was a very good people manager with people that he trusted," Lawrence said.

"If he didn't trust you, he couldn't manage you. I can only speak from where I was, but you trusted him implicitly; you knew he was always going to do things for reasons that were inherently the right ones, which were looking after and supporting athletes in getting performances."

Your grandad had laid the foundations for an Institute that would become the benchmark of Australia's network. He did it with the top priority always in mind: the athletes. And while all the state institutes assisted in building each other, he and Mike Nunan led the charge.

Your grandad's background in the media gave him a firm grounding in the importance of preparation, knowing the facts and forming an opinion, as well as the tools with which to argue that opinion coherently. That became a valuable asset for the state institutes, especially before the 1993 formation of their official body and voice the National Elite Sports Council, with Nunan remembering him as being "so passionate and articulate that he was a strong ally for us and, when I say 'us', I mean all the state institutes and he soon became probably our best spokesperson for the group".

Wilma Shakespear said that ability to form a persuasive and coherent opinion was coupled with your grandad's contacts in, and acceptance by, the media, which was important to the fledgling group. Shakespear was among your grandad's closest friends and allies from his time at WAIS and, while Queensland's institute did not appear until 1991, the pair remained close colleagues right to the end of their tenures – both resigning in 2001.

It undoubtedly helped that Shakespear spent 10 years living in WA alongside her Olympic rower husband Peter and her experience as a national netball representative before switching into administration gave her a unique experience from which to draw as the states found their way. She saw the disputes from both sides; she had worked as the Australian Institute of Sport's netball coach for nine years, before becoming its Manager of Elite Programs and eventually leaving Canberra to head up QAS.

Shakespear's friendship with your grandad extended well beyond work; she made the trip west for his 50th birthday, she organised a farewell party for him upon his resignation from WAIS and he was among the first to know that party was secretly also for her. Shakespear spoke with great respect for your grandad, particularly with regards to what he and Nunan helped Australian sport achieve in those developing days.

"I don't think even they understood that what they were teaching was that there wasn't one way to the destination and in a country like ours, we really needed a system of both centralised and decentralised," Shakespear said.

Your grandad had a vision for WAIS. He fought for that vision and he marked some amazing achievements in realising it. It was a different vision to what existed at the time; different philosophies and different priorities. As Shakespear said, those differences eventually resulted in a strong sporting system across Australia, but those differences also guaranteed conflict.

Chapter 13

There is More to Life Than Results

THE WORDS OF INAUGURAL SOUTH Australian Sports Institute director Mike Nunan were poignant: "We were wanting athletes to be successful for a career, not successful at 18 and then on the scrapheap by 20," he said.

He was discussing the merits of decentralising programs out of Canberra. His comments were made around the ongoing battle between the state institutes and the AIS and one of the main contributors to that view was the gymnastics program.

The differences in approach to sport that your grandad had experienced at the national level made him believe there had never been more need for state institutes. WAIS was fulfilling its mission to support its athletes in achieving internationally competitive results and it had also gone into fight for the rights of those athletes against national bodies that seemed happy to play fast and loose with those rights.

A poignant example of that was the battle for the rights of a cyclist named Tony Davis around the 1988 Seoul Olympics. It was a conflict that centred around a national body – Cycling Australia – its people, its governance and its programs. It was a conflict that impacted both Davis and your grandad significantly and I encourage you, or anyone reading this, to take some time to learn about that incident. However, for legal reasons, that story was not able to be told in these pages.

Seoul had barely subsided before the rights of West Australian athletes were again tested. Again by a national body. And, again, it was because of one underlying issue: an inadequately prepared national system failed to adapt to life alongside state institutes.

The national body – this time, the Australian Gymnastics Federation – was fast becoming redundant. Not because it had no place in the system, but because it refused to adapt itself with the system that was evolving.

The same could not be said for the Western Australian Institute of Sport.

Your grandad remained steadfast in his view that athlete results would and should always be the barometer with which to judge WAIS's performance. That barometer was constantly rising.

The state contributed 13 per cent of the national team at the Barcelona Olympics – well beyond its target of matching its nine per cent of Australia's population, or the 10 per cent of the fancy catch phrase – and its representation of 41 athletes reflected more Western Australians than ever before marching behind their country's flag at the opening ceremony. The number increased slightly for the Atlanta Games and across the three Olympics encompassing WAIS's first decade of existence, WA's representation at the pinnacle event of world sport went from 21 athletes in seven sports at Los Angeles in 1984, to 41 athletes in 14 sports at Barcelona in 1992.

At the close of its first 10 years – the end of 1994 – WA had more athletes inside the world top 10 in a wider variety of sports than ever before and the state's growing pride and investment in its high performance system put it in a position to bid for the 1998 Commonwealth Games; a significant effort, despite having not been successful in the bid.

The Institute was financially strong and your grandad had overseen its budget increase from the initial $300,000 government grant to one of $2.2 million in a decade, with WAIS having amassed almost $3 million in contributions from the corporate sector alone in its first 10 years. That strong financial position had the Institute employing 31 fulltime and 15 part-time staff by the end of 1994. That growth was at times difficult to maintain – such as having to house the sports science department in a conference room – but it led to the commitment of $2 million in the mid-90s of the Liberal Government that had taken power to build a dedicated, three-storey standalone facility adjoining the Superdrome.

That building allowed WAIS to house all its staff in dedicated sports science, strength and conditioning and administration areas. They were departments and programs that had developed and positioned themselves as nation-leading, particularly the work of sports scientist Steve Lawrence and his team. The downside to the significant and rapid growth was the Institute's inability to maintain pace with funding requirements and it was forced to close four programs in 1991, while pulling back in all others.

As your grandad said at the time: "WAIS is a victim of its own success".

But funding was always among the ongoing issues your grandad had to face from Federal to State level. The money was there, but your grandad remained convinced its allocation was inadequate: "the sports funding cake in WA is big enough, the way it's being cut remains a problem". He was again referring to the focus on recreation spending in WA and the top-heavy investment of bureaucrats.

The setback of reducing programs ultimately assisted in strengthening WAIS's contribution to its strongest sports. The access in the late 1980s to Federal funds for the first time through the Australian Sports Commission's Intensive Training Centre program – developed with strong assistance from WAIS Board Member and Federal Member of Parliament Dr Ric Charlesworth, as well as the ever-present David Hatt – ensured key sports continued to grow.

Ever the driver of better performance though, your grandad was as thankful for the money as he was committed to the message that "access to this funding source must be further improved". The direct result of the funding was the appointment of full-time coaches in athletics, hockey, rowing, swimming and gymnastics. WA's results in athletics in 1991 were of particular significance because of the credit your grandad paid not only to WAIS's new coach, England's Tudor Bidder, but also to the "invaluable support from the AIS athletics unit". It was evidence that your grandad could work with those from the national system who wanted to be worked with.

The recruitment of Olympic basketballer Michelle Timms into the WAIS Breakers program resulted in the team's first playoff appearance within her first year of 1991, before helping the Breakers to their inaugural WNBL championship the following season. The fact that WAIS had a side in the national basketball competition was significant: it had been a concerted effort of your grandad's to strengthen national competitions, with his belief that they created a more successful national program and he often pointed to the Sheffield Shield in cricket and its effectiveness in producing a strong national team in justifying that belief.

The institute's hockey, athletics and rowing programs all experienced boon years in the early 1990s and WA's reputation as a strong sporting state had again been restored.

However, while the growth of the institute overall had made a significant impact to the state's sporting performances, it was the development of one sport in particular that had begun to send shockwaves across Australia: gymnastics.

WA's evolution into the country's gymnastics powerhouse can largely be credited to one woman: Liz Chetkovich. Although she would probably tell you it was mostly your grandad.

Chetkovich's involvement with gymnastics began as a 14-year-old in one of those fate-wields-its-hand moments: she was the babysitter of a woman named Nelleck Jol, who coached gymnasts at the 1960, 64, 68 and 72 Olympic Games. Jol's recreational classes were bursting at the seams and Chetkovich was recruited from the sidelines to assist. She was immediately hooked on the sport.

"I was destined to become a gymnastics coach," Chetkovich said.

Chetkovich then obtained a physical education degree at UWA and accepted a coaching job in the late 1970s in New Jersey, US. She returned to Perth in mid-1981 and opened her own academy under her maiden name, Liz Golding's School of Gymnastics, before changing it after marriage to Chetkovich Academy of Gymnastics "because it sounded foreign and specky".

Jol had remained involved in the scene, coaching her beginning classes, so Chetkovich identified the potential pathway and catered her academy accordingly, taking the best eight to 10 gymnasts from Jol's group to further develop their talents. It was a gutsy move and one that was "highly unusual for a woman to do so at the time" in borrowing $10,000 from the bank and starting the business.

It started small, hopping from suburban recreation centres around Perth and even operating out of a park opposite the Freshwater Bay Yacht Club once a week. The conversion of a trucking warehouse in Subiaco into what became Lord's Recreation Centre provided Chetkovich's academy with its first dedicated home, with one of the trucking bays becoming a pool and the other a foam pit for gymnastics use.

The small business of a former babysitter had moved into its own facility – a warehouse at 473 Scarborough Beach Road in Osborne Park, where Harvey Norman stands today – and was producing nationally competitive gymnasts when in 1984, Chetkovich began receiving curious questions from government representatives as to what would need to be done to better establish gymnastics in the state. Her response was simple: providing an opportunity for the best gymnasts from all clubs to train together as a WAIS squad under advanced coaches would likely accelerate their development

The WAIS squad system served its purpose for a little more than three years until the completion of the Perth Superdrome, which had included a gymnastics arena in its plans. The facility created a custom-designed, centralised location and the program evolved. WAIS had engaged Chetkovich in its earliest days to establish an Institute squad, making it just the third program operating nationally after the AIS and South Australian Sports Institute.

The WAIS gymnastics program operated out of Chetkovich's Osborne Park warehouse for three and a half years before the opening of the Superdrome. WAIS supported the operation of a gymnastics squad from mid-1984 until the end of 87. The squad, which comprised the best gymnasts from all clubs, trained two sessions a week out of the Chetkovich Academy of Gymnastics. The increases in funding in the late 1980s to WAIS and the previous relationship with the program had Chetkovich become the Institute's first employed coach, alongside swimming mentor Gerry Stachewicz, on a part-time basis.

The major development for the sport in WA came in October 1986, when Chetkovich received a Sir James Cruthers Scholarship valued at $10,000, facilitated by Channel 7 and named in honour of the broadcaster's founding general manager. Chetkovich's application had been based on her proposal to conduct a six-week study tour of the gymnastics stronghold of the USSR, with visits to Moscow and Minsk, to examine the nation's training system.

Your nana and grandad were invited to dinner immediately upon Chetkovich's return and they sat in the small dining room of the latter's federation style home in Maylands, listening to the passionate outlining of what WA needed to implement in the sport.

"I said, 'Wally, this is what we need to do with gymnastics. We've got a venue, we need a centralised program (in the state), we need coaches in place, we need to bring all the kids into one place to train in one location. They can't be training out at the clubs; we need to get them in, we pick the best kids and we train them in a central location. I've been on this tour, here's the evidence'," Chetkovich said.

"Wally said, 'Ok, we'll do it'. Mike Nunan (inaugural South Australian Sports Institute director) said at the time – and we still talk about this – 'You're crazy; why would you back a sport like gymnastics? It's going nowhere and it's not possible to be successful'. Wally went against that, because I'd given this compelling argument that we should do it.

"But there was no money to employ a coach at the time, so I mocked up this budget and said if we charged the kids fees and WAIS put this little bit of money in – our original budget was $7500 a year – there'd be enough to employ a coach and we could get the program started. He said I couldn't guarantee that I could bring the money in, so I said I would work for nothing and if we brought the money in, he could pay me, but if we didn't, I didn't expect to be paid.

"That's how we started it off."

Your grandad was amidst one of several debates for funding. He was arguing with the Minister for Sport Graham Edwards, complaining that he needed more money for the sports science division.

He sought to highlight his financial frustrations by stating that WAIS "couldn't even afford an international gymnastics coach". The irony was that the government provided WAIS funding for the gymnastics coach, but not the sports science division. With that, the Institute employed its first international mentor with the appointment of American Larry McDonough in 1988.

McDonough took over as head coach of a program for which Chetkovich had already developed a methodical and successful approach, encompassing three key aspects: the availability of a suitable facility in the Superdrome; the appointment of appropriately qualified coaches; the establishment of an appropriate talent base.

The lesson for your grandad in the development of gymnastics was that it provided clear evidence of the value in operating proper programs – ones that provided a pathway from talent identification, through to development, through to elite performance – instead of complementary training sessions and feeder programs.

"I always remember the great conversations, the great discussions and looking at what the possibilities could be," Chetkovich said.

"He (your grandad) would take that leap of faith with you and the way I operate is that I require that leap of faith from people. I'll say, 'Let's get an overseas coach', without having it all on paper. It was exciting times.

"He took the time to give his people time and he never got so caught up in paperwork that he didn't have time for you."

WAIS was operating the most comprehensive gymnastics program in the country. It was more comprehensive even than that of the Australian Institute of Sport. At any one time, it had three streams working towards three different Olympic cycles; in the mid-90s, it had groups targeting Atlanta, Sydney and Athens, for example.

Chetkovich's experience from the USSR study tour impressed on her the importance of world-class coaches at every level of the pathway and your grandad's trusting of his staff ensured that advice was taken. The program's credentials were further enhanced when WAIS in 1991 secured Andrei Rodionenko, considered the mastermind of the USSR's individual and team gold medals at the Seoul Olympics, as its technical director in the sport.

To say it was a coup would be an understatement: it marked the first appointment anywhere in the world of a Soviet coach outside their home country. Rodionenko's arrival acted as a floodgate and WAIS soon had four internationally renowned and exceptional Russians on staff: Rodionenko as its women's head coach after McDonough returned to the US; Melic Tichabaev as its specialist acrobatics coach; Sergei Shelest as its men's coach; Nikolai Lapchine as head coach of the junior program.

One of the hallmarks of Chetkovich's days running her academy was the strong relationships her program had built with clubs around Perth and that proved invaluable to WAIS's operations at the talent identification level and in forming a united voice and vision for gymnastics in WA.

"With Liz, we had someone there who was pushing gymnastics," said Bruce Elliott, WAIS Chairman for the Institute's first decade of existence.

"She had a similar vision to your dad – not as global – in that she felt you could make a program that was similar to those found in the Eastern Bloc countries. We talked to high schools so that we could get all the kids going to the same high school, then have a bus take them in so the parents didn't have to be there all the time and steps like that to help the program."

The experience it had on staff, coupled with its strong network around the state had WAIS producing consistently outstanding results.

WA won the Australian Senior Teams Championship in 1988 and defended its title in 1989. By 1990, the average scores of WAIS gymnasts had increased from 9.0 to 9.6 and WA's Sallyanne Hargrave had become the first non-AIS athlete to win the national title since the Canberra institute's establishment in 1981.

"When we started off in 1988, the AIS thought, 'Oh that's great, you'll send your kids to Canberra', then in 89 when we had half of the world championship team – three of the six gymnasts – and we were making it quite clear we weren't going to hand the kids over, they started to dig their heels in," Chetkovich said.

"Ju Ping (national and AIS coach) said to me, 'You should give the girls to me, because you can never produce a world champion. You don't even have good coaches'. So, I asked what if we got a good coach and she said: 'Even if you get a good enough coach, you can never do it'.

"That was when we got Andrei Rodionenko out, but as we got better and better, they began to turn the screws on us."

The first turning of the screws came on Christmas Day 1989. Your grandad and Chetkovich exchanged several phone calls.

A highly deserving WAIS athlete was set to be overlooked for the Australian team for the 1990 Commonwealth Games. Much like the cycling controversy of the Seoul Olympics in which WAIS became embroiled in defence of Tony Davis, it was again a case of the national coach having discretionary powers and wielding them in a way that appeared biased.

This time, the athlete was Jane Warrilow. She had achieved 9.812 on the vault at the national championships to record the equal-highest score ever marked by a WA gymnast, yet she had not been selected in the initial team. She was eventually selected as the travelling reserve.

But the ringing of those phones, like the Christmas bells around them, was a portent of what was to come.

While WAIS was making major inroads in gymnastics, the Australian Institute of Sport was steaming ahead in its program at the same time. And the two major movements in the sport were on track for a head-on collision.

The AIS had marked a significant achievement of its own when in 1985 it appointed Chinese coach Ju Ping Tian to head up its women's gymnastics program and to oversee the national team. Ju Ping was a hard taskmaster, but she had also helped Australia accomplish greatness; Australia's sixth-place finish at the 1991 World Championships in Indianapolis, US, was the best result in the country's history – well above its previous world ranking of 16 – and for the first time qualified it a full contingent for the subsequent Olympic Games in Barcelona.

However, success can sometimes have a habit of hiding the shortcomings of its methods and the same could be said for the coaching style of Ju Ping. The 1992 headline of a *Sydney Morning Herald* report demonstrated that: "Why Australia's girl gymnasts are happy to cry for Ju Ping".

Success brought the happiness; the methods brought the tears. The article was referring to Ju Ping's reduction to tears of 19-year-old Commonwealth Games silver medallist Kylie Shadbolt on three separate occasions during a training exercise.

It described the coach's penchant for intimidating remonstrations and that "not only does she speak fractured English, but her words pelt like hailstones". The response to the Shadbolt incident from Jim Ferguson, executive director of the Australian Sports Commission, was: "She is the epitome of toughness. She won't let her girls be anything but focused. Every day I see her girls outside the gym crying because they can't meet her standards".

It was common theme at the time on the national level: rivers of tears could flow, as long as they floated success.

Ju Ping's methods were possibly the result of a hardship that most Australians were oblivious to. Journalist Roy Masters' piece for the *Sydney Morning Herald* went on to explain that "during the Chinese revolutionary war, her father, Zu Ching Tian, was a high-ranking officer in the Komintang Army that opposed Mao Zedong's force. After the surrender in 1949, he was arrested and imprisoned on suspicion of being a counterrevolutionary. His imprisonment, for 25 years, together with frequent torture, led to his death in 1975."

Ju Ping's family was required to denounce her father lest they be executed as traitors and her mother was forced to work as a labourer to feed the two children. Ju Ping had shown enough talent as a gymnast to be taken as a 14-year-old to live with the national team in Beijing, where she later in life became a part of the national coaching structure.

Ju Ping immigrated to Australia in 1983 with her husband, living in Sydney before securing the job at the AIS in Canberra.

Perhaps it was the heartbreaking aspects of her past that founded the personality, actions, methods and philosophies that she brought to the AIS and Australian gymnastics. Those methods and philosophies helped Australia achieve some major milestones in the sport and in addition to the world championship and world ranking rise that qualified it for its first full team at the Barcelona Olympics, Ju Ping also developed the country's first international gold medallist – Shadbolt – and its first world championship apparatus finalist, Julie-Ann Monaco.

At the end of her coaching tenure with the national team, she oversaw Australia's first Commonwealth Games team gold medal in 1998. The results were there, but the methods created tensions – especially with your grandad – and a feud that turned bitter and at times personal erupted in the lead-up to the 1992 Barcelona Olympic Games.

Barcelona was supposed to be a watershed moment for gymnastics, not one mired in controversy, but the latter happened when WA's dominance in the sport again came to the fore.

WAIS was considered to have the strongest gymnastics program in the country: media reports labelled its progress as having taken "giant strides" in the 15 months under Russian coach Andrei Rodionenko and coaching partner Liz Chetkovich leading into the Games. Those strides led to WAIS having an overwhelming representation in the competition for Olympic berths, with its four gymnasts accounting for a third of the country's 12-person squad competing for the seven places at the Games.

The four WA athletes entered the selection period with strong credentials: Michelle Telfer had competed in two world championships – including the historic sixth-place finish in the US – and was a member of the silver medal-winning team at the 1990 Commonwealth Games, where she also won bronze in the uneven bars; Jane Warrilow had world championship experience; and 14-year-old pair Brooke Gysen and Tracey Gibbs had both won silver medals at the Pacific Alliance titles as juniors.

There was certainly strong competition from interstate, with several gymnasts demanding their place in the team ahead of WA's competitors. Victoria's Joanna Hughes and AIS pair Shadbolt and Monique Allen were considered the country's best gymnasts: they had been among the group that helped Australia qualify for Barcelona. Hughes, at just 14-years-old, had achieved the best placing by an Australian at a world championship when she finished 19th, with Allen two places behind her, and Shadbolt became the country's first international gold medallist with her success at the 1990 Konica Grand Prix in Brisbane.

The trio was considered an automatic selection for the team, leaving three spots plus reserve up for grabs. The squad for the Olympics was to be named after the national titles, which were held in Melbourne from 28-31 March 1992.

Telfer did not compete at the Australian Championships due to injury, but her training partner Warrilow won the all around section with a performance that Melbourne's *Herald Sun* labelled as "a near perfect display". Gysen was also putting her hand up, having won the state elite championships all around title in the lead-up to Barcelona, while having been WA's best performer at the Olympic training in Canberra and the China Cup in Beijing.

A train-on squad of 10 gymnasts was named for a six-week camp in Canberra to identify the final squad that would compete at the Olympics. Highlighting their dedication and passion to the sport they loved, Year 10 students Gibbs and Gysen enrolled in the newly-introduced distance education program, allowing them to continue schooling around their seven-hours-a-day training sessions. WAIS's four gymnasts were all among the train-on squad that operated under AIS and national coach Ju Ping Tian's ever-watchful eye and ever-stringent hand.

It was a tense and intense time for all involved and those tensions soon erupted, with a headline splashed across national papers – from *The Australian* to *The West Australian* – reading: 'Fat' gymnast dropped from squad.

West Australian Tracy Gibbs had been told she was no longer a part of the training squad due to the results of a skinfold test being too high.

It was a move from Ju Ping and the AIS that contradicted the national body's own selection criteria, which outlined that the skinfold test was to be used in cases where two gymnasts of equal standing could not be separated in selection trials, in which case "preference will be given to the gymnast at or below the recommended skinfold". The actions of Ju Ping, sanctioned by the AIS and Australian Gymnastics Federation, were confusing and drew outrage from several quarters.

The issue made it all the way to Federal Parliament, where WAIS Board Member, revered Olympian and Perth MP Ric Charlesworth delivered a scathing address to the House of Representatives that labelled the national powerbrokers as heavy-handed and as having utilised an "imprecise selection process".

"For the sake of one or two millimetres, in a test which has a margin of error of plus or minus three or four millimetres, she has been excluded from the possibility of continuing in the trial," Charlesworth told the House.

The testing in itself was contentious. It was far from the more precise methods of modern sports science – testers usually allowed a seven per cent variation to account for discrepancies – and Gibbs had returned results that were both under and over the AIS's recommended range of 40mm across seven sites.

Steve Lawrence had conducted the first set of skinfold tests at WAIS, returning measurements inside the accepted range, before they rose upon retesting at the AIS in Canberra soon afterwards.

"Doug Tumilty, the guy that did the skinfolds in Canberra, and I agreed that the difference was such that they were basically the same," Lawrence said. "Ju Ping decreed that the athlete was going to be deselected from the team, based on this measurement. We were in an argument saying it was an inappropriate use of science. She was only using Tumilty's scores and even Doug was saying, 'You can't do that'."

Adding to the confusion was that the selection criteria had clearly been put in place to assist in instances of a stalemated selection process, when two gymnasts displayed equal skill and performances through trials that a preference could not be reached. However, in the case of the 1992 Olympic selection, the trials had not yet been completed.

Gibbs' latest skinfold test was also returned as 38mm, but was not being used by selectors. Furthermore, what Ju Ping and the AIS had not revealed was that another West Australian – Jane Warrilow – had returned skinfold results higher than Gibbs, but had not been dismissed. The premature ruling out of Gibbs was also in contrast to the patience the selectors had shown to Victoria's Joanna Hughes, who was recuperating from an elbow operation and had not competed in 11 months to that point.

"They are giving Hughes every chance and rightfully so," your grandad told *The West Australian*. "Why, then, take a pedantic position with Gibbs?"

The irony was that Hughes was eventually ruled out of the Games through injury, but your grandad's support of the patience shown towards the gymnast again highlighted what his priority was above all else: the athlete.

People over process.

The same mantra did not appear to exist for the AIS. It seemed the priority for the gymnastics establishment was to execute whatever plans the coach desired and to whittle down the squad.

Gibbs was the first target to be dismissed, either with legitimate cause or otherwise. The inconsistency in the approach towards Gibbs (expelled) and Warrilow (retained), who had both returned skinfold results above the recommended range, was telling of the true motives behind the premature omission of the former.

Gibbs was an outstanding gymnast who, on a good day, was among the best in the country. However, on a bad day, she struggled to make it through training exercises. Warrilow, on the other hand, was among a group of athletes favoured by Ju Ping and was considered an essential member of the national team. It was a clear contradiction that could have easily been resolved with honesty and transparency: consistent performances must be a required pre-requisite for selection and Gibbs did not meet that criteria at the time.

However, instead of honesty, Ju Ping, the AIS and the AGF opted for a confusing approach that resulted in the national public humiliation and embarrassment of a 14-year-old girl, who first had to endure her expulsion being read out in front of the trialling squad through a pre-prepared statement, before having had newspaper headlines splashed around the country labelling her as being too fat to go to the Olympics. The even more heartbreaking part for the athlete was that she was stuck in an environment and with people that appeared to show no empathy towards her or her situation.

The strict approach of Ju Ping's training methods demanded a complete communications blackout, with the exception of one phone call a week. That included restricting gymnasts from having any contact with their families while in camp.

"We are not allowed to talk to the girls over there except on their day off once a week but she called Monday and she was most upset," Gibbs' mother Cheryl told *The Australian* at the time the story broke. "She was very confused and she didn't know where she stood or what she wanted to do – whether she wanted to fight or give in. She said she couldn't sleep and it had upset her training. There's no one there to comfort her at a time like this except her coaches."

Her coaches weren't there, though. They had been. They weren't anymore. They had been expelled, too. WAIS mentor Liz Chetkovich had been at the trials assisting the WA contingent, but had been expelled from the AIS after fighting for the rights of Gibbs.

"When it came to 1992, it was clear we were going to have half the team, but some people weren't happy about that," Chetkovich said.

"I actually didn't agree with Tracy being in the team, because her performances were too inconsistent, but Ju Ping tried to get rid of her because of her skinfolds. She should have been up-front and said, 'The process requires you to do your work consistently and Tracy doesn't sit inside that' and I would have thought that was fair enough, but the way they went about it had it front page news that Tracy Gibbs was too fat, when she was beautiful.

"I got kicked out of the Olympic training camp, because I was saying that either she lets Tracy trial, or neither Tracy nor Jane can trial. Ju Ping needed Jane for the team, so I took Jane out of the training environment and went and trained her in the strength and conditioning gym and I said: 'I'm taking her, because according to your criteria, she's too fat to train'.

"So I took her away and then in the residences, Warwick Forbes (AIS head coach) came up to me and gave me a letter saying, 'You've been banned from the AIS, you should pack your bags and leave immediately'. So I was kicked out of the Olympic Games trial and I had to look on from the stands, because I stood up for that principle and said either both were in, or neither were in.

"I went and stayed at the Canberra Motor Village and I was banned from travelling with Australian gymnastics for about 12 months. That was the lowest point, in my opinion, where Gymnastics Australia allowed a girl's name to be splashed all over the papers that she was too fat."

It was a challenging case that had perceptions of a conflict of interest: an AIS coach was doubling as the national coach and had been given unfettered discretion on selections to the point they were contradicting the sport's own criteria. And there seemed to be little consideration given for the potential emotional and psychological damage being inflicted on an athlete – in this case a 14-year-old girl.

Your grandad had seen enough. He penned a column titled "Selection fast-track – to court" for *The West Australian* in which he labelled the selection controversies of athletes such as Gibbs and 1988 Seoul Olympics cyclist Tony Davis as being far too frequent, despite being easily avoided. He wrote the warning of, "To proceed on our current path is a fast track to court – and not the court on which sports should be played".

Your grandad's aim took in two targets: first the Australian Cycling Federation, for not only its involvement in the Davis issue, but also in the fight for the selection of Darren Hill, who had been overlooked for Barcelona. He also attacked the sport for its employment of Charlie Walsh in the dual role of AIS coach and national coach, which he argued created clear conflicts of interest.

His second broadside was fired at gymnastics, following on from the conflicted interests of Walsh with the identical situation that Ju Ping was in with her sport. Your grandad pointed out that funding was tied to the performance of athletes and if an athlete was not selected for a team, then they could not post results that, in-turn, drew that funding. That created a significant impetus for AIS coaches working as national coaches to select their own AIS athletes for major international competitions.

Even if the conflicts of interest did not eventuate, they remained clear, created negative perceptions and made it impossible for anyone – athlete or administrator – to have full confidence that selections were being made objectively.

Your grandad wrote the piece because he felt the number of selection controversies had increased dramatically in the years leading up to the Barcelona Olympics. He himself had been involved in several and he listed reasons for that, one of which was that "organisations (such as WAIS) now assist athletes to fight for their rights. Previously, it was left to the individual, who had neither the time, the resources nor the clout to get a result".

Your grandad was ready to lead the Western Australian Institute of Sport into whatever battle it needed to fight in order to protect the rights of its athletes. And the AIS had just entered his crosshairs.

"From 92 onwards, that was when we were clearly at war with gymnastics and the AIS," Liz Chetkovich said. "That was when it all started."

Western Australia ended up with strong gymnastics representation at the 1992 Olympics, with Michelle Telfer (travelling reserve), Jane Warrilow and Brooke Gysen helping their country to a seventh-place finish. The state accounted for just under 50 per cent of the national team.

The addition of WAIS coach Andrei Rodionenko to the coaching staff was also a credit to the work of the Institute. The representation was reflective of a positive Olympic cycle across the board for WAIS, with WA making up 13 per cent of the 292 competitors and 146 officials that Australia sent to Barcelona – well above the nine per cent target.

However, the battle for the rights of Tracy Gibbs had been lost; she had not received a reprieve and an option to continue trialling. And while the next Olympic cycle began and brought with it a focus on Atlanta, the episode did not sit well with your grandad and the tension between WAIS and the national setup was palpable.

"The issue of Olympic team selections is another recurring problem at the national level," your grandad wrote for the WAIS 1991-92 Annual Report, which took in the Barcelona Olympics.

"Subjective selection criteria and the inconsistent interpretation of published criteria stained too many team selections in the lead-up to Barcelona. It is inevitable that these matters will end up in undesirable court battles if the Australian Olympic Committee

(AOC) and the ASC (Australian Sports Commission) don't insist on selection criteria that ensure all athletes receive their basic rights."

The continued growth of the state institutes also resulted in a new wave of confusion around the national structure.

The Australian Institute of Sport that was constructed was not done so in accordance with Professor John Bloomfield's original vision, but was more of a broken-down, simplified and cheaper version for the Federal Government to implement. The state institutes that were supposed to be so crucial to the success of Bloomfield's network were never created alongside the AIS, causing several issues, one of which was the ongoing uncertainty of roles and responsibilities.

Had the network of state-based bodies been formed by the Federal Government at the same time as the AIS, there likely would have been a far more cohesive and collaboration working relationship. However, that was not the case and it had been left up to the state governments to form their own institutes and then, in-turn, up to those institutes to develop and build a vision for sport in their state.

For WA and WAIS, that resulted in a highly-successful institute with a gymnastics program that was competitive with the national body, yet supported by far less resources.

"There was constant war," said Ric Charlesworth, Olympic icon, former Federal Member of Parliament and, at the time, a board member of the Australian Sports Commission.

"The WAIS gymnastics program got $40,000 a year from the federal body, but was producing half the national team, so they were being funded by WAIS and by chook raffles, yet producing as many elite athletes as the AIS, which consumed the majority of the sport's funding. That was a constant source of aggravation.

"Rationalising the state institutes and the federal institute was one of the constant struggles of that time. I would have had my battles with Wal, I'm sure, but that would have been five per cent of the time and most of the time, we were fighting for the same thing: a fairer distribution of the funds from the Sports Commission and the value of decentralised programs."

The national system was fragmented. The Canberra mentality was such that it believed it had a right to dictate national initiatives, however, the body had no justification to do so. The states had been left to fend for themselves and, in the case of WA and Victoria, they did not want nor need intervention from the AIS. Your grandad had a very clear opinion of the AIS: it was an equal – a state-based/territory-based institute – nothing more, nothing less.

"The role of the AIS in the national system is another issue that must be resolved," your grandad wrote in the 1992-93 WAIS Annual Report.

"There remains a clear role for the AIS in providing a residential program where necessary, a national training centre and research programs. However, the AIS is no longer pre-eminent in the national system and to avoid confusion, it must be prepared to accept a role alongside other institutes as an equal player in each sport's national plan."

Gymnastics and the AIS's program in the sport had reached a stalemate with the states, but it was about to play a move that was so radical it was bewildering that it was ever proposed. Yet, not only was it proposed, it was approved.

AIS and national coach Ju Ping Tian had grown up in a country that had a very different view of the world to Australia. It was a country that was willing to implement systems that would unlikely align with the values of most Australians.

One in particular was the initiative to remove talented athletes from their homes and families and send them to national training centres – in Ju Ping's case, that was the gymnastics group in Beijing. The athletes were housed at the training centre and were to dedicate their lives to achieving success. It was a system that resulted in many talented athletes disappearing; burnt out and cast aside.

However, the sheer population of a country like China,

coupled with the incredible financial contribution into systems that operate in that way, particularly from communist countries which looked at international sport as a way to portray an image of political and societal superiority, guaranteed it success on the international stage.

Australia's own Olympic icon Ric Charlesworth said in the interview for this book that two aspects make a country successful in sport: numbers and money. The methods of countries such as China – and it was not alone; the USSR operated similar methods – utilised both to great effect.

The cultural difference in the weighting of the negative effects against the positive results ensured the methods were viewed as nothing but successful. That would never be the case in a country such as Australia, which would view the social isolation as potentially having a long-term negative and dangerous psychological impact on the athletes and that would make the system unsatisfactory, regardless of the results it achieved.

Yet the Ju Ping plan, sanctioned and supported by the Australian Gymnastics Federation, which was supported and sanctioned by the Australian Institute of Sport, had proposed exactly that: gymnasts who were identified by the national coach for training at the highest level were to relocate and take up residence at the national training centre in Canberra for an unspecified duration of time. If the athlete elected not to relocate, they would forfeit access to funding support and their potential selection for national teams would be impacted.

When your grandad took aim at dual-role coaches who mentored at the AIS as well as guiding the national team, he did so in part in objection to the funding filtering to institute programs being tied to the performances of athletes. Therefore, the model proposed for implementation by Ju Ping had the potential for a top-end athlete exodus out of the states, which would result in performance-based funding being withdrawn given there would be little to no representation remaining from the states, which would result in the closing of state-based programs or restructuring them into feeder systems.

It was the AGF's endgame: it not only brought the best athletes to Canberra, but also ensured the states became feeders into the AIS system instead of elite bases in their own right.

"I was on the board of the Australian Sports Commission and John Coates, now heavily involved in the Olympic movement, he was deputy chairman of the Australian Institute of Sport," said David Hatt, former WAIS board member.

"I was told I had to represent the Board in the negotiations between the States and the Commonwealth over the gymnastics program. I didn't believe that our program at a national level was where it should have been, so I went to see Ju Ping. Many things were happening inside gymnastics – it was like a nest of vipers.

"WAIS had good programs, good facilities and we were producing good athletes. This huge fight erupted and I went to Coates and said, 'We can't do this; there's no solution'.

"Ju Ping had limited English and she told me this story about all these little trees, with one big tree in the middle and if you water all the trees, the water doesn't help the big tree grow. The big tree was the gymnastics program in Canberra. I could understand the analogy, but she was arrogant, she was used to centralisation and she'd come from China and her way was the only way."

The proposal made little sense to states such as WA and Victoria, which were regularly producing internationally competitive gymnasts: the system was not broken, why fix it?

Then there was the concerning issue of athlete welfare: the AIS was demanding WAIS send its best athletes east. This was a demand coming from a body that just sanctioned treatment of a 14-year-old WA girl that resulted in newspaper headlines labelling her fat. The strict regime had prevented the girl from having contact with the support system she so desperately needed and, when the state coach had attempted to stand up for the girl's rights, the coach was banned from the AIS.

There was no merit in the proposal, no justification for it and your grandad saw it as holding an absurd potential to devastate the lives of children and their families. There would be nothing the AIS or the AGF could say that would satisfy WAIS or your grandad that the system would be executed with diligence around athlete welfare: the entire country had just seen first-hand through the Tracy Gibbs issue how the national system dealt with young athletes.

"The conflict was all a question of: do you need to leave Western Australia to be selected for the Australian team?," WAIS Chairman from 1984-94 Bruce Elliott said.

"We weren't stupid enough to say they'd never leave the state and we knew they needed to go to camps and what-have-you. Ju Ping brought a Chinese view. She wasn't trying to hurt the kids, it's just what she knew; in China, if you want them to be successful, then you pick them and move them.

"One of the other problems was that it wasn't like we had 200 kids and 50 would go to Canberra; we might have had eight and if they left, then it's not a viable squad. We needed to ensure depth in a squad to ensure our athletes were competitive nationally."

It was an issue that was bubbling away behind the scenes in 1994 as WAIS was celebrating its first decade in operation and, as if attempting to fortify its position for the battle that was about to begin, curious stories began appearing in the media, such as *The West Australian*'s piece titled "WA program keeps happy star at home". The story discussed how the investment and results of the WAIS gymnastics program had allowed athletes such as the successful Jenny Smith to remain and thrive in the support of her home state.

"Andrei (Rodionenko) and the other Russian coaches at WAIS have the know-how to take me as far as I can go in gymnastics," Smith told the paper. "Mum and dad are always there to help if there is a problem. I can't imagine what it would be like to rely on strangers for every need. I don't think I would be happy training without someone who really cares to go home to at night".

It was a piece that, with the benefit of hindsight, had a clear agenda being driven by WAIS. Particularly as it included the suggestion that Smith would prefer to "give up (the sport) than go without the security of her family". The message was simple: the national system being proposed was not wanted by athletes and would result in careers ending, not flourishing.

"Once you start playing with the lives of young girls, you get some pretty powerful people involved and the media loves controversy," Elliott said.

"This was at the top end of the controversy scale. Ju Ping: she was a bit like (national cycling coach) Charlie Walsh, really, because they vehemently believed what they were doing was right, they didn't believe they were screwing anybody. I honestly believe Ju Ping thought this was the way and it was the only way she knew.

"She then got bitter to the point they were saying it was their way or the highway. It really should have been the AIS saying, 'This is not the way and we need to develop something else in Australia', but they weren't willing to. I say they got nasty, but to me it was more peripheral with the odd phone call.

"To your dad, it was blood on the floor stuff."

Comments by your grandad around the approach the governance of the Australian Gymnastics Federation and the Australian Institute of Sport were littered throughout the WAIS Annual Reports spanning its first decade and he urged both to "take a realistic approach" in the national strategy. He was particularly pointed in his remarks that the AGF's actions were a "blot on the sport" and believed the body's "integrity in this matter has been brought into question".

It must be mentioned that your grandad understood that not every sport was able to have a base in every state. He commented that "it is recognised that limited talent bases might not justify an Intensive Training Centre program in all states in all sports". However, WA was a highly successful state in gymnastics: WAIS athletes made up two of the five competitors at the 1994 Commonwealth Games and its gymnasts dominated the medals, achieving two gold and one silver, with the AIS contributing just one bronze to the tally.

The state's program was critical to Australia's success. It was imperative it survived, but it was doomed to fail, because, despite the heavy resistance from WA and Victoria, publicly in parliament and the fiery rhetoric from parents, the AGF approved the proposal to relocate and centralise athletes at the AIS and used the threat of funding cuts to ensure obedience from the states.

The AGF and AIS refuted all of those assertions, claiming that while the wording of the national plan permitted that action, neither body had any intention of acting in such a way.

"It is simply not the case. We are keen to develop a network where state and national institutes work together to achieve a common objective," AIS boss John Boultbee told *The West Australian*.

"In gymnastics, the national plan is clear and relocation will only take place in consultation between the athlete, coach, the parents and national coach. If the parents object, a program will be worked out with the gymnast and he or she will not be denied funding. We're about achieving top results and if an athlete does not operate within the national plan he or she cannot expect to get the same level of assistance."

Despite the promise of "consultation" and the assurances that athletes and their parents would first be spoken to before any plans were implemented, the AGF dispatched letters to gymnasts who were expected to relocate to the AIS.

It listed WA gymnast David Schneider on the document, however, neither Schneider nor his parents had been consulted over the move. If they had been, the AIS would have known the athlete's preference had always been to remain at WAIS, given at that time he was in the second year of a mechanical apprenticeship.

Schneider was 16-years-old at the time and had never been beaten in national competitions. It was yet another example of the misalignment between AIS and AGF assurances and the subsequent actions taken.

Tempers were flaring and the actions of Ju Ping Tian was not helping.

The closed-shop that was the gymnastics program reached new heights of secrecy when at the 1994 World Championships in Brisbane the national coach excluded Western Australians Salli Wills and Cathy Keyser from competing in the all around competition. She then refused to explain why, telling *The West Australian:* "I don't want to, or need to, say anything".

Each nation was permitted three gymnasts to compete the all around competition and Australia would have lost nothing had Wills and Keyser competed, regardless of their placings. Instead, Ju Ping only allowed Joanna Hughes to compete in the event and the WA pair lost the opportunity for valuable experience.

It was a poor look for the national establishment, which appeared to be taking out its frustrations over the standoff with the states and WAIS on the athletes. Ju Ping's decree around communication-blackouts when in competition and training also meant there was a total media ban on all athletes and staff. The blackout was an ongoing issue, but it was one that was again supported by the sport's hierarchy.

President Jim Barry claimed: "It is like trying to speak to a footballer at half time – no player or coach would allow that".

Well, it was not like that at all. It was more akin to the media speaking to a cricketer at the close of play of a day of Sheffield Shield, which prior to the 90s, during the 90s and ever since the 90s has happened at the close of every day, for every match. And footballers and their coaches are now regularly interviewed at all breaks, while cricketers are mic'd up for TV audiences and interviewed during actual play.

The ultimate irony is that gymnastics would these days bend over backwards for the level of coverage being asked of it at the '94 Championships. As one Dutch reporter who was frustrated at the ban told *The West Australian*: "One would think the host country would be delighted with the opportunity to use a high profile event like this to expose their own competitors. The old Soviet team used to do this, but that does not happen any longer".

The only person permitted to talk to the media and explain why Wills and Keyser had been omitted from the all around competition was Ju Ping, yet she refused to do so until constantly pushed by *The West*'s reporter on the ground, Gene Stephan.

"The world championships are for results, not experience," Ju Ping said. "If their training is not ready they should not be given the opportunity to compete in the championship".

The ban left the media with no choice but to do what the media does whenever it is shut out of something: find alternative sources. Those sources were telling a very different story to that of Ju Ping, one which indicated assistant coaches Andrei Rodionenko – from WAIS – and Victoria's Fiona Bird were "furious at the decision" and that "the Chinese coach ... is concerned that the regional programs look to be having more success than her own".

Ju Ping's decision was made to appear even more irrational when just four months later Geraldton's Wills became the first Western Australian to win gymnastics gold at a Commonwealth Games when she took out the beam at Victoria, Canada. Wills' family was unable to congratulate or even talk with their 14-year-old daughter because of the communications ban. The first time in three weeks that the athlete spoke to her family was when she arrived home from the Games on 26 August.

Wills' performance had come after another strong year from WAIS when Jenny Smith in May 1994 became only the second Australian gymnast to win an international all around title when she claimed the China Cup in Beijing, defeating competitors from powerhouse countries such as Romania, Russia and China.

The Institute's status was growing within Australia – reflected in Liz Chetkovich being named Western Australian Coach of the Year – and midway through 1994, talented 15-year-old South Australian and World Championships representative Rebecca Stoyel overlooked the AIS in Canberra in favour of moving to WA to prepare for the Commonwealth Games. It was a move that was encouraged by Stoyel's coach, but one that again showed the AIS program as a less attractive option to that of WAIS, even in status among the states.

That point was driven home when WAIS identified an urgent need for its athletes to gain international experience ahead of the 1995 World Championships in Japan; a view that was as logical as it was in contradiction to the stance against Wills and Keyser competing at the previous year's Championships due to insufficient experience. The Institute organised a month-long competition and training tour of the US, beginning in Reno, Nevada. When the other states heard about the initiative, they requested to join and the group expanding to include 12 of Australia's best gymnasts.

A power shift was occurring and the AIS was losing. WAIS coach Andrei Rodionenko was among the first to bear the consequences of this feud, as his selection for any national team was constantly shrouded in uncertainty.

Your grandad had made up his mind that the AIS and AGF were immoral in the plan they wanted to implement and could not be trusted. The evidence to him was too clear to ignore.

The AGF and AIS claimed to be accommodating to athletes around its national relocation and training plan, yet they dispatched letters without warning demanding those same athletes relocate to Canberra. They claimed to be consultative, yet banned coaches from training sessions and complained that "people have taken entrenched positions" – Boultbee, quoted by *The West* – when views contrary to their own appeared.

They claimed an athlete's national selection would not be jeopardised by a refusal to relocate, yet two Western Australians had for reasons known only to the national coach been barred from competing in the all around event at a World Championships they had every right to compete in. They claimed to have the welfare of gymnasts in mind, yet they sanctioned actions that resulted in a 14-year-old girl being labelled fat in newspapers across the country.

"It was a vicious fight nationally," said current WAIS Director Steve Lawrence.

"Wally got into huge stoushes with guys like Jim Barry, who

was the president of the AGF and Jim Ferguson, who was the CEO of the Australian Sports Commission. I remember Wally coming back from (a meeting) and saying that he thought Jim was going to hit him.

"He was visibly shaken by it a couple of days later when he came back from Canberra."

WAIS continued to produce elite performances and introduce innovative initiatives. However, that meant the issues with the national movements reached flash point. In May 1995, WAIS announced its gymnastics program would be closed by December.

It would have seemed like a sudden turn in fortunes for a state that was still producing outstanding athletes, but it was a decision that had been forced. WAIS and the parents of the state's gymnasts had been lobbying and attempting to fight the implementation of the AIS and AGF's national strategy for years, but their cries had achieved nothing.

"The AIS was a very average organisation in those days," said David Hatt, former WAIS and Australian Sports Commission Board Member.

"Robert de Castella (Australian Institute of Sport Director from 1990-95), he's a great person, a wonderful athlete and a national hero, but he didn't understand this issue and whatever Ju Ping would say, that's what he would say. So, Hawke and Keating (former Prime Ministers Bob Hawke and Paul Keating) and whoever else got involved, would be faced with de Castella saying these things, while we're saying he wouldn't know.

"But how do you do that? I'm David Hatt from Narrogin and this is Wally Foreman, from Bruce Rock – who gives a shit? This is Rob de Castella, a national hero."

There was little other option than to publicly concede defeat and shut the doors, which would mean the sacking of up to 14 coaches, including the internationally renowned Russian contingent WAIS had recruited.

"It is simply a case of stripping us of our best gymnasts and if we don't comply we will be deprived of federal funds," your grandad told *The West Australian* when discussing the impact of the AIS and AGF's actions on WAIS's program.

"The AGF's relocation plan is totally inappropriate for 12 to 16-year-old children. The AGF and Australian Sports Commission, which has supported this plan, can now hold themselves responsible for the demise of one of the country's leading gymnastics programs. The proposals are designed to preserve the AIS gymnastics program and destroy those at State institutes – it is gymnastics genocide."

It was a move that undoubtedly contained a level of politicking: your grandad had been in the media for far too long for him to be oblivious to the storm the decision would create. It was more likely that he was counting on it, because he was not winning the battle behind closed doors and he needed the media to carry the message further.

That passing of the baton was editorialised when *News Chronical* on 19 April 1995 published a cartoon depicting the AIS as a fierce bear swiping at a character representing WA and saying, "To Canberra she must go!", with large words beneath reading: "An Eastern Bloc". An editorial titled "No place like home" was run in *The Sunday Times* and lambasted the Australian Gymnastics Federation and the Australian Institute of Sport, saying their centralisation policy "tears at the very heart of Australian society – the family unit" and adding that "the move neglects one basic ingredient to the whole callous affair – the young athletes themselves".

The Federal Government was soon involved in the situation as a result of a combination of the media attention nationally, the lobbying from parents in both WA and Victoria, and the engagement of the State Government's Minister for Sport Norman Moore. Moore was particularly aggressive in seeking a resolution and, as quoted by the *Canberra Times*, advised Federal Minister for Sport John Faulkner that the plan intended for implementation by the AIS and AGF put the "welfare of young children at risk".

Another ally also emerged. Your grandad was a 12-year-old selling ice creams during the British Empire and Commonwealth Games in Perth, watching on as Australia's best athletes took on the world. One of those athletes was high jump silver medallist Chilla Porter.

Porter, 35 years later, had taken up the role of WAIS Chairman, following the resignation of Dr Bruce Elliott, and was a crucial ally in fighting the AGF's plans. "The folly of this whole exercise is that there is no evidence to support the argument that our medal prospects will be better if the program is centralised in Canberra," Porter said.

The pushback against the national bodies was gaining momentum and Senator Faulkner ordered an urgent inquiry when claims of abuse at the Australian Institute of Sport began to surface from the parent groups around the country. The groups alleged the AIS program was operating a "concentration camp" that physically and mentally abused young female gymnasts and showed them how to vomit to avoid putting on weight.

The inquiry largely dismissed the claims and any wrong-doing by Ju Ping as head coach, but the allegations served as a clear example of the underlying current of disharmony being felt by the crucial stakeholder groups.

The States did not want this plan, the parents didn't want it and neither did their children – the athletes – while governments at both state and Federal level were rapidly increasing their involvement. AIS boss John Boultbee had claimed that opponents to its plan had taken "entrenched positions". That was debatable, given the only people seemingly for the plan's implementation were those at the AIS and AGF.

Boultbee's presence and influence were among the main drivers of positive change in the culture of the AIS and its relationship with the states. He helped shift the national system to a far more cohesive and positive place, but on this issue, he was caught in a difficult situation.

The outcry across Australia was also beginning to gain traction. The Australian Gymnastics Federation's Annual General Meeting was approaching on 17 June 1995 and Victoria was preparing to move a motion of no confidence against the 24-year incumbent president Jim Barry, executive director Peggy Browne and women's technical director Kim Dowdell.

It was a controversial meeting: the constitution did not permit a vote of no confidence to take place, so Victoria instead nominated a challenger, South Australia's Lance Otto, for the presidency. It was a clear sign of the lack of faith in Barry's leadership that Otto had been the former's vice president for 24 years.

However, two rounds of voting failed to give either candidate a majority, which resulted in Otto taking a moral stance and withdrawing, as he believed only a clear majority vote could end the disharmony tearing the sport apart.

Barry retained his position by default, but his authority had been struck a damaging blow, with WA Gymnastics Association president Bob Biltoft later saying: "We are extremely disappointed with the outcome of this meeting and feel it will have a lasting effect on the future of Australian gymnastics".

However, one positive out of a meeting described as "bitter and nasty" was the election of 1968 gymnastics Olympian Murray Chessell as vice president. In Chessell the AGF had a new member of the leadership who wanted a consultative relationship with the states.

The changes made under Chessell's guidance were enough to convince your grandad and the WAIS Board to continue its gymnastics program. However, the funding cuts – or redistribution out of the states into a centralised Canberra model – already dealt by the AIS and AGF under the Olympic Athlete Program and through the Australian Sports Commission were telling and required the sourcing by the institute of an additional $80,000 a year.

The position gave birth to the WAIS Fliers initiative: a marketing campaign that made heroes out of WA's gymnasts and provided the corporate sector with a range of benefits in exchange for a $250 contribution. It was an innovative and successful campaign and the Fliers program remained a part of WAIS until the closure of the gymnastics program in 2016.

The intensifying political intervention further developed in 1996 when WA Premier Richard Court wrote to Prime Minister John Howard. He urged Federal Government intervention and the feud approached its end. The AGF had made a mistake that would cost it its national strategy.

One of the policies outlined in the centralisation plan threatened to revoke the Olympic Athlete Program funding from any gymnast who refused to relocate to Canberra. The fact the AGF argued it would never enforce the caveat was irrelevant; the caveat itself was in direct opposition to the Coalition's sports policy, which spelled out the need for developing athletes to have genuine choice between entering residential AIS programs or receiving support at home-based training facilities without feeling disadvantaged.

The Federal Government had been reluctant to intervene in the stoush, but the AGF's approach to the states had left it with little option. Federal Minister for Sport Warwick Smith said: "It is important that the AGF and the AIS offer an effective choice without heavy-handed action or approach".

The Federal Government ripped Australian gymnastics from a state of destructive in-fighting and prevented its demise. The "gymnastics genocide" was coming to an end and was officially over in May 1996. It was heralded by *The West Australian*'s headline of: "Officials forced into gym back-flip".

The article quoted WA Liberal Senator Ian Campbell as having made the strong statement of: "The AIS, Australian Sports Commission and gymnastics officials are beginning to understand we are fair dinkum about our policies which are designed to achieve a good outcome for sport."

The intervention of the Federal Government had forced a board meeting of the Australian Gymnastics Federation, which unanimously passed a new national plan for women, which *The*

West outlined as having "removed national coach Ju Ping Tian's absolute control over the relocation of gymnasts". The plan removed any ability for the national bodies to apply funding penalties to athletes who refused to relocate, as well as the states to which they belonged.

"We've moved to get the wording of the national plan correct, but the spirit of the plan is no different," AGF President Jim Barry told *The West*.

Barry then conceded the structure of funding for state-based programs had changed, but the AGF acted like it did not understand what all the fuss was about. The State Government took the new proposal to clubs and associations, consulting with parents and the WA Gymnastics Association, and ensuring they were satisfied before it endorsed the changes.

The changes ended a bitter feud that emerged publicly 18 months prior and produced few winners. The bid to stop the implementation of an ill-thought-out, or at the very least, inappropriately prioritised plan had been won by the states and that was largely due to the work of your grandad and the unrelenting, loyal staff around him, in particular Liz Chetkovich.

However, WAIS paid a heavy price. When it announced it would close its gymnastics program, it was forced to close both its male and female programs. The former never reopened in its original structure. The recruitment by WAIS of former Soviet head coach Andrei Rodionenko in 1991 had marked an incredible achievement for Australian gymnastics, let alone the state institute, but that achievement had been lost by the end of 1996.

Rodionenko had endured as much disrespect from the national hierarchy as he was willing to accept. Instead, he accepted a job offer from Canada to become head coach of its national women's program. It is bewildering to think that Rodionenko, a man who was considered the architect of the USSR's highly-regarded women's program, was only included in national teams after fierce debate and protest from WAIS and was only ever rarely consulted by the AGF.

"He has waited for the past six weeks in the hope that the AGF would develop a new structure for women's gymnastics," your grandad told *The West Australian* at the time of Rodionenko's departure.

"This hasn't occurred and he now has no option but to reconsider his professional integrity and his future. The manner in which he was treated by the previous AGF hierarchy was a disgrace. There were obviously people threatened by his record and achievements."

The AGF refuted those claims at the time, but as journalist Gene Stephan wrote in her piece for *The West Australian* covering the departure of the coach: "Rodionenko's record is unrivalled in international gymnastics and his results dwarf those achieved by Ju Ping".

But perhaps it was Chetkovich who paid the biggest price of all. The loss of funding and Rodionenko forced a coaching restructure to plug holes. That involved moving junior coaches into head coach roles and Chetkovich volunteering to move sideways and take on a part-time position to manage the program.

It took 10 years for WAIS's gymnastics program to recover to a point where Chetkovich could move up to four days' work a week, but she never worked full-time for the gymnastics program again. At the time of her move out of coaching and into program management, the Olympic cycle for Sydney had begun.

Like any Australian athlete or coach at that time, it was Chektovich's dream to represent her country at the home Games. The impact from the feud with the AIS and the AGF had torn those dreams apart. Chetkovich went to Sydney, but as a commentator and not a representative of Australia or WAIS.

"I never got the opportunity to coach at my home Olympics, because the previous budgetary constraints effectively forced me prematurely into a program management role," she said. "It took me quite some time to get over the fact that I had to hand that opportunity on at that time."

WAIS was, of course, not the only body to suffer collateral damage from the battle. The losses that occurred on the other side were as significant as they were a catalyst for change.

AGF President Jim Barry had been lobbying for the top job in international gymnastics, but the near-miss he suffered at the Australian body's AGM, his subsequent weakened grip and the bitter in-fighting that had been waging for the better part of a decade in the sport in his own country had derailed any push for election as president of the International Gymnastics Federation.

Barry secured less than 10 votes of a possible 102 in his attempts to become that body's president. He had been a member of the international executive for 12 years and junior vice president for eight years, but lost those roles also. Barry resigned from the Australian Gymnastics Federation shortly after, ending a 25-year tenure.

His departure was followed by those of some of his closest allies: executive director Peggy Browne and financial director David Wood. In a domino effect *The West Australian* labelled as a "gymnastics fallout", the resignation of the three top officials was also accompanied by "the fall from grace of controversial head coach Ju Ping Tian", who was retained as the AIS women's head coach, but removed as the national women's head coach.

Ju Ping was not at the helm for the Sydney Games and the coach's profile continued to suffer through her methods, with a lengthy column in *The Australian* in July 1996 detailing how a Ju Ping outburst reduced two 15-year-old girls to tears in the Georgia Dome in Atlanta during an Olympic training session.

Ju Ping's national position was filled by affable American Peggy Liddick, the former coach of Olympic gold medallist and world champion Shannon Miller. Liddick had already been in Australia prior to her appointment, working in a visiting role with state institutes throughout the year; she was, of course, hosted by WAIS and the VIS.

Liddick brought a completely new and consultative approach to national gymnastics. From the start, she said every state had something to offer and that her first course of action would be to engage the top coaches from around the country – a year too late to save Russian Andrei Rodianenko from being lost to Australian gymnastics.

Her statement of, "I want them (the states and nation's top coaches) to make a wish list and I will try to make it happen", was a collaborative gesture that had been missing from the sport for some time. Liddick's appointment was significant not just for her attitude, but because it marked the first time since Ju Ping joined the AIS in 1984 that the role of AIS head coach and national head coach had been split.

It was also only one of several appointments that began the sport on the road to the cohesive, well-oiled and cooperative unit it evolved into. The hiring of Jane Allen as the AGF's executive director, plus Murray Chessell being elected as the body's President, completed the assembly of a new administration while, as mentioned, John Boultbee's influence at the AIS was a fresh and welcomed change.

"We were successful in gymnastics in proving to them they were wrong, but it really did take a long, long time," said Bruce Elliott, WAIS Chairman throughout the majority of the feud.

"It wasn't until they replaced Ju Ping with the American coach (that we began seeing change). So, maybe we weren't successful, but she (Liddick) had a different view and all of a sudden our view blended perfectly with hers: you could train in the west and then go to a camp for a few weeks over east.

"No-one ever argued with that. The argument was that you can't take a 10-year-old and move them to Canberra. It might work for some kids and give them that option, but don't say to them if they don't move then they won't be selected."

The period had a significant impact on your grandad. In 2001 upon his resignation from the Western Australian Institute of Sport, he told *The West Magazine*: "What that really impressed on me was the win-at-all-costs attitude just wasn't acceptable. Up until then, I'd always thought, you know, you do everything within reason to win.

"But then I saw people who were quite prepared to do things that were completely anti-social and unacceptable to our society to try and get a result."

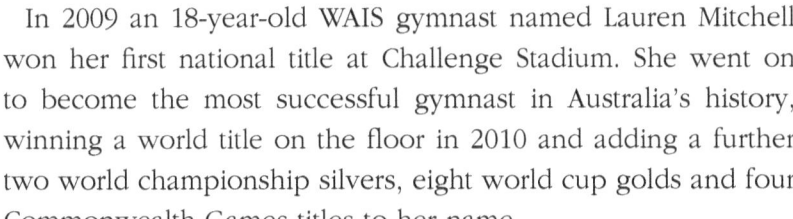

In 2009 an 18-year-old WAIS gymnast named Lauren Mitchell won her first national title at Challenge Stadium. She went on to become the most successful gymnast in Australia's history, winning a world title on the floor in 2010 and adding a further two world championship silvers, eight world cup golds and four Commonwealth Games titles to her name.

I covered that 2009 national championship. It was one of my first jobs covering an event as a journalist and it was arranged by Liz Chetkovich.

Everything that happened that day did so because in 1984 a man named Wally Foreman became the director of the Western Australian Institute of Sport. Everything from the nationals being held in the Challenge Stadium gymnasium, to Liz Chetkovich remaining involved in gymnastics and Lauren Mitchell having the opportunity to develop and compete in her home state. And even to me covering the event, having got the job because of a coach he put in place.

Your grandad brought into the Institute the people he believed could direct WA sport down the path it needed to go and he trusted and backed them to the hilt. He fought battles that emotionally and physically drained him and he did it because he believed in the people he had around him. And they all believed that the rights of WA athletes and coaches were worth fighting for.

"When we got the new WAIS administration building – I don't know if this was the same for everybody – and you walk up the windy steps, the first thing I would do was look to see if Wally was there," Chetkovich said.

"Truthfully. If he was there, it gave you this sense of safety. Wally was always ready to fight the fight, without a view of how he would look to others. He never concerned himself with how he would look to others, with keeping up appearances, or being politically correct; there was none of that and his motivation was always the athlete.

"Ju Ping Tian said to me before Sydney: 'You are so lucky to have Wally Foreman and I wish I had Wally Foreman fighting for me'."

Everything that happened that day in 2009 in the Challenge Stadium gymnasium – three years after he passed away – happened because of your grandad.

Chapter 14

Actions Have Consequences

Your grandad was not a universally loved person. That's important for you to understand, because pleasing everyone or being everyone's mate is an impossible idyll to pursue. You will only end up disappointing yourself if you try.

There were some who did not like your grandad's opinions and there were others who felt character traits of his left him overly stubborn and blinded to the merits of ideas that weren't his own. And there were some who did not enjoy your grandad's commentary on the radio: I witnessed that first hand when I was about 10-years-old.

I was woken by an immense, thunderous crack and the screeching of tyres. It was the night of the Western Australian Football League grand final and someone was unhappy their team lost and obviously was upset by your grandad's commentary of the event, because they had launched at our window a fist-sized rock with an obscenity-laced note elastic-banded around it.

Thankfully, their aim was as poor as their spelling and grammar and the rock had missed the window. It hit the wooden support beam holding up the gutters. We had a private phone number and address from then-on.

Your grandad achieved some amazing feats and helped progress Western Australian high performance sport to a level at which it had never previously been, but in doing so he moved against other people and he was never hesitant in publicly berating them if he felt it necessary. People such as Charlie Walsh, Ray Godkin, Ju Ping and Jim Barry probably all had moments where they wanted to throttle your grandad.

And by the early 90s they were not alone.

The achievements your grandad helped WAIS and WA mark were also made rapidly. Your grandad was aggressive in his pursuit of the betterment of the WA high performance sport system, but that aggressiveness could also come across in his personality.

On a local front, one of his first targets were clubs and associations.

One of the primary issues that drove the founding of the Western Australian Institute of Sport was your grandad's perception that the Department of Sport and Recreation and the clubs and associations of WA sports were mismanaging funding and inadequately utilising it. He believed there was too much needless spending, too much red tape and too many people looking out for their own interests instead of the interests of the sport.

In his characteristically honest – others would call it, "abrupt" – manner, your grandad did not hesitate in making those feelings known. In the very first WAIS Annual Report, he wrote: "One area of concern apparent in the first year is the fact that some WA Associations appear to have lost sight of their real purpose: the well-being and development of the athletes.

"The reasons for this are varied – domestic dissention, complicated committee structures, apathy and reluctance to challenge the national body are some of them. None of them are acceptable and collectively they are doing as much to retard high performance sport in this State as the problems mentioned earlier.

"Most will be satisfied that WAIS's first year goals have been achieved. But in all honesty, the lack of assistance to high performance sport previously made it easy for WAIS to make an early impact. The real task of establishing WAIS's credibility is just beginning.

"There are less excuses than ever before for West Australians not to win medals, score runs, throw goals or break records. The onus rests squarely on those entrusted with the money and those receiving it to make this development a success."

Athletics and swimming were among the first to be brought to task.

In addition to his notes about the sports in the WAIS Annual

Reports, your grandad suggested publicly that swimming should consider restructuring its club system. He said the eight major metropolitan clubs needed to be based at a 50m pool and have an indoor, heated facility, while the smaller centres should be zoned.

Your grandad believed the plan would allow for more successful talent identification, while the zoning would re-focus the sport on providing identification and development opportunities for as many swimmers as possible, instead of clubs and coaches attempting to identify and develop athletes they believed could be internationally successful. It was a system that was operating in Queensland to great effect and the QAS to this day is regarded as one of the strongest swimming programs in Australia.

Your grandad saved some of his most pointed comments for the administrators of athletics.

"The Athletics Association has the opportunity to encourage and promote the elite WA athlete and must be accountable for future performances," your grandad wrote in a column for *The West Australian* in 1985.

"There is just not enough top class competition here for our better athletes and they do not have the incentive to lift their performances. The association has done little to promote either the sport of athletics or its athletes. As a result, there is little glory associated with the sport in this state.

"By comparison, track and field athletes overseas, particularly in Europe, are heavily promoted by their associations and, thus, huge crowds come to watch meetings. When was the last time the AAWA attempted to promote one of its athletes through the media? It is essential that elite athletes are encouraged because as we find in other sports, one world-class competitor encourages others to follow.

"Governments, both at Federal and State level, are at long-last doing their bit to aid sport with financial aid and, in the case of athletics, it's time they started to be more professional and positive in their approach to producing world-class competitors. I also believe Little Athletics has had a detrimental, not beneficial, effect on the production of top-class athletes.

"In effect, little athletics defeated its purpose because its participants are pushed too hard by over-zealous parents and coaches. Unlike senior athletes, these kids are getting too much competition in their formative years and, as a result, injuries such as stress fractures and tendon problems, unheard of in youngsters a few years ago, are common-place.

"Given the number of world-class competitors WA produces in other sports, it's hard to justify the lack of top athletes produced here, particularly over the past 25 years. The AAWA has a new board structure and they are trying to make changes that will boost standards of competition.

"Hopefully we will see some world-class athletes as a result."

The State Government election of 1993 meant little more to your grandad than the event it was. His position at WAIS meant politics had become far more important in his life than it had in previous roles, but your grandad's view on the world was never politically linked.

He would have undoubtedly been apprehensive about the change of government, but that apprehension would have simply been in light of the positive contribution the previous government had made.

Your grandad was not naïve to politics, but he was trusting of people. He believed that he should and would be judged on his merits and achievements. It was perhaps that ideal that was naïve, because some people involved in the incoming Court Ministry instead preferred to prioritise politics and policy over merits.

I must state again: the issues that arose for your grandad throughout the 1990s had nothing to do with politics, it was to do with personalities. In fact, both sides of government had their strengths and weaknesses when it came to WAIS: Labor was more supportive and forthcoming with funding on a day-to-day basis, but the Liberals were the only party to ever contribute to capital works specifically for the Institute, leading not only to its standalone facility in the 1990s, but also its new, current facility built a few years ago.

They were issues linked to personalities, not parties, and the first of those personalities was the new Minister for Sport and Recreation, Doug Shave. He held the position for barely six months before resigning from the front bench for personal reasons, yet in that short time he instigated a process of opening the WAIS directorship position to the public market, forcing your grandad to reapply for his job.

It was a move that almost succeeded in removing him from the Institute and it was a process that continued with Shave's successor, Norman Moore, before your grandad was finally reappointed. And the drama haunted your grandad until the day he resigned, playing a significant role in him doing so.

Your grandad was interviewed for the WA Sports Federation publication *Sportsview* upon his resignation from WAIS in 2001, but before it went to print, he sent a private memo to the writer with two points, the second of which read: "Doug Shave. May I ask that the difficulties encountered with this Minister not be over-emphasised.

"I don't have any difficulties in saying that his period as Minister was one of the more difficult periods for WAIS and that I had to re-apply for my job during that period. However, I would prefer to focus on positives rather than negatives, if possible."

Out of respect to your grandad's wishes, some of the more intricate, personal details of this saga have been withheld. But, at the same time, this was a period of time that changed the course of your grandad's life and it led to a couple of major changes for WAIS and, therefore, should be told.

The Western Australian Institute of Sport is a QANGO: a quasi-autonomous non-governmental organisation. It received partial funding from the government, supported by funding from the corporate sector, and conducted work to benefit Western Australia and its citizens, but its employees were not government appointments.

Your grandad was employed at WAIS on three-year contracts from the moment he began in June 1984. Those contracts included a clause that permitted the Minister of Sport of the day to simply roll them over and initiate the next term as they approached completion and so long as everyone was satisfied to do so. If the WAIS Board was satisfied the director was leading the organisation in the right direction and the director was happy to continue, it would recommend the rollover to the Minister, who invariably obliged without debate.

That was how it worked for the first nine years of your grandad's employment, before different personalities had different views. There were concerning signs for your grandad almost immediately upon the change in government. Those concerns left a paper-trail among a series of lever-arch folders that your grandad kept for his entire life and even the existence of those folders is testament to his concerns over his position.

The first piece of paper among those documents is dated 14 April 1994. It was a fax from your grandad to WAIS Board Members John Inverarity – also a close friend of your grandad's and a highly respected former State cricket captain – and Jack Busch. It outlined the demands from Moore, through his Policy Officer Hallam Pereira, that even after having successfully reapplied for his position, your grandad's supposed three-year term was to be backdated to the time his previous contract expired – 30 June 1993.

The Minister was effectively attempting to place him on a two year and three-month contract. The date on that piece of paper alone tells the weary tale of the drawn-out trial your grandad was put through. He was adrift in uncertainty for 18 months, before being told his contract would be backdated, ensuring he would have to go through it all again just two years later.

Your grandad began keeping those personal files under the instruction of David Hatt and WAIS Chairman in the latter part of the 1990s Neil McKerracher.

"They were out to get him," Hatt said. "So I told him he needed to start keeping everything – everything – in case they tried to unfairly dismiss him and he needed a defence."

Hatt had been on the receiving end of the differences in personalities, as well. Ric Charlesworth, too. Albeit, both for more political reasons.

Hatt had a significant impact on the establishment of high performance sport in WA, but a week after the change of government he received a letter formally advising him "you are no longer a member of the WA Institute of Sport Board". It was an unceremonious end to an involvement in WAIS for one of the most pivotal people involved in establishing the Institute.

Hatt was not even invited to a WAIS function until the late 90s.

"I was really hurt by it and I was never invited to any functions, until the late 90s, because Wally was told he was not to have anything to do with me and Richard Charlesworth," Hatt said.

There is, of course, always two sides to a story and the more passive Dr Bruce Elliott, who was WAIS Chairman at the time, denied there was anything untoward in the process of requiring your grandad to reapply for his position. Elliott needed only to use himself as justification of that.

"In my 11 years, the issue of Wally's position only came up towards the end, but that wasn't because of your dad, that was because we were doing it for everyone," Elliott said.

"We did it for me: we were saying we needed to find someone to replace me, because I'd been there too long. Everyone has a use-by date. I don't know that they actually thought your dad's use-by date was up, it was just they were looking at a few people's positions. By then, your dad was starting to rub a couple of influential people up the wrong way and that's usually all you need: someone that's politically minded and who knows how to play the game.

"There were evaluations and interviews. I'm sure he felt quite bitter. It was difficult for me then. It was just a question of whether he was still the right man for the job and those things always turn out a bit nasty, but it turned out alright in the end."

Your grandad would have disagreed. He still considered it one of the most challenging periods of his professional career when discussing it with media almost a decade later. However, he kept his job and, while Elliott was measured in his response to the issue, it must also be noted that it was he who saved your grandad's position.

The three-person interview panel was split at one apiece; Elliott cast the deciding vote that ensured your grandad remained Director of the Western Australian Institute of Sport.

Athletics and swimming were the sports locally your grandad most took to task and in which he rubbed those "influential people" the wrong way.

Politics was not so much the issue as the people involved in those politics. So, while many of the personalities involved in the turmoil around your grandad's job were involved in the Liberal Party, that was not to say that the Liberal Party was out to get your grandad, more that it was the connection that brought the personalities together. The change in government therefore created opportunities for some disenfranchised quarters to rock a boat that had, until that moment, been sailing along quite smoothly.

Swimming was a sport that enjoyed those political ties and had strong Liberal connections in WA at the time. Dual Olympian Peter Evans, a gold medallist from the Moscow Games, retired from swimming after missing selection for the 1986 Commonwealth Games and unsuccessfully stood as the Liberal candidate for Perth that same year. It was a move that had him attempt to follow his father, Max Evans, into politics, with the latter a shadow minister for the Liberals until the 1993 election win, after which he became Minister for Finance, Racing and Gaming.

Then there was the McKenzies: Lyn McKenzie, nee McClements, achieved butterfly gold at the 1968 Mexico City Olympic Games and moved into coaching in the WA system and her husband, Alex, had close ties with the Liberal Party, in particular future-Premier Colin Barnett.

Your grandad's challenging of swimming led to disagreements with people whose connections and influence became more significant with the change of government.

There were coaches within the swimming club system, such as Lyn McKenzie, who were making a living by identifying athletes and seeing them all the way through their careers. Learn to Swim programs were established to identify potential world-beaters as early as possible, before progressing those who were talented and interested enough into competitive training.

The early days of WAIS were relatively painless in terms of integrating with the existing setup, as the tiered scholarship program simply provided valuable funds for talented swimmers to assist with training and competition costs. However, it was when WAIS began to grow and implement its own in-house swimming program that problems emerged, with scholarship athletes expected to join the Institute's program at the Superdrome under international coach Gerry Stachewicz.

"A lot of us coaches had put our lives on the line for this – we were running swimming pools, swimming programs and coaching – and our athletes' successes were what was drawing (new swimmers) into our programs," Lyn McKenzie said.

"So, when that was threatened to be taken away from us, that's when we (club coaches and your grandad) started to butt heads a bit. He appointed Gerry Stachewicz, much to the horror of everybody else, and many of the swimmers moved over there for no apparent reason, other than the fact they were going to get better funded and taken away from the home coaches that had produced them.

"Gerry – or whoever it was – was then going to get the glory. So then our swimming programs suffered every time. It means that if you've got aspirations, then bad luck, because you're only producing athletes to a certain point, but I've got aspirations to produce an Olympic champion, because I felt I had experience to pass on."

McKenzie's concern made a lot of sense in a lot of ways and the setup that clubs were running prior to the establishment of WAIS's swimming program undoubtedly demanded an enormous commitment and investment of time and energy from the state's talented coaches. However, it was also a prime example of the failings your grandad believed were taking place.

Your grandad saw the system of swimming – and sports like it – as blurring the lines between recreation and high performance and inefficiently splitting the resources available. He no doubt would have seen tremendous value in talented coaches such as McKenzie, but his argument would have been that such a talented coach should not be having to concern herself with Learn to Swim programs and the operations of a swimming club and should instead be focused solely on coaching the athletes.

The counter-point to that is that the money to enable them to coach high performance needed to come from somewhere. However, that was not your grandad's focus and he believed the athletes were being neglected as they were not receiving 100 per cent of the coach's attention. Whether he was right or wrong depended on which side of the debate someone was on.

McKenzie remembered your grandad fondly, saying she "thoroughly admired what he did and although we didn't always agree, I always knew what he stood for". But your grandad's approach in achieving that betterment of sport put people offside and on at least one of those occasions, he put the McKenzies offside.

"I really believe he had the best interest in WA sport and I don't know what other way he could have chosen to structure it, but I know there were a lot of coaches that weren't happy about it," Lyn McKenzie said.

"I was the one who was very vocal, that's all. There was an issue to do with selection trials for the Commonwealth Games and WAIS. I'm not going to say Wally, although Wally was the director of WAIS at the time. There was a deal struck, which was about the inclusion of a certain swimmer within the WAIS team.

"Alex's (Alex McKenzie) argument with Wally was that he felt Jacqui (Olympian swimmer and daughter of Alex and Lyn) was treated very poorly. In the selection trial, Jacqui beat this particular girl – who got fifth in the event – and Jacquie got third, yet the fifth place swimmer got selected over Jacqui.

"Alex was very angry. It was utterly appalling and unjust and that was where the big blow-up was, but we got over it."

Lyn McKenzie insisted that the feud with your grandad "never amounted to anything". However, personal documents kept by your grandad suggested they at least stoked some already-burning embers of discontent.

The Minister for Sport and Recreation Doug Shave on 5 August 1993 wrote a letter to then-WAIS Chairman Bruce Elliott stating: "I have asked my Senior Policy Officer to contact you and arrange a meeting between you, Mrs MacKenzie (sic) and other appropriate persons to re-examine the four specific complaints made by Mrs MacKenzie about WAIS".

To suggest the issues in those disagreements were solely responsible for the threat to your grandad's job would be unfair, but it certainly made influential people aware of your grandad and courted their involvement. It would be fair to count it as one strike against him.

And it was a strike in a sport that proved an ongoing challenge for your grandad; as close friend, confidant and former boss of the Western Australian Sports Federation Mick Aitken recalled, it was "one specific sport that was forever – forever – at the core of his problems".

"He believed that the system had badly let down high performance athletes and high performance sport and that the system was not capable of putting that right, so he needed to not only wrest power from the state government, but also to a certain extent from the state sporting associations, whose rather benign and maternalistic view of sport was an affirmer to Wally's get-up-and-drive for what he saw sport should be all about," Aitken said.

"That was typical of the sorts of battles that Wally would always have, where the sports were trying not to relinquish authority over the athletes and felt they were their possessions. Wally was like: 'Well, you've had a hundred years and stuffed up, so I'm going to do it for you. You can fight me all the way, but that's how it's going to be'.

"There was no doubt that some of the state sports bodies felt very much threatened by Wally."

The extent to which the feud with swimming impacted your grandad's job was also a point raised by current WAIS Executive Director Steve Lawrence, who at the time was the physiologist for the Institute's swimming program.

"Wal made some enemies in a couple of other people that ended in him having to re-apply for his job," Lawrence said.

"That issue was created around the swimming program. In essence, WAIS had achieved another stepping stone and employed a full-time coach in swimming, paid for by WAIS. That upset a lot of people in the swimming community.

"It became very successful and the more successful it became, the less and less support it got from the broader swimming coaching community. A bit like in athletics, the coaches become very protective of their athletes and it's an unfortunate trait of those particular sports, where the coaches perceive their worth based on the quality of athlete they have at the time, not about the role they can play to assist somebody.

"There were political connections between a couple of the swimming coaches and they had a direct line into Doug Shave, the Sports Minister at the time. Shave called WAIS into account about why it was doing certain things and that led to a couple of the Board Members not supporting Wal, so he got really dirty about that.

"He felt he was undermined. Then, in the end, basically, the line was given to the Board that they wanted the director's position advertised, so Wal had to go in and fight for his job."

Strike one for your grandad with members of the incoming government could have come in the form of his friendship and long relationship with David Hatt and Ric Charlesworth. Strike two came from his run-in with personalities within the swimming community. Strike three came when he approached the incoming government with the same tenacity and forthright devotion to high performance sport that had steered WAIS so well for so long.

Your grandad was in the crosshairs.

Governments keep everything.

It was probably that trait that led to David Hatt instructing your grandad to build the mountain of personal files in order to protect himself from any threat to his position. It was also that trait that led to your grandad becoming the front-runner for the position of inaugural director of WAIS, when Hatt inherited a storage of archived documents in the early 1980s and found several with your grandad's name on them.

And it was also that trait that would have had a 1991 letter written by your grandad to the then-Sports Minister the Hon Graham Edwards fall into the wrong hands upon the change of government.

The letter opened with, "I am writing to express my concern at the current climate in which sport is operating", and went on to lambast the Ministry of Sport and Recreation for its operations that your grandad perceived as having made no improvement since the Burke Government moved to water down its authority and influence.

He stated that "nothing has changed" and "many of the same people have been put back in the same positions". The Ministry of Sport and Recreation was, like WAIS, meant to be an apolitical body. However, it had historically been empowered and was a key body under Sir Charles Court's Liberal Government, before Labor took office in 1983 and systematically watered down its influence. It might have been apolitical, but it would not require too much scratching of the surface to work out which side of politics the Ministry preferred.

Your grandad was very good at what he did and his experience was invaluable. That led him to helping Hatt produce Labor's sports policy at the end of the 1970s. It also led the incoming Court Ministry (Richard, son of Sir Charles) requesting he do the same for the Liberal Party. The move undoubtedly unearthed his previous comments around the Ministry for Sport and Recreation, while the policy itself pulled no punches.

However, he did so for a reason. In a personal cover letter, he explained that he produced the policy in the hope that "the future of the Western Australian Institute of Sport is guaranteed by the eventual Liberal Party Policy and an improved funding and housing arrangement for WAIS is developed". In a further example that politics was not the cause of your grandad's disharmony, those improved "housing arrangements for WAIS" were later realised as a result of the Liberal Party.

Your grandad outlined his beliefs on the importance of sport, from health advantages of an active lifestyle, to the societal benefits and international appeal. However, in his recommendations for the pursuit of sport becoming "financially self-sufficient", he stated that "an important feature of this policy is the annulment of the long-standing marriage between sport and recreation".

He laid it all on the table: "The policy recommends the disbandment of the Ministry of Sport & Recreation and the establishment of the Western Australian Sports Commission and the Western Australian Recreation Commission."

Your grandad was seeking to remove all government influence from high performance sport in Western Australia by removing any association with its sports body, the Ministry of Sport and Recreation. Under the proposed structure, WAIS would answer to the WA Sports Commission, which would sit alongside the WA Sports Federation and be answerable directly to the Minister for Sport.

It was strike three.

The Hon Doug Shave took on the Sport and Recreation portfolio on 4 February 1993 and immediately began a process that destabilised your grandad's position as the longest serving and most successful state institute director in the country. He handed over the portfolio to the Hon Norman Moore on 25 August 1993.

In a little more than six months he took actions that haunted your grandad for the next 18 months. It was a process that knocked the wind out of him; this was a man who had fought intense and public battles and been personally attacked for the sake of Western Australia's athletes and he had never relented, yet he was almost floored by someone from his own state.

However, there are always two sides to the story and it is important to hear both.

"The minister has a lot of advisors and everyone has a view as to whether someone is doing a good job, or someone's not doing a good job, but my understanding – and you're asking me to go back 20 years – is that there was never any doubt in your father's passion for what he was doing and your mother's involvement in sport, of course," Shave said.

"So, people would have been feeding me lots of different views. Sport itself is an area where everyone is an expert and if someone's son in a football team doesn't get what he wants, then all of a sudden the coach isn't doing a good job. That's all thrown up to the minister and, in the end, the minister has to make a decision.

"I can't recollect anyone putting pressure on me not to reappoint your father. If I thought your father wasn't the man for the job, I wouldn't have reappointed him, it's as simple as that. I didn't know the politics of it all, but there could have been someone who had a grievance – either legitimate or illegitimate, in their view – towards your father and they may have expressed that to me."

The insistence of Shave was that the actions taken were simply process and were only taken as a result of the directions of his advisor on the WAIS Board, who he named as Jack Busch.

"But I'd be surprised if Jack did do that (recommend against appointing your grandad), because I thought he was a reasonable judge," Shave said.

However, others close to your grandad insisted process was not the motivation.

"That wasn't process: that was a vindictive witch hunt … for no good reason," said David Hatt, whom it must be mentioned sits on the opposite side of politics to Shave. "They were after Wally; no question they were after Wally. Wally was really worried, because he knew they were after him."

Even the softly-spoken former WAIS Program Manager Craig Davies remembered the incident as one that arose from the specific personalities aligned to the incoming government.

"There was a change in government from Labor to Liberal and Doug Shave was the Sports Minister," Davies said. "He made the decision to advertise Wally's job, because he thought he had an allegiance to Labor. That caused Wally a great deal of stress. He was shattered by it; that someone could actually make him re-apply for his job because there was a perception he had a Labor allegiance."

Shave was advised of the comments and the belief from some that his actions ranged from being politically motivated, to him, personally, being "on a witch hunt".

"You see, they underestimate me, because I would always choose someone on merit," Shave said.

"There were some people who remained as advisors who were suggested to me were Labor people, such as Jack Busch; he retained his job. I reappointed him, as I remember. But the boards that were dealing with money, making government decisions to be involved in business deals, they would have been the ones that I would have been concentrating on, such as LandCorp.

"When it came to the Institute of Sport, because the government is the biggest business in Western Australia, it should be focused on financial control, so because of my background of balancing my budget every week and not going broke, my normal instinct would have been that I would have said to people, 'What's this Wally Foreman like, does he know how to handle money, is he doing a good job?'

"They are the questions I want answered first up. And, 'What are his politics?'. I would have known automatically that if your dad had been there under Burke and under Dowding and under Lawrence, that there was some chance his leanings might have been towards the Labor Party. I never knew, I never found out and I never asked, other than I would have asked my advisors and I mean the Liberals.

"When you're a minister, you have all these people telling you what to do. If I'd had real concerns about your father, I would have gone to John Inverarity, because I knew him at school, he was a very ethical person and his father was very ethical, too, and I would have suspected – I may be wrong – that Inverarity was probably a Lib.

"I never did that, so my concerns weren't that great. If you go through the statistics on your dad, apart from the fact that he happened to marry a very successful athlete, his love was in the game and whether he was Labor or Liberal, if someone put it to me and said – and they would have – that they had an inkling he was very aligned to the Labor Party, I would have said they might have been right, but I don't think he can do me too much damage.

"At the end of the day ... he's producing the results. What are you going to do: axe a bloke who's doing his job correctly for political reasons? Some ministers have; the Labor Party were particularly good at it. I didn't believe in that policy and that's why your father got reappointed by me."

However, your grandad did not get reappointed by Shave. And he only narrowly got reappointed by the WAIS Board once his successor took charge of the portfolio.

The process of reapplying for his job dragged on until 29 March 1994, forcing your grandad to reinterview and survive the voting process by the smallest possible margin before his reappointment. The office of the Minister for Sport and Recreation then attempted to backdate his contract to the time when he first came out of it – 30 June 1993 – like the previous 18 months had never happened.

And while it was Doug Shave behind the initial actions, it was Norman Moore who picked up the baton in August 1993, with the offer in a letter to then-WAIS Chairman Bruce Elliott that "if Mr Foreman, who is the current holder of the position accepts the new terms and conditions of the contract referred to above, he is most welcome to apply for the appointment".

It was a point in time that Moore remembered well, proactively addressing the issue in the interview for this book before a question had even been asked.

"Before we begin, let me just tell you something: when I became Minister for Sport, Wally's contract had expired and everybody said I should just renew it, but I thought, 'No, bugger that'," Moore said.

"Whilst I knew of Wally, I didn't know him very well and so I went out to the market place again and said the position was open if anybody wanted to apply. You wouldn't believe the correspondence I got saying, 'You must reappoint Wally', from all over the place. I thought, 'Well, that's fine; let's just see if Wally's the best and if he is then he'll get the job and, if he's not, then someone else will'.

"Wally was a bit upset about it, too, because he felt he should have just had it rolled over. I know Wally was upset about it, but he won it hands-down – there was no-one who came even close – and I said to him after, 'Wally, that now proves to everybody – and you, in particular – that you're the best man for the job. Instead of just rolling it over, you've now proven it'."

Moore seemed sincere in his outlining of his motivations for continuing the reapplication process of your grandad's position. However, it was still a bitter pill for your grandad to swallow. Moore might have felt your grandad was required to prove himself, but your grandad felt he had been proving himself to WA sport for the better part of a decade.

The timing of the fight for your grandad's own survival coincided with the fight for the survival of the WAIS gymnastics program and Moore was integral in that battle. The Minister carried that same belief as your grandad in regards to national and state sporting bodies.

"I'm a federalist and I was keen to have a West Australian Institute of Sport going really well, as opposed to AIS, which was seeking to be dominant," Moore said.

"Wally and I actually formed a good relationship in promoting WAIS in competition with AIS. In a federation, you shouldn't make everything the same in every jurisdiction, because otherwise you might as well just have one government. So, the beauty of federalism is that all the states compete against each other, within the loose boundaries of the federation, to see who can do things better than everybody else.

"That creates a competitive environment. If you just have one overarching body like the AIS and everybody is just a subsidiary of that, then you don't get any competition. They argue we get international competition, but sport's more than that, it's domestic as well as international. So, Wally and I had similar views in that and we were prepared to argue the case for WAIS."

Moore also proved crucial to the history of WAIS itself: he was the Minister responsible for securing the funds for a purpose-built standalone facility for the institute. It was a proud moment for WA sport at the time of its opening in 1996, as it was the only facility of its kind in Australia, with all other institutes retrofitted and operating out of colleges, teaching institutes or hidden away in the bowels of a stadium.

The strategic appointment of Charles "Chilla" Porter – the man your grandad watched at Perry Lakes Stadium during the 1960 British Empire and Commonwealth Games – as WAIS Chairman following the resignation of inaugural Chairman Bruce Elliot was also an important step in securing funds for the facility, with Porter heavily involved in the governing Liberal Party. However, once your grandad convinced Moore that the government needed to spend money on WAIS, it was Moore who pulled the strings and it was a significant achievement, given the persistent Liberal view of high performance sport and bias towards the Department of Sport and Recreation's participation goals.

"It was actually difficult to get the money for it, because there was a bit of a view around that you didn't need to spend money on elite sport and that you needed to spend money on participation, rather than elitism," Moore said.

"Within the department itself, there was the opinion that any government money should be concentrated on participation in sport, rather than big amounts of money going to WAIS, because I think the department – some of the officers, not all of them – had the view that if WAIS was going to get money, it was going to come out of their budget.

"It was a no-brainer, to me: what's the point in having an elite institute if it doesn't have the facilities?"

Moore managed to find $1-million to fund the construction of a new standalone facility for the Western Australian Institute of Sport, which was tacked onto the south west side of the Superdrome. It had to compromise significantly on the design, given $1-million, even then, was not a lot of money to build a two-storey building with a subterranean strength and conditioning area, but it still stood for almost 20 years and was the best state institute facility Australia had at the time.

Your grandad and Moore had worked together to achieve that feat and, together, they had fought a bitter national war to save the WAIS gymnastics program. In those ways, the stubborn approach of Moore's character proved invaluable. In the background, that stubbornness was still plaguing your grandad until his eventual reappointment as WAIS Director in March 1994.

I do not remember much of that time – I was only 10-years-old – but I do remember there was a party at our home in Duncraig, with several of your grandad's colleagues and friends. Neither Shave, nor Moore were among them.

"I have great admiration for what he did at WAIS and it was sad when he left, because Wally was WAIS," Moore said.

"Maybe, like everything, an individual can't be an organisation and there comes a time to move on. He became a great commentator, of course. One of the best. It was terribly sad when he passed away. An absolute tragedy. But I think the reputation that he forged for himself was demonstrated by the funeral service: it was amazing."

There was genuineness in Moore's words, particularly in the context of his actions and his approach towards reappointments within his portfolio, when he claimed: "I would have had no idea what Wally's politics were and I never thought about it at the time. The view was, when contracts expired, you go out to the marketplace and then you could justify in your own mind that you've got the right person for the job".

In a personal letter to friend Mick Aitken, even your grandad said of Moore's actions: "I obviously have some concerns ... but I am also realistic enough to know that WAIS can't expect to sit on its own outside the system".

However, the concern that remained with your grandad was why the process began in the first place. That was a point for which he always felt personally slighted.

"If I had of been vindictive and I had the power – and believe me, I'm not a vindictive person – your father wouldn't have been there," Shave said.

"The Liberal Party didn't have it in for your father. Mind you, if he was a Lib, that wouldn't have surprised me either, because if he was good at his job, we'd have reappointed him. The Labor blokes might have eyed me off and said, 'He's a hard bastard, he takes no prisoners', but there wasn't a necessity to take that approach in regards to your father, because he was doing his job."

Exactly what motivated the process to begin and if it was anything other than process might never be known. But it was a significant moment in your grandad's professional career.

"If you're talking about times of uncertainty, for Craig and I – and there were others involved by then, too – it wasn't a comfortable time," said Steve Lawrence.

"His contract was up and you might find some explanations saying that it was just process, but that wasn't the feeling at the time. It might have been an opportunistic time for them to do it, but it was the only time he had to reapply for his job.

"He felt more than a bit hurt, he was disappointed and felt quite betrayed. He felt the Board hadn't supported him in his fight to do what was best for the athlete. I know there were people on the Board who he never trusted again."

Your grandad's return to the position of WAIS Director was announced publicly in an article in *The West Australian*, which declared "none of the applicants matched up to Foreman".

The short and specific reign of Chilla Porter as WAIS Chairman had ended as WAIS's standalone building was completed and Neil McKerracher QC entered the position. A significant number of correspondence kept in your grandad's personal files to and from the Minister's office are testament to the role Neil McKerracher played in finally ending the torturous 18-month process of your grandad having to reapply for his job.

McKerracher was a no-nonsense chairman, whose extensive background in the legal system had him dealing with people far more intimidating and on matters with far greater consequences than those he ran into in sport. His vast experience and understanding of law also allowed him to end the convoluted process of appointing WAIS's director. He also helped implement some important changes to policy that had been long overdue.

Your grandad had not received a pay rise in five years, partly because he elected not to, due to the financial situation WAIS had been in and partly because "I did not feel I was in a sufficiently strong enough position to debate the issue at the time" of his reappointment. That five-year pay freeze was corrected.

Your grandad and McKerracher also moved to change all termed employment contracts to a duration of four years to align with Olympic cycles and avoid future instability caused by the process around reapplications. The understanding of the legal system also allowed McKerracher and your grandad to ease the shackles of some government involvement that had begun to creep into WAIS operations.

As your grandad's next term of employment neared an end in 2000 and with another 18-month reapplication process always a possibility, the Institute had found a new, firmer footing in its position with the government. Following an investigation by the Crown Law Department into the rights of the government over a body such as WAIS, it was made clear that the interference of the past would no longer be tolerated.

"The Crown Law Department has advised that WAIS is not governed by the provisions of the *Public Sector Management Act*," read a line in a note from the WAIS Board to Moore.

"Accordingly, appointments of its officers and employees do not come within the scope of that Act".

The letter was conveyed with respect by insisting WAIS would always engage the Minister for approval prior to officially appointing a director, but the message was clear: the Institute engaged the government by way of courtesy, not necessity. No unnecessary interference from the government would be tolerated, because it had been discovered that the government legally had no rights in the matter.

Your grandad's 2000 employment contract was subsequently rolled over without the need for any reapplication for the position. It was the polar-opposite of the period he had endured previously.

The 1993 contract debacle was the only time your grandad was ever made to reapply for his job. But, as has been stated throughout this book, politics had nothing to do with it. Your grandad was as appreciative and as forthright in his challenges of the Liberal Part as he was the Labor Party.

It was simply the personalities who found their way into the system and into positions of influence. They perhaps made assumptions about a man who had been entrenched throughout several years of rival rule.

But in that assumption was a great irony: your grandad was always a Liberal voter.

Chapter 15

Sometimes, We Must Let Go

THE FIGHT FOR A JOB he should have never have had to fight for was the beginning of the end for your grandad at the Western Australian Institute of Sport. He continued for another seven years after his reappointment in 1994, but the toll taken on his spirit was significant.

It was an incident that marked a shift in your grandad's experience and vision for WAIS; one that contrasted with his values of prioritising the coaches and athletes – the people who mattered most to a state sports institute. You'll find in life, Charlotte, that some people enjoy using buzz words such as "process", "efficiency" and "strategy", in a bid to achieve a perception of professionalism.

Layers of middle-management get introduced and businesses are broken into "silos" – managers managing managers – and Key Performances Indicators are used to judge the performance of people, reducing them to numbers, with "manager reviews" replacing simple conversations. The entire workplace becomes riddled with anxiety, dehumanised, sanitised and devoid of inspiration. Processes are prioritised over people.

The saga your grandad was put through was an indication of the way the world was heading – including WAIS – and that prospect proved exhausting for him. That exhaustion was compounded by the resumption of battles that had already been fought and won, only to repeat under new administrations. WAIS's independence from government and ongoing funding challenges were a couple of those.

WAIS was riding a wave of success in the lead-up to the Sydney Olympics: the Institute had produced a record number of medals at the 1992 Barcelona and 1996 Atlanta Olympic Games, while achieving the same at the 1994 and 1998 Commonwealth Games.

It had increased its Intensive Training Programs from 11 to 18 during that time and had moved from supporting 300 athletes to 480 as Sydney drew closer.

However, despite this, Sports Minister the Hon Norman Moore in 1999 – the eve of the home Olympics – told your grandad and WAIS Board Members that he had a "non-negotiable position" on the funding of the Institute and that it was no longer a priority for the State Government. It came at a time when the Queensland Academy of Sport, the Victorian Institute of Sport and the New South Wales Institute of Sport were all reporting increases in budgets.

Concerns were raised by the Minister over WAIS's financial management, despite the Institute having never had an audit query. The lack of investment had WA steadily slipping behind the other states in terms of sporting infrastructure. That latter issue proved irreparable to a point mentioned previously: WA will not be in a position to bid for an event it held in 1960 – the Commonwealth Games – until the completion of the new stadium in 2018.

The issues also began to play on your grandad's mind and he wrote to Moore that "it appears that someone is undermining WAIS in regards to the advice you are receiving". It had the potential to sound paranoid, if not for the concern of other Board Members, who labelled Moore's objections over finances and funding "totally unsubstantiated" and as coming at a time when he had smothered the Institute in platitudes following the release of the annual report, which documented all finances as well as athlete achievements.

"The timing of those remarks ... are in complete contradiction with each other," one Board Member commented. Government red tape was beginning to tie up an Institute that should have had very little influence – at least in operational matters – from the Minister. Issues such as your grandad's salary, which had been identified as "very inadequate", had been sat on by Moore for three years with inaction until the Government's own salary advisor discovered the below-par situation and took action.

WAIS began to feel like a gimmick to your grandad: it was there when the Government wanted a boost to its image, but forgotten when the Institute needed the government's support. The Minister's meddling also began to reach peculiar levels when Moore dictated such decisions as WAIS employees not being permitted to use Frequent Flyer points accrued through work travel.

The situation began to create a rift between WAIS and the Government. A rift that had never existed under previous administrations. Your grandad had gone from dealing with ministers and personalities throughout the 1980s who were mostly proactive and supportive, to ones who appeared determined to act more as roadblocks, often despite reason.

And your grandad was not the only one feeling that way.

"It seems to me that there is a misunderstanding as to the legal position of WAIS," wrote one senior Board Member to your grandad.

"We are not a Government body. We are a separate body. The Government has been persistently in all public statements and in stationery issued by WAIS fully recognised for its financial contribution, but it does not make the decisions. It is not the Minister who appoints the Director as a matter of law. The Board appoints the Director. The Board sets the conditions of the Director's salary. The Board is ultimately responsible for all decisions in relation to expenditure.

"Governments tend to take a pragmatic approach, namely if they supply the funds, they call the shots. Most people in society would understand that this works fairly well, but that pragmatic approach cannot supersede the role that directors of boards are obliged to play at law which is to make proper decisions concerning, amongst other things, the welfare of their senior people.

"It is probably time to take over these things and tell the Minister who is going to make the decisions. I am not prepared to continue under a scheme under which we are incapable of discharging our obligations at law."

Members of the WAIS Board were ready to walk.

The ongoing angst between WAIS and the Minister Norman Moore led to your grandad and Board Members becoming concerned that there were parties actively working behind the scenes to disempower the Institute. There was evidence they were right.

The Ministry of Sport and Recreation had established a body it labelled the High Performance Sub-Committee, which subsequently produced a "Strategic Plan for High Performance Sport". The document opened with statements such as "a coordinated approach to a comprehensive high performance system is necessary" and "Western Australia needs to provide an efficient and effective system that is able to respond to the rapidly changing market". Buzz words to create a perception of action and importance.

The irony in the Ministry's plan and desire for a "coordinated approach" was that it neglected to invite anyone from WAIS – the state's high performance sport body – to sit on the high performance committee. In fact, it neglected to even advise your grandad of its existence. In December 2000 – at least six months after the committee's formation – your grandad had still not received any formal communication from the Ministry or the committee.

Yet, this was a body whose September minutes reported that its purpose was "not only a review of WAIS", indicating that it was at least in part a review of WAIS, despite the Ministry having no rights to oversight or review the Institute.

Leading that review was a curious contingent of members, whose qualifications to conduct such activity made little sense to your grandad. He described as "laughable" a group which comprised of government officers and people with limited experience in elite sport administration. Those inadequacies were shown in basic factual errors founding the "review" of a system the committee believed needed changing.

The committee in September 2000, for example, discussed the increased funding to WAIS, but the reality was that WAIS had not received a funding increase since 1996 and its funding had, in fact, been decreasing in real terms in that time. Your grandad raised a simple and valid question in an email to WAIS's then-chairman Neil McKerracher: "Why wouldn't someone talk to WAIS about this?"

The committee also believed universities were being underutilised for sports science analysis, but again failed to consult WAIS or your grandad on this view, despite the Institute having spent its formative years housed at the University of WA and maintaining a constant working relationship. WAIS had moved from the University premises because its growth led to an inability of UWA to cater for both students and the Institute's athletes, yet there were retained Memorandums of Understanding which enabled both to work closely together.

And then there was the entrenched belief from the Ministry of Sport and Recreation that a "statewide system" should be put in place for high performance sport. It was the same view that had years previously led the Ministry to claim the $20-million made available by the State Government should be used to construct 20 sports centres around WA, before Prof John Bloomfield promptly advised that it was not up for discussion: the State Sports Centre – the Superdrome – was to be built.

"That shows their ignorance," your grandad wrote. "It's the same as education: if you live in Albany and you want to do dentistry, you move to the university. You can't take a university to every student."

Perhaps most concerning was some of the seemingly underhanded activity. One of the committee's members approached your grandad's secretary and requested a list of former WAIS Board personnel and, when he discovered that the secretary had mentioned the request to your grandad, promptly asked "what Wally's reaction was".

The committee was also setting up meetings with the Minister, as well as briefing sessions for the media. That was, in your grandad's view, all being conducted by a group unqualified to do so. A group charged with investigating the performance of WAIS, yet which had zero oversight of the Institute at any point in history and failed to notify WAIS.

"I must say I am becoming more and more suspicious of all these activities when I hear things from interstate and read between the lines," your grandad said. "I'm just about ready for a real 'blue' if that's what they want – publicly."

Ultimately, WAIS was included in the sub-committee, with its chairman Neil McKerracher assisting the works. And, despite your grandad's initial and highly agitated reaction, he eventually accepted the work that was being conducted. That reaction, though, was telling.

There's a term used in warfare called "war weariness"; it refers to the physical and mental exhaustion caused by an ongoing battle. Your grandad was getting weary.

Happiness has no place in high performance. That was a belief previously mentioned by WAIS foundation staffer and your grandad's successor as director Steve Lawrence. The theory is that happiness leads to complacency and, instead, happiness is an emotion best left for the retired.

So, how do those involved in high performance survive a life of never-ending underachievement? They use sign posts: events that serve as micro-goals along the way. They can be targeting personal bests, gearing up for a national championship, or even simply achieving a training session's requirements.

In your grandad's case, the 2000 Sydney Olympics were a major sign post and from the day the city was announced in 1993 as the host, the entire country's sporting system was invigorated with an injection of renewed purpose. And funds.

Your grandad firmly believed that sport had a power over people: it could unite the divided like few other events in life could. It also has a power over politicians who enjoy seeing their pictures in the paper and, from the Federal Government's implementation of the $135-million Olympic Athlete Program through to State Government cash injections – such as that which led to WAIS's standalone facility – high performance sport hummed with activity.

Marketing went into full swing with athlete events and appearances and fundraising activities rarely absent from a calendar. This was an opportunity for WAIS and the state institutes like it to unite and show how far out of the Montreal quagmire they had dragged Australian sport.

"The Sydney Olympics: there is something incredibly different about a home Olympics," Steve Lawrence said.

"It's close, you're talking about athletes competing in a town we all know about, the number of media and publicity was huge around it and WAIS was providing a huge contribution to the team. Compared to '88, when it was all about trying to claim something and create an opportunity, by then, we were well-established, we were in a purpose-built facility, we had good representation.

"We were having farewells to athletes. That Annual Dinner was huge and, from memory, it was the first time we had vision of our athletes competing. We changed the way we celebrated: before that, it was either Wally or Tom Hoad, or someone like that, giving a 15 to 20-minute oration and now we had five minutes of vision of athletes competing. It was a continuation of success. We didn't falter and we had a lot to celebrate.

"We had a huge number of athletes we were looking after – I even remember having Danny Green in the lab. It was a really proud Olympics for Australia and we were really proud of our contribution. I know your dad was really happy with it and we celebrated that. We probably celebrated a bit too much."

And the athletes did not disappoint. A team of 628 competitors across 34 sports led Australia to 16 gold medals, 25 silver and 17 bronze, with a final ranking of fourth: the country's best result since the 1956 Melbourne Olympic Games, where it finished third, and to date its second-best effort in more than 100 years of competing the Games.

It was a result built on inspiring performances such as Cathy Freeman's gutsy 400m triumph, streaming to victory in an attention-grabbing body suit that belied the weight of expectations on her shoulders. Your grandad's close mate Ric Charlesworth coached the women's hockey team to a defence of its Atlanta Olympic title, while Australia's most successful Olympian, swimmer Ian Thorpe, scooped three gold and two silvers from the pool.

It was also a proud moment for WA: a record 51 athletes – more than double the 22 who represented their state at WAIS's inaugural 1984 Games – returned home with another record of eight gold medals across hockey, swimming, water polo and sailing. WA contributed 11 medals in total to the country's tally and it was a point of pride for your grandad: "This was a remarkable achievement for a state with less than 10 per cent of the country's total population".

Your grandad was also there to witness the feats by Australia, taking leave to work in commentary for Channel 7. It was because of Channel 7 that your grandad took his first steps into the modern world: he was required to have a mobile phone. When you're old enough to understand, I'll play for you the audio recording the ABC took of your grandad attempting to use an Automatic Teller Machine for the first time.

He had a disinterest – close to fear – of most forms of technology. Channel 7 convincing him to have a mobile phone was a major milestone that the broadcaster would not fully understand. Years later, it led to a comical moment for your grandad and me. My phone rang. The screen flashed: "Dad Mobile".

"Dad?" I asked, with the question in a tone that expected no answer, assuming he had forgotten to lock the phone and it had called me from his pocket.

"Glen? Glen, is that you?" he replied, equally unsure whether he had managed to place a call.

During those Olympics, though, his phone rang with another question. At the subsequent Games in Athens in 2004 your grandad broadcast what ended up being his most famous piece of Olympic commentary, calling Australia to its first ever men's hockey gold medal for the ABC. But it was a moment at Sydney that best reflected why he was so respected for his calling.

An archer named Simon Fairweather, undoubtedly inspired by his home Olympics, had stormed into gold medal contention. Channel 7 had – reasonably – not expected an Australian to be in such a position and therefore had not allocated a commentator. Your grandad was asked to do the job, despite having never been able to make it through a Robin Hood movie without falling asleep, let alone analytically describing an archery competition.

Nonetheless, armed with a rule book and an hour's silence to prepare, he called Fairweather to the men's individual gold. Channel 7 commended his commentary and received similar plaudits from viewers.

Your grandad respected everyone, but he worked in sport and therefore reserved his highest respect for the athletes he strived to assist. That respect meant a lack of experience was never an excuse: it simply required greater preparation. That day, your grandad ensured that nobody knew he had never broadcast archery before.

That day, he ensured all the focus was on the athlete who deserved it.

Only fate knows where its road will lead us.

That moment calling Simon Fairweather to victory had your grandad drawing on everything from his "Training by Numbers" program at Scheyville's Officer Training Unit, to his repetitive football preparation. It also marked the culmination of something greater.

Your grandad in 1984 had felt a burning desire. He had become fed up of reporting for various media outlets on the continued failure of Australia's – and more specifically Western Australia's – sporting system and yearned to help change it. To correct it.

Australia finished 32nd at the Montreal Olympics: its worst ever finish at a Games, with no gold medals, one silver and four bronze. Western Australia alone at the Sydney Olympics contributed 11 medals to a tally that had the country finish fourth on the global scale. It was arguably the country's best result, despite being one peg below the 1956 Melbourne finish, given the evolution and professionalisation of sport at that point.

The ghosts of Montreal had been vanquished and the success of the state institutes were pivotal to that. The Western Australian Institute of Sport had come of age. Crucial to its success was the athletes, supported by the coaches, who were backed by the programs, which were built and reinforced by WAIS. They were all put in place by your grandad.

"Sydney was a huge milestone for us and, as a home Olympics, it meant a lot for any Australian sportsperson," said your grandad's long-time friend and WAIS foundation employee Craig Davies. "For WAIS to have made such a significant contribution was really important and, for Wally, I think that would have been the pinnacle."

Happiness has no place in high performance: there is no ceiling, the job is never done and a performance can always be improved. Instead, there are sign posts. Sydney was a sign post for your grandad.

All the places we go and all the people we meet in life take pieces of our hearts. That is where nostalgia comes from. It's where mourning comes from. When we yearn for those places and people who are gone, it's like our hearts are aching for the pieces they took with them.

Age is one of life's little ironies. Or perhaps it is better labelled as a paradox: the older we get, the richer our lives become through the family, experiences and memories we gain. Yet, at the same time, the older we get, the more of those same things we realise we have lost to the past.

A few events took place towards the end of your grandad's time at WAIS which undoubtedly made him think about the past, about what time had taken from him and about what the future would bring. The first was his 50th birthday – a major milestone for anyone – on 4 January 1998 and which came with your grandad's almost neurotic attention to detail.

It was held at Caversham House and brought together people from all the major moments in his life: his childhood in Bruce Rock, the family's move to Perth for his teenage years, high school, the army, the bank and the Fremantle Courts, his time in the media and, of course, his time as director of WAIS. There was a table arrangement as obsessive as that of a wedding and the correspondence kept by your grandad to and from Caversham House showed the level of detail to which he planned the day.

There was even a run sheet. Your grandad could be pedantic on details when he wanted to be and, despite the Perth weather turning out one of its hottest Januarys on record (a few days after the party, the mercury tipped 42.6 degrees), he insisted that the poor two-piece band Rick and the Fox continue playing through sweltering conditions. There was a patio area where the food was set up, an area on the paved path for the band, tables and umbrellas placed on the grass and, of course, "there will need to be an area for dancing".

He was pedantic about the details because this event was special: not because it was his 50th birthday, but because of the people and memories it was bringing together. Even people such as Wilma Shakespear, your grandad's counterpart from the Queensland Academy of Sport, made the journey west.

Every person there returned pieces of your grandad's heart. Nostalgia was strong that day. As it was a few years later when your grandad reunited Trevor "Red" Riley, who had grown from childhood Bruce Rock football buddy into Chief Justice of the Northern Territory's Supreme Court.

They had seen little of each other until a trip north by your grandad in the months leading up to his resignation from WAIS brought them together again.

"Just a quick note to thank you for your hospitality on Tuesday night and to say how thrilled I was to be able to renew an important friendship after 41 years," your grandad wrote to his friend. Note the specification of "41 years". It was a clear sign of how much the past was tugging at your grandad that he did not simply round the number to 40.

"I have become quite nostalgic about my childhood in recent years and I have especially fond memories of Bruce Rock and my friends from those days," he continued. "I am so pleased that we have made contact again and we must make the effort to stay in touch. I suspect it will take several such occasions to replay all of the footy matches, Test matches and school yard 'scandal', so I will look forward to the next one."

Piece by piece, your grandad's heart was reminding him of a time that had disappeared, despite what his life during his time at WAIS had brought him. And there was no doubt that it had brought him a great deal: your grandad was very good at what he did. He was a leader and he had the rare ability to take those around him and those he needed on the journey with him.

It also brought challenges, not only to your grandad, but those who were on the journey with him and at the turn of the century, one of his dearest friends and allies had faced enough challenges. Craig Davies – the third longest serving WAIS staff member behind only your grandad and Steve Lawrence – walked away.

"My resignation came because I basically became disillusioned with the elite sport system," Davies said.

"I felt I wasn't really enjoying the work as I had before. I wanted to get out of that situation and get back to grassroots, so decided to go back to teaching. It was a great working environment, working with Wally and Steve. You'd go to work and know there'd be quality work done, but you'd also have fun as well.

"I think I learnt a lot about dealing with people, a lot about elite sport and a lot about how important values are and being true to those values, not meandering from them."

Davies was the program and athlete coordinator at WAIS: when your grandad was fighting battles over political meddling and funding withdrawals, that position was directly affected by the outcomes. WAIS had grown to a point that Davies could not have imagined when he first began in its early days, but the changes to sport, sports governance and sports administration – policy over people – that impacted your grandad so much, had also become too much for Davies.

Your grandad understood the reasons for leaving, because he was feeling the same way, and accepted the resignation, but not before taking aim at those he believed had caused the loss of one of WAIS's most valued people.

"I write to you to express WAIS's increasing concern at the level of interference and disruption being caused to the Institute primarily by the Ministry for Sport and Recreation," your grandad wrote to Sports Minister Norman Moore.

"These problems have now reached a level where they are causing WAIS to waste a significant amount of time in dealing with them and they have contributed to WAIS losing one of its most senior and valuable staff members, Mr Craig Davies."

The loss of Davies was telling for your grandad.

"I always felt that when Craig left, there was something in Wally that said, 'Time's a-comin'," Steve Lawrence said.

Lawrence was right: the time was "a-comin'" for your grandad. It arrived as one more piece of his heart departed. Wilma Shakespear – your grandad's closest ally among the state institutes and a woman who had fought alongside him in some of his most significant moments at WAIS – resigned in 2001. The pair were at a function together when Shakespear told your grandad the news.

"It wasn't public knowledge, but I told him," Shakespear said. "I said, 'You and I are going to have a good night tonight, because we're both on our last hurrah'."

All the places we go and all the people we meet take a little piece of our heart. And when the people leave and we find ourselves standing alone in those places – well, our whole heart just isn't in it anymore.

Your grandad paced around the offices of the Western Australian Institute of Sport with his right hand in his pocket, jiggling the loose change he always kept there. It was his habitual routine whenever he was troubled and deep in thought. Funding was again the issue.

This time, it was the announcement that there would be severe cutbacks to state institutes at the conclusion of the Sydney Olympics, as the Olympic Athlete Program would be dramatically reduced. Millions of dollars were going to be lost. It was a horrendous time for a people-person such as your grandad, because the effect was that people were going to lose their jobs.

The changes had to be made, though, and WAIS had been proactive: it conducted a review in 1999 to identify the priority sports and subsequently abandoned its programs in baseball, softball, basketball, water polo and volleyball. The corresponding staff were retrenched.

"That wasn't a pleasant time," Steve Lawrence said.

"Wal had one trait that we had an argument about: he always felt it was his responsibility to deliver the bad news. We had to let a staff member go who was working in my team – I was managing him – and I wanted to be able to tell him, but Wally said, 'No, I'm the director, I'll tell him'.

"This guy goes upstairs because he's been asked to see the director and when he comes back down, he looks at me and before I can say anything, he's walked out the front door. I went upstairs and Wal and I had a discussion about it. I said, 'That's the last time that happens, Wal. I'm not doing that again'."

Your grandad always felt it was his responsibility to fix things and as a result he shouldered a lot of stress and pressure. The shallow and sometimes unintentionally callous ways that governments work then rubbed salt into the wounds left by the OAP decision. If WAIS had begun to feel like the state government's gimmick that was always good for a photo opportunity, then Australian sport as a whole was the same to Federal counterparts.

The Sydney Olympics were in full-swing, with Australia performing well and the nation transfixed on the Games, so Prime Minister John Howard used the opportunity to announce that the funding to sport would stay. The loss of good people, the irreparable dismantling of programs and the rescaling of operations had ultimately been unnecessary.

It was the same battle your grandad had fought plenty of times before and lost copious amounts of energy over, only for sport to be treated like the shiny toy in a government's portfolio. It was the same on all fronts: Federal, State, the Department of Sport and Recreation, the Australian Sports Commission, funding, independence, the rights of athletes. The fights that had already been fought were doing the rounds again.

And your grandad's contract required renewal. Yet again, he would have to plead his case to Sport and Recreation Minister Norman Moore in order to justify his right to continue at WAIS.

"He got tired of the fight and he got tired of people letting him be a front-runner," said Liz Chetkovich, a long-time coach at WAIS under your grandad and a close friend.

"He fought the fight so often that he got tired of the fight; he never got tired of the Institute. When a new wave of people came through, I think Wally said: 'I'm tired of fighting, I don't want to fight anymore'. What he did was 17 years of high energy. He crammed 35 years into 17 years, quite truthfully, because the volume of work he did, the intensity of the work he did, the passion of everything that he did, it was worth two of what everyone else did."

The correspondence your grandad kept showed a significant difference in the concern and anxiety he had around his 1993-94 contract renewal compared to the renewal six years later.

It would be untrue to say he no longer cared, but it was apparent the sting had gone out of the process. He was no longer willing to submit large chunks of his life and energy to it. If Moore was going to reappoint him, that would have made your grandad very happy, but he wasn't going to sit through another 18-months of disrespect, waiting for that to happen. So, for the first time in almost two decades, he explored his options.

The support of your grandad from Neil McKerracher throughout the latter's tenure as Chairman was unprecedented and ensured your grandad would not only be treated fairly, but that a passion for the job remained. In his letter applying for reappointment (a requirement of the process) your grandad wrote: "Having just been through the most difficult times in the Institute's history, I am particularly keen to assist with its recovery. I must say the difficult times have been made easier and the job has been made more enjoyable working with the current Board and in particular under your Chairmanship".

But his scars from the past remained. Your grandad was highly experienced and respected in his field and, in the lead-up to the 2000 Olympics he had even been approached for the position of Group Manager – Sport by the Sydney Organising Committee for the Olympic Games (SOCOG), but he had also been made aware of an issue during his previous contract farce.

Having been made to reapply for his job, your grandad approached a Human Resources group to help him piece together an updated CV and assist with the process. They were obviously valuable as he held on to the job, but the advisors also mentioned the experience and respect he had was limited to a narrow skillset: not many companies were in the market for an almost 50-year-old former journalist-turned sports administrator with no qualifications.

It was disheartening for your grandad to hear. It was another reminder, amidst the professionalisation of sport, administration and the world around him, that times were changing. However, his currency in sport remained strong and his respect could not have been higher.

Iconic Australian cricketer Justin Langer, an amazing man who held a high level of respect for your grandad, once gave me a booklet. It was the program for the 2014 Western Australian of the Year Awards, which Langer subsequently won in the Sport category. In it, he wrote a note and highlighted a name at the back. It was that of your grandad, documenting his winning of the same award from 14 years earlier in recognition for all he had done for sport in the state and the tremendous growth he had led WAIS through.

A few years after, your grandad was given the honour of being named a Member of the Order of Australia. So, if the government was going to choose not to hold onto the experience that led to those honours, your grandad was prepared to take it elsewhere.

An opportunity with the New Zealand Institute of Sport that was circling an enormous salary of about $200,000AUD was floated, among others, but interestingly – and despite the bundles of correspondence he had around these positions – your grandad mentioned very little of the job offers to your nana. They were, presumably, a safety net in the event the reappointment was not forthcoming and leverage against Moore in those negotiations.

Then, suddenly, Moore was gone.

Labor returned to government under the leadership of Premier Geoff Gallop and WAIS found itself under a new Minister for Sport and Recreation: Alan Carpenter. Carpenter was a man who went on to become Premier himself and who delivered a touching address at your grandad's memorial service, but, at the time, he was a respected journalist who had crossed into politics and carried a reputation as a tenacious reporter.

His career had taken him from newspapers into television, where he had been the State Political Reporter for both Channel 7 and the ABC, before hosting *The 7:30 Report* and *Stateline*. If ever there was a Minister who could have played the hardest of hardball with your grandad's position, it was Carpenter.

"Alan Carpenter came in and we were both a bit concerned," Neil McKerracher said.

"We'd seen him on TV and he'd been a pretty tough interviewer and interrogator. We thought, 'Gee, we've got problems here'. Then from Day 1, he was just fantastic and really supportive."

Carpenter didn't give your grandad any special treatment and, really, it had nothing to do with Liberal or Labor: it was to do with people. In stark contrast to the 18-month process Moore put your grandad through, the Gallop Government took office in February 2001 and by May, Carpenter had reappointed your grandad.

People over process and policy. Carpenter marked the first return to that mantra for your grandad after the better part of a decade under Doug Shave and Moore.

"I think Wally almost got a second wind with Alan Carpenter," former boss of the WA Sports Federation Mick Aitken said. "I think he felt he got some of the respect back that he felt he had lost with some of the previous government ministers. I'm not politicising this at all; it was about the people, not the governments."

Mick Aitken was right: Alan Carpenter did almost give your grandad a second wind. Almost.

He wrote to Carpenter following his reappointment and stated, "We have all been invigorated by your enthusiasm and support for the portfolio", but followed with, "As I mentioned at our most recent meeting, I am considering other professional options that have arisen during the past few months". And the pull of one of those "professional options" was strong.

It was an option to return to the Australian Broadcasting Corporation. An option he had always wanted for the end of his career. Despite all WAIS had achieved under your grandad, it was never his intention to end his professional career there. He always wanted to end his career in the media, calling the sport that he loved.

Your grandad first began at the ABC in the late 70s. Thirty-five years later, a young broadcaster named Dan Lonergan was returning to Melbourne and a position had opened.

Lonergan already had a relationship with your grandad, who sought permission from the young commentator's boss at the time, Glenn Mitchell, to assist him with his sometimes-erroneous cricket commentary. Lonergan would often dissect Sheffield Shield calls alongside your grandad in the director's office at WAIS, where a shiny, new desktop computer sat for years with the plastic protector still draped over it.

Much as he had the first time your grandad joined the ABC, he had received an early warning from the departing broadcaster that a position was about to open up. Not only was it an opportunity to return to the media and the ABC, it was a position based in Perth. And, if your grandad wanted the position, it was as good as his: he was basically holding down two fulltime jobs between WAIS and the ABC, given his assistance with WAFL, AFL, summer requirements and Sports Talk broadcasts.

Your grandad ideally wanted to see WAIS through to the Athens Olympics before returning to the media fulltime, but it was an opportunity that might not have come around again if he let it pass.

"Longevity is something in life these days that is unusual to the point of being unique," Aitken said of the decision your grandad was faced with.

"Staying that time takes its toll on you. Wally was worn down, because the battles were battles he'd fought before and won, only to have to fight them all over again, just with different people. He probably found it difficult to have to replicate those battles and to have the same respect for his adversaries, if you like, that he would have had in the past.

"If you play for Man United for 17 years, you don't want to find yourself playing for Accrington Stanley, trying to make a living."

It all happened very quickly. Perhaps, too quickly.

Your nana was with one of her athletes overseas in Hungary for an athletics meet and the first phone call your grandad made on the subject was to let her know he had resigned and was returning to the ABC fulltime.

"He was exhausted, I knew that, and he always wanted to return to the media," your nana said.

"The issues with reapplying for his job wore him out more than anything and, looking back on it now, it was a sign of depression: we very rarely went out for dinner during that time and we always used to be going out with somebody. He said one day that it was dragging him down and then the next thing I know, he'd resigned.

"He was home by himself because I was away, so he was looking after both you boys (me and your Uncle Mark) and it might have become bigger than Ben Hur in his head. He probably should have waited until I got back and he probably panicked a bit."

The WAIS senior management and Board had a strategic retreat at The Vines and it was there that the longest-serving director of a state institute of sport broke the news to some of his closer colleagues. The wider staff and a press conference in the executive suite on the ground floor of Challenge Stadium followed in the days after.

The announcement came in early July, with *The West Australian*'s headline reading: "WAIS ace will not miss the drama cycle". It was a reference to the national and public clashes your grandad had with the Australian Cycling Federation and Charlie Walsh, beginning with the selection furore surrounding Tony Davis at the 1988 Seoul Olympics and flowing into the 1990s. But it also referred to the repetitive nature of the battles he was having to fight. Sitting alongside your grandad at the press conference was WAIS Chairman Neil McKerracher.

"Oh God yeah, he was emotional. I've seen tears in his eyes on many occasions. I would consider him quite an emotional person," McKerracher said.

"He was very emotional about Australia's success. He was very considerate and thoughtful with people, he enquired about them and he knew names and what people were doing. He did a lot for athletes behind the scenes, who had had difficulties or tragedies or what-have-you.

"Wally was just a hell of a good bloke and left such an indelible mark. I mean, he knew and was always nice to all my kids. Yes, he was very emotional."

The time was no longer "a-coming"; it had arrived.

Your grandad's final day at WAIS was Friday 7 September 2001. And, while several farewell parties were thrown in his honour, this wouldn't be a complete story if I told you he was universally missed. As Steve Lawrence said: "There was no crying in the hallways". Even your grandad's closest friends would admit there were several people who were happy to see the back of him when he resigned.

That's not necessarily a negative, but it was reflective of the way he went about his business. Your grandad could be dogmatic in his pursuit of whatever goals he was pursuing and gave little concern to his own image or what people thought of him. It was a selfless drive, but it was also one that impacted WAIS, because, by 2001, the bridges he had burnt meant his pursuits were becoming that much harder to gain traction. People were becoming that much harder to convince to listen.

There were even moments when his closest staff members were put offside, as was the case with his longest running co-worker and eventual successor, Steve Lawrence. Lawrence had been headhunted by the New South Wales Institute of Sport for the position of assistant director in the late 1990s and was offered the job, but turned it down.

Your grandad claimed it as a victory for WAIS's preeminent status among state institutes, but the real reason was that Lawrence could not see him doing the north shore-to-Homebush journey every day of his working life and that he remained committed to his position with the national hockey teams – based in Perth – in the lead-up to Sydney.

"He then went and told all the staff and I thought, 'You dickhead, why'd you go and do that?'," Lawrence said.

There were also some suggestions that your grandad was a "director for the time" and that his method was outdated by 2001. There were an equal number of people who refuted that belief, but the fractures were appearing.

As Neil McKerracher said, his passion, talents and abilities were never questioned and he showed a great ability to adapt to changes, "but I think it might be the case that he would have needed some people around him that would have operated a bit differently".

Lawrence, who at the time of writing this was nearing your grandad's record as the longest-serving state institute director, did not feel the same way and said "Wally would probably find himself out of step now with our view". He believed there was a "difference in philosophy and a difference of time" from your grandad's approach to what WAIS became. He was probably half correct.

Your grandad's approach was no longer having the same impact, but that was because it was him – a man who had repeatedly fought the same battles for 17 years – pushing the barrow. There's no reason to suggest a different person with the same approach as your grandad would have been hitting the same walls.

The difference in philosophy Lawrence was referring to was your grandad's propensity to fight the national bodies and systems and to do everything in his power to ensure a WA athlete had the ability to remain in WA, yet still achieve their dreams, if they chose.

"Western Australian-based and fighting for that," Lawrence said.

However, it is important to note that your grandad was never blinded by misguided parochialism. He spoke often about the higher goal for Australian sport, which was to ensure Australia succeeded on the international stage. Often, that was best achieved by creating a strong support network for athletes within their home state and he fought passionately for that. Equally, though, there were times he acknowledged athletes needed to move away and on from WAIS to achieve the best results for Australia.

Perhaps it was more your grandad's view on the structure of WAIS that was "out of step". He held a view that the athlete and coach were the primary players and the lion's share of support therefore needed to be expended on them.

"Our view is that the coach is a manager and middle-management has a role to play, but it's not their view solely, because in essence the athlete is the most important person and it's about empowering athletes to make decisions for themselves," Lawrence said.

"We are still first and foremost athlete-focused, but sometimes, you have to tell the athlete that their best option sits somewhere else. 'Don't stay here, go to Canberra, go to Brisbane'. I think that's a recognition of an evolution in the world."

Lawrence saw WAIS as a stepping stone to bigger opportunities, be that interstate or internationally, and he argued that the AIS was no different. However, your grandad believed the same thing: during the fight to save the women's gymnastics program, he commented that "it is recognised that limited talent bases might not justify an Intensive Training Centre program in all states in all sports".

And in argument against the Department of Sport and Recreation's strategy to take training bases to all corners of the state, he argued that "if you live in Albany and you want to do dentistry, you move to the university. You can't take a university to every student."

Sport was changing and so was the world in which it was administered, but there were those, such as Liz Chetkovich, who believed that world desperately needed people like your grandad.

"I think sport has gone too far in the way of categorising this, KPI that, Winning Edge this; the thing that makes people perform at the highest level is what human beings do for human beings," Chetkovich said.

"I heard an interview on the radio about Ross Lyon (Fremantle Dockers coach), in that Ross Lyon was able to sell his vision to his coaches, to his players and to his club and make them follow him unconditionally. Other coaches might have come and put in these structures and systems that looked very sound, but if you can't get the rats to follow you, if you can't play the Pied Piper, you can't get the results.

"I think it's underestimated what's required to get people to fully embrace what's required of you and go with you unconditionally. You will not find one successful athlete that is not following a coach or a system that is inspiring them to work the way they need to work. Wally did that.

"I would challenge any opinion that he was a director for the time and say: yes, he would have needed to have been led into the brave new world, but there's a possibility that we've gone too far into that other realm and we're so over-regulated that we've lost the feel for the sport.

"What's Justin Langer done that's different (to WA cricket)? He's inspired the players. What did Darren Lehman do (to Australian cricket)? In six months, did the KPIs change, did the structure change? No, the inspirational leader changed.

"An institute is no different: if you're not inspired by the leader, what are you getting out of it? Wally's method of leadership is more valid now than ever before."

That, unfortunately, was not the point. The point was that, for whatever reason – be it being "out of step", be it weariness, or be it a result of bridges burnt – your grandad was not having the same impact and it made every battle that little bit harder. The effect of that was given even more significance due to the way in which WAIS had operated for 17 years.

Your grandad was the face of WAIS. Another way of expanding the acronym of the institute was: Wally's Australian Institute of Sport. That was mostly referred to light-heartedly and your grandad never set out to make it the case, but it was a result of his high profile. He had been a successful journalist and had existing relationships with the media, while also continuing his media work while at WAIS.

The media liked him because he was one of them and it was happy to give the Institute – through your grandad – airtime and column space. WAIS was often a leader and its voice was heard in a wide, public domain. That had some major benefits for WAIS, especially in the form of the corporate investment that the Institute was able to attract as a result of its ongoing media coverage and public profile.

WAIS has not been able to match the investment of the corporate sector since your grandad left. That could be the result of many factors – the Global Financial Crisis, for example – but undoubtedly one of your grandad's strengths was his profile. It was a cornerstone of his directorship. It helped WAIS make inroads where others could not. When that power waned – when people stopped listening to the squeaky wheel – so too did WAIS's profile.

"It was his singularity and sense of purpose and his clarity and vision that was at the core of everything that WAIS was, stood for and, in many ways, still is," Mick Aitken said.

"He was WAIS. The Chairman, the Board, the staff, they all come and go. He was WAIS. I wouldn't say Wally was omnipotent, because he was very respectful of the Board and everyone involved, but he didn't suffer fools and if anyone disagreed with him, they better have a bloody good reason and he wouldn't want to waste too much time with people who didn't share his vision.

"WAIS, in a way, had become a victim of its own success under Wally."

The Western Australian Institute of Sport was the leading state institute in the country when your grandad left. Your grandad took up the position of director on 4 June, 1984 and finished on 7 September 2001.

WAIS in that time had grown from a one-person organisation with a budget of $300,0000, to one comprised of 50 staff and a budget of more than $4-million. The state's Olympic representation expanded from 22 athletes in six sports at the Los Angeles Olympics, to 51 competitors in 20 sports and a record eight West Australian gold medallists in Sydney.

WAIS had created precedence and played a lead role in defending the rights of athletes against national selection policies and strategies that were perceived as unjust: a lead role and battles that unlikely would have been played and fought to the same extent had it not been for your grandad and WAIS. He then ensured athletes would not have to hope individuals such as him would take up their fight by being pivotal in the establishment of the National Elite Sports Council (NESC): a body comprised of state institutes and academies that combined for a more powerful voice.

Your grandad chaired NESC for several years. He also, specifically, was a key player in securing Federal Government funding for the states in the late 1980s. He was involved in the process around the construction of the $20-million State Sports Centre – the Superdrome, which became Challenge Stadium and is currently HBF stadium – and was crucial in initiating and securing the planning and building of the standalone WAIS offices that sat adjacent to it for the better part of two decades.

But WAIS was ready for your grandad to step aside, even if parts of your grandad were not ready to step aside from WAIS. And it was ready because of the work your grandad had invested. As Olympian Ric Charlesworth said, the end for your grandad at WAIS was inevitable at some point, "but it was a pretty damned good image that he left".

The press conference was called. Murmurs filled the room, before silence as your grandad announced his resignation. "Purely personal," was a phrase used in explaining the decision. That was later interpreted by many as "family time". That was not necessarily true.

In a television special on your grandad's life produced by the ABC after he passed away, one former colleague explained that the decision to leave WAIS was based primarily on a desire to spend more time with your nana, your Uncle Mark and me. That was not correct.

Your grandad and I, at that point in our lives, did not get along well. I fought him at every turn and I devoted far more energy to friends than I did family. Your grandad and I did not spend much time together, but that had nothing to do with his work. That was to do with our relationship.

And it would probably be more appropriate to say that it had more to do with me: your grandad attempted to forge a relationship with me on several occasions, even organising weekend fishing trips down south for just us. The problem was, I didn't really like fishing and would have preferred to play the latest computer game. Our interests were too far apart.

Well, not even that is totally accurate. I deliberately feigned a lack of interest in sport – and in his interests – as a way of challenging him to the point that I believed it. Part of the reason I played ice hockey from 15-years-old was that it was a sport I believed he knew little about. The irony came later when he told me he once commentated an Australia-v-New Zealand ice hockey match at the now-demolished Mirrabooka Skaters On Ice.

It was not until after your grandad passed away that I allowed my love for his same passions to come out. That was when I entered sports journalism. And it was not until after he passed away that my best friend told me a secret your grandad had kept for almost a decade: he used to sneak into the ice rink after my games had started and would watch me, before sneaking out at the end.

I never knew he was there; he didn't want me to know, because he knew I would challenge it. My friend knew, because he saw him and spoke to him. He kept the secret he was asked to keep.

Your uncle and your grandad had a very different relationship. Your uncle was much younger than me – he was born in 1992 – and that was probably a contributing factor, but he also allowed himself to love your grandad's passions. Your grandad coached your uncle's cricket team and was always there to help at junior football. He would take him to trainings and take him for extra trainings – just them – either after school or on the weekends. And, as I mentioned previously, your nana and grandad loved and respected each other very much.

Despite how busy both of their lives were, they always had Friday dinner together, Saturday dinner with friends and Sunday dinner with all of us. I frequently chose to stay home. Your grandad was always there for the family, when the family wanted or needed him to be there. Undoubtedly, there was probably part of him that felt he was so tired from WAIS that he was not with the family as much as he could have been. But that was not why he resigned from the Institute. That reason was simply to do with the battles that exhausted him and the opportunity that arose to return to the ABC.

In announcing he had taken that opportunity, the tears welled in his eyes. WAIS was his baby and, despite the growing pains, it's always difficult for a guardian to let go of their baby.

"It's not going to be easy to let that go, to step back from it," he told *The West Magazine*.

Your grandad was emotional in walking away from WAIS but he was also pragmatic in pointing out the fact that "my new position at the ABC will give me the opportunity to do something that I enjoy doing for the next 10 years". And he did enjoy it. As immensely as he enjoyed his time steering the Western Australian Institute of Sport.

The tragedy was that it was for far less than 10 years.

WA Sports Federation boss Mick Aitken (above, right), described the environment of sport in WA in the 1980s as "tense and intense" – but he and your grandad helped the state achieve amazing results, including the development of the Perth Superdrome. WAIS has called the Superdrome home since 1986, including when it developed its first standalone building, at which your grandad is pictured below with Sports Minister Norman Moore (middle) and advisor Halem Pierera (right).

Life is a balancing act and your grandad and nana perfected it. They lived and worked together, whether that was as a journalist and athlete (above, courtesy NINE Network and State Library of WA, and below, ahead of the 1982 Brisbane Commonwealth Games), or director and coach (right). Both were immersed in a life they loved, which was only enhanced by their love for each other.

A life driven by passion is rarely an idle life and that was certainly the case for your grandad.

Not only was he balancing his life and love with sport and your nana, but at the same time he remained a working journalist and broadcaster, regularly contributing to newspapers, broadcasting sport and talkback radio on the weekends and even anchoring TV sports news during Olympic and Commonwealth Games, when the usual anchors were abroad.

He did all that around his "regular" job as the inaugural director of WAIS. And he was a leader in every field.

One of your grandad's greatest strengths was in encouraging and empowering others to achieve greatness, such as three-time Olympic hockey champion and 1995 WAIS Athlete of the Year Rechelle Hawkes (above).

However, in helping others achieve greatness, your grandad was also recognised for his contributions to the state when in 2000 he was named West Australian Citizen of the Year in Sport (below, back row, second from left). He was awarded the Australian Sports Medal in the same year, before being named a Member of the Order of Australia in 2003.

PART THREE

Chapter 16

Follow Your Heart

It was August 2001. The questions came thick and fast.

The man answering them was different: he was talking about Bruce Rock, fifth grade teacher Colin Smith and the army, but he was no longer the mischievous, scrawny 21-year-old who graduated a 2Lt from the Scheyville Officers Training Unit. He was a man who had steered the Western Australian Institute of Sport and WA high performance sport for 17 years to unprecedented success, with an unbroken three decades in the media covering countless internationally and nationally significant events.

He was a loving, devoted husband and had been for 20 years. He was father to a moody 17-year-old preparing to graduate high school, and an adoring nine-year-old infatuated with his dad and the world of sport he was immersed in. His hair was as thick as ever, although the jet black was now speckled with grey and the scrawny teenage frame had matured into that of a fit and strong half-centurion.

And that face: it had rounded, but remained home to a pursed-lip, cheeky grin that seemed hooked at its edges to his ears, with the eyes a mirror of the smile. It was a smile that made several appearances that morning, sitting in the main studio of 720 ABC Perth as Mornings host Liam Bartlett stated that "the boy from Bruce Rock has come a long way" as part of a WA Story interview less than a month before your grandad's final day at WAIS.

"It's been a long journey, but it's been a very exciting one and I've always just felt so privileged to be able to be pursuing a professional career in an area that has, really, always been my hobby," your grandad replied. "It's been a lot of fun."

This next part goes quickly, Charlotte. Not for a lack of activity – your grandad jammed a lot into a short amount of time, as he always did – but he was 53-years-old. In just five years, the main studio of

720 ABC Perth would be renamed the Wally Foreman Studio. In just five years, the world as we knew it would change forever.

These were the final years of your grandad's life.

Convincing your grandad to take part in that interview was no small feat for Liam Bartlett. One of the main reasons your grandad endeared himself to so many people was that he rarely conducted himself with a motivation of ego. So taking part in a 30min show about himself was not overly appealing.

"He would always say things like, 'No, Liam, not me, surely there's someone better', and would invariably end up saying, 'Oh, ok, when do you want to do it?'," Bartlett said.

"He fit the criteria perfectly: he had a reasonably high profile, he'd done things that had caused him to come into contact with a lot of people over the years, he'd achieved some good things through WAIS, public achievements, public profile – notoriety to an extent – and his own story hadn't been told."

That story had plenty to it, as well. Your grandad returned to the ABC a far more experienced man than when he first left in 1979. His time at WAIS never halted his momentum in the media and, instead, further built on his understanding of sport, adding administrative nous, a vast array of contacts and an enormous amount of respect and credibility for his achievements.

Those achievements were later recognised with the Order of Australia Medal for Services to Sport and the WA Citizen of the Year for Sport awards, but they also accompanied the ever-growing list of experiences he had taken in through broadcasting. Even before your grandad's return to the ABC in 2001, he had already commentated Test cricket, Olympic and Commonwealth Games, Davis Cup tennis, international hockey tournaments, AFL and WAFL football, rowing and swimming.

I know I'm biased, but I also truly believe it is fair to say that there was no-one like your grandad in Australian sports broadcasting and there likely never will be again. The reason for that is due to the professionalisation of sport and the levels of bureaucracy as a result.

It is unlikely a state high performance body will ever again appoint a director or chief executive straight out of the media, with no university qualification and no previous relevant administrative experience. Even the age of 36 would be borderline too young and a candidate would be lucky to get an interview these days without a Masters of Business and Administration (MBA).

Yet, your grandad was given the opportunity to effectively pursue two separate career paths – the media and sports administration – at the same time and in a way that allowed them to complement each other. The results he achieved stand as an example that, sometimes, the modern world is not as efficient as it believes it is in comparison to the past.

"The ABC gained a bit of gravitas and credibility when he came back," Bartlett said.

"He was perfect to come back, because, to me, that's where you (the audience) go for that sort of experience. You don't get that as much these days because those people are no longer there. That's what he brought to the ABC. That's why he was perfect."

Quantifying what it was your grandad brought back to the ABC was one of the most challenging parts of this writing process. How do I quantify an intangible talent?

What made your grandad so skilled at painting word pictures of an event that was in front of him and in a way that engaged an audience that was not there? Was it as simple as giving the scores at the correct time? Or the appropriate rise and fall in the level and tempo of his voice, as opposed to incessant shouting? Did he read more dictionaries than anyone else and simply have a bigger repertoire of words at his disposal?

Perhaps it was your grandad who summed it up best.

"Well, you can do a lot of research before an event, but I think you'll find the really good commentators have accumulated a wealth of knowledge throughout their lives," he told *The West Magazine* in 2001.

"I know that when I used to sit there and talk to people like Dennis Cometti, he was doing much the same things as me as a seven or eight-year-old. You just have to have this passion for sport and it goes back as long as you can remember. And you end up with this huge amount of knowledge.

"Certainly, you must do research before a major event, but I don't think you can suddenly go out at the age of 20 or 21 and acquire knowledge that people have acquired because they've been doing it as an interest from a very young age."

Your nana, in putting on her coaching hat, would tell you that "perfect practice makes perfect". The double-use of "perfect" is not an error: many people reel out the adage of "practice makes perfect", but if you practice something the wrong way 1000 times, that certainly does not make the end result perfect. Your grandad, beyond who he was as a person, was a trained journalist, he was a trained 2Lt officer and had self-trained as a manager of a hundred staff for 17-years; all required strong communications skill. He had a lifetime of perfect practice.

"Wally is in the same category as people like Dennis Cometti and George Grljusich, Tim Lane, as well as Glenn Mitchell," Liam Bartlett said.

"Those people are trained communicators: that's what they were trained in first up, they were trained very well and they learnt their craft and then they went out and applied it. The trend has been that you take people from the ranks of retired sports stars, but I'm sorry: playing the game is not the groundwork, the foundation, for communicating the game. The communicators are the ones who should be communicating the game."

Dennis Cometti himself in his eulogy for your grandad delivered a similar observation.

"A couple of years ago I heard him broadcasting the Australian Open tennis; Juan Carlos Ferrero was playing Wayne Ferreira," Cometti said. "They were having these incredible rallies: Ferrero, Ferreira; Ferreira, Ferrero. I drove home and sat in the car transfixed to Wally's call, it sounded like a sobriety test, but Wally didn't miss a beat. I was exhausted and rang him the next day and said he was great.

"But, then again, Wal was my favourite broadcaster and, in so many respects, I felt his career had mirrored that of his sporting hero Dennis Lillee: Wally had gone from a tearaway quick, to a craftsman, to an elder statesman. Wal understood broadcasting is a shared experience; it's supposed to be entertaining. He was a humble broadcaster and quite happily made fun of himself.

"There was no, 'I told you so', in Wally Foreman."

Or perhaps your grandad, as a broadcaster, was an oxymoron: did his ability as a commentator actually have little to do with his commentary ability? Was it more about who he was and how that combined with his skills? But, then, that was the same challenge; attempting to explain why he "was such a good bloke".

That came down to character and the two people responsible for instilling that in him were your Great Grandad Eric and Great Grandma Norma. And when it came to engendering that character on the microphone, it was the former that first guided your grandad.

One of the hidden gems uncovered in this writing process was the revelation that your Great Grandad Eric had a short stint as a sports broadcaster. Your grandad was, of course, not around to remind everyone and your great aunties were not old enough to remember, which is why many of the family had no idea it had taken place. Your great grandad remembered, though, and he was quick to recall – even at 97 – the influence it had on his only son.

"When he was on the radio, did you used to listen to him?" I had asked.

"Oh, yes," your Great Grandad Eric responded. "I used to listen to him and was able to correct him quite a bit, because I used to do quite a bit for three years as a radio announcer myself."

We were sitting in your great grandad's loungeroom by the electric heater on a cold winter's morning. I was taken aback.

"On the radio? You were on the radio?"

"Oh yes, as an announcer. I used to do a bit on Kalgoorlie sports, *Night Like Day Sports*, as they used to call it."

It would have been nothing more than an interesting point in your great grandad's life, if not for the fact your grandad went on to become one of the most loved sports broadcasters in the state. Your Great Grandad Eric commentated every Tuesday night for a period of about three years around a local sports meet, he said, and followed it up with some coaching once he was off the air. There would be other times when he broadcast a 30min sports show to the region. The time in broadcasting ended as your great grandad's work responsibilities increased.

Your great grandad was 97-years-old when he was interviewed for this book, so he must be given a little slack, as some of the dates he mentioned did not align. If your grandad took as much of an interest as was described, it was more likely that Great Grandad Eric's broadcasting days were after the family moved to Bruce Rock in 1950, otherwise your grandad would not have been old enough to understand what was happening. And the recollections suggested your grandad knew exactly what was happening.

"He did used to listen to me, as a matter of fact, and he was probably one of my greatest critics: 'Geez, dad, you gave him a bit of a bad run, didn't you', or, 'You didn't praise him enough'," your great grandad said.

"He was quite critical of what I did, but it showed he was listening. I think that's where he got his passion for radio from. He saw, if I say so myself, that I didn't do a bad job of it, that I handled the situation and it can be handled, provided you put preparation into it. You don't just get on the air and read a script, because you're not worth a two-bob watch if you do that.

"I loved it, but I don't think I ever had the yearn to be a radio journalist; it was just a job they wanted done, they thought I could do it, and so I did it."

The decades passed and the country turned into the city and your grandad turned from a mischievous child into a mischievous professional. And your great grandad's voice in sports broadcasting turned into that of your grandad's.

"I never really criticised him; I more tutored him than being a critic," your great grandad said.

"With Wally, it wasn't hard to hurt his feelings. In other words, he didn't like criticism very much. He was terribly nervous the first time he went on, until he became a bit harder and that's when he started to blossom; when he got the confidence that he could do it.

"When I listened to him, I was as proud as punch. I always thought he did a far better job than what I did. I had nobody to tutor me, though. There was a script and away you go. I knew very well what it was like – being before the public – even though you couldn't see them and I knew it was fairly confronting. I knew he had to overcome that and, to overcome it, he had to be pretty smooth in what he was saying.

"That was the angle I took (in my advice to him): 'Don't jibber about what you're trying to say, otherwise you're going to foul it up. Be sure about what you're trying to say and put it in the finest words you can think of'. I used to encourage him that if he had some sort of slant on something and he could make a joke of it, then use it, by all means and that's par for the course, to be able to pick a hole in something.

"When he got into a tight corner and was battling for words, I think he took the nettle by the hand and I think that made Wally; he was pretty smart that way. If he got cornered, he could wiggle his way through it."

The remarkable part of your great grandad's words is the reality they reflected. They contained the message of the importance in preparation that makes a good broadcaster, because, for all the talent your grandad had, he would not have been worth "a two-bob watch" without the preparation to back it up.

They contained the challenges for your grandad in being a public voice, as despite his thorough enjoyment of his job, it was something that was not always easy for him. It might surprise many except those close to him to know that your grandad was a sensitive person and conflict or criticism never sat well with him, regardless of the battles he fought for the benefit of others and the criticisms he wore as a result.

The words of your great grandad also contained the importance of measure; the advice not to jibber, to be sure of word and to "put it in the finest words you can think of". And, of course, "make a joke of it". Anyone who listened to your grandad broadcast would recognise every piece of that advice in his style.

Perfect guidance. Perfect practice.

The guidance of your great grandparents also taught an innate respect for people. Those values also came with country life. It is engrained in those who work the land, because whether it's battling a bushfire, fundraising for the local sports club, sowing a paddock or mulesing a flock of sheep, everyone is in the same situation and the only way through is together.

There were, of course, people your grandad did not like. But his default starting position was always respect and collaboration. He would alter as required from there.

And while all that sounds trivial and inconsequential, it was another important trait your grandad brought to the ABC and a legacy he left there. Newsrooms and media organisations are an interesting place to work. Technically, everyone is on the same team, but it rarely feels that way. Most journalists and broadcasters view their self-worth as the most important aspect of their job and in many ways that's fair; it is not an outlet's worth that helps them obtain and keep their jobs, it's their own.

When I was working as a journalist, one of the biggest sources of support for me was, ironically, from a man who worked at a rival outlet. He always phoned me, gave me pointers and even introduced me to contacts. He had the benefit of experience on his side and had already proven himself to the point where he was comfortable with what he offered professionally and had no hesitation in helping others reach that point.

It was the same for your grandad. By the time he returned to the ABC, he had achieved so much in such a diverse range of jobs, including media, that what others did was inconsequential to his career. While always remaining ambitious, he was also the sort of person who never felt threatened by the ambitions of others.

That was as true for the next generation as it was his peers. One of your grandad's closest friends at the ABC was Russell Woolf, the former Drive presenter who shared a partition with your grandad in the office. Woolf recalled the willingness of your grandad to help, before pulling up a chair alongside his mate to run him through the three pages of handwritten notes he had prepared. Your grandad was a stickler for detail, which was another trait he believed was important, but above all else, he was always there for his colleagues.

"He had an attention to detail that was fantastic," Woolf said.

"In fact, I can remember because of his association with Lyn and therefore with Kylie Wheeler after she was accepted to a national team, he asked if I'd be interested in speaking to her. He'd say I didn't have to, but explained why it was such a good story and what she'd achieved, then he'd deliver his notes, then when I did the interview with her, I called her a decathlon athlete instead of heptathlon.

"I came off air and he called me on it and was getting all indignant about it, but I was like, 'What's five sport make a difference?'. He never got angry about it, but it stays with me to this day, because it was about being a journalist with the ABC, broadcasting to an audience that expects you to give the right information. That was exactly how I read it and he wouldn't have said that, but I think that was the message that I took away from it.

"I still, to this day, think about it, because in the rush to get to air every day with 15 stories or whatever, sometimes there's slips here and there, but we make sure we try to be accurate. It still, in fact, makes my skin crawl a bit when I think about it. It's good for me, though, because I do feel like I still have Wal sitting on my shoulder every now and then."

Clint Wheeldon, the man who filled the position with ABC Sport made vacant by your grandad's passing, remembered the collegiality of your grandad well. Wheeldon was working for ABC TV at the opposite end to your grandad of the East Perth building. He leaned on your grandad and Glenn Mitchell almost weekly – every Tuesday – for story ideas, when the commercial stations "would go and talk to whatever footballer they happened to be paying that season".

The pair struck up a friendship and your grandad even suggested to Wheeldon, who always held ambitions to get into sports commentating and made no secret of it, that he was intending to retire at 60, giving the young protégé a clear timeline with which to prepare.

"Both Glenn and Wally were very helpful, always," Wheeldon said.

"I'll be honest, I thought, 'Ok, well I've got three years to get myself into a position that when Wally retires I can take his job'. Unfortunately, it ended up being quicker than any of us expected.

"I don't know if you can give a bloke a bigger rap than this: it was an impossible job to step into, because of what he meant to everyone. I almost got drowned in well-wishes. Talk about big shoes to fill; they were impossible to fill, not just because of a him as a broadcaster, but him as a human being."

Wheeldon was not the only one to experience that warmth and welcoming nature of your grandad. Roanna Edwards was a 20-year-old budding broadcaster when she joined the ABC Local Radio sports department in East Perth as an indigenous trainee. She had initially wanted a job out of Geraldton, as it was closer to home, and had hoped for the general news rounds.

"I remember my interview, I remember waiting to hear back and I remember the excitement of being told I had the job. But above all, I remember a message left on the voicemail of my mobile phone a few days before I started," Edwards said.

"It went: 'Oh, hi Roanna, it's Wally Foreman here from ABC Radio Sport. I just thought I'd call to say congratulations and welcome to our team. I'm looking forward to meeting you when you start with us in a few weeks. No need to return my call. OK, bye'. I knew nothing about radio, but I knew a bit about the ABC and, in particular, Grandstand. Dad had made us listen to it on all those car trips from our various homes across WA's Mid-West and Wheatbelt to Perth.

"I'll be honest, though, I didn't know much – except *that* voice. I got a rush of excitement as I listened to the message, I was so awestruck. I knew this voice more than I knew most of my families'. Those smooth tones. That warm, cheery, knowledgeable, trustworthy sound. The beautiful, distinct sound of Wally Foreman. I can hear that very voice 10 years since I last heard it in person."

Edwards was immediately absorbed into the ABC Local Radio Sport family, just as Bruce Rock had absorbed your grandad and his family throughout the 1950s. In her first week on the job, she joined your grandad at the WACA Ground for the Test Match between Australia and South Africa, accompanying him from the Level 5 Broadcast boxes to the press conference area on the ground floor, passing through the members' area on the way. The walk was an eye-opener, with your grandad either greeting or being greeted by almost everyone in attendance, even being asked for autographs by the younger crowd.

"Every person he stopped and talked to, he introduced me to," Edwards said. "He made me feel included and important. That was Wally."

And that was one of his lasting legacies, according to Deborah Leavitt, who during your grandad's time was promoted from producer to Local Content Manager and was your grandad's boss.

"I always felt really honoured that he was part of our team," Leavitt said.

"The thing that always stood out for me was his collegiality; he was always the person there with a phone number to help another program if they were looking for a specific person to interview. He was there for News or Television, there was no sort of silo mentality in the way he would look at his responsibility.

"He was able to leave a real legacy around that, because up until that point I think there had been quite a bit of division in radio and television news and he was one of those people who could seamlessly and effortlessly move between the two types of platforms. It never mattered to him, it was all about the audience being the most important thing, so if it meant helping TV get the story, then he was onto it.

"Media is notoriously competitive, so that was probably the gift of someone who had a whole career before coming into it."

And then there was Sports Talk.

A broadcaster can connect with their audience only so much through one-way commentary. The true bond comes from the two-way relationship of talkback radio and, for your grandad, that avenue was primarily the weekend show Sports Talk; a program exactly as it sounds, dedicated to discussing all issues of sport.

There was a host, or facilitator – such as your grandad – and two experts. The experts were often former players of particular sports, but could also be people such as current athletes and journalists. And there was one particular combination your grandad was very fond of: himself facilitating the forthright Ken Judge and the rambunctious Kim Hughes.

Sadly, two of that trio have already passed away. Your grandad was the first to leave us, in 2006, before Judge passed away on his 58th birthday, the 15 January 2016, after a lengthy battle with multiple myeloma – a type of cancer. Both Judge and your grandad were the same age when they died.

The connection in death reflected the connection in life, because your grandad and Judge built a strong relationship through the ABC, while your grandad also had an extensive history with Hughes. When the three combined for Sports Talk, they created an atmosphere of in-depth knowledge, unmatched experience and utter enjoyment of each other's company.

"Sports Talk, it was fantastic. It was fun," Judge said when interviewed for this book in 2012.

"There was always a bit of banter and the times when I loved it best was when Hughesy, me and Wally did it, because we just had great fun. It was three blokes, sitting around, talking sport and shooting the breeze with a few backhanders to one another.

"Wally knew Hughesy quite well from when he was a kid, so

he knew a few things that he could hang on Hughesy and things like that. Of course, I worked with Hughesy, so I could put shit on him from that. So, Hughesy was a good fall-guy, because we could both put shit on him.

"It was the most enjoyable two hours you could have talking sport, because it wasn't like you were talking to anyone, it was just like you were talking between the three of you. I think the listeners loved that, because we often had listeners call up and say, 'Love the show, you guys sound like you're having a ball', and that was exactly what it was about. It wasn't working; it was having fun."

That enjoyment was a deliberate focus for your grandad, but it was not necessarily altruistic. Of course, your grandad wanted to have fun and enjoy what he was doing, but as many of his colleagues have pointed out in describing the art of a good broadcaster, insincerity is quickly recognised and rebuked by listeners. The Sports Talk team needed to enjoy what they were doing in order for the audience to enjoy it as well and that responsibility largely came down to your grandad. Your grandad was personable and had a good rapport with his experts, but the group was not there for a comedy gig.

Judge was a premiership player with Hawthorn and later coached both the Hawks and West Coast Eagles, so had an intimate knowledge of football. Hughes in 1979 became the first West Australian to captain the national cricket team and the second youngest at just 25-years-and-57-days-old, gaining great experiences and insight into cricket.

The natural Australian affinity for cricket and football ensured the two experts were sufficiently versed in each other's sports, but they could not be expected to be proficient in the eclectic mix of whatever else had the potential to be discussed at any moment and, with such a small panel, your grandad needed to ensure that everyone was prepared. Both Judge and Hughes recalled your grandad's meticulous efforts in ensuring all three of them combined to produce the best possible show for the listener.

"I loved Sports Talk," Hughes said.

"We had good chemistry and the listeners can tell that; we knew each other well so we could hang shit on each other. With Wally – and he's the only one who's ever done it – he'd call me up on a Thursday or Friday and say, 'Right, these are the topics, have a read in *The West* of this, that and that, so you're up to speed'.

"Wally was the perfect MC: people who call up want to hear from the experts. Wal would of course come in with some statistics and what-have-you and we'd have a good rapport. The way Wally did things wasn't the same way everyone else did things."

It was a point with which Judge concurred.

"Can I tell you another thing about working with Wally: Wally was a very knowledgeable person himself, but he respected that we were the experts," Judge said.

"He could hold his own on any sport people called up about, but he knew that he was the host and that people wanted to talk to the experts, so when people rang up, he would direct the questions to us. If it was something we didn't know, such as cycling and sports like that, then he would take that, but if it was footy or cricket, then he would direct it to us.

"Every Friday he would call up – and Clint Wheeldon does it now, too – and say, 'This is who we've got on, tomorrow' and he'd give you a chance to think about it and prepare. Wally wanted us to prepare, so that the show could be as good as possible. We didn't always get that."

Of course, it was not only the experts and athletes your grandad had a rapport with and, as Hughes said, he was "one of the few people who can mix with politicians, sponsors, athletes and the media". There is a belief rolled out often that boldly declares "sport and politics should never mix", but the reality is that they are rarely independent of each other.

Your grandad understood that probably better that any other commentator of his time, given his vast experience in dealing with government, both federal and state, throughout his tenure at WAIS. It enabled him to bring a unique and learned insight to the listeners when administrative and political issues breached sport's field. Few politically-associated sports issues polarised the

WA community like the debate over the city's requirement for a new stadium.

It was an issue that your grandad was passionate about and he had been an advocate for the construction of a replacement for Subiaco Oval since the 1990s, when Perth failed in its bid to attract the Commonwealth Games and it was becoming abundantly clear that the city's infrastructure was inadequate for local needs, let alone hosting international events. The stadium debate has thankfully and finally ended, but it waged for decades of inaction.

Reports were produced – slowly – then sat on shelves. Decisions were made, then overturned by a new government. The site continuously shifted, from Subiaco, to East Perth, to Burswood and even had an area in Cockburn being entertained as an option. "Entertained" is an appropriate word, because placing the state's prestigious, top-tier stadium in Cockburn would have seemed like something out of a sitcom. A major turning point for the issue came with Labor taking office in 2001 under Premier Dr Geoff Gallop and Alan Carpenter being appointed Minister for Sport and Recreation.

It was a turning point on a few levels and you will remember the impact the previous Liberal Government had on your grandad, as well as the personal impact Carpenter had on him second-guessing his decision to leave WAIS. However, in terms of sport in the state, WA again had a minister of action and Carpenter commissioned the Langoulant Report in 2003 to finally arrive at a decision around the "where" and "how big" aspects of the stadium.

Your grandad played an important role in that report as a contributor and consultant, due to his experience from WAIS, but he also ensured the public was kept aware of the subject every step of the way.

"The role your father played, in my thinking, was keeping the issue in the forefront of people's minds, otherwise you could keep talking about it for the next 35 years," said Carpenter, who went on to become Premier of WA in 2006.

"My view was that we needed a multipurpose, world-class stadium, so we needed a report; it was going to be chaired by Ron Alexander, it ended up being John Langoulant. It took a bit longer than I hoped it would (four years). There was a preliminary process – a gap analysis of what we needed – and we started to identify the need for a stadium, which didn't really need to be identified, but it was answering the questions of, 'How big?', and, 'Where?'.

"My clearest recollection of your dad around the stadium was having a face-to-face meeting with him and then being interviewed by him. We'd announced a 60,000 seat stadium and the first thing he said was, 'It's not big enough', because one of his things was that we wanted to attract big events. I was prepared for it, because I think the World Cup was on in Germany at the time and I'd had a look at all of their stadiums and there were only a couple that were more than 50,000.

"Your dad had strong views on the stadium and had it as a running topic on Sports Talk every week. The thing that I would say is, not so much the specifics, but the fact that he was agitating to get it done was very important."

Roanna Edwards produced many of those Sports Talk shows. She saw first-hand your grandad's depth of knowledge on almost any topic that arose and she witnessed his ability to form and retain the relationships he did, from politicians like Carpenter, to his expert panel of Hughes and Judge. Regardless of who it was he was dealing with, there was always mutual respect.

"There's a common theme there: Wally was a country man with an enormous heart for regional West Australians," Edwards said. "It's why I admired him so much and why his listeners admired him in return."

Your grandad never lost his love for the bush and a piece of his heart always remained in Bruce Rock. It's difficult for city dwellers – and make no mistake, I count myself in that category – to understand the connection regional Western Australians have with the ABC. Smartphones, apps and higher-powered radio towers might now mean there is a greater selection of listening options in the country, but for much of our history the national broadcaster was the only major station that reached into the regions.

Your grandad never lost sight of that. He knew that when he uttered the words, "720 ABC Perth", that he was often not talking just to the people of Perth and he was determined to acknowledge that.

"Wally always would talk about people from the bush and he gave them a voice," Hughes said.

"That's why he was so loved. There'd hardly be a country town where he hadn't done a sportsman's night or a Sports Talk. In fact, he used to tell a story that he was doing a sportsman's night out in the country and had asked, 'Can you hear me up the back', and some bloke piped up, 'Yes, but I'm happy to swap with someone who can't'.

"I use that story now when I do talks and every time I think of Wally. I of course mention him and say he told me the story, but all of a sudden you've broken the ice and the crowd relaxes. Everyone knew Wal. And they loved him."

The sportsman's night Hughes referred to often occurred around an initiative of your grandad's to take Sports Talk out to the country. It was not often – once or twice a year – but it was an important recognition of the regions and, while I cannot conclusively say that it was an idea started by your grandad, no-one I spoke to could recall it happening before his return to the ABC in 2001.

"It was a thing they (the ABC) were going to do regularly and he was really keen to do it, to take Sports Talk to country towns," Judge said.

"It was Wally's idea, just two or three times a year, because we had great audiences in the country and, of course, everyone in the country loved him. I remember doing one at the shopping centre in Geraldton and there were people everywhere. Of course, him being there, it was, 'Wally this' and 'Wally that'. People loved it."

Your grandad's devotion to the country was ever-present, but it also came with its challenges. Hughes recalled him as a "sensitive soul", who wanted to help everyone and fix every problem. The more he engaged the regions, the more he wanted to engage them and the more they wanted to engage him.

Your grandad probably wouldn't want those challenges discussed, because it was just the person he was that he never looked at requests for assistance as a burden. However, the demands were taxing on him at times. It was only his love for the people of the country that kept him going.

"I remember how many Drought Buster forums and men's group talks for farmers Wally did that year before we lost him," Edwards said.

"Wally was a man of the people: the audience adored him and his listeners were so loyal. Whether it was Jean in Geraldton stirring him up with that easily recognised thick accent – 'Vollleeyy, come on Volley, you can't talk about my Eagles like dart' – or some random thought for the week from dear old Dave in Albany, who passed away not long after Wal, and even the likes of Bob in Mt Barker.

"They listened every week, they called every week. And Wally loved to take their call."

It was easy for the listeners to like your grandad. He made it easy.

He understood that broadcasting was not about him, it was about the experience for the listener. At the same time, being talkback, there was a relationship with the audience that needed to be built and relationships are two-way. So, while he needed to share parts of his life, he did so in a way that made it about the listener.

He revelled in that and it was those parts that he shared that endeared him to the public. Your grandad was happy to laugh at himself and make himself the punchline of jokes, which often centred around his inability to operate modern technology. And he did so to the point that he exaggerated his incompetence at his own expense for the enjoyment of the listener. Well, mostly exaggerated his incompetence, as Russell Woolf remembered.

"I think everyone knows he was a luddite and hopeless with technology, so he used to always write long-hand," Woolf said. "His writing was not always that easy to read, actually, but it was always pen and paper. He'd go up to the printer and you'd think, 'Oh, he's printed something off, well done Wal', but he was just grabbing a hundred pages out of the cartridge to take back to his desk and write."

Your Uncle Mark, at barely 10-years-old, often had to record football games for your grandad, because he could not work out how to do it. However, given he was attempting to use a VCR and that technology no longer exists – it was born and died off within your grandad's lifetime – it's possible you might need to give me the same assistance at some point. And possibly even help out your Uncle Mark, too.

However, regardless of whether or not his incompetence was overplayed, the audience enjoyed your grandad's tales and exploits to the point where the ABC put together several multiple-minute segments for broadcast and could have created a weekly series. There was the time producer Alicia Hanson recorded your grandad's running commentary of his first-time use of an ATM machine, complete with sound effects of the machine beeping incessantly at him, asking if he needed more time, and a member of the public telling him, "It's like sex, Wally: don't rush it".

Then there was the time Afternoons presenter Bernadette Young announced to the audience that your grandad had lost his filing cabinet keys. The ensuing avalanche of suggestions on where to find them and how to find them – including praying to Saint Anthony, the Patron Saint of returning lost items – demanded a follow-up when your grandad eventually found them.

"So, you're actually at the point now with these where you'd prefer not to find them, is that the case?," Young asked your grandad, again providing running commentary as he walked into the ABC building in East Perth.

"If these are the keys, I'd certainly have rather not found them where I found them," he replied.

They were in the centre console of his car; a place your nana told him to look at the very start of the month-long search and which he vehemently asserted he had checked.

They were stories that your grandad collated into a larger world of incompetence for the entertainment of the listener; a world he introduced immediately upon his return to the ABC in 2001 and into which he often dragged his friends and subsequently named the "Duncraig Domestic Dyslexics", as he explained to Liam Bartlett.

"It's a group of people who have distinguished themselves through appalling performances around the house," your grandad said. "A lot of them are ducking for cover these days and not wanting to be a part of it, because we have aired some of their worse performances."

To which Bartlett queried: "Is it true that you really did call in an electrician to change a light globe?"

"That is true, but the main reason for that wasn't my inability to change it, Liam, it was that I couldn't reach the light globe.

"Probably my worst performance relates to Dynamic Lifter: I was trying to do the right thing by the P&C and buy a bag of this stuff and I sprinkled three quarters of it around and had a quarter left, so I was wondering what to do with it. Lyn wasn't around to advise me – she's in charge of all things handy in our house – so I thought the best thing I could do was put it on the indoor plants."

"But you also put it on plastic indoor plants," Bartlett interjected.

"They didn't grow, either! I tell you what did grow and that was the blowflies, we couldn't get rid of them three months later. I am hopeless in that department, I must admit."

The Duncraig Domestic Dyslexics was a trademark of your grandad's and a hit with the listeners if talkback response was anything to go by. In fact, probably the only people whose interest in the group started to wane were the members themselves and one in particular was forced to request of your grandad that he no longer be dragged into the on-air sideshow as it was impacting his business dealings, with clients thinking he was an idiot.

Your grandad's tales of dysfunction endeared him to the audience because of the reality they brought: no longer was he a ghostly, unattached voice hovering in the ether of radio, he was a real person – as incompetent as the rest of us – and capable of doing more than his share of stupid things.

There was his music taste, as well.

The single song selection he was permitted on Liam Bartlett's Mornings show after doing a sports segment alongside friend and ABC Grandstand's Karen Tighe even came with an advisory: "The ABC wishes to warn listeners that the following program may contain music tracks picked by Wally Foreman. Unfortunately, the ABC's charter insists that we must give our presenters a certain latitude with the selection of music they play during their broadcasts as a way of adequately reflecting the unique attributes of their personality – and, for this, we apologise in advance."

It was all a part of who your grandad was and why he was liked so much: he knew his music was from a bygone era that was lost on many people (although, I argue that everyone secretly has a little love for country and western in their hearts) and he knew his antics were so incredulous they were humorous. But he accepted all of that and played upon it – played it up – choosing to laugh with the audience at his own expense. He was just good fun to listen to as a listener, to talk to as a caller, and to be with as a co-worker.

"What your dad had and what not everybody has, was that natural warmth," said friend and former co-worker with ABC Grandstand Sport Karen Tighe.

"He was that loveable, larrikin rogue, who could get away with doing things in his downtime with Dennis (Cometti) in his young days. You'd think, 'Oh, Wal', but he was too loveable to get into any trouble. On the other side, there was this complete passion and want to get things right and you see that when you look at something like the formation of WAIS or his passion for wanting a new stadium.

"He had an ability to take a complex issue and break it down into laymen's terms for broadcast – he could make it understandable – and I think that is such a skill for communicators. That ability to tell a story well, it's an ability that the very best commentators have and he had that; you could close your eyes and feel like you were at the event.

"And there was that lovely banter he was able to have with other broadcasters ... especially when he liked to tell stories from his times at Bruce Rock, or when he would tell stories of his times with the Duncraig Domestic Dyslexics. I think he revelled in that refusal to understand technology, because I think there was part of him that did understand it, but he liked to have that aura, because people would come to help him and he played the game.

"He had that ability to connect and to tell the fun stories that people really warmed to, while having that connection to rural WA and emphasising how important sport was and continues to be - it was the bond of communities. There was also his music and I remember I used to do the sport with him, particularly on a Monday when Liam Bartlett was doing the Mornings program, and he would play Patsy Cline or whoever and I remember I joked that we should perhaps update our music selection.

"There was one woman who called up afterwards and said, 'Well you listen; you can just take your modern music and take it straight back to Sydney. You do not criticise our Wally'. It was so funny."

Chapter 17

Take Time for Family

It was around this time, from 2001 to about six months before he died, that my relationship with your grandad was at its most strained. I was leaving high school and wanting to be independent, yet feeling like a failure because I had no TEE score and therefore no ability to join the hoard of my friends going to university, no job prospects other than my casual work at Zeno's Café (our Sunday dinner fish and chip shop) and no idea of what I wanted to do.

The less I did about the problem, the worse I felt about myself and the result was pushing people – especially family – away, instead of asking for help. I told you at the start of this book that I owe you a debt of thanks, because I have got to know my dad – your grandad – better than I could have ever hoped. Part of that learning was exactly what his life entailed before he became the man whom I knew.

My feelings of insecurity and fear existed because I did not know everything that came before me. All I saw was the success of my parents everywhere around me. I had no idea, for example, that your grandad flunked high school and was as misdirected as I was when he graduated and that was probably why he got so upset at me when I repeated his mistakes. And I had no way of knowing that your grandad was reliving another part of his life he regretted.

One of the most poignant moments in my research for this book was when I was going through your grandad's personal files and found a set of speech notes he had prepared for a school's graduation ceremony, for which he had been asked to discuss the importance of male role models. He discussed his dad – your Great Grandad Eric – and how he "always pushed him away", how they fought and how he "used the family home like a hotel".

Your grandad and I were going through the exact challenges your grandad and Great Grandad Eric had gone through.

It was a revelation for me, because all I ever saw was a devoted son (your grandad) to his elderly, kind and gentle father (your Great Grandad Eric). I never saw the chaos that a teenager brings. Your grandad wanted more and a better start for me than he gave himself. Knowing all of that would have been incredibly reassuring, however, your grandad and I never got to arrive at that conclusion together.

The result was that your grandad and I had the strained relationship we had. I felt an enormous pressure that followed me everywhere and felt crippling. I got angrier at the world and more incapable of action with every inaction that I took. It got to the point where your grandad said to your nana that he was going to leave, because, with no way of knowing what was going on in my head, he believed he was the problem.

"He was so funny – 'I think I'll leave, but I'll come back when he's grown up' – because he said I got on better with you and you didn't like him," your nana said.

"I said, 'No, it's just that somebody's got to love him'. You know what he was like, he just always wanted to make things right and you weren't happy, so he thought by him leaving you'd be happy."

I will forever be grateful that my relationship with your grandad began improving dramatically about six months before he passed away. We were even able to have conversations about sport without arguing. There is, of course, a deep regret that I didn't do more to enjoy the company of my dad for longer, but I know I can't be too hard on myself; for the same reason a teenager's challenges have no perspective, the concept of death and genuine loss has no context until it's experienced.

There were other factors at play, as well. The blood condition that I was diagnosed with meant I was unable to play contact sports for much of my childhood, taking away a bonding experience for most fathers with their children. And while life was privileged in many ways growing up, that privilege came with certain costs and I didn't see your nana and grandad as much as I would have liked. Neither were likely to be home from work before 7pm, both had work commitments on weekends and they were often away interstate or internationally.

It left your Uncle Mark and me often in the company of babysitters, or staying at the houses of family and friends. Much of that changed by the time your grandad resigned from WAIS and returned fulltime to the ABC, but I was already 17-years-old by then. However, the greater flexibility of time helped him be far more engaged with your Uncle Mark, who was only nine-years-old.

Don't misunderstand me: that life brought us tremendous experiences, as well as teaching me independence from an early age, but it had its challenges which impacted my relationship with your grandad. The turning point was when your grandad took the action for me that I seemed incapable of: he helped me get a job.

Your grandad was invited to a private dinner to give a speech on leadership to a small collective of Perth's business leaders, one of whom was a man named Bruce Morgan, the former chief executive and part owner of logistics company Courier Australia. Morgan asked him what his biggest challenge in life was at that point and he had said me, his relationship with me and the lack of direction I had. He said he felt that if I could just get a proper job, that it might give me enough stability and purpose for everything to start to improve. Morgan handed him a business card, with a request that I call him.

I worked for Courier Australia for the rest of your grandad's life. I "picked-and-packed" magazines for about two years off a conveyor belt, sorting them into a series of 52 palletised metro runs and 12 country tubs, which would be collected in the afternoon by the drivers and trucks, taking them out to the newsagents.

I worked alongside some of the most honest, funniest, but rough-as-nails blue-collar workers in the middle of a Belmont warehouse that could feel hotter than Hell in summer, regularly 10 degrees hotter than outside, and like a freezer in winter, before being given an administrative role in the office for three years. That was where I met a man named Dylan Henderson, my manager who was one of the most supportive and helpful people that could have ever entered my life. He put up with some silly behaviour of mine when your grandad passed away, but never let me get away with it, at the same time as never holding it against me.

That job was never going to be my life and it had its challenges, but it gave my life the structure it needed. And your grandad was right: the rest started to fall into place.

"He was so concerned about you and he was so proud when you got your first full-time job," your grandad's friend and ABC co-worker Karen Tighe said.

"I think he felt some guilt in terms of that he had Mark, who would follow him around like a bee to a honeypot and we would welcome him into Sports Talk. I think he felt he hadn't done enough to connect with you when you were small. He just wanted you to find your niche and he felt he wasn't good at communicating with you and I know he used to tussle with that.

"When you got that job, he was really happy. He wanted you to be happy, but he totally acknowledged at times you were like chalk and cheese and I know he was thinking, 'How can this little one be so enamoured and I don't have to do anything, but my first born; maybe I wasn't around enough'."

But as Tighe suggested, my relationship with your grandad was only part of our household's dynamic. That was why it was important to tell you all of that, because, just like I had no way of putting my teenage challenges in perspective, a life restricted to sunshine and rainbows has no perspective. And it is not a life. Life balances its challenges with its successes; its heartache with ecstasy.

He found life a little easier with your pre-dysfunctional teenager Uncle Mark.

It was like your grandad did not even need to try with your Uncle Mark. If anything, he had to try and dissuade him from taking such an interest.

Your grandad was very skilled at compartmentalising areas of his life. He had to be; there was too much going on to allow his thoughts to overlap. Work time was for work and family time was for family. The times they do coincide can be mentally exhausting and frustrating. It can turn clear thought and planning into emotional chaos.

Those compartments for your grandad were breached when your Uncle Mark became old enough to want to accompany him to games of football or cricket. The result was some very strict ground-rules.

"From the time Mark was four, he went to his first cricket game," your nana said.

"Dad would say, 'Make sure you come at lunchtime and pick him up', but Mark wouldn't want to come home. Poor Mark, dad would say, 'You sit there and you're not allowed to speak a word, you're not allowed to go to the fridge, you just watch', and he did; he just wanted to watch. He did that throughout and he was so well behaved."

The strict rules did little to dampen your uncle's enthusiasm and he would regularly join your grandad at AFL and Sheffield Shield matches, as well as for the weekend morning routine of preparing for and conducting Sports Talk. Saturdays in winter – Sports Talk followed by an AFL match – were your Uncle Mark's favourite day of the week. He would wake at exactly 6:50am, at which point your grandad would prepare his toast, cut into thirds, before he packed his bag full of Eagles paraphernalia if the game was a West Coast match.

They left the house at exactly 7:45am, with Uncle Mark testing your grandad's knowledge of the players and their numbers on the way, repeating as necessary to ensure they had been memorised for the game later in the day. Final preparations for Sports Talk were completed on arrival at the former ABC studios on Adelaide Terrace, before your Uncle Mark, your grandad,

Glenn Mitchell and the expert/s would head for coffee at 9am at the shop around the corner, discussing at length the issues of the day – usually why soccer was rarely a hot topic on Sports Talk, despite it being the "world game" – with Italian owners Vince and Dave.

Your uncle, being too young for coffee, had something different, but – another quirk of your grandad's – he was only ever allowed a combination of two of the three options: an ice cream, a packet of chips and/or a soft drink. The group then returned to the ABC and, while your grandad finished some work, your Uncle Mark kicked his treasured soft Eagles football up and down the halls of the relatively empty building with Glenn Mitchell and even former Fremantle Dockers captain Ben Allen, who always made your uncle kick with his left foot for practice. The game would progress from straight kicks to trick shots, dribbling the ball in and out of doorways.

Sports Talk began at 10am and Uncle Mark sat in the control room alongside Karen Tighe, with your grandad ordering him every week, without fail, to "stay out of Karen's way". He never got in anyone's way, of course, and the inoffensive Tighe would barely have batted an eyelid even if he did. In fact, she regularly encouraged your uncle to answer the phone for talkback callers, before patching them through to the panel, but he was too nervous to ever try.

Your uncle instead sat silently, either taking in the show or monitoring sports results from around the country and the world, relaying them through to the panel. There was usually some time to kill before heading to Subiaco Oval for the AFL call and, depending if it was the afternoon or late game, there was also WAFL requirements, much to the chagrin of your uncle, who found the second-tier competition as a tedious curtain raiser to what he truly wanted to watch.

Your grandad bought your Uncle Mark a copy of the matchday program every weekend, before sneaking him past the occasional overzealous elevator guard at the stadium and being greeted by the Media Level security chief, Marcos, who in his thick Italian accent always said: "Oh, hi Wally, have a good call today". Glenn Mitchell got your uncle to write down his predictions for the game – exact score: goals, behinds, margin, winner, leading goal kickers and leading ball winners – and once mentioned the prediction on air, as Mark's efforts were so close to reality.

Your uncle then disappeared into the soundproof telecommunications room adjacent to the ABC commentary box; his own private sanctuary, with the best view in the house, heating, sliding windows for atmosphere and rarely disturbed. Your grandad and uncle then kicked the footy in the parking lot after the match, while they waited for the seemingly endless stream of traffic to clear, before heading home to watch the replay of the game, with a detour to Hungry Jacks for dinner. They were special moments that grew in significance with time.

"I think this only became clear a few years after dad had passed away," your Uncle Mark said.

"I voluntarily went to work with my dad; I don't think many kids did that. And I loved it. It was sport, it was footy, it was West Coast and it was my dad. I had the best time and I was lucky. I never realised dad was working either. For me, it was fun, so I just assumed it was fun for him. And I rarely got to hear him because I was always in the studio with him so it just didn't seem like he was on the radio.

"These experiences are also becoming more and more important with time, too; I only got 14 years with him, but I suspect we packed a lot more in there than most 14-year-old boys would with their dads."

Passion. That was what drove your grandad.

That was what made him want to compartmentalise areas of his life. To dedicate them to work and family. He was passionate about his work, his role and sport and he wanted to ensure the appropriate respect through his focus was shown to reflect that. It was also what ensured his utter enjoyment of time away from work, because he was equally passionate about family.

He preferred separation so that he could throw all of his passion into what he was focusing on at a particular time and that was especially the case for family time. Your grandad could be overt in that distinction between family and work, in the case of a comment he made to Russell Woolf, stating that "I really keep work and family separate, but I'd love to have you over and have you out for a wine with friends of ours". But it was also a clear distinction made through his actions.

"In this world where we talk about work-life balance and not working 70 hours a week and denying yourself an opportunity to be with your family – companies talk about it, people talk about it – but Wal really did do it," Woolf said.

"He would bend over backwards to help you, but if all of a sudden it was 3-o'clock and Mark had to go to cricket training or something, you couldn't hold Wal back with a dozen stallions. There was nothing that was going to stop him from putting the pen down and walking out the door, to make sure he didn't let anyone down, especially his family.

"I used to remember what day of the week it was that Mark had cricket training, or football training, because Wal wasn't available after that time on those days of the week, every week and he would turn things down rather than give up those opportunities. He used to talk about Sunday night fish and chips at Zeno's and what a great night it was, despite doing the same thing every week, and he always came back radiant.

"When he talked about Lyn it was really different: he'd get a twinkle in his eye and tell stories about how they first met, her hairstyle and, 'They were the most amazing legs I'd ever seen'."

Your grandad designed such clear opportunities for family time. It made it easy to manage and energised him, be it the Friday night dinner with just your nana, or the Saturday dinner with friends, or the Sunday family dinner (we ate a lot), be it short family breaks or big family holidays.

I remember sitting around a table at a restaurant in Fremantle for a Sunday dinner when your grandad and nana broke the news to us that we were going to Disney Land (well, America as a whole, but Disney Land was the important point to me) as part of their work commitments to the Commonwealth Games in Canada. I was no older than 10 and your uncle was barely old enough to talk.

They had gone to the effort of gathering brochures so that when they unveiled the surprise, we had something to look at. They were also determined to return when your Uncle Mark was old enough to enjoy it and that opportunity arrived after your grandad's move back to the ABC. The rescued time from the responsibilities of WAIS also meant the trip was solely for the purpose of a holiday; there was no 'tagging it on the end' of a business trip.

I enjoyed the freedom of having the house to myself, as I was working by then and preferred to stay home, but the trip was also being planned with family friends the Kings, whom your nana and grandad had met through your Uncle's schooling at Poynter Primary School, with their daughter Emma the same age as Mark and equally sports mad. Emma eventually went on to represent her state in cricket and at the time of writing this, was still holding a contract with the Western Fury and Perth Scorchers (WBBL).

Your nana and grandad and Jeff and Heather King showed the next generation the same excitement that was given to me in revealing the new America trip, prefacing the unveiling by asking the three children – Emma, her younger brother Sam and your Uncle Mark – over a breakfast at the Kings' house what was the one place in the world they most wanted to go.

Your uncle, ever the realist, said Dunsborough, while Sam in his eight-year-old wisdom sought the action packed excitement of a trip to Afghanistan. Emma nailed it and said Disney Land. "I remember looking up at the sky to every plane that passed overhead over the next four months and thinking, 'That's me soon'," your Uncle Mark said.

He did not have to wait long to look up, because compartmentalising as he did, your grandad flew out later that day to Melbourne to broadcast the Australian Open tennis.

Your grandad shook your Uncle Mark awake. He was clearly concerned.

"Why'd you wake me up?"

"Well, it's been almost 14 hours, so I wanted to make sure you were alive."

It was San Francisco and one of the first stops for the Foreman and Kings on the American jaunt, with your uncle suffering from terrible jetlag. However, your grandad's fear was real and stemmed from the original trip to America that the family took. Your nana had gone ahead on that trip, having had an athlete competing at the Commonwealth Games in Victoria and therefore needing to concentrate on work.

While your grandad could compartmentalise family and work, he was not necessarily the multitasker in the former that he was in the latter, so it was a challenge for him to have to get a 10-year-old me and infant Uncle Mark from Perth to Los Angeles, up to Vancouver and across to Victoria by himself. For some reason, we went via Cairns, too. And I was sick.

Thinking he was doing the right thing, your grandad asked my teachers to load me up with homework as I was missing a week or so of school. He then suggested that if we do all of that homework on the plane, I wouldn't have to worry about any of it for the rest of the trip. He forgot how badly I suffered from motion sickness and that suggestion quickly became a bad idea when I succumbed to that and your Uncle Mark was not dealing well with the pressure changes of altitude. And we had barely left Perth.

His solution was a soft-drink for me (the gas and bubbles did help) and a little dash for Mark of some medication called Phenergan, which is a powerful antihistamine, but has strong sedative effects and can also help with motion sickness. The rest of the flight was a calming sanctuary of travel, until we finally arrived in Victoria, Canada, and your nana, impressed at your grandad's ability to keep everyone well behaved, asked how long your Uncle Mark had been asleep for.

"About a day," your grandad replied.

Thankfully, there was no Phenergan involved in the 14-hour jetlag nap 10 years later. Your grandad and Uncle Mark explored San Francisco's Fisherman's Wharf for the morning. That included, of course, finding an internet café to check the football scores, as West Coast was playing Essendon. Your uncle was temporarily upset he had missed a classic showdown, with James Hird dominating the final quarter and kicking the winning goal to steal the game for the Bombers, high fiving a member of the crowd along the way.

Then your uncle remembered where he was and the disappointment quickly faded. There was a trip to Las Vegas and Nevada, before the group arrived at the destination for which it was bound: Disney Land, Anaheim. I have vivid memories of the Disney trip your nana and grandad took me on, mostly centring around the latter's inability to stomach anything that would qualify as an exciting ride.

His worst performance was making us line up for two hours – and that's not an exaggeration – for Space Mountain, only to leave the line at the last available exit after speaking to a Disney addict, who excitedly told him it was her favourite ride because of how scary it was. Your poor nana looked at him in disgust, grabbed my hand and lined up for two hours again. However, one memory I had forgotten until your Uncle Mark mentioned his similar experience was your grandad's propensity for the tame-to-the-point-of-boredom rides of Fantasyland.

And one ride stood out more than the others.

"Of course, we all had to have a couple of goes on It's a Small World," your Uncle Mark said. "The bloody ride barely does a thing and you just end up sitting there listening to dad sing 'It's a small world'."

Your Uncle Mark was not exaggerating. Your grandad's flat refusal to go on any ride that slightly increased heart-rate meant he had to fill the time at Disney Land with something and that something was It's a Small World. Very rarely would he go outside that comfort zone; even the soft melodies of Splash Mountain were "ruined" by the surprise waterfall drop and gotcha-style hidden camera at the end. We're talking about a man who took me to a pop-up fun park in Rockingham one night, then spent more time vomiting in the carpark than he did enjoying the rides, because he had one round on a particularly dizzying attraction.

To paint a picture of It's a Small World: it's a simplistic and very slow boat ride through tunnels and scenes of animatronic dolls dressed in the national garb of hundreds of cultures. Over and over again in varying languages they sing the same song: It's a Small World. Reading the history of the ride itself on Wikipedia, which someone has incredulously taken the time to write over several pages, would probably fill you with the same sense of thrill as the ride itself.

Your grandad loved it and even on our original trip to Disney Land insisted that we go on it several times. Your Uncle Mark, at just two-years-old on that holiday, was a convenient excuse: "Well Mark needs a ride, too, it's not fair on him, so I'll take him on It's a Small World. Again".

On the rare occasions we managed to get him on a decent ride, his summary of whether or not he enjoyed it was always the same: "I have no idea, my eyes were closed the whole time."

Overseas holidays were, of course, the exception to the rule.

We were lucky to go on about three as a family – the US twice and Europe – but the majority of time, we had just as much fun in the backyards of Western Australia. And most of the time with other families, be they Bryan and Steph Cousins and their children down south, or Jeff and Heather King and their children up north. Canal Rocks Beach Resort in Yallingup was the regular every Easter holidays throughout my childhood and that later changed to include Coral Bay with the Kings.

Your grandad had always loved the ocean and as long as the

destination was near the beach, he was pretty content. It surprised me when, in writing this book, I discovered your grandad was a keen surfer when he was younger. It of course aligned with his passion for the beach, but he never mentioned it and instead we spent our time in the ocean on bodyboards, either out at Smiths Beach or Injidup Point down south. And on that trip to the US, he even taught your Uncle Mark and Emma King how to surf during the stopover in Hawaii.

But, despite his country roots and his love for the rugged, genuine Australia, he often struggled with the realities that brought. He was more than happy to "rough it" camping, or the likes, and loved enjoying the country, but it was the task of getting there in the first place that had the potential to cause drama.

"One of the funniest moments was the 'Bloody Jesus' story," your Uncle Mark said.

"We re-tell this often, mum and I, but nobody understands besides the Kings, because I think it's one of those had-to-be-there moments, although anyone who knew dad could imagine the way he looked and spoke throughout the 'ordeal'. It happened on another trip with the Kings, this time to Ningaloo Station up north.

"To get to Ningaloo Station you had to drive along a dirt road – it was about 15km from memory. There was nothing challenging about it, except dad had just bought his brand new car – a Honda CRV. It was a big deal for dad to upgrade to an all-wheel drive, but we always knew it would never be taken off road. Except this time it had to be."

Your uncle described the tension in the car as palpable. The rains in the northern part of the state had carved corrugated grooves into the gravel road. There was nothing unusual about that; it does exactly the same to the roads out east where your grandad was from.

But this was his new Honda CRV – very much a city-dwelling people mover disguised as an off-roader if ever there was one. It took some convincing from your uncle and nana not to turn the car around.

"The second we got onto this dirt gravel track, you could feel the stress in the car immediately rise," your uncle continued.

"Every time we went over the bumps, the car would rattle and dad kept his loose change in the middle console, so it was rattling around loudly and not helping the situation. It didn't help that to try and reduce what he thought was damage to his car, we were going at barely 20kmh. Dad probably didn't realise that slowing down meant he'd hit every possible bump on the gravel road.

"It pushed him to breaking point and he was at his wits end. It finally got unbearable and he just let out this huge shriek of 'BLOODY JESUS'. As scared as we were, mum and I couldn't help but laugh. It was so funny and was a story that was told around the campfire that night."

Having a famous father involved in sport in a sports-mad country like Australia had its advantages. It also had its drawbacks.

Your Uncle Mark might have felt its impact differently, but for me, the pressure of expectation was the most unbearable. I mentioned that the blood disorder I was diagnosed with at about 10-years-old ruled me out of a lot sport and your grandad was still at WAIS while I was growing up, so I didn't have to endure that pressure to the same extent as your uncle. However, one memory clearly stands out for me and it was around junior football.

It was one of the most miserable winter days you could imagine; it was not just raining, it was hailing, and I was yet to be diagnosed with my condition, so I was less than 10, decked out in nothing more than a football singlet, the shortest of shorts and boots. I was sitting in the car with your grandad in the warmth of the heater, discussing whether the game would be cancelled or not.

My memory of the conversation involved him hopping out of the car with the intention of finding out whether we were playing and he would then return to get me or drive home, but his understanding was clearly different, because he returned in a fuming state of disappointment, accusing me of abandoning my friends and teammates for the comfort of the car. I never had a chance to defend myself and, to be honest, I can't even remember if I ended up playing. I can just remember how unfair it felt, having been accused of something incorrectly, simply because he had not given me the opportunity to explain.

Sport was always intense with your grandad. And when he returned fulltime to the ABC, it meant more time to be involved in the sport of his children. Given my propensity for independence and my age, that meant the majority of his energy was focused on your Uncle Mark's sport, including coaching the teams. Of course, that was a wonderful opportunity for them to spend time together, but as mentioned, it had its challenges.

Technique was one issue: both your uncle and I were late developers physically, so through our teenage years we looked like primary school kids surrounded by men. That never stopped your grandad making us "crash packs", or go for the ball in football, or, in your uncle's case, attempt to straight-drive boundaries in cricket with the forearm strength of a wilted lettuce leaf.

Coaching was another issue and your grandad took the approach when it came to football that, as the coach's son, he needed to give your Uncle Mark less – not equal – game time to avoid any perception of favouritism, despite your uncle being a tremendously talented footballer (he later kicked four goals off a wing in his First Grade debut for North Beach). He spent the most time on the bench and the most time playing in the defence.

Your grandad coached your uncle's footy team for one year and never again; it was that unpleasant a season for both of them. And, when it came to cricket, your Uncle Mark endured an almost identical situation to the one I described.

"It was my first year of if-you're-out-you're-out," your uncle said.

"I'd just got out and I was walking off – I was probably actually taking this a bit better than I usually did – then, out of disappointment more than anger, I went to hit my bat on my shoe. Unfortunately, as I did this the bat fell out of my hands and, from then, nothing I did could have saved me from what was about to come.

"I walked over and started taking my stuff off and dad walked over. Usually a discussion about my dismissal would ensue but instead, I just got, 'That was an absolute disgrace'. Tears quickly flowed and they did nothing to ease his anger.

"At the end of a serious lecture, I was bloody scared, and he said, 'If you ever want to play again, you will apologise to all your teammates and the parents, in front of everybody'. I did, but he didn't talk to me for the rest of the day.

"I understand that it must have looked to dad like I threw my bat, but I stand by my version of events and when I come face to face with him again, whenever that may be, I'll tell him that. We never got to talk about it again."

All of that stemmed from good intentions, of course. I described earlier the strict discipline with which your Great Grandad Eric oversaw your grandad's sporting exploits, sternly chastising him for any show of dissent to an umpire in cricket and he was given several lashings with a belt for throwing his racquet during a junior tennis match.

Your grandad's intent came from a desire to instil good sportsmanship; an extremely positive trait that he learnt from his parents. But, sometimes, that intent could leave him narrow-minded. If there was one lesson I would hope your Uncle Mark and I can teach you through these experiences with your grandad, it would be this: always start by giving someone the benefit of the doubt, especially when it comes to family.

People, friendships, helping-hands and even mere acquaintances criss-crossed eras in your grandad's life in such a way that if they were illustrated, they would resemble a crime scene board from an overplayed police drama. But one of the most poignant of those criss-cross moments, personally, came during his return to the ABC.

Your grandad and nana were in the midst of designing their dream home. It was to be their retirement home, perched one street back from the ocean, with 180-degree views of the sea. It was what they had been saving and hoping for their whole life. Your grandad was focused on the construction and had blueprints sprawled over the commentary desk of the ABC box at the WACA Ground.

He was stationed by himself to feed live score crosses from the Sheffield Shield back to the daytime programs. That day, though, he had to rush off for a meeting with the builders for the house. He asked the WACA's Communications Manager, Simon Moore-Crouch, to do the crosses for him. He said would be back as soon as possible.

Much like you, Charlotte, your mum – my wife – never got to meet your grandad. He died before even I had met her. On that day and several others throughout that summer, he met and passed the microphone to a man who a decade later became my brother in law and your Uncle Simon.

Chapter 18

Regrets, You'll Have a Few

A STORY IS LIKE A sports broadcast: it needs balance to be complete. The volume and tempo require changes, highs and lows, to reflect and describe the evolution of the game unfolding.

Your grandad's story had its changes and it had numerous highs. It also had its lows. A few of those came throughout his time at the Western Australian Institute of Sport, but they were external lows. Like someone broadcasting the same event, but talking a different language to your grandad.

The changes he experienced and the lows he found himself in shortly after returning to the ABC were internal. For a brief period in his life, your grandad suffered depression. Not many people knew. In fact, only your nana did. And it was not clinically diagnosed, but it was the belief of your nana; the person who knew and understood him best.

It began to grow from the regret he held over leaving WAIS and was compounded by issues around his relationship with the Institute upon that resignation. He was also troubled by his relationship with colleagues at the ABC and was heartbroken by the death of his mother – your Great Grandma Norma.

All of this might come as a surprise to some people, because your grandad was forever buoyant on air and rarely negative off it, especially to the colleagues around him. However, your nana, with the benefit of hindsight, could recognise the illness because your grandad did what many people are hesitant to do: he talked about how he was feeling.

His depression was not chronic and did not linger, thankfully, as it can for others. And, thankfully, we now live in an age in which more is known about conditions such as depression, but it's important that you know it can affect those we assume most unlikely to experience it, such as your grandad. And he need only have looked around his office to see that it was a condition capable of impacting anyone, be it as a standalone illness or a symptom of a larger issue.

Friend of your grandad's and highly respected ABC broadcaster Eoin Cameron, who dominated breakfast radio before his retirement in 2016 and passing just months later from a heart attack, openly discussed his battles with bipolar disorder – a mental condition marked by alternating periods of elation and depression, or extreme highs and lows. And that was also the condition suffered by one of the colleagues working closest with your grandad, Glenn Mitchell.

It was one of Mitchell's greatest regrets that he never told your grandad and that it impacted their relationship in the way it did.

Glenn Mitchell is regarded by some as one of the greatest sports broadcasters Western Australia has produced, but by his own admission, he stumbled into the trade.

He was an executive officer at the government printing office on Station Street, Subiaco, when he got involved in coaching the state women's cricket team. It was in his cricket role when in 1989 he was interviewed by Fremantle Radio about the team and came across so well that he was subsequently offered a co-hosting role, which he fulfilled every Saturday morning.

Broadcasting was a passion of Mitchell's, but was nothing more than a voluntary hobby until under encouragement by family and friends he applied for an advertised commentary position with the ABC later that year. He had never commentated a thing in his life, but "more as a joke I put in for it". It was no laughing matter when George Grljusich interviewed him over the phone, put him through a voice trial and offered him a job.

Mitchell didn't even know if he wanted to be a sports broadcaster, so he was granted six months leave without pay. It only took three; he called the government and told them he would not be returning. The ABC team at the time was Grljusich, Trevor

Jenkins and Mark Cutler, with Mitchell as the junior understudy.

By the time your grandad returned to the ABC fulltime a decade later, Mitchell was head of the department.

Your grandad and Glenn Mitchell shared more than just their passion for broadcasting, they also shared weekly visits to Kennerton Green. Kennerton Green was the complex in Wembley where your great grandparents lived. It was a peaceful sanctuary, with units forming a crescent around a central, shared pool. It was a short walk out the back gate to the bank, grocery store and café strip and a road-crossing out the front to the evergreen, spacious Henderson Park.

Your great grandparents lived in the unit adjacent to Mitchell's parents and that meant he and your grandad frequently bumped into each other and discussed sport before Mitchell had even made the move into broadcasting and to the ABC. They would have been confusing conversations for any eavesdropping parents, because later, when both men were on the radio together, neither set of guardians could differentiate the voices, believing they sounded so similar.

Your grandad and Mitchell also shared weekend WAFL commentary and Sports Talk requirements, with your grandad enthralled in the intense and frenetic life brought about through the combination of his radio work and fulltime role with WAIS.

And they shared the experience of Mitchell's wedding to ABC Grandstand's Karen Tighe (ABC Grandstand was the national sports program, as opposed to the local content requirements fulfilled by your grandad and Mitchell), for which your grandad was asked to be Best Man. Your grandad engaged the reception with his usual wit when he opened his speech with, "Years ago, Karen's father put her to bed with a dummy and he's doing the same thing again tonight".

The pair knew each other well.

Well enough that your grandad was the first person Mitchell contacted when a position on the ABC Radio sports desk was about to open up with the return east of Dan Lonergan. Your grandad's relationship with Lonergan meant he was already aware, but Mitchell's advice was enough to make him apply and, of course, he was offered the position and accepted it.

The timing was not perfect. Your grandad had wanted to remain at WAIS until the Athens Games, to make sure Australian sport did not suffer the hangover of a home Olympics, the glory of which had the potential to blind governments – state and federal – to the lasting and damaging effects of funding withdrawals should they be convinced that Sydney was the high and it was acceptable to pull the rug out from athletes thereafter. But given the unique media market in Western Australia and the limited positions with ABC sport, opportunities such as the one Mitchell was offering did not come up often.

"I got the impression that he was starting to get a bit jaded with the workload and everything at WAIS, so as soon as I heard Dan was going, I rang your dad," Mitchell said.

"He made quite a few comments to me that he felt he didn't really do the right thing by you and that your mum, to an extent, felt the same. Your dad was always at meetings until 7pm and your mum was the same (with her training squad) and given the age-difference between you and Mark, one of the driving things behind your dad's decision to leave WAIS was to, as he put it, was to not have Mark grow up the way you were forced to.

"For us, it was a huge coup. If your dad hadn't of been in the running, I'm buggered if I'd known who we'd have given the job to. At the 11th hour, if we said, 'Congratulations, you've got the job', and he said he'd decided not to take it, I would have sat there and thought, 'What the hell are we going to do?'. It was a Godsend that he came in.

"In the space of five years, we'd had George (Grljusich), we'd had Clinton (Grybas), we'd had Dan (Lonergan). Three people sitting alongside me. We were the only two when he came back."

Your grandad and Mitchell shared many enjoyable moments

together – as many variances of highs as there were lows. They held a great respect for each other's abilities, with your grandad particularly reverent of Mitchell's encyclopaedic knowledge and talent for referencing moments in sport – a trait for which he was dubbed "the Oracle" by Grljusich – and he often commented to your nana that "he's better than me in terms of his knowledge and history".

Mitchell, conversely, admired your grandad's values and the tenacity with which he fought for his moral beliefs. He respected your grandad's refusal to ever put himself ahead of an athlete, be it the public battles such as those around gymnastics and cycling, or discrete actions such as not attending an international event that he could easily have justified attending to instead spend the money on an athlete.

"It was the principled nature of your father which I admired most," Mitchell said. "The stance that he took on what he believed in, he would not be swayed and he wouldn't care if it cost him his job; he would say an injustice had been done and he would not rest until it had been righted. He would never walk around looking for a fight, but he would never back down from a fight."

It was their combined talents that made ABC Sports Talk such a successful and enjoyable program for the listeners. Your grandad's storytelling ability and unique understanding of sport gained through his role at WAIS, combined with Mitchell's encyclopaedic memory, created an enormous bank of experience across a diverse range of sports from which to draw.

However, despite the mutual respect, they also had their challenges and both men regretted the way in which the relationship developed. Both would have preferred a different outcome. And it's important for you to understand your grandad's life as a whole, so that when you're in a similar position – and you will be – you will know that you're never alone.

The fact that your grandad was subservient to Glenn Mitchell upon returning to the ABC never bothered him. In fact, there was an aspect of that which appealed to him, because it meant he would not be burdened by the workload of administration and management issues. Your grandad believed he would be engaged for consultancy work with state institutes, particularly WAIS, national bodies and government groups and he would have an ability to accept that work as he would not be mired by paperwork and logistics at the ABC.

But the personalities of your grandad and Mitchell were night and day. The situation was certainly not untenable, but it was one borne of difference in operations and sometimes a lack of communication. Mitchell, for example, would occasionally take holidays and the first your grandad would know about it was that his colleague was not in the office on a work day.

Your grandad, who found it easy to be open always with people, felt confused. He wondered how he could fix a problem that he had no idea he had caused, yet could presume nothing else than being the cause. Karen Tighe observed that "at times, because your dad had such great warmth, people connected to him and Glenn would become more insular", while Mitchell freely acknowledged the contrast.

"Your dad was very different to me in that he had a vast network of friends; I didn't and don't," Mitchell said. "Your dad was a very gregarious person and I'm not and neither is Karen. I mean, my idea of a good night is to stay at home, but your dad, if there was a dinner party to go to or people to socialise with, he would prefer to do that."

There is an irony in that difference of personality: the harder you try, sometimes the worse you can make a situation.

Your grandad longed for a closer relationship with me and he wanted his relationship with Mitchell to be different and stronger, but he was never able to work either one out on his own. Part of that is because my personality is more akin to Mitchell's than your grandad's. Your grandad enjoyed the company of anyone, it was like he gained energy from spending time with people. I'm the opposite; large crowds – even medium crowds – leave me feeling anxious and apprehensive.

Your grandad's relationship with me improved when I started getting myself and my life together and his relationship with Mitchell was as it was because of issues he was unaware of. Sometimes, there's nothing you can do for someone, because it's not about you. Then again, everyone appreciates support and your grandad was forever determined to help those he perceived could benefit from support. For that reason, his relationship with Mitchell ate away at him as much as his relationship with me.

"Wally was quite a sensitive guy, he didn't want to be bluing with people, especially Glenn Mitchell," said Kim Hughes.

"He couldn't understand, because Wally was happy with what he was doing, he was happy with his place in the world, he felt no-one a threat. He was a big softie, not weak, but gentle and caring. But that was one of his great characteristics, I felt, and was why so many people warmed to him, because he was gentle and kind.

"When you were in Wally's presence, he just made you feel good."

But your grandad would not be able to "fix" the situation, mainly because he was never aware that Mitchell was battling his own demons. It's also important to remember, especially in the case of mental wellbeing and illness issues, that in some ways it's disrespectful to assume others need help or fixing, let alone that we can be the ones to help or fix what we assume they cannot.

However, all of this only became known the year your grandad passed away and came to a head five-years after.

Glenn Mitchell's career with ABC Radio ended in 2011.

He resigned after a heated exchange with a colleague and a string of incidents that he described himself to *The West Australian* as "angry, grumpy and sometimes reprehensible behaviour". His resignation was accepted by ABC management, having previously been rejected after similar incidents.

It was a decision that was followed by a suicide attempt, fortuitously prevented by a passer-by and one which ultimately led to a correct diagnosis of bipolar type two. It would have been a hellish period for Mitchell and his family, as well as those around him. The subsequent treatment began awakening him and his family from the nightmare that had begun to crescendo throughout the time Mitchell worked alongside your grandad.

Mitchell and your grandad worked together fulltime for five years, with the challenges to their relationship growing as that time wore on, but it wasn't until the final two months of that period that the former begun to find answers as to why he was behaving and feeling the way he was, be it towards your grandad or otherwise. He was diagnosed with depression in September 2006. Alarm bells rang for his wife, Karen Tighe, when he told her he had no interest in going to the Commonwealth Games.

"That was when I knew something was wrong. That whole year wasn't good for him and then your dad died; 2006 was a hell of a year," Tighe said.

The depression was an incorrect diagnosis, as it was a symptom of the bipolar and not the cause of how Mitchell was feeling, but it was a step towards the answer. However, your grandad never knew as he passed away two months later and his relationship with Mitchell was never given the chance to mend.

"One of my greatest regrets was that I never said anything to your dad," Mitchell said.

"Lyn was very nice and she said, 'Don't worry, he knew'. I said it before, but he was one of my closest friends; I mean, we used to have coffee together every day. He was always very kind to me, but I'm sure there would have been days when he would have gone home to Lyn and said, 'I don't know what's wrong with him and whether he's just grumpy, or whatever', but that was a real regret for me.

"There were times when we didn't see eye-to-eye, but a lot of that was predicated by my illness, but there was never a time when things weren't patched up. We never talked about it, though; if it happened on a Monday, we'd be back on a Thursday and it would be like it never happened. I enjoyed working with your dad more than anyone else; he always had his little anecdotes and he was always the life of the party. There's still times where I could be sitting reading and I wish I had your dad to talk to about something.

"I inflicted a lot of my mood swings on people and your dad copped more of it than anyone else, with the exception of Karen, because she was copping it at home and at work. Because of what your dad had to endure, that's why I regret to this day that I never told him I went to the doctor and was being treated.

"Your dad had to put up with me being in a grumpy mood, being non-communicative, sitting in a corner and being detached from the world. I talk to everyone now about trying to take my own life and what-have-you, I do talks about it, but for whatever reason I didn't tell your father. I don't know why, because if I had of told him all I would have got was support."

Time takes a lot from us all and it leaves us all with regrets. It's inevitable. The best we can do is try to make the most of the time we have so that it leaves as little room as possible for regret. Sometimes, though, we run out of time.

When that happens, forgive yourself and others.

Chapter 19

The Hardest Part Is Letting Go

CHRIS MARTIN, LEAD SINGER OF the band Coldplay, belted out a line in 2005: "And the hardest part is letting go, not taking part".

It is as true for the abstract reflections of regret as it is for the more practical situations in life, such as that which your grandad faced in resigning from WAIS. And it is true for the ethereal moments in which we farewell loved ones from the physical world, while our heart desperately attempts to hold onto them.

When it came to WAIS, your grandad had needed a holiday, not a resignation. That was the belief of your nana – and she would know. You will remember that when your grandad made the decision to leave WAIS, your nana was overseas at the time. She had been on-hand throughout the build-up to breaking point, so an element of her would not have been surprised, but she was not on-hand to talk through the decision. Your grandad had already resigned by the time he made the phone call to her in Hungary.

When moments of major change occur through opportunity, people often go through a period of euphoria – often referred to as the honeymoon period – in which negative thoughts or challenging considerations rarely present themselves. It was that period that had your grandad neglect fully considering his decision to leave WAIS.

"When he left WAIS, I said to him to remember how he felt that day and what drove him to the decision, because he might need to call on it later on if he regretted it," your nana said.

That is not to say that if he had of been in a different state of mind, he wouldn't have made the same decision anyway. But, without a doubt, he would have better considered all aspects of the decision and been more mentally prepared for what was to come.

Your grandad struggled to let WAIS go.

As your nana said: "He really missed it, but he was there for so long that it was understandable". And that is correct. Your grandad helped found the place and turned it into one of the most successful state institutes in the country for a long period. It was his baby, but as with any parent, we all need to learn to let our babies go at some point.

Your grandad entered his new career at the ABC with a strong belief that he would remain heavily involved with WAIS on a consultancy basis. That did not eventuate. There were two schools of thought around whether or not it should have, but both centred on the same reasoning: WAIS needed to move on from your grandad as much as your grandad needed to move on from WAIS.

There was a strong argument for your grandad to have been better utilised to sell WAIS and garner corporate support. WAIS has not been able to come close to achieving the levels of corporate support it had under your grandad since his departure, even to this day. The funding sources for WAIS currently are almost entirely government related. That is a model completely opposite to the one which operated under your grandad and which was mandated to sustain a 50-50 split between government and corporate funding.

The modern-day model, of course, has its advantages: WAIS can simply focus on its core business requirements – supporting athletes and coaches – without having to worry about selling the Institute to corporate bodies, knowing that its income is being taken care of by one of the most stable sources possible. Any fluctuation to that supply will, in the context of government funding, be minimal.

The counterpoint, though, is that WAIS could be seen as compromised.

Under the current model, it would be very difficult for WAIS to criticize the state or federal government for decisions it makes in relation to sport – funding or otherwise – when that government is its primary source of revenue. As the saying goes: don't bite the hand that feeds.

WAIS's proud independence and your grandad's staunch defence of that independence, combined with his willingness to engage in any issue of the day in sport – including critical commentary of government decisions – was a major contributor to the Institute's image at the time as the outspoken, objective voice of high performance sport in the state. The model enabled your grandad to publicly criticize any decision made by government that impacted sport – an opportunity he frequently took – without fear of death knell repercussions. If the government wanted to use WAIS and its athletes as a showpiece and publicity pawns, that was fine, but your grandad was going to make the government earn every opportunity.

He demanded that the government not shirk its responsibilities to the high performance sporting sector because, after all, under his directorship the government was contributing no more or less than the corporate sector. And WAIS led the country in its strong financial position. No other institute had been able to attract the same level of support from the corporate sector.

However, regardless of what role your grandad and others believed he could have played in WAIS, none of it eventuated. WAIS began to move in a different direction.

Your grandad perhaps would have felt differently – more philosophical – about WAIS, his involvement with the Institute after leaving and the new direction it was taking had its new director not been a man he anointed.

Steve Lawrence had been with WAIS for as long as your grandad had. He had long been the acting director whenever your grandad was away from the office and he was viewed as the natural successor. That came with advantages upon applying for the job, but it also had its drawbacks: by the time your grandad left the Institute, he had burnt his fair share of bridges and his close association for almost two decades with Lawrence meant the latter could have been tarred with the same brush.

However, Lawrence had a very different personality to your grandad. The WAIS Board was satisfied that difference was significant enough that Lawrence would still be capable of bringing "fresh blood", while retaining "all the familiarity with WAIS and its objectives".

Lawrence did take WAIS in a different direction and he had every right to do so, but because he was a man that had been so close to your grandad for as long as he had been, your grandad at times perceived that change as a personal slight towards him.

At the minor level, your grandad was upset over Lawrence's decision to change the Institute's Year Book cover from sepia to full-colour. "It wouldn't be fair to say he went ballistic, but he was very concerned," then-WAIS Chairman Neil McKerracher said.

The one ongoing involvement your grandad retained with WAIS was his hosting of the Hall of Champions inductions at the WAIS Annual Dinner. His orating abilities and deep, passionate knowledge of sport made his speeches and the subsequent on-stage interviews a highlight of the evening for most in the room. However, he – and even some members of the Hall of Champions selection committee – felt that your grandad's involvement there was being whittled away, with reductions in the time allocated for the segment.

Your grandad was the Chairman of that committee after he left WAIS and David Hatt took over after his passing, but even before then, there was a request to cut the segment from 15min to 10min. "Or lose the interviews," said Glenn Mitchell, who was also a committee member. At a deeper level, your grandad felt staff who were seen as being aligned to his administration and allied with him personally were being wedged out of WAIS. People such as Liz Chetkovich, but more personally your nana.

Your nana was one of the country's most qualified and successful athletics coaches – that is why, at the time of writing this, she remains the national junior coach – and WAIS was lucky to have her. However, she was made to feel like her position at WAIS was always on a knife's edge and there was nothing your grandad could do, despite his concerns.

"Your dad perceived that your mum was copping what she was copping because she was married to Wally Foreman; it had nothing to do with her abilities, it had nothing to do with her philosophies, it had nothing to do with her as a person," Glenn Mitchell said, after your grandad had confided in him over the issue.

"That affected him greatly and he was very hurt by it."

Perhaps your grandad was jumping at shadows, but it was how he was feeling. He believed certain people were not receiving the support and full-backing they needed, simply because they were perceived as being aligned to him. Ultimately, your nana was made redundant from WAIS after your grandad passed away.

Her position was jointly funded by WAIS and Athletics Australia and when the latter wanted to move the funding to have the position based out of Athletics WA instead of WAIS, there was little she could do to stop it. By that time, your grandad was no longer with us, but if he was he would have felt – rightly or wrongly – it was another move towards dismantling the culture of WAIS that he had created over 17 years; the approach that it was a family more than a business.

"Your dad every week, without fail, would have spoken to every person in that building," Mitchell said.

"It wouldn't have mattered if it was the guy down in the gym, or the girl on reception, or the cleaner that came through when he was still there at 6-o'clock. Your dad had a natural ability to build a team and make a team feel good and that everyone had value. Your dad had the common sense of management, but not necessarily the expertise and by that I mean he didn't have an MBA or what-have-you. He had the street smarts on how to bring the best out of people and allow people to make their own mistakes to learn from.

"He had no formal experience, no skill in management and yet he's gone from himself and a half-time secretary to building up an organisation with a multi-million-dollar budget. That's an amazing thing and the main thing was that he cared about people. Because of the way your father genuinely cared and spent time with others, I think it came home to him when he left the impact that he had.

"I don't think he ever got to realise that from the ABC."

Your grandad's inability to completely let go of WAIS – regardless of whether he should have had to or not – eventually meant that even the cordial, semi-regular coffee meetings between him and Steve Lawrence ceased.

"In the end, we stopped catching up," Lawrence said.

"I think because of the way things turned out at the ABC, he regretted leaving WAIS. What was clear to me was that he still loved commentating and it was what he wanted to do, but he regretted leaving WAIS, for sure. It's probably the same for any person: you need to recognise that, like a child, you can bring them along to a certain point, but then you're not there to tell them what to do anymore, you're there to listen. It'd probably be fair to say that your dad was more a teller than a listener.

"That ability to tell was his strength and what made him as good as he was – as successful as he was – so it's not a bad thing. In the end, we stopped catching up, because he so wanted to tell me, but he didn't tell me, but I could tell that he so wanted to. He'd have the leg going at a million miles an hour, twirling the hair, and I could tell it was frustrating him and he didn't agree with things that were going on in the national system or things I was doing at WAIS.

"He did make a couple of cutting comments, which I spoke to your mum about afterwards. When he was in control, he was usually ok, but if he'd had a couple of reds, you found out pretty quickly what he thought.

"Probably through my own personal background, but also through being involved with your dad, it was like, 'Be your own man'. I took the job on because I was really confident that I had a view of the system that was best for the future. I was confident about that. The fact that, going into that, I was heavily promoted by Wal almost made me a bit concerned it might align me with one side.

"I think he was also disappointed, because he thought he would get more consultancy roles, but they didn't appear, probably because he'd burnt a lot of bridges with people in fighting the good fight. He'd burnt a lot of relationships and people didn't want him back in. If someone from the national system said, 'Oh, we could use Wal for that', there would be these points of opposition.

"To some extent, although I don't consider it to be true, he was considered too focused on his perspective and not broad enough. The difficult part around it all was trying to establish a new approach. The other way of saying WAIS was Wally's Australian Institute of Sport. Wally was the face, he would promote the athletes, but because he was such a good talker, often the performances of the athletes were heavily aligned with Wally's presentation of them.

"That's not because Wally was looking for that, but it was just his ability and skill to articulate. So the director did the interviews, he was there with the Hall of Champions at the Annual Dinner, it was very much Wally's show."

Your grandad was open about his inability to let go of his emotional hold of WAIS. He said as much to *The West Magazine* in the year following his departure.

"I'm finding it really difficult at the moment," your grandad said. "It has just been so much a part of my life. I'm actually trying to disassociate myself. I find that I'm just talking to people and I suddenly do get quite emotional about something they'll be talking about or something they've raised."

However, while your grandad felt abandoned by the new direction of WAIS and his lack of involvement with the Institute after his resignation, there was also the other side's perspective.

Your grandad had been such a central pillar to WA's high performance sport system for almost two decades and taking the reins from a person who had made such an impact would have been an imposing task for anyone.

That was why your nana, who could be forgiven for being unapologetically one-sided, preferred to remain philosophical over the issue. There were, of course, moments that raised even her eyebrows, but mostly she believed your grandad needed to give Steve Lawrence space as much as she believed WAIS could have better used him.

"He felt WAIS could have used him a bit more and he felt a bit shut out and I tried to explain to him that Steve was probably trying to put his stamp on his way of doing things," your nana said.

"Dad was a hard act to follow. Dad had such a big following and whoever was going to step into that role was going to have a hard time. I tried to tell him that Steve just needed to get on and do it his own way.

"We can all put our own biased stamp on these things, but Steve has his own personality as well and if I was to put myself in his shoes, with everyone saying, 'WAIS isn't as good', and, 'WAIS won't be the same', I mean, how would you like it? That's how I looked at it.

"To me, dad got depressed after that; he got quite down."

There could be point and counterpoint made almost endlessly, but it would make no difference to the end result. Your grandad, for the first time since his decision in the 1970s to leave the ABC and join the NINE Network, was holding onto regret and was uncertain of where he was in life.

He was feeling lost and abandoned and those feelings were reinforced when his mother, your Great Grandma Norma, suddenly lost her life.

Your Great Grandma Norma passed away at dawn on 15 October 2003.

She had been unwell for weeks, but just breathless, flu-like symptoms and nothing that suggested she would be lost to the family. She had been admitted to hospital after feeling faint, but her condition rapidly deteriorated thereafter.

Losing a loved one is different for everyone, but for many of us it can be a strange experience. It is gut-wrenching, but not at first. That comes later. Along with a flood of other emotions. It was the same for your Great Grandad Eric, your grandad and his sisters, who switched into organising-mode in the days after.

The family met with the funeral director and minister in the loungeroom of the Kennerton Green unit. The same loungeroom that retained for protection the plastic covers on the floral-patterned sofa, which now acted as a fond remembrance of your Great Grandma Norma. Your grandad tracked down a former St Nicholas' Anglican Church minister, Canon Frank Watts, to conduct the service, as your great grandparents were very fond of him through their 40-year association with the church. Great Grandma Norma had even documented her desire that Minister Watts oversee her funeral service.

The service was at Karrakatta Cemetery, where your grandad was later buried alongside his mother and father, and the wake was held at Dalkeith-Nedlands Bowling Club, where your Great Grandma Norma's name adorns the honour boards around the room. Your Great Aunties Sandy and Jill organised the catering, which was of course handled by the Bowling Club ladies. The club was a comforting setting for the family and the turnout was overwhelming.

It was an emotional day for all involved and, for the children, there was the added concern for their father, your Great Grandad Eric, who seemed lost, yet resigned to the fact he had to farewell his soulmate. They sang your great grandma's two favourite hymns, "Abide with Me" and the "23rd Psalm (The Lord is My Shepherd)" and remembered the love and support she brought them through the uplifting ballad "Catch a Falling Star".

Your grandad rose during the ceremony to deliver the eulogy on behalf of his family. His lapel was adorned with the Order of

Australia pin that he had received a month before. It was the first time he wore it and did so "just for her", because he knew how proud his parents were of the honour. His words were the perfect dedication for the family and expressed all of their tremendous loss and love.

While those words in their entirety are best left between family and those in attendance at the funeral, they ended with the following moving tribute:

> *Her life might be likened to a tennis match. Scheduled for five championship sets, which women don't actually play, but she could have. She won the first set in Kalgoorlie – convincingly. There was the odd service break against her, as when her brother died, but she won it. She breezed through the second in Bruce Rock and while the third set in Perth was longer, I suspect she was just savouring the moment. Straight sets – mum's match.*
>
> *In cricket terms, there are many elements to a classic innings.*
>
> *Longevity is one. Hers had that. She was stoic and determined when the situation demanded, but she had all the shots and she used them to keep the innings moving. At no stage did she bat for herself. The team came first. She formed important partnerships. She showed courage when she had to and was always encouraging the person at the other end. Helping them to achieve the team goal and to fulfil their potential.*
>
> *She's been dismissed but the game was won long ago. We've decided to bat on, mum. We're not going to declare. The bloke at the other end reckons it would be a waste of one of the finest innings of all time if we called it off now. Our*

only concern is whether we can find anyone good enough to last the distance with him.

We're hurting, but we have the most wonderful memories to sustain us and the most perfect example to follow.

As dad said, they threw away the mould after they'd made you.

Rest in peace, mum. And God speed.

They were words filled with emotion for a lost mother that only a child could write and your Uncle Mark vividly recalled finding your grandad in the midst of writing them.

He walked into your grandparents' room and found your grandad hunched over at the end of the bed, crying. Mark clambered up and gave your grandad a hug, asking what was wrong and being told of the eulogy. He attempted to comfort your grandad as best as an 11-year-old could, then went to find your nana.

"I remember him curled up on the bed and I tried to comfort him and put my arm around him," your nana said. "It was like putting my arm around someone who didn't want your arm around them. A part of dad died the day she died; she was such a big part of his life.

"He was not the same after that. A little bit of him had gone with grandma."

The matriarch of the family had been taken and it hurt your grandad deeply – it, of course, hurt the entire family deeply – rocking his already fragile world at the time. The regret of leaving WAIS and new challenges at the ABC would have faded into insignificance. But it was a crushing blow at a time when your grandad was searching for the end of the round.

"It knocked him, because let's face it, grandma Norma was particularly proud of the way he'd followed his profession and the success he'd found," your Great Grandad Eric said.

"He was the No. 1 boy, sort of business. He was very close to his mother and he was pretty close to me, too. But I know that he missed her terribly. We were very proud to have Wally and I think Wally was very proud to have his parents, which was very pleasant. He used to think the light shone out of Sandra, too.

"However, that's life and now Wally's passed on, too, and we all miss Wally just as much."

And, now, your Great Grandad Eric has joined them and we all miss him just as much. Mothers hold a special place in a child's heart – particularly a son's heart. A place that can never be filled by anyone else. When your grandad lost his mother, he lost a piece of his heart.

But this is the story of your grandad.

You never knew him – that is the point of this book. But, if you had, you would have known that depression and grief could never hold him for long. Your grandad was blessed by the support of the people he had around him, his family and friends, his faith and love in life and his refusal to ever give up.

The hard times, personally, were replaced with the stoic support he had to offer athletes and friends in the coming years and the passion that he brought for that support. Not to mention experiencing the exhilaration of calling the West Coast Eagles to the 2006 AFL Premiership.

Coldplay might have sung, "The hardest part is letting go", but as your Great Aunty Sandy said of the loss of Great Grandma Norma, they all eventually did. And so too did your grandad let go of the regret he felt for leaving WAIS and the uncertainty he held in his return to the ABC.

Life goes on. It must. And he let it all go. He never forgot any of it, but it no longer held him back.

In fact, two chapters from a total of more than 20 should more than suffice on the topic. Let's move on.

Chapter 20

Always Keep a Sense of Humour

It did not take long before normal broadcasting resumed and the smiles returned.

And the consultancy roles came along, too. Perhaps not in the number or – with all due respect – significance that your grandad had been initially expecting, but he treated every one of them as important.

One of the last projects he worked on before he passed away – and one he was passionate about – was helping to establish the South West Academy of Sport in Bunbury. SWAS opened its doors after your grandad passed away and now operates as a cohesive pathway option for regional athletes with the potential to progress to the Western Australian Institute of Sport. The Academy continues to recognise and honour your grandad's role in its history through its annual Wally Foreman Coaches Award, while your nana was named a patron of the body.

And there were plenty of smiles for the ABC audience, too, such as the time Liam Bartlett and your grandad used April Fools and the former's Mornings program to convince listeners that Tourism WA and Main Roads had combined to begin work on a clear-top tunnel beneath the Mount Henry Bridge, so people could "drive with the fish" on their way to work. Congestion issues were plaguing the current bridge, the pair discussed, but because of a lack of funding for infrastructure, Main Roads convinced Tourism WA to provide a portion of its budget to solve the problem and create a tourist attraction at the same time.

Your grandad took his mobile phone onto the street outside the ABC's new East Perth building, with the passing traffic providing the required sound effects to continue the ruse that he was "on location". "Yes, Liam, the Main Roads people are here with the surveyors," your grandad said. The feedback resulted in some rather irate callers, who were fuming at the government's money wasting, before the penny dropped and the ruse was up.

"He was a champion stirrer," Bartlett said. "I used to call him King Wally and because we had a state-wide audience, it caught on and the audience would start calling up asking, 'Is the King there?'"

Your grandad's sense of humour rarely hid, whether that was in the more public instances of the April Fools prank with Bartlett, or the hilarious "snorkelling" incident with Kim Hughes, during which both men were left stranded for minutes live on-air in a fit of uncontrollable laughter after Hughes asked your grandad the innocuous question of, "Are you a bit of a snorkeler, Wal?". And his humour was always on display at the regional sportsmen's night and Drought Busting, where he of course shared the country blood.

"I understand the hardships of the country. I come from Bruce Rock, although in about 1967 a cyclone went through and caused $40,000 worth of improvements," he used to say, in one of several one-liners he had a tendency to repeat. Your grandad was a creature of habit and, having found hundreds of speech notes in his personal files, it was humorous in itself to see the stack of go-to icebreakers he used throughout his career.

However, that humour and cheeky streak was capable of landing your grandad in his fair share of trouble.

This must be prefaced by saying that domestic violence is never a laughing matter and I accept that making jokes around the subject can serve to normalise a dangerous plague on society.

But, equally, sometimes things get taken a bit too far and if anyone knew your grandad and the adoration he held for the women in his life, they would understand that there was never an ill bone in his body towards the fairer sex. Nonetheless, fury erupted one morning when Liam Bartlett's replacement on the Mornings Program and your grandad's long-time friend Geoff Hutchison decided to play a song by Perth-formed, Melbourne-based rock group The Blackeyed Susans.

It was the 9:35am music track, leading into the 9:40am sports segment. Having briefly listened to the band's music, I'm confident it was not to the taste of your grandad and he probably attempted to shut out every word of the song, but when it was over and Hutchison back-announced the artist, your grandad quipped: "Treat 'em mean, keep 'em keen, as they say, Geoff".

The fourth instalment of the Mad Max movie franchise was not released until 2015, so very clearly the inspiration for *Fury Road* occurred this morning in early 2006. It was a bewildering experience for Roanna Edwards, the young trainee sports broadcaster working alongside your grandad.

"I was gobsmacked," Edwards said.

"I was gobsmacked because in the gruff world of 'blokey blokes' and egomaniac broadcasters, Wally was a gentleman of the highest order. I knew his adoration for his wife, Lyn. I knew his love and respect for his sisters. I knew if Wally had daughters or daughters-in-law they would be fortunate to have such a beautiful man as their father or father-in-law."

And, if it was a courthouse trial, your grandad would have had no shortage of character witnesses.

"I have to say, something that I always thought was so beautiful was the way your dad adored your mum," ABC Grandstand's Karen Tighe said.

"He delighted in recounting the story of how they met and whenever one of them had been away, they would meet each other at the airport and just want to get their hands on each other. You could just see it. Not everyone in life gets to meet their soulmate, but very truthfully, he did."

But this was not a courthouse trial. It was closer to a public execution. And, while I write much of this with dripping sarcasm, the situation for your grandad became very serious.

Your grandad was finding out quickly that the ABC he returned to was not the same organisation he first joined in 1975. In the 70s, he, Dennis Cometti and George Grljusich respected their positions and brought an unequalled talent to the microphone, but they also got away with doing whatever they wanted, to an extent. They were on the frontier of a new era in sports broadcasting in Western Australia.

It would have looked like the Wild West compared to the ABC of 2001, which had turned into a professional, stern and regimented fortress of the Fourth Estate. In fact, the comparatively-stifling environment and the previously-mentioned challenges he was going through were potentially the reason he applied for other jobs.

For example, in the personal files he left behind were applications – and, in some cases, offers – for roles heading up the Wellington Institute of Sport in New Zealand, Athletics Australia and even the Western Australian Cricket Association. However, it was perhaps an indication that his passion still lay in broadcasting that he never pursued the positions.

It was, nonetheless, a different world to the one he was used to. The ABC had developed policies that required management to investigate any on-air incident if an official complaint was received. That day, there was at least one official complaint received. The person who received it was Liam Bartlett's former producer, who had been promoted to Local Content Manager, Deborah Leavitt.

"It was a comment that was misinterpreted," Leavitt said.

"That was at a time when the audience couldn't go and listen back, whereas now we have the systems where you can do catch-up listening with podcasts and downloads. Someone heard something he said and took it out of context (and complained), so that had to be worked through the processes that we have around our editorial policies.

"I know I had discussions with Wally about it, because he felt really frustrated by it and felt it was really asinine because it had been misconstrued. I understood that, but we still had to go through the process. I knew that comment was not representative of Wally, but you have these adjudicators saying, 'Well, not everyone who listens to the radio knows that person'.

"So we have a responsibility to maintain certain standards and keep that in check, because the person listening isn't always going to be the person who is able to make that easy assessment. I think that was the thing that was a challenge for me to explain to him, because I knew damn well it was not intended in that way, but a lot of times when you deal with media, it's about perception."

Being hauled into the manager's office was not the end of it, either. For your grandad's three-second gaffe, he was ordered to make an on-air apology and was required to speak at a White Ribbon event – an organisation that seeks to raise awareness for and end domestic violence. Well, he was invited, but he was also instructed by the ABC that his RSVP would be "yes".

It was an event championing women's rights and I can't imagine he felt too comfortable being there, given the events that had occurred. And that was before the saga began to crescendo.

The details have been lost in time as to whether he was required to deliver a speech, or actually host the event. Either way, it required a run-sheet and several email correspondents. Your grandad was never good with technology. Especially email.

Your grandad took his values very seriously – that should have been well established by this point of his life story. So when those values and his attitudes towards women were brought into question, he was infuriated. And I mean that; this saga angered him immensely, especially the point that any punishment required him to go beyond an on-air apology.

He recognised, though, that while he believed it had been blown out of proportion, the people who held his purse strings had a very fine line they needed to toe when it came to issues such as this. Sections of the public could easily become menacing and your grandad, as a high-profile media figure, would be an easy target if the situation was not handled in the correct way. And, as the public broadcaster, the ABC was equally vulnerable to public opinion.

So, your grandad played the game. Publicly. Privately, he remained seething. And that anger, combined with his inability to harness technology, almost cost him his job.

"Wally was sent some information from organisers of the event advising times and locations and his expectations," Roanna Edwards said.

"He scoffed away at his desk as he read the email, still shaking his head and muttering about what he believed to be the injustice of it all. He couldn't take it any longer and used his limited Microsoft Outlook experience and capability to forward the message to his great mate Russell Woolf. Wally wrote a couple of lines before sending.

"I never got to see exactly what it was he wrote, but I know it was cheeky and I know it wasn't an email he wanted read by management or the listeners that had taken exception to his original comment. But I also know Wally thought his comment was quite amusing. As he clicked send, he popped up from his desk against the window of our open-plan office like a meerkat and peered over to Russell's workstation to enjoy what he assumed would be an entertaining reaction from Russ.

"Only problem was, Russ wasn't reacting. Wally's look changed from one of the cat getting the cream, to slight concern. Russ got up and wandered over to the photo copier which was midway between his desk and the corner that the sports team occupied. Wally said: 'Russ, I've just sent you an email. Did you get it?'.

"So Russell wandered back, had a look and casually replied, 'Nah Wal. What was it?'. 'Are you *sure* you haven't got it?', Wally asked again and again was told, 'Nah, nothing mate. Is it important?'. At this point, Wally's face lost a little colour. He shook his mouse frantically, and his breathing was becoming a bit deeper.

"I asked him if he was ok and if he needed some help. He got up and started pacing behind his desk. I took it as a call for help and wandered to his PC and poked around, asking what his concern was. He said to me: 'Ro, I don't know, I was sure I forwarded the email to Russ. But I think I must have hit reply and it has now gone to the organisers. Stupid bloody thing. I hate computers. Oh, Ro, I could be in big trouble here'.

"His pacing was more frenetic and he said, 'Ro, I think I'm going to be sick'. I quickly opened his sent items to put an end to it all and told him the good news was it didn't appear to have gone to anyone. 'Are you sure you hit send?,' I asked him, to which he replied, 'Well, I thought I did, but the window didn't close so after I hit send I hit the X in the corner and closed the message'.

"I went into the Drafts folder and there was Wal's emails. Drafted to Russ, as he intended, but never sent. After that, it went straight in the trash. Russell never received it and, more importantly, neither did the event organisers. And Wally paid his penance – in a variety of ways."

I can only imagine the knot that would have tightened in your grandad's stomach at that moment. We've all done something similar, whether it's email or text message; sending the message to the person who is the subject of the message, simply because they're the ones on the mind, and not the intended recipient.

Given the way the saga unfolded, it was remarkable your grandad made it to November before his heart attack. And along with Russell Woolf and the event organisers having not received the email, it was a blessing ABC management never laid eyes on it either.

"I don't know how he felt about it all in the end, but I don't feel it had any impact with the people who knew and loved him," Deborah Leavitt said.

"They probably looked at that and thought, 'There but for the grace of God go I', because it happens to a lot of the broadcasters, when something is taken out of context. In some ways, it's a leveller. I think he did come to that conclusion eventually, understanding how it could have been perceived if he'd listened to it blindly."

Maybe. Probably not, though.

Your grandad had another talent he had developed over time: knowing which battles were worth fighting. That one had dragged on to the point it risked becoming a bigger joke than the one it grew from. I am certain that what he would have taken from the situation was that there is a time and place for everything.

It might have made him slightly more cautious when choosing his words. But like the great broadcasters before and after him – such as his good friend Eoin Cameron – your grandad was unlikely to ever let policy, perception or opinion ever shackle who he was.

Because the larger lesson was this: keep a sense of humour and always laugh, but also know that not everyone will laugh with you.

Chapter 21

People Come First

Two people. One belief.

In the closing years of his life, your grandad had two final battles to fight for others. The first centred around the Athens Olympic Games and a woman named Sally Robbins, the second around the AFL and a man named Ben Cousins. They were vastly different scenarios, but both were based on one belief: people come first.

No story, no win, no loss – nothing – no matter how big or small, was more important than the welfare or general wellbeing of a person and, your grandad believed, it was the responsibility of everyone to uphold that value, even if there was no obligation to do so.

That was the case with Sally Robbins.

"JAMIE DWYER. JAMIE DWYER"

There are the comedic calls and gaffes of your grandad, such as "the snorkel piece" alongside Kim Hughes, which get played on air repeatedly to remember your grandad. They reflect his humour and relaxed approach to life as much as broadcasting. Then, there are the other pieces which reflect his skill in commentary and, when it comes to those sound clips, there are two that stand out.

Coincidentally, they both relate to the lesson and events of this chapter. But perhaps, by now, you realise that is because whether we're discussing a broadcast or a life, significant moments and significant people are so much more than just that. They are developed. Built. They are multi-layered and crafted. By the time a significant moment or person is described, they are already significant. The description simply adds another layer.

That was the case for the second (chronologically) of your grandad's most remembered broadcasts: the West Coast Eagles' triumph of the 2006 AFL Grand Final. Your grandad, with a voice faltering from exhaustion as much as excitement and anticipation, detailed the heartbreak of the 2005 decider and the rise of a brigade of unparalleled young players, before delivering a passionate call that was punctuated with a perfect 10-word finish of, "Let your hair down Western Australia, the Eagles have landed", pausing between "Eagles" and "have landed" for effect.

And it was the case for the other oft-replayed soundbyte: the breakthrough gold medal win for the Australian men's hockey team at the Athens Olympics. The medal marked the first time the men had basked in Olympic glory and was not significant because of that moment alone, but because of layers of disappointment in the seemingly countless decades that had preceded it. So often, Australia went to the Olympics either ranked as the best team in the world, or being more than capable of winning gold, only to have faltered under the expectation to do so.

That was not so in Athens, as Jamie Dwyer, the best player in modern history, converted a penalty corner to snare the elusive medallion for his country. Your grandad's description only added to it: "IT'S IN! JAMIE DWYER. Jamie Dwyer has scored the winning goal for Australia. Australia wins its first ever men's hockey gold medal". It was a memorable moment for your grandad. He loved hockey – life in the country and the friendships he made through life ensured that – and he loved Australia winning.

Significant moments. Multi-layered. Built and developed over time.

Yet, as significant as those moments were, they were also just games. And that is in no way intended to belittle the often-lifelong pursuit of athletes, whose talents inspire generations. This entire book is based on a lifetime of passion for sport. It takes nothing away from those celebrations, but life has an innate talent of its own: perspective. And it likes to remind us of that when it feels our judgement gets clouded.

Athens had another significant moment for Australia. One that wasn't as basked in glory as our hockey team, yet one that was equally multi-layered. One that had been developed and built into a significance far greater than it deserved, because the moment was given precedence over the person it involved.

It was a moment when, for whatever reason, rower Sally Robbins, was unable to complete her event, which impacted her team. Not a big deal, when put in perspective. No-one died. Although, the world could have been forgiven for thinking someone had, because the vitriolic treatment of Robbins and the mismanagement of the situation that erupted in the aftermath was another heartbreaking moment for Australian sport.

Concern for the welfare of one of our own made way for narcissistic indignation. Then again, we as a nation have a track-record of turning on our own when the bright lights of the world's biggest stage blind our perspective.

The women's eight rowing final of the Athens Olympics was held on Sunday, 22 August 2004. Australia had slipped into the contest. It finished last in Heat 1, more than six seconds behind the world record-setting leader USA, and took the third of four Final spots available through the repechage with a time that was understandably slower than its Heat mark, but still more than five seconds off the leader of the repechage group and eventual gold-medallist Romania.

So, far from favourites. Still, we're brought up to believe it is the Australian way – and the way of most competitive athletes – to throw caution to the wind in the face of adversity and give everything to a challenge. The Australians did. They were coming third at the halfway mark of the 2000m race, but the talent in the boats of their rivals eventually began to overwhelm the underdogs and they had slipped to fifth with 500m to go.

That was when Sally Robbins collapsed. She released her oar and lay back onto one of her teammates. Her teammates unleashed their wrath, suggesting Robbins get out and swim. Crew member Julia Wilson told media after the event, "We had nine in the boat but only eight operating. I just want to stress there was not a technical problem. No seat broke. There was nothing wrong with boat".

Wilson received a reprimand for her comments from Australian Olympic Committee president John Coates, who labelled attacks on fellow teammates as having no place in the Australian team.

Robbins received little reprieve. A prime minister weighed in, the callous moniker "Lay Down Sally" was coined and splashed across newspapers. And probably the largest pile of salt to be dumped on the wound came a month later at the Australian Olympic team's returning celebrations, when instead of the issue fading into history with time, the flames were once again stoked when crewmate Catriona Oliver slapped Robbins in a fit of anger.

In the years that followed, Sydney "shock-jock" broadcaster Alan Jones was reportedly ordered to pay $1.7M in a defamation case brought by Coates for comments made at the time in relation to the incident. Newspapers continued to take every opportunity they could to rehash the story and the "Lay Down" label – it sold papers. A book was even written.

Robbins, at the time of the Athens Games, was 23-years-old. People can hold whatever opinion they want to hold over the incident, but I doubt any of them would be able to endure as Robbins did the endless flood of negative, vitriolic abuse regularly issued by seemingly an entire nation without hesitation. Eventually, it would get to anyone. Even those far older than 23.

And for what; a rowing race in which we were never going to win a medal? Nine people in a boat, eight with sticks and one with a microphone? Please. It sounds more like a cheap karaoke setup than a matter of grave significance.

Every now and then, it's important that life reminds us of perspective.

Your grandad was sharing a cab with your nana in Athens when his mobile phone rang. It had become a requirement of the job that he have one, otherwise he would have undoubtedly gone his entire life mobile-free. They were spending what little time they had together, being in the city for the same Games, but different purposes.

Your grandad was broadcasting for the ABC, while your nana was there as a private coach (she was not officially a part of the Australian support team) to her heptathlete Kylie Wheeler and only in the city for as long as the event took to complete. Your grandad was informed of what had taken place and the abuse Robbins had endured from her own team afterwards. "Oh no," your nana said, as she shared with your grandad the dread of a repeat of any number of incidents littering sport's history in which perspective has been lost.

The precise involvement of your grandad from that moment on is relatively unknown, because your nana, as mentioned, was only in Athens for a few days and Robbins could not be contacted to share her memories. She has been rather interview-shy since 2004. Few could blame her.

But those close to your grandad recall it as a significant issue for him. Your nana remembered the efforts he went to in Athens to influence his colleagues in the media on messaging and coverage, particularly around the way in which Robbins was portrayed, and probably most poignantly your Uncle Mark recalled the day as a 12-year-old, with no-one else home except him and your grandad, he opened our front door to Robbins.

Like most people, your uncle had only known what he had been told by the media, which was usually confined to the "Lay Down Sally" tag. He was promptly informed by your grandad that "there was more to it than that". That day, your uncle showed Robbins into the kitchen, where she waited while he found your grandad, and was then told, more than asked, "Are you just watching TV?". Robbins and your grandad sat for an hour in privacy in a separate lounge room, talking.

For my part, I remember the term "Lay Down Sally" being strictly banned in our house. Not that we had any great cause to use it. But whenever the subject came up, your grandad spoke in tones of hurt and disappointment; those slow, low patterns that come close to defeat, but never quite reach it.

That was because your grandad refused to ever be defeated on any issue, let alone that one. And as long as Robbins was still breathing, he was going to ensure she knew the world was not against her – it was just a vocal minority too caught up in their own disappointment to understand the hurt and potential damage they were causing.

It was around the time of Robbins' visit to our house that your grandad penned an article for *The Sunday Times* in an effort to restore perspective.

> *Enough's enough. When is someone in Rowing Australia going to take control of the renegade members of the women's eight before they do irreparable damage to their target and their sport.*
>
> *The crusade that Catriona Oliver and Kyeema Doyle, in particular, have been allowed to conduct against their teammate, Sally Robbins, since they stepped out of their boat at Schinias on August 22 is nothing short of disgraceful.*
>
> *The physical attack on Robbins at a welcome-home function this week was the last straw.*
>
> *And it demonstrates again that some national federations in this country are not capable of managing their own affairs.*
>
> *Whether Robbins did the right thing or the wrong thing in that race is largely irrelevant.*
>
> *What is important is that the manner in which she has been crucified by her coach, her teammates and sections of the Australian media could have dire consequences for the victim of such attacks.*
>
> *David Beckham wasn't subjected to these levels of vitriol when he missed a penalty in*

Euro 2004. Paula Radcliffe didn't finish a race in Athens she was expected to win but wasn't assailed by coach or teammates.

People have suffered breakdowns and even committed suicide when subjected to this level of intense, personal persecution.

Are Oliver and Doyle going to persist until they break her?

And where is the safety net for Robbins and her crewmates?

It was there after the first appalling outburst. AOC president John Coates, a rowing stalwart, stepped in.

But since the Games finished, the assault has continued at every opportunity, unabated.

I don't know what happened in that race. I don't know if Robbins suffered an anxiety attack, if she misjudged the race, or if she simply tried too hard.

What I do know is that the coach, Harald Jahling, was part of the panel who selected her. He did so with full knowledge of her training and competition record. She didn't select herself.

I also know that Robbins isn't a quitter. Her ergometer tests in the laboratory were the best of the entire crew. The ergometer is known among rowers as the "lie detector". You're on the machine on your own and you can't crib your scores. It measures power and pacing.

I also know that going into the Games the women's eight was given a 50-50 chance of making the final. A medal was never a realistic possibility.

So, if Oliver and Doyle are trying to convince the world that Robbins should apologise for her *collapse because it cost them a medal, who are they trying to fool?*

I also know that Jahling's comments, as the crew's coach immediately after the race, were totally out of order and bereft of the leadership expected of the head coach of the national women's program.

His comments did nothing but incite a group of highly emotional athletes when he should have been the calming influence.

I'm not here as Robbins' godfather. I haven't had anything to do with her since I left WAIS three years ago. For what it's worth, I knew her then as a very decent, retiring but personable young lady.

And I don't know why she stopped rowing when she did. I'll be very surprised if there's not a reason, either physical or psychological, for it.

But I do know that the fierce and relentless attacks on her are inappropriate and potentially very dangerous.

At the end of the day, it was a rowing race, for heaven's sake.

It was not a matter of life and death but it would seem that some of her teammates might be happy to make it so.

Their behaviour and that of their coach has been most un-Australian and the lack of control shown by Rowing Australia has been breathtaking.

We're an interesting bunch, Australians.

We take great pride in that title, "Australian", and all we believe it encapsulates. And we take just as much pleasure from berating anyone we believe has not met those values, counter-labelling them "un-Australian". The problem with both terms is deciding exactly whose definition of "Australian" and "un-Australian" is the definitive one.

The labelling of a person with external beliefs is like an accepted form of mass-bullying and, beyond that, they're terms that must bring into question the intelligence of anyone who uses them, because they're so subjective that they're meaningless. What's the point in using one-word terms that require an appendix to define? I write that knowing that I just quoted your grandad using the term. That's ok; we all disagree at times.

The irony of even having terms of "Australian" and "un-Australian", marginalising our own compatriots, is that I would have thought one of the highest values of being an Australian would be "mateship". Clearly, I would be wrong. See, meaningless.

It was an issue that was part of the debate surrounding Sally Robbins. She courted fury, headlines and accusations that she had not acted out the values expected of Australians. To fight until the end or, if that was not possible, the death. But if someone doesn't achieve those expectations, why do we, as Australians, believe we have the right to label a compatriot un-Australian? To presumably speak on behalf of the more than 23 million other Australians and denounce their citizenship and worth to the country?

Why do we take pleasure in marginalising our own? And why do we seem to be the only country that does it? Elsewhere, there are of course civil wars around philosophical differences, yet in terms of terms, I've never heard spoken the words "un-British", "un-Indonesian" or "un-New Zealander".

Australia only needed to look at the same Olympic Games to see that it had confused its priorities and lost its perspective. That it was projecting a very poor image comparatively to the rest of the world. In fact, it didn't even need to leave the rowing venue. In the same event, just different gender, and with far greater credentials than the Australian women, the Canadian men's eights rowing team entered Athens unbeaten for two years.

However, crewman Ben Rutledge succumbed to the intensity of the moment and stopped rowing. "I panicked ... I've never done something like that before. I just couldn't move," he said at the time. Canada finished fifth. Rutledge admitted he "panicked" and "just couldn't move" with the honesty of a man seemingly devoid of any fear of retribution and hostile accusations. Especially from his teammates, let alone his own country.

And far from ordering him to the gallows, he was instead provided support and the result was that Rutledge helped his country win gold at the subsequent Olympics in Beijing. Back home, in Australia, Robbins' own attempted comeback for Beijing was drenched in reworked material and fear-mongering from Athens and she hasn't felt comfortable to speak openly and honestly for more than a decade.

Another piece of irony in the whole affair is that, the last time I checked, no-one from Australia has ever selected themselves for an Olympic Games. Not in my lifetime, at least. So, while everyone was scrambling to crucify Robbins, the fact was that a panel of people were responsible for first sending her to Athens, before another group selected her to sit in the boat for the Final. That was even though she had shown signs in the lead-up to the Games of being susceptible to extreme and crippling fatigue, be that psychological or physical.

Of course, the hierarchy was not to blame for her selection – and I mean that – because Robbins had put the performances on the board and earnt her place. They couldn't not select her. It was interesting, though, that despite exhibiting those signs that she perhaps required support, Rowing Australia in the lead-up to Athens ceased funding the sports psychologist it had employed since the lead-up to Atlanta (1996). And even when that psychologist, Jeff Bond, was on-board, he recalled to the ABC in an interview that the head coach of the women's program, Harald Jahrling, had not wanted him involved with the women, so he worked with the men.

However, there seemed to be an apparent unwillingness to accept responsibility for those aspects. It was easier for the nation to turn on one of its own. To ridicule and abuse a 23-year-old. To label her un-Australian and, ironically, hold her up as an example to the rest of the world of what not to do. To hold her solely accountable and make her the scapegoat.

Solely accountable and the scapegoat for finishing last in a Final in which we were fifth-placed before Robbins even stopped rowing and in which we never stood a hope in hell of finishing on the podium, let alone winning. But Robbins was apparently the un-Australian one.

We're an interesting bunch, Australians.

Chapter 22

Always Look After Your Mates

If we are watched over in this life by those who have graduated to the next, I have no doubt that there would be one friend in particular your grandad would be watching over: Bryan Cousins.

The Cousins name was already well known in football through the exploits of Bryan with Geelong in the VFL and Perth in the WAFL, before the next generation put that name in lights, with Ben Cousins having won a Brownlow Medal and the 2006 Premiership with the West Coast Eagles, a club he also captained.

But Ben also had a troubled side and he slipped into a world of methamphetamine addiction that sent him to the brink of oblivion and, at the time of writing this, it is hard to know if he will ever return. We can only hope. It has been an addiction that has brought immense pain to his family and friends and in probably the only parallel the situation shares with the events involving Sally Robbins – aside from your grandad's actions – it has also emboldened almost every Australian with the belief that they have a right to expel whatever judgements they have on Ben and his family. Very rarely are those judgements founded on a full understanding of the situation.

Every part of Ben's battles would have left your grandad heartbroken, not only for Ben himself, but for Ben's father and your grandad's close mate Bryan, who along with wife Stephanie, their other son Matthew and daughters Sophie and Mel, go through the nightmare of drug addiction on a regular basis in an unforgiving and public arena. It would have hurt your grandad to watch it, but it would have been important to him to be there for the family.

And I know that the Cousins would have equally appreciated that support. They always did. Bryan referred to your grandad as having been one of the few members of the media that he trusted. There were others, such as Seven's Sean Menegola, Jeff and Peter Newman, and Nine's Sonia Vinci. But your grandad was the only one Bryan ever entrusted with the totality of what was engulfing the family.

It might have seemed a long bow to draw to have earlier connected Sally Robbins with Ben Cousins, but it wasn't that long at all. The connection they shared with your grandad was one and the same.

"I remember when Sally Robbins was going through her tough time and there was so much coverage about her in the media – she seemed to be being almost crucified," Bryan Cousins said.

"Then, some time after, I heard an interview with Sally and she said the only support she ever received from anyone in the media connected to sport was from Wally Foreman. It really resonated with me when I heard her speak about Wally's support and I have no doubt that getting support from a person like Wal would have meant so much to her.

"But that's how your dad was. In Ben's case, he knew he was a human being, he'd met him and knew he had a terrible issue to deal with and, in the case of Sally Robbins, she was a human being too and he cared about the individual person. He showed great mateship to both Ben and me. When things were at their worst, Wal as always there for us."

But the story of the Foremans and Cousins didn't start with Ben's addiction or heartbreak. Friendships, like any significant issue, is built, developed and multi-layered. That building began even before I came along.

Bryan Cousins and your grandad had crossed paths when the former was a football player for Perth and the latter was a journalist with the ABC and NINE Network, but the true friendship began with your nana. It was the early 80s and your nana had established herself as one of the country's best runners.

Her credentials and talents had a mutual friend, Ian Miller, recruit her to Perth as the club's pre-season fitness coach. It was the first time a woman had been appointed by Perth and she could have faced a challenge in controlling a raucous hoard of footballers if it wasn't for two people.

The first was, of course, Miller, who was a highly respected and decorated member of the club – with the exception of a brief period in which he joined rivals East Perth – having won a Premiership and Sandover Medal with the Demons. He was also the coach. The second figure of support for your nana was Bryan Cousins, who had returned from the VFL a few years earlier and had been appointed captain.

"Your dad said to me one day that he appreciated everything I had done in that regard, because I made sure the boys treated Lyn with great respect. You know, when the boys are all mucking around, sometimes it's difficult to get a group of footy players under control," Bryan said. "Lyn was great and the boys really responded to her, but that was really the start of our friendship and it grew from there."

The association began a long friendship that enveloped in your grandad when he accompanied your nana to the numerous club functions. The friendship strengthened when your grandad recruited Bryan as a special comments provider for the ABC and it later solidified when our families regularly shared Canal Rocks Beach Resort, Yallingup, as a holiday destination.

"Shit, they were funny days," Bryan said.

Funny mostly because of your grandad's incompetence and humour. Like the time he spent the holiday hobbling around. He had awoke early to polish up on his boogie boarding skills, but as he made his way to the beach in semi-darkness, he booted a rock wearing just his thongs and broke his big toe. Painful for him; hilarious for the rest of us, given his overplayed theatrics. Or the time he went body surfing by himself, was dumped and knocked out on the seafloor and had to be saved, legitimately, by two kids who held him up until he spluttered back to consciousness. One of the two boys exclaimed, "Mate, that was the wipeout of the week".

Both events grew in grandeur with every retelling your grandad gave. And the laughs would continue whenever the families made the regular trip for lunch to a winery, loading up on merlot – or "mer-lot" as your grandad and Bryan called it. The wine also assisted in the commentary, if not for the alcohol, then for the fact that both men's lips had a habit of soaking up the tannins and turning purple, aptly making them look like the pair of clowns they often acted like.

It was during one of those lunches that an elderly couple was celebrating a 50th wedding anniversary with family at a nearby table. They continually glanced at the Foreman-Cousins group, before gathering the courage to ask your grandad and Bryan where they knew them from. With half the winery's supply under their belt and the other half on pre-order, the dynamic duo thought it would be a fun idea to switch places; your grandad became Bryan and vice versa.

The problem was, both were so used to "taking the piss" out of each other, that the façade turned into a couple of monologues that did nothing but make them both "look like dickheads", with your grandad insisting that not only was he a champion footballer himself, but he had taught Ben Cousins – his faux son, in that conversation – everything he knew about football. Bryan, in-turn, proclaimed that he – Wally Foreman – was undoubtedly not only the country's best commentator, but also the most knowledgeable sports journalist.

"It sort of became a competition between us to see who could make the other look the most stupid. I said to Wal, 'I'm not too sure we know what we are doing here, mate, other than making us look dopey'," Bryan said.

"We told them the truth and we sat there for about an hour with these people. I remember when they left, one of the sons came back and said it would be great if Wal could send the parents a cheerio on the Saturday WAFL footy, which he did. Anyway, they left and suddenly a carton of merlot arrived at our table from them, which we promptly set about trying to consume. Gee, that was a funny day."

Bryan was often the butt-end of your grandad's jokes. On one occasion, your grandad convinced close friend and renowned practical joker Peter Sweeney to phone Steph Cousins, pretending to be from Canal Rocks Beach Resort, and inform her an error had occurred with the Cousins' booking. The Cousins family used to book one of the apartments with ocean views and, in their ongoing banter, Bryan would tell your grandad that he could only come up when invited, otherwise was required to stay down in the tentland area. So, your grandad had Sweeney place a call to the Cousins, pretending to be a representative of the resort and advise they had been "double-booked".

"Poor Steph is trying to be polite and angry at the same time, so I've come home and she's said, 'You're not going to believe what happened, but they've double booked and we're down in tentland'," Bryan said. "Wal just happened to call me the next week and when I told him what had happened with our booking at Canal Rocks, he just burst into laughter."

Even a kind invitation to join the Cousins for a barbecue dinner courted your grandad's snide humour, as he saw Bryan at the grill and announced his concern that "knowing you, you'll drop the lot on the way up".

"Sure enough, no word of a lie, I dropped the lot on the way up," Bryan said.

"He mentioned it on air, too, because I'd just had the lawn mown and he says, 'We had sausages and grass clippings'. Whenever I would do anything stupid – which was rather frequent – he would never miss me on his Sports Talk show, to the extent that people started asking me about my 'friendship' with Wal.

"We were at an Eagles function one night and Mark Seaby's dad said, 'Do you mind if I ask you a question you might not want asked? Are you and Wally Foreman mates, or are you not good mates?'. I said, 'No, we're real good mates – why do you ask'. And he said, 'Gee, I wasn't sure because he gives you a real hammering on the radio'.

"My major client is a farmer/property developer, with whom I probably do 70 per cent of my business. He spends a lot of his time driving machinery and enjoyed listening to Sports Talk. He genuinely became concerned about Wal pulling the piss at my expense and said to me, 'Wally makes you sound like you're an idiot'. He suggested I speak to Wally about it, but when I did Wal said, 'Thank Christ the message is getting through'.

"One of Wal's favourite put-downs of me was when the Interdominion was at Gloucester Park and Wal was coming down to watch the Final. He rang me to see if I was going to be there, as I was training a couple of horses at the time. I had the great Fred Kersley driving for me and I had my best horse, Global Force, racing that night. Wal came down and was hanging around with us and he obviously knew Fred well, so they had a good old chat while I was gearing my horse up – the normal practice.

"So as Fred and Wal had a long chat, the time came for Fred to take my horse into the Parade Ring prior to going out onto the track for his race. So I followed Fred and Global Force into Parade Ring and walked alongside Fred, having a bit of a chat and telling him that I felt the horse was well and hopefully would race up to his best.

"When I come back, Wally and the two blokes are laughing their heads off and Wally says something like, 'You take being a wanker to a new level. Mate, you've driven one winner in the country, this guy is the greatest driver in Australian history and you've spent the last 10 minutes telling him how to drive the horse'. I said, 'Wal, I wasn't telling him that at all'. Wal just cut me off and said, 'Don't start'. Unbeknownst to me, Wal had another story he could tell about me.

"So, the next day on Sports Talk he tells the story and it's all the things you would hate to be said about you: 'Can you imagine a bloke who can't drive to save himself trying to instruct the best driver in the country?'. He once again did a good job of pulling the piss at my expense, but it was always a good laugh. He'd do it so eloquently.

"But he was the greatest one at telling stories against himself, too, and there was no-one better at it. Oh, shit, he was so funny.

Again, that was another part of the bond. You know, you have these times in your life – I do, anyway – where you sit there and reminisce. And I think, 'If I could have one week back in my life, what would it be?'.

"The weeks and moments I shared with Wal are some of those that I think about."

Friendships are multi-layered. They're developed.

The Cousins-Foreman friendship had been built on 20 years of laughs, mer-lot and football. Your Uncle Mark was a beneficiary, too: having capitalised on your grandad's lifelong friendship with Kim Hughes to have one-on-one batting lessons with a former Australia captain, he followed it up with one-on-one pointers on football from Brownlow Medallist and then-Eagles captain Ben Cousins.

They were good times. But towards the end of your grandad's life, the good times had become a little less frequent. The laughter had all but stopped and was replaced with concern for a mate and his family.

Ben had begun accruing a laundry list of indiscretions, each one seemingly more severe than the next. They were indicative of the larger battle that was waging within him, but no-one knew any of that at the time. And how could they? Despite all we know now, be that about Ben Cousins or the scourge of methamphetamine, this was occurring at a time when the drug was nowhere near as prolific as it is today and perhaps nowhere near as understood.

Ben's actions were considered troubling, without doubt, but not necessarily a reflection of an issue that was out of his control. Regardless, by February 2006, Ben had stepped down from the West Coast captaincy, having three days earlier abandoned his car and run from police near a breath-testing station. A year before, he had been caught up in a police investigation around a nightclub shooting. They were trying times for the Cousins, but your grandad was also finding it increasingly difficult.

Not because of Ben's actions, but because of what was being said, what was being reported and the implications it had for his close friend's son. Your grandad retained faith in Ben, because he knew he was a good man at heart and every indiscretion was considered an opportunity for the turning point that would lead to recovery. But little did your grandad – or Ben's support network, including Bryan – know that the athlete was caught in the grip of the early stages of drug use, which was rapidly turning into addiction.

This was a time before methamphetamine had entered the consciousness of most Australians, so your grandad was not alone in having never identified patterns of drug use. He was also a country boy – they weren't exactly handing out the stuff on Johnson Street in Bruce Rock. Drug addiction being the root cause of Ben's troubles unlikely entered your grandad's mind in the early stages of the former's battles.

Drug use was the habit of those "zombies", as he used to call them, who roamed the city, streets and public transport in the early hours, who clearly were searching "for nothing but trouble". It certainly was not the habit of a friend. Ben was a friend of your grandad's and he was the son of an even closer friend, Bryan. And Bryan now acknowledges that he was as unaware of the larger problems as your grandad was.

He reassured your grandad that, while he was disappointed in Ben's actions, there was no insidious problem at the root of the misbehaviours, because Bryan had, in turn, been reassured of that by Ben directly. What more could your grandad or Bryan have believed? As Bryan said himself: "The biggest mistake most people around Ben made was that we all made a judgement call on his health based on how he was playing his footy. There were really two processes; his initial outright denial and then when we started finding out."

Your grandad knew more than most the troubles engulfing Ben Cousins, but he flatly refused to engage in the rumour and innuendo, which were rapidly gathering speed. On many occasions, he proved an invaluable counsel to Bryan. However, no matter what he knew and how close he was to the Cousins family, the media still had a job to do and the evidence was mounting against Ben.

Two important characteristics to acknowledge of your grandad were his honesty and balance. Despite his relationship with the Cousins, he stood for right and wrong. Your grandad did not attempt to justify or defend Ben's actions, but instead chose only to engage in fact. He was not blinded by his loyalty to friends, but instead chose to stand by them and support them, privately and publicly, in the face of the knowledge he had.

That was the case in your grandad's personal life, when the jovial atmosphere of a Sunday dinner at Zeno's Café with family and friends took a sudden turn with the conversation, which began angling towards Ben. Ben had been witnessed by this friend's son – a first-hand account – taking drugs at a party. Instead of brushing the accusation off, as he often would have done, your grandad became incensed. It was not normal behaviour for your grandad towards a friend.

But it was probably the result of the pressure that was beginning to mount at work. Even in general news reporting, there were challenges for your grandad. His friend, Liam Bartlett, had been among the first to bring to light the story of Ben running away from the police breath-testing station. The office environment was "a little bit tense" that morning, as the station manager Deborah Leavitt recalled.

The format of Sports Talk had also changed. For a period, Glenn Mitchell and your grandad were on the panel at the same time, but it ultimately did not work. They were both extremely knowledgeable, but the best format was one host and two experts. So, Mitchell made the decision to take himself off of the program and leave your grandad with, more often than not, Kim Hughes and Ken Judge. "Your dad had the ability to connect with people," Mitchell said. "I loved Sports Talk, but it was better for the audience that your dad did it."

That raised issues, though. When the misdemeanours began emerging, your grandad was attempting to voice his support of Ben by sticking to the facts in the face of some damning and repetitive rumours in a forum easily susceptible to the mob-mentality. Of course, there were legitimate conversations taking place, but it was the more opinionated, unsubstantiated claims that got to your grandad the most.

"There were times at the early stages, when Ben did the cross-country exercise (running from the police) and swam across the river, that your dad was very pro-Ben," Mitchell said. "There were people who were calling up and shit-stirring him and I remember saying, 'Wal, he's spending a lot of time with some unsavoury people, I've seen it with my own eyes', but he would refuse to believe it.

"Something else would come up and I'd tell Wal and he'd say, 'Bullshit, mate, it's tall-poppy syndrome'. I said, 'Wal, there can't be this much smoke without fire', and then even Judgy said, 'Mate, when I was at the Eagles, I was getting phone calls from punters telling me we had a problem'. Wal would flat-out refute it."

Even with those words from Judge, your grandad still would not lower his defence.

"He had the strong affinity with Ben Cousins as well and so there were those emotions and poor old Wal, he just couldn't see that there was anything wrong with Ben," Judge said. "Hughesy and I used to speak to him about it, the things that we'd heard were going on, and he just wouldn't hear it. In the end, I said, 'Wal, you've got to listen. This is what's going on. I know you like him, but you've got to accept that this is what's going on'.

"And, of course, he was close to Bryan and so that made it harder. You always want to believe in the good in people and there was that strong emotional attachment for him to what was going on in Ben's life, as well. He loved Ben Cousins and he loved the family and it was one the harder things for all of us to accept."

Your grandad was becoming increasingly aware that something serious was going on and it put him in a difficult position, but he also used that position to offer balance to the story. Emotionally, your grandad might have been compromised, but he would not allow himself to be conflicted professionally; he was too intelligent for that and had experienced enough similar situations through the Western Australian Institute of Sport to know how to handle it.

The facts of events – such as Ben running from a booze bus – were irrefutable, but the speculation around them were not. Those were the moments your grandad seized upon and in which he became most aggressive in his defence. There were claims, for example, that when Ben ran from the breath-testing station, he had been in the car with underworld figures and doing drugs. In fact, the car was full of old school friends from Wesley.

The Cousins family had been at a wedding for one of them. Ben was driving a group into town afterwards. Your grandad knew this, because Bryan had told him. Your grandad called Bryan regularly, mostly to simply enquire about how Ben and the family were going, but he would often make a call to his friend to also advise of the latest story doing the rounds, to which Bryan would either provide the truth to be relayed publicly, or the truth in confidence. Bryan did that, because he felt your grandad was one of only a few people in the media he could trust and he was the only one the former fully confided in.

As Bryan reflects now, a significant number of the rumours were, in fact, true. Ben's issues were escalating – mostly behind closed doors. Bryan and your grandad were always open and honest with each other, but they probably both wished they had placed more credence on the stories and rumours that were doing the rounds.

AFL in Perth is a unique market. It's likened to a fishbowl. Its best performers are scrutinised to an extent unmatched anywhere else in the country. This was also a time when Fremantle had yet to mature from the "little brother" of West Coast and had only played one finals series prior to 2006.

That scrutiny was even greater for Eagles players, particularly the elite midfield of Cousins, Chris Judd and Daniel Kerr, who had helped engineer another grand final appearance for the club in 2005, falling short by four points to Sydney. The spotlight was already on Ben Cousins, but it's one thing to adapt to that spotlight focusing on football and another to have it start shining like highbeams into every corner of a personal life.

Ben's behavioural issues occurred at a time when the game was in a sort of transition phase, in which the expectations of clubs and players were required and demanded to be of the highest standards. Previously, there were opportunities for clubs that so wished to cover up player indiscretions and, even if an issue made it into the public forum, the consequences were not as dire as they are today. AFL and cricket share many examples in that transition; much the same as it is no longer accepted that professional cricketers attempt to set alcohol consumption records on long-haul flights to an international tour, so too are AFL players expected to conduct themselves in a fashion conducive to high performance.

Those standards and expectations were not always so professionalised. Over the years since Ben's issues, there have been several initiatives introduced by clubs and the AFL around Codes of Behaviour, the introduction of sound club structures, core values produced and leadership groups formed, not to mention training and education programs around mental and physical wellbeing and drug use.

This transition phase for the athletes rightfully increased public expectations on those athletes and, in turn, resulted in a higher level of scrutiny from the media. The Cousins family were having a difficult time adjusting to the reporting, particularly as the challenges facing their son became clearer. By this time, the family had received counselling, guidance and advice from medical and addiction professionals and were more aware of the serious health and wellbeing issues rapidly consuming Ben's life. Others outside the family were not as informed.

As Ben's misbehaviours increased, the media scrutiny intensified and that went as much for the legitimate coverage as it did the rumour and innuendo. Among the worst was a phone call from a journalist placed to Bryan at 1am advising him that they had been informed that Ben had passed away and requesting he confirm it. Another time, a story was published without confirmation stating that Ben was on life support after a heroin overdose. Neither story held any truth.

"In my case, I was open with the media if I felt someone was honest and open, but in the end, it was relentless," Bryan said.

"On reflection, I may have been a bit hard in my views on the media at the time. Certainly, around that period, I had very little knowledge of the nature of addiction, but I was equally sure the media didn't either. I started seeking as much advice as I could and after some time and realisation by me, I became fully aware of how serious Ben's problems were.

"I appreciate in many cases it was as difficult for the media as it was for us – the journalists had a job to do – but the only one I fully trusted and felt comfortable speaking completely honestly to was Wal. I think Ben was a bit the same. Wally could call me and I would tell him, even if something was private and confidential, because I knew it would never go any further and not once did he betray my confidence.

"I even rang him on occasions and asked him how I should deal with some situations. There were times when I became aware of an indiscretion by Ben and I would ask Wal for advice on how to deal with it publicly. Where Wally stood alone among some of the media that we dealt with was that every time he contacted me, his No.1 concern was Ben's welfare and the welfare of the family, not getting a story. Our friendship was so strong at that stage that it was like Ben was his nephew or something.

"Wal was like that with everyone, but I would always keep him informed and he would always ask. I think he would have found himself in a tough situation at times with his media colleagues, but he never let on to me."

Significant moments are built. They are developed over time and they are multi-layered. There were many layers to the moment for your grandad in September 2006 in which he described from an MCG commentary box West Coast's Ben Cousins and Chris Judd holding either side of the AFL Premiership, hoisting the cup in celebration. It was emotional for him, for many reasons.

The 2006 AFL Grand Final was the last major sporting broadcast of your grandad's life. It was his first call of an AFL Grand Final. It involved a close friend, whose friendship had grown stronger over the years preceding the win and it involved the West Coast Eagles, a club he enjoyed seeing taste success.

There were layers of pain and frustration that had led to that moment, layers that focused on his connection and love for the Cousins family, but there were also layers that didn't involve the Cousins at all. Layers that didn't involve pain, frustration or anger. Layers of jubilation and joy. The fact that your grandad was there at the MCG was one of those layers.

Fate and destiny are interesting concepts. They are built around a belief that we do not necessarily have control over the ultimate destination of our lives. That our lives are, instead, led like the sections of an orchestra, whose individual sounds weave in and out of each other under the guidance of the conductor to create a perfect moment of harmony. They are concepts that usually rely on occurrences of chance and coincidence, that appear too coincidental to be coincidence or chance.

I don't know if I believe in fate or destiny, but there were several moments of chance that were seemingly orchestrated to have your grandad's final major sporting broadcast end in harmony. For one, it was the first – and last – time the ABC sent two teams of broadcasters to an AFL Grand Final: one for the national audience and one for the WA audience.

That was the result of a strong push from Glenn Mitchell, head of the ABC Perth sports department, and Deborah Leavitt,

Local Content Manager for Perth, for there to be an audience-tailored experience. The pair was fortunate to have the ear and agreeance of Peter Longman, the founding Executive Producer of ABC Grandstand's national programming.

The argument was that, for a three-year period, there had been grand finals that did not involve a single Melbourne-based team, yet the ABC had repeatedly turned to Melbourne-based commentators. That was not to say they weren't worthy of calling the game, but they were calling teams they might have commentated a few times at most throughout the season, while broadcasters who had the local knowledge of the players, with 11 or more games under their belts of a specific team, and who had a greater relationship with their state's audience, were left behind.

The push began in 2004, when Brisbane played Port Adelaide. It continued in 2005, with West Coast and Sydney. And it was finally realised for the 2006 rematch between those sides, when the ABC was advised they had finally been given a box for the game, a makeshift position on the opposite side of the ground to the usual broadcast boxes. But it never happened again.

Then, there was the fact your grandad was chosen to call the game. It was a combination of his talent and timing. Mitchell, as head of the department, could have easily chosen to go himself. He had every right to. He had sent himself, along with former Fremantle captain Ben Allan, the year before to host Sports Talk from the MCG ahead of the 2005 Grand Final. But a year later, he decided to send your grandad and Dan Lonergan instead.

Despite their moments of difficulty, your grandad and Mitchell were friends and often worked as a strong team. The latter had a healthy acknowledgement of his own talents, like any good performer in the media, but he also respected your grandad and all he had achieved in his career. And he knew that at 58-years-old, it might have been the last chance your grandad had to call an AFL Grand Final. It was a humble decision, made more so because of the decision to also send Lonergan, but it was also one he had to fight for.

"I called up Peter Longman and said, 'Yep, we've got a team: it'll be (Ken) Judge, (Jon) Dorotich, Foreman and Lonergan'," Mitchell said.

"He came back to me and said Dan wasn't doing it and that I had to do it, but I went back and said that, no, Dan would be doing it. I've always said Dan is a better football commentator than me. I mean, I'm a better cricket commentator, but Dan is better at football.

"I said, 'All this time I've argued with you saying, why the hell isn't Dan doing the Grand Final, because he's better than the blokes you've got doing it and he's better than I am'. I said I couldn't then say, 'Thanks, I'll take the Grand Final', so Peter said, 'Fine, then you should be doing it in place of Wally'.

"I said, 'No. Wally's 58, I'm 45, there'll be plenty more grand finals for me to call down the track and I want Wally to do it and I believe Dan should be doing it'."

Mitchell had no idea how correct he was that it was your grandad's last chance. As fate would have it, it ended up being Mitchell's last chance also.

Then, there was West Coast contesting the final. Of course, had they not been, none of this would have eventuated from a WA perspective, but there is the fact that in your grandad's lifetime, a WA team had made the grand final just four times and, of those times, he only had a realistic chance of being selected to commentate one of those matches. And West Coast won.

Your grandad died less than two months later.

Fate? I'm not sure I believe in it. But a lot of individual moments of chance had to work together in harmony to make it happen.

There was a lot to do. Not just for the fact it was an AFL Grand Final involving the West Coast Eagles, but also for the fact that your grandad worked for the ABC. If there was any body as fiscally frugal as your grandad, it was the ABC. The broadcaster wanted to make sure it got every possible bang for its buck.

And your grandad was as excited and nervous as if it was his first broadcast. It was like it was his first day at school, or his first business trip. Even after all he had seen and achieved in his life and career, the AFL Grand Final – that particular AFL Grand Final and everything that went with it – and the opportunity to call it meant so much to him that he was giddy beyond measure.

He had rushed into the East Perth offices Thursday morning, frantically scraping together his last-minute preparations. Gathering all the required documents, printing others out, collecting his AFL Year Book and, of course, writing out the players and notes he would need to complete a successful broadcast. Then he dashed to the airport to make his flight, leaving it all behind at the office.

"Many people will reflect on the 2006 Grand Final as they reflect on Wally's life and could the script have been written more perfectly; that his final football call be his beloved West Coast Eagles winning the premiership? How perfect is that," your grandad's work colleague Roanna Edwards said.

"I remember listening as I drove to Geraldton for the weekend. I remember his voice disappearing on him in those final minutes. I remember pulling over somewhere near Eneabba because I couldn't bear the tension and it was making my pressure on the accelerator fluctuate. It was unbelievable.

"But really, when I reflect on it all, I giggle. Because no one else got to see the childish excitement Wally had in the days leading up. No one else saw him come into work on the Thursday morning, frantically putting things together to catch his midday flight to Melbourne. No one else got a phone call from Perth Airport summing up all the craziness that was Wally's grand final preparation.

"He called my desk phone: 'Ro, its Wal. I need your help. I'm such an idiot. I've left pretty much everything on my desk. My team lists, my preparation and all the information about the next couple of days'. I could only laugh. He was laughing, too, but in an almost panicked way. 'Ro, I've also forgotten my itinerary. I have no idea where I'm staying when I get to Melbourne'.

"We laughed some more as I fossicked through the paper on his desk to find everything he needed. I found the name of the hotel and provided him with it, as well as the address and contact number. Of course, I had to wait as Wally wrote it all down – this wasn't a man that could simply open a text message at the other end and have all the information he required.

"I wished him well and hung up the phone. I then had to put all his paperwork together and contact the hotel and advise I had a 13-page fax coming through that needed to be given to Mr Wally Foreman upon check in. It's impossible to know if he collected his paperwork. I'll assume he did, but let's be honest: he could have called that match with or without it.

"He was destined to call his Eagles to victory on that last Saturday in September, 2006."

Your grandad could relax a bit once he was on the ground in Melbourne and the informalities of the build-up to the 2006 AFL Grand Final were completed with dinner in Chinatown with Russell Woolf and friends on the Thursday night. Your grandad's misconception of a "Chinese restaurant" was on full display as he arrived at the alley-based, pop-up style yum cha in some of his more formal evening clothes – contrasting Woolf's trademark shorts and thongs – holding a bottle of red wine, which was promptly consumed from brightly coloured plastic picnic cups, on a fold-out picnic table.

Friday night was less of a culture shock: dinner with the Cousins family and their friends in South Bank, followed by more red wine with his ABC colleagues. The formalities of the build-up to the 2006 AFL Grand Final weren't completed until it was almost bouncedown.

Your grandad and Woolf provided interviews and crosses from the Grand Final Parade on Friday, the day before the game, into the Mornings program with new host Geoff Hutchison, who was broadcasting from Parliament House, near the Windsor Hotel. Woolf hosted his Friday Drive program from Melbourne, then assisted your grandad on the morning of the decider with Sports Talk from West Coast's Grand Final Breakfast function at Vodafone Arena.

A few more interviews were gathered and prepared for the pre-match preview and then it was time to get ready for the call. No trip to the football in Melbourne is complete without taking part in the march to the ground, so there were no taxis that day as the ABC Perth commentary team of your grandad, Dan Lonergan, Ken Judge and Jon Dorotich were joined by Woolf and producer Damian Rabbitt in treading the path to the MCG.

Destiny, it would seem, was fast approaching.

Your grandad called a lot of sport in the years of his fulltime return to the ABC. Countless AFL matches, Davis Cup and Australian Open tennis – including some particularly significant matches – and the international successes of an Olympic Games, the 2002 Commonwealth Games and its successor, the 2006 instalment in Melbourne.

The men's hockey gold medal in Athens would have marked one of your grandad's most memorable moments, without doubt. But top of that list would have been the 2006 AFL Grand Final. It was a remarkable game for those who had nothing invested in it, let alone those for whom it was a multi-layered affair.

Even the match-up itself was layered in history. In 2005, West Coast won its qualifying final against Sydney by four points, but then lost the grand final to same opponent by the same margin. In 2006, although the result was yet to fully play out at that time, Sydney had defeated West Coast in the qualifying final by one point, then went on to lose to the Eagles – you guessed it – by the same margin.

I'm no mathematician, but the odds alone of that happening and the symmetry would surely be so improbable that it was another gift to those believing in fate and destiny. There was no love lost in a rivalry that repeatedly produced tight contests, be they in a finals series or not, with the four previous results between the sides decided by less than a goal.

Even the week before the decider was tight: Sydney's Adam Goodes had won the Brownlow Medal, with West Coast's Daniel Kerr and Chris Judd in third and fourth place, respectively. It appeared that trend might have been changing though, with the Eagles dominating the opening half and holding a convincing 25-point advantage at halftime.

The ABC Perth commentary team did not have the best vantage point, calling from the makeshift media centre that had been set up in 2004 in the Great Southern Stand. It was a tiny space, long and narrow, barely two seats deep. Russell Woolf, an avid West Coast supporter who had a media pass but no seat, was perched at the back with producer Damian Rabbitt, while the broadcasters squeezed into the front row.

But with the contest that was about to unfold, few would have been complaining. Sydney had cut the margin to 11 points at the final change and, when Goodes kicked a goal in the first 15 seconds of the final quarter, the differential was just a kick.

"The grand final was quite funny," said special comments provider Ken Judge of the day.

"Your dad was quite emotional about it, I mean, he was a great commentator and he commentated really well on the day, but there was a feeling that he was almost playing himself. You just felt that he rode every bump, he jumped around in his seat and it was funny watching this person on the edge of his seat in a close game of footy, being so emotionally attached to it and wanting to call them across the line to win it.

"He's up like this," Judge rose to his feet and started moving his arms around animatedly, "And waving his arms about. He was never as into it as he was that day, especially when there'd been nothing in it all day and a goal was like gold. He wasn't biased in his call, I've got to say that, he was professional enough that he didn't show anything like that. But if you could actually see him during the call, I mean, he was drained at the end of that, because he'd played it himself."

Almost 100,000 people watched as the match evolved into one of the most thrilling grand finals in history. Goodes had opened the scoring early in the final quarter, but for the next 20 minutes the teams traded goals, even behinds, in an at times congested affair that ping-ponged between forward lines. Both teams' defences often seemed impenetrable.

In a sign of just how tight the contest was, after Goodes' opener, neither team scored another major until Adam Schneider crumbed and kicked truly about 12 minutes later to drag Sydney within a point. The match then briefly turned ironic, with West Coast answering within a minute and Sydney kicking another goal 30sec after that to defy to previous scoreless trend, but still maintaining the tightness of a one-point scoreline to the advantage of the Eagles.

There was five minutes to go and the Eagles were holding the slimmest of leads of a point, when West Coast's Daniel Chick make a crucial smother of Ryan O'Keefe as Sydney attempted to exit defence. The loose ball was pounced on, handballed to Adam Hunter and slotted through to restore a seven-point advantage. It appeared enough, until Nick Malceski responded at the 27-minute mark.

The score was 84-85 in West Coast's favour and would not change for the rest of the game. One point the difference. Just under four minutes to play.

"One of my lasting memories was that Wal was always going to call the end of the game, but we didn't know how long was left and they were a point up for about four minutes. Normally you cycle every minute or 90sec or whatever," Dan Lonergan recalled.

"I was a little bit worried he was going to burst, mate, because it was an eternity. Sydney kicked the last goal and I reckon there wasn't another score – certainly not another goal – for three or four minutes. He just had to keep calling and calling, until it was on the half-forward line."

The players were "out on their feet", as your grandad described, with many cramping up as the game began its crescendo. The players were struggling to keep their footing – even an umpire went down in the closing stages – and your grandad was struggling to keep his voice; the nature of the game in its entirety, let alone the final four-minutes straight of calling, had left it raspy and thin.

It had almost faded completely when the ball tumbled over the boundary line near centre wing.

It was a brief moment of respite. It was a time when the commentators would have usually subbed for each other. Your grandad glanced at Lonergan who shook his head.

"Bring 'em home, Wally."

"There's a lot of tired boys out there, Wal," said Ken Judge.

"Very tired," your grandad responded, then continued his commentary.

"Nearly 30 minutes played in the final quarter of the grand final. It comes down to Malceski, he's caught with the ball. Kerr goes in solidly and there will be another ball up. Barry Hall is calling everyone up. He wants someone in the gap. He realises that a full kick will land in no-man's land, so it's Dempster who comes up and Embley comes with him.

"Cox palms it down. Chance for Cousins; runs onto it, handpasses to his own advantage and picks it up inside the boundary line. He comes in-field but is tackled. Handpasses to Fletcher; Fletcher to Kerr. Kerr needs to kick – and he does – but he's exposed them."

Judge groaned at the error that resulted in a loose ball in the centre of the ground. Your grandad continued.

"It's in the midfield. In goes Rowan Jones, handpass to Lynch; Lynch can't get rid of it, but gets a kick-of-sorts away. It's with Waters; Waters handpasses wide in the direction of Cousins. They're very tired. Sydney with the ball; it's with Fosdike. Fosdike kicks towards full forward; the contest is critical. Opportunity for West Coast close to the boundary line."

Jon Dorotich interjected: "Out of bounds". The seconds were ticking away. The suspense and the energy coming through the airwaves was palpable. Your grandad resumed.

"It's going to be a throw-in on Sydney's 50 metre line. Nearly 31 minutes played."

Judge again: "Gees, the heart's racing here". Your grandad pursed his lips in agreeance, the closest sign he could manage to a smile, as his whiting knuckles held a vice grip on the binoculars that were tracing the play and pressed firmly against his eyes.

"Boundary throw-in. Sydney in attack. West Coast lead by a point. Cox gets a hand to it."

Suddenly, a long, droning wail let cry around the ground, like the game of football itself could no longer sustain the suspense.

"THERE'S THE SIREN," your grandad shouted, as Judge let out a noise of surprise himself and the roar of the 100,000-strong crowd filled the effects microphone.

"There's the siren. West Coast have won the 2006 Premiership by a solitary point. West Coast avenge last year's defeat. West Coast: the premiers for 2006 – 12.13 (85) to Sydney 12.12 (84). The West Coast Eagles came to Melbourne on business and that business is now complete."

The sounds of the celebrations of the crowd continued to echo in the background of the broadcast. A smile finally spread across your grandad's bewildered face, hidden only barely by the arm and sock of the microphone. His legs were jigging like the pistons of car engine.

"Let your hair down Western Australia – the Eagles have landed."

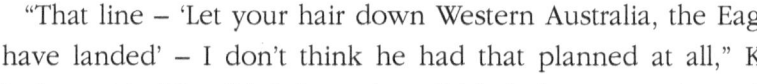

"That line – 'Let your hair down Western Australia, the Eagles have landed' – I don't think he had that planned at all," Ken Judge said. "He didn't have it scribbled down anywhere, but it was a great line, and I think that was a culmination of all his emotions. That was an outpouring."

It was 10 words that encapsulated immense emotion. The scenes of celebration were tremendous and would be etched into the history of that day, particularly the iconic image of Ben Cousins and Chris Judd, former captain and current, holding either side of the Premiership Cup. Your grandad drank in the moment. Interviews with the team were conducted and the listener was given their conclusion. Then the broadcast came to a close.

You might think that with a West Coast grand final win, particularly given the way in which the match played out, the connection with the Cousins and all the layers that went into building the significance of that moment, that your grandad would have partied the night away with whoever wanted to party. The truth was a lot tamer, simply because of the significance of the moment. It left your grandad as drained as if he had played the game himself.

"He called it, played it, he'd done everything," Judge said.

"I actually said to him after, 'What position did you play today, Wal?'. He displayed all of the emotions of someone sitting in Row 1, who was the most passionate Eagles supporter of all time, but calling the game at the same time.

"It was a WA thing, but he loved the Eagles, you know that, and he loved Ben Cousins, so it was a WA thing, but there's no doubt that the Eagles part of it was more emotional for him."

Your grandad had an immense passion for anything Western Australian and so he enjoyed seeing Fremantle win, just as he did West Coast. But Judge was right: he loved the Eagles. In fact, it wasn't widely known, but he had earlier that year been asked to sit on the Board of West Coast. He lobbied his case for acceptance with ABC management, but they believed it would have been a conflict of interest and refused to allow it.

Your grandad pointed out that the ABC had been fine with him working on air for more than a decade while holding the position of director of the Western Australian Institute of Sport, a job that put him in countless conflicts across the country with countless organisations, but it was to no avail. It also made little difference to the significance of that day.

He openly recalled the opportunity to have commentated the 2006 AFL Grand Final as a career highlight – if not *the* career highlight – upon his return to the Perth office. That was a point that meant a lot to Glenn Mitchell, who had pushed to have your grandad anchor the broadcast.

"When I look back, I think that's wonderful, because it was the only grand final he ever did and it was the last major piece of commentary that he did. It was important that he did it, but it only came about because of what I learnt from your dad and the way he treated people," Mitchell said.

"I'm just so happy that it turned out the way it did and even when you listen back to the recording, you can hear the sheer joy in his voice at the end. He did a lot of things – Olympic gold medals and what-have-you – but I look back and I'm thankful that it turned out the way it did, but I also note that it did happen that way, because of the time I spent with your father."

That day was a moment of ideal serendipity to cap an immense career. As Karen Tighe recalled: "How blessed were we that the Eagles were able to break through in that grand final and your dad was able to be there? Someone was looking down on us all then."

Significant moments are built. They are developed over time and multilayered.

Your grandad left the ABC broadcasting box that day and made his way to the Eagles' dressing rooms. He, of course, went straight to Bryan and Ben Cousins and shook their hands and embraced them in a display of understanding and affection that only close friends can share. Russell Woolf had joined your grandad and was introduced to the father and son.

"He did it in such a way that Bryan trusted me immediately, like he felt if Wally had introduced us, then it meant I was ok," Woolf said.

"That helped, because Bryan and I then spoke on a number of occasions and I always treated him with respect. Wally would always talk about Sunday night fish and chips at Zeno's, Christmas on the farm. And he would always talk about Easter with the Cousins at Canal Rocks.

"In the back of my mind, I always think of your father and that it's because of him that I was talking to Bryan Cousins and to always respect that. I've had some good conversations with him, on and off the record."

Then, the group parted ways.

Woolf's requirements of having run his own Drive show from the ABC studios in Melbourne, coupled with assisting your grandad, followed by the drama of the grand final itself, had him exhausted and he "flaked out on the couch". The whole Cousins family was in Melbourne and enjoyed the celebrations of the official Eagles functions and your grandad had the ABC's function with his colleagues.

He and Bryan intended to catch up later in the night, but it never eventuated. Instead, they spoke on the phone at length the next morning, before your grandad's flight back to Perth. That day was the last time they saw each other. The phone call was the last time they spoke to each other.

The joy held in those moments of celebration began to disappear and have all but vanished in the days since. Ben's drug addiction gripped his life in a way that every parent fears. It laid waste to his hopes and dreams and his fight against it will never be over. Drug addiction never is. It might offer glimmers of hope and moments of reprieve, but it is a lifelong battle that will forever haunt the entire Cousins family.

The true nature of that battle began to be revealed to the public in the months after your grandad's death. Ben was arrested in Melbourne in December 2006 for charges of being drunk in public – the charges were eventually dismissed – and Bryan and Stephanie revealed the following March that their son's challenges were related to substance abuse.

He was indefinitely suspended by West Coast and travelled to a California rehabilitation centre to achieve some level of privacy in overcoming an incredibly personal battle, but he was never afforded that luxury. The media followed him everywhere.

Ben, of course, was no saint and often courted the media's attention with his actions, but where most people would be able to attempt to piece their lives back together without external pressures, that was just not possible for the Brownlow Medallist.

The pressure, instead, continued to mount and compound his challenges.

He returned to football with West Coast, having issued a public apology and assured the AFL he was no longer addicted to drugs – an issue that is far more complicated than a person simply deciding they are no longer addicted to drugs – but was later linked to being at the house of another former Eagles talent, Chris Mainwaring, on the night he died from a drug overdose.

More police charges followed, he was sacked by West Coast, suspended by the AFL as a whole, made a brief three-season return to football with Richmond in 2008 and appeared to be recovering, before relapsing and plunging to a state worse than before. Ben has since repeatedly been arrested and charged by police, admitted to mental health units, rehabilitation clinics and hospitals, but all have appeared to make little difference to his state of mind, or ability to lead some form of normal life.

The same goes for his family, who face challenges the rest of us would dread to face. It was repeatedly said to me that, in a way, a silver lining of your grandad's passing – always qualified with, "if there was one" – was that he was not alive to see the tragic events that engulfed Ben's life.

People believed that your grandad was adamant the whole saga was a beat-up, that it would have torn him apart because, as Glenn Mitchell said, "in your dad's mind there was nothing in it and he believed Ben wouldn't be involved in it". Mitchell believed it would have had such an impact that your grandad would have had to have been given time off, away from the microphone, because the public fallout would have been too intense for him to balance his love and loyalty to the Cousins with his work requirements.

Aspects of those opinions were correct, such as the fact the saga would have torn your grandad up, but he was not naïve to the problems and he was blinded by loyalty to the point that he believed Ben was innocent. He knew probably better than anyone outside the Cousins family the challenges the football player was going through. He knew about the drug addiction.

He might not have known for how long the battle would have drawn out, or how dramatic some of Ben's actions and events would become. He might not have said any of it publicly – even off the air to colleagues – and he might have even contradicted that knowledge with his words, but he already knew how bad it was and how bad it was looking. He chose not to bury his head in the sand, or to create distance between himself and the problem, but instead he stood by his friends through it all.

"The 2006 Grand Final is special to me for a number of reasons, but particularly with regards to Wally. It was unfortunately the last time we saw each other," Bryan said.

"It meant a lot to him, the Eagles winning; with Ben playing and it being a WA team. For his last major sporting event that he called to be the 2006 Grand Final, I suppose that's fitting in a small way.

"To your father's eternal credit, he never told me how much it affected him. We used to talk to each other and I never, ever didn't tell him the truth; we never fell out about it and, if anything, I think our friendship strengthened over that time. Quite frankly, without his support, I'm not sure I would have made it through. Now, as I look back, he would have been torn between a friendship and a job and you know where your dad's priorities in life were.

"I remember Ben saying to me one day, 'I just wish I had a terminal illness; someone might at least then try to understand me and the extent of my problems'. Some people would make me feel like I was part of the problem, or that I caused the problem. And I felt like that at times, too, but when I looked at my family, I thought, 'Well hang on; I've got four kids, if I was a bad parent I'd have four drug addicts'. As I've been told by many counsellors during this time; addiction does not discriminate. It can happen to anyone and anyone's family.

"Getting the support and understanding of someone like Wal, who I believe was universally respected for his balance, his fairness and his openness – the public of WA probably knew more about the Foreman family than you did yourself – was so important. He was one person that never made me feel part of the problem, only because he was so even about it; he was never looking for an angle, it was all love and care."

Your grandad had such a profound impact on the lives of the people around him, through the genuine love, care and support he always showed to others. That love, care and support lived on after his death, through those same people who were impacted by it. They surrounded our family, became our safety net, in ways that made ensured we could come out the other side of an event as tragic as losing your grandad. In particular, many of the male friends of your grandad's rallied around your Uncle Mark.

He was only 14-years-old when your grandad died. He lost the man who spent countless hours helping guide his sporting ambitions, with precious bonding time disguised as strict rules for everything from accompanying his dad to games, to how to hit a straight drive with the correct technique. Men, particularly men of your grandad's era, are not necessarily trained to deal well with discussing emotions, but being there for a boy at sport, helping to fill a place that no-one had asked be vacated? That, to so many of them, was easy.

Friends of your grandad's such as Jeff King – friends from your uncle's school, who had holidayed with our family – and George Young, Glenn Mitchell and your Great Uncles John Raynor and Steve Young. They would all frequently make the weekend pilgrimage to whatever cricket or football ground your uncle was playing on, there to support their mate's kid, because their mate could no longer do it himself.

And, often, a figure would be standing on the opposite side of the ground, occasionally wandering over, particularly if members of our family were there, to say hello. Despite the heartache that was unfolding for his own family, Bryan Cousins made sure he was there when he could be for ours, because your grandad had always done the same.

It's just what mates do for each other.

Your grandad resigned from the WA Institute of Sport in 2001 as the longest-running state institute director in the country, having held the position for 17 years. He had hoped to steer WAIS through to the 2004 Athens Olympics and always intended on returning to the media, but when a dream position at ABC Perth came up shortly after the Sydney Games, the offer to join Glenn Mitchell and Grandstand's Karen Tighe was one he couldn't refuse.

The Wally Foreman Story | 449

Upon his full-time return to the ABC, your grandad eventually settled and became very comfortable with his new identity. As Dennis Cometti said at your grandad's memorial service: "Wally understood that broadcasting was a shared experience; it's supposed to be entertaining". And entertain, he did. Alongside close friend and former Australia cricket captain Kim Hughes (above, back row, second from left) and football expert the late Ken Judge (above, front row, left), your grandad revelled in the informative – yet, very entertaining – Sports Talk. He and Hughes were also involved in one of the more humorous exchanges – "are you a bit of a snorkeler, Wal?" – when both men were left in uncontrollable fits of laughter live on air (below-left). Of course, his self-effacing humour was not confined to work, as Snow White found with Grumpy (below, right).

Your grandad felt privileged for the way in which he spent his working life, but he also had an acute sense of balance. For every broadcast completed, there was a dinner party, or holiday with family and friends, be it at home with the Duncraig Domestic Dyslexics (above) or abroad, to destinations such as North America with the King family (below).

Above all else for your grandad was family. Your Great Grandad Eric's 90th birthday in 2005 with sisters Jill (above, second from left) and Sandy (far right) was cause for celebration, but so too was a Sunday dinner at Zeno's Café, Hillarys (below).

Just four days before he suffered his heart attack, your grandad hosted the induction into the WA Hall of Champions of close friend and former national hockey captain Craig Davies at the WAIS Annual Dinner. It was one of the last photos captured of your grandad and the emotion of both men highlights the moment's significance.

Tributes flowed from every corner of the community following your grandad's passing and included tributes such as the above in *The Sunday Times* (courtesy/credit Greg Smith) and the below in *The West Australian* (courtesy/credit Dean Alston).

However, the response of the public was equally poignant. Notes from people who had "never met him" flooded in and a crowd of about 3000 attended your grandad's memorial service, with even more listening to the state-wide broadcast on ABC.

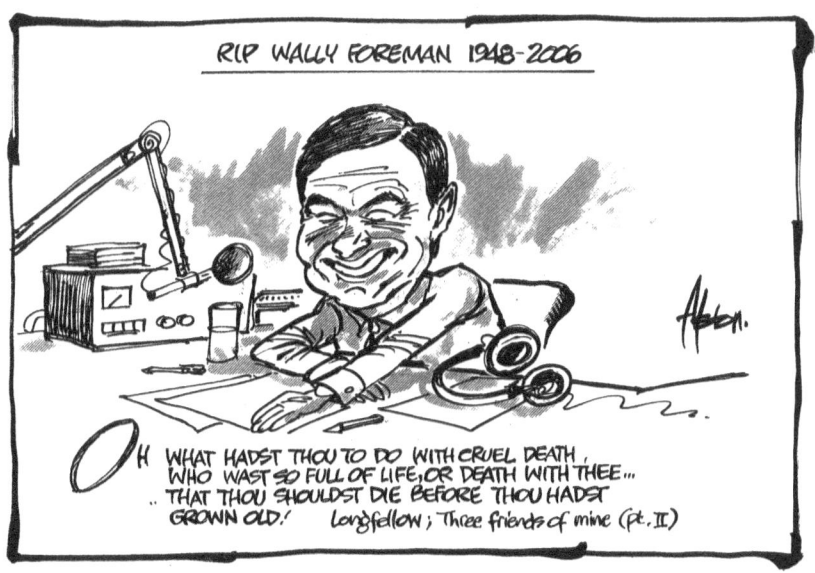

PART FOUR

Chapter 23

Every Ending Has a Beginning

You might have pictured the day we lost your grandad as devoid of colour. So overcast and gloomy that the sky appeared to wash away his vibrant life with a grayscale flood. The truth was more ironic than reflective. It was a near pristine day, with spring warming temperatures to the high 20s beneath an almost cloudless sky in its final charge towards summer.

But perhaps we're skipping too far ahead, because while the 2006 AFL Grand Final was like your grandad's closing remarks in the broadcast that was his life, the credits still had to roll. The closing sting still had to play.

When a person gets to 58, like your grandad, they're certainly not expired, but they're also not the fit, young specimen they once were. They begin to slow, or at least find it increasingly difficult to keep the same pace as their younger self. Issues with their health begin to emerge; issues that require a little more attention than bed rest. And they might find their mind is not as sharp as it once was.

Time posted a reminder of that fact to your grandad in 2000, care-of the Seven Network. It was ahead of the Olympic Games and the broadcaster required its staff to undergo a basic GP screening to ensure the rigours of media – particularly the action-packed, high-pressure deadline world of sports media – was not going to send any employees to an early grave and lead to literal dead air.

Your grandad's screening identified a cholesterol issue and he was referred to a cardiologist, who highlighted some concerns. Aside from the high cholesterol, there was some build-up of calcium in his arteries. It was concerning news, of course, but not life altering; it could be treated with medication, which your grandad was prescribed. The medication was Lipitor – a statin used to treat high cholesterol and lower the risk of heart attack in people with recognised risk factors.

Fast forward five years and the medication was perceived to be having some unexpected side-effects. I must say "perceived" there, because at the time of writing this, statins have again hit the headlines, with science refuting side-effects such as those your grandad experienced. Your grandad was always an active man; he would go for a minimum 30min run at least four days a week, yet the drugs had weakened his muscles to the point where they were regularly cramping and often – comparatively to the times of non-medication – tearing. That occurred even in conditions not necessarily considered strenuous, such as boundary umpiring at your Uncle Mark's junior football.

The most concerning issue, though, was related to his brain function. Links between statins and memory loss are constantly raised, investigated and refuted, but those links were not as publicly debated at the time your grandad was taking the medication. It's important to stress the positive impact statins have on the health issues they are prescribed to treat, but it is concerning the apparent reluctance of the medical profession to at least accept a link exists between the drug and memory loss.

In the case of your grandad, there had been no issues off the medication and there suddenly were issues when he was on it. America's Food and Drug Administration (FDA) acknowledged the link in 2012. Lipitor's official website even warns of it. Regardless of any debates over the issue, your grandad experienced the side-effect.

A year before he passed away, he was due to give a speech in Esperance and he and your nana had arrived the same day and checked into their hotel room. Then, something happened that sent streaks of panic through both. Your grandad sat on the end of the bed, with no understanding of where he was, no recollection of why he was there and no idea what he was supposed to be talking about that night.

Your nana was close to calling an ambulance, before they opted instead for rest and to reassess if the problem did not dissipate.

Your grandad awoke with his full memory, like the episode had never happened, and delivered one of his trademark engaging talks.

There were other indicators of issues, as well. While the Esperance episode was by far the worst, your grandad's colleagues had noticed little uncharacteristic mistakes in his commentary. Kim Hughes, alongside your grandad in cricket broadcasts, recalled errors such as calling the ball being struck to "mid off, I mean, mid on". Your grandad himself, ever the perfectionist, was upset at his call of the 2006 AFL Grand Final, because of occasional errors in player names, despite Ken Judge insisting and reassuring him that it had no great impact on the call.

And then there was the 2006 WAIS Annual Dinner.

Your grandad stood at the lectern that had been set up at the front of the room. It was the main arena of Challenge Stadium and had been converted to a large function area, as it was for every WAIS Annual Dinner.

These were the moments that many people enjoyed the most about the Institute's annual dinners; the induction of new members into the Hall of Champions and the spectacle that was made of the event through your grandad's hosting. Of course, that is not to take anything away from the evening's proceedings. Everyone was there to celebrate the achievements over the year of Western Australia's sporting community.

Your grandad's passion, however, was undeniable. His induction readings drew people in, engaged them and made them want to give the special acknowledgement that was deserved for the unique achievements of the Hall's members. Your grandad would motion around the room, reciting from memory – mostly – the trials and tribulations of the Hall's existing members and achievements that led to their inductions, before welcoming the new members, with an orating ability that put world leaders and their speech writers to shame.

Except for Saturday, 30 September 2006 – the night of that year's WAIS Annual Dinner. As your grandad stood at the lectern, motioning around the room and reciting the achievements of the members of the Hall, there was a vague sense of disorientation. The usually precise and flawless delivery of your grandad was a little erratic, with some stutters and errors.

It would have meant little to most people in that room, but those close to him noticed it. And when they approached your grandad after to reassure him that it was again a good segment of the night, they were met with a frustrated response. The frustration of a man who knew he could have – should have – done better, yet had no explanation as to why he had not.

He was feeling off, he told them. He did not want to stay. And for one of the only times in his life, your grandad left the WAIS Annual Dinner early.

It was four days before his heart attack.

There is a cause for every effect.

If the concerning health issues were the effect, your grandad believed the cause was the medication. The issues became intolerable for your grandad and, believing it was the medication causing them, 12 months before he died he committed one of the most severe crimes a patient can: he elected to stop taking it without consulting his cardiologist.

Your grandad had been speaking about the adverse effects of the medication with fellow ABC broadcaster Eoin Cameron, who was on the same tablets for high cholesterol and had been experiencing similar effects. Cameron had suggested your grandad try psyllium husks, a natural fibre. It undoubtedly was never the intention of Cameron that your grandad cease his medication without consulting his cardiologist, though.

Despite the failure to report the change, the change itself succeeded in addressing your grandad's cholesterol issues. The psyllium husks reduced his numbers from 9.2 to 4.2.

But back to that cruel, pristine day. That almost cloudless, warm breath of summer. The same breath I felt on my face as I slid open the flywire door in the laundry and poked my head out to the backyard, turning it left to face the clothesline.

It was Tuesday, 31 October 2006 – one of your grandad's days off. Tuesday and Wednesday were the ABC sports department's weekend, given they had to work everyone else's weekend. Your nana was busying herself in the kitchen, getting ready for her day as head track coach at the Western Australian Institute of Sport. Your grandad, having never been able to sit still for longer than a 10min sports news bulletin, was putting his neurotic idiosyncrasy to good use, hanging out the washing.

It was a good time for our family, or at least your grandad and me. And when there was peace with us, it usually meant a more pleasant environment for everyone else. For the previous six months, we had begun to get along. Even enjoy each other's company.

We could sit and watch the news together and have a civil conversation about the world, instead of a civil war. As bewildering as it might seem, we couldn't do that until I had grown up enough. There were, of course, relapses, but for the most part we were on our way to building an adult father and son relationship.

For that, I will always be grateful. Because on that Tuesday, having asked your nana where your grandad was, being advised he was hanging out the washing and being on speaking terms with him, I made the small effort to double back. To retrace my steps through the house, poke my head out the side-door of the laundry and shout, "Bye dad, have a good day".

He was hidden by white sheets and pillow cases, with only his legs visible beneath. There is a song, "Welcome Home" by Radical Face, with the lyrics: "Sheets are swaying from an old clothesline, like a row of captured ghosts". Your grandad's spirit could have easily been among those sheets, billowing in the breeze attempting to break free from that which was holding it, because his seemingly disembodied voice replied through the flapping fabric: "You too. See you tonight".

As I walked past your nana, I kissed her goodbye and told her I loved her, which made me realise I had not done the same for your grandad. "Can you tell dad I said I love him," I asked your nana, before leaving the house and driving away. For the first time in a while, given the uncertainty of direction in my life which I described earlier, I smiled.

I remember all of that as vividly as it was yesterday, because that was the last time I spoke to your grandad. The warm breath of summer continued to whisper throughout the morning. The sheets continued to sway. Within hours, the hold the world had on your grandad would begin to be released.

Glenn Mitchell walked out of the ABC Perth studios. It was 6pm on Sunday, 29 October and he had just finished a show called Sports Extra – the younger brother of Sports Talk. He turned the corner and saw your grandad, working at his desk.

"What the hell are you doing here?" Mitchell enquired.

"Mate, they've got me as the bloody ambassador for the aging and I've got to do a talk tomorrow, so I'm just getting some stuff together."

Mitchell rolled his eyes at the ever-increasing workload and remarked that he hoped "they're paying you well".

"No, but they've given me this gym membership."

It was the last time Mitchell ever spoke to your grandad.

"Did you tell him I said I loved him?" I asked your nana.

"What do you mean?"

"Remember, when I was leaving the house, I asked you to tell him that I loved him, because I forgot."

"Oh, yes. I did, darling."

It was all I could think to ask. All I could think to do. I doubt your nana remembered whether she told him and the answer didn't really matter, to be honest. If she had of said no, I would have been upset, but I was ultimately relieved and thankful for the larger turn our relationship had taken over the previous months.

And, anyway, any emotion I gave at that moment would have been feigned. A show of an emotion I thought I was supposed to show. The truth was I was numb. I felt nothing. And I felt confused because I was so numb. Your nana, Uncle Mark and I were at the hospital. We had been told your grandad had a heart attack while using a treadmill at the gym.

He didn't usually use gyms; he was more inclined to just strap on the running shoes and go for a run around the block. However, he'd been given a membership as payment for a talk and felt obliged to at least give it a try. It was the first item on his checklist for that day. Your grandad, typically, had to fill every waking second.

The plans for your nana and grandad's dream home were coming together. They had been saving for the house for much of their lives. It was to be their last major project before retirement, or as close to retirement as someone like your grandad can get.

Architecture and design were probably the furthest skills from your grandad's forte, but your grandparents had found a builder capable of deciphering his curious descriptions – "I want a Hollywood bathroom" – and they had received the final plans. The last step was to have them reviewed by close friend Stuart McKeown. McKeown had served during Vietnam, having been dispatched to the country on operations. He was a close friend of Morey Grafton and, in-turn, he and his wife Marie-Anne had become friends with your nana and grandad.

McKeown was also a successful builder, hence his involvement in helping your grandparents throughout the planning process. He and your grandad had both agreed it would not be a good idea for McKeown to actually build the house – friends becoming involved in business together is rarely a good idea – but he had no problem providing some trusted oversight. Part of that oversight had been helping the builder decipher the "Hollywood bathroom" request.

"I was thinking, 'What the eff is a Hollywood bathroom? Do you want Angelina Jolie or something in there, Wal?', but what he meant was that he and your mum had been in some flash hotels with beautiful designer en-suites," McKeown said.

"After it all happened (the heart attack) and your mum came back with the plans, I remember we made that bathroom pretty flash. A lot more open than you'd usually have."

Your grandad finished hanging out the washing on Tuesday morning, drove your uncle to school, prepared his gym bag and a change of clothes, then picked up the phone. He called McKeown. His intention was to go to the gym, then on to McKeown's to review the final plans.

"I remember thinking, 'Shit, that really doesn't suit me', because I had some reports to do," McKeown said.

"I nearly said to him to give the gym a miss and to come and see me. I didn't do that. In the afternoon, I was sitting in the office going about my business, looking at my watch and I was thinking, 'You bloody asshole, Wal. You better have a good excuse'.

"Unfortunately, he had the best excuse he could have had."

Your grandad had ended the conversation, hopped in his car and drove to the gym. That was the last phone call your grandad ever made. McKeown was the last friend he ever spoke to.

My mobile phone rang and up flashed the name, "Mum Mobile". I was sitting at my desk in Courier Australia's Belmont offices on Robinson Avenue.

It was a good day and I had left the house smiling. So instead of answering in the gruff manner with which I usually responded to calls, I picked up the phone with a cheery, "Hi mum". The cheer vanished in seconds. I could hear your nana's breath shaking; it was erratic and she was clearly rushing somewhere.

"Glen, dad has had a heart attack," she said, trembling. "I'm getting in the car now, but I don't know what to do. I need to go to the hospital, but I need to get Mark. I don't know what to do."

"You go to the hospital, I'll get Mark and meet you there," I said. "It'll be ok, mum. We'll be there as soon as we can. Dad will be fine."

I hung up and turned from my desk, just as my manager Dylan Henderson was about to walk into the room. I met him at the door and told him what had happened. He said to leave everything, grab my stuff and go and to worry about nothing else but my family. I quickly phoned your Uncle Mark's school. I asked them not to tell him – I didn't feel it was appropriate he heard the news that way – but to get him to gather his things and wait for me at the front office. I would be there in 20min.

I jumped in the car and raced north to your uncle's school in Duncraig.

Your Uncle Mark jumped in the car alongside your grandad.

I had just left for work, your grandad had finished hanging out the washing and was driving your uncle the short distance to school. They talked about the day and your grandad said he intended to go to the gym, before doing a few other "bits and pieces". They farewelled each other, saying "I love you", before your grandad drove off.

It seemed no different from any other day. Tuesdays were assembly day for your Uncle Mark – a House assembly, as opposed to full-school, so confined to sections of the students who had been divided into three houses across the campus. It was the second period; mid-morning.

Your uncle was congregating with friends outside his designated House, sitting on a wall, when he was signalled by one of the teachers. He approached cautiously, unsure of whether he had done something wrong and was facing discipline, and was told to "pack up your things; your brother is coming to get you".

Your uncle was bemused and confused. Not only was he not expecting to be picked up, but I was the last person he expected to pick him up for anything. My relationship with your Uncle Mark when we were younger was full of sibling rivalry. The rather extreme eight-year age gap between us certainly didn't help, given other families would usually fit one, maybe two, extra children in an age-range such as that. We were fiercely competitive.

That was why your uncle met the news that I was coming to pick him up with a large dose of scepticism, before refusing and insisting the teacher must have interpreted the message incorrectly.

"Maybe you've forgotten a dentist appointment or something," the teacher said.

"No, I don't forget anything."

"Well, he's coming to get you. Please collect your things."

"Can you tell me why he's coming?"

"No."

Your Uncle Mark finally submitted and gathered what he needed, packed his bag and headed to the front office. As he walked across the large open quadrangle area in the middle of the campus, he began to worry. He hadn't forgotten a dentist appointment, he knew that. And he knew I was the last person in the world who would collect him for anything. Unless something was wrong.

The ladies at the front office were as kind as always as your uncle signed himself out. Then he waited, sitting on a cushioned chair in the main reception foyer which provided a clear view of the drop-off/pick-up area. He did not have to wait long before my white Toyota Corolla Seca pulled up.

I had been reciting in my mind different approaches I could take on breaking the news to your Uncle Mark the entire drive up to his school. He was only 14-years-old, so should I try and ease into it – "Now, something's happened, but I don't want you to worry, because it'll be ok" – or tell him straight out, so that we could begin moving on to how we would deal with it?

I opted for the latter. I was trying to be positive in my mind and my rationale was that there was no need to ease into anything, because all we knew at that point was that your grandad had a heart attack. He certainly hadn't died and there was no reason to believe he wouldn't be fine. Your uncle opened the door, sat in the passenger's seat and asked what had happened.

"Dad's had a heart attack," I said. "Don't worry, it's going to be ok. He'll be fine."

Your uncle choked up almost straight away and a look of anguish washed over his face.

"He'll be ok," I tried again.

"You don't have a heart attack and be ok."

The worst-case scenario had not entered your uncle's mind, though. He believed it would be difficult for the next few weeks, or months, but that ultimately life would return to normal. Scheduled broadcasting would soon resume. Your uncle asked where your nana was.

"Mum's at the hospital. We're going straight there."

Very little else was said. Very little needed to be.

I still get a knot in my stomach as I drive past Sir Charles Gairdner Hospital. Your uncle is the same, yet unfortunately he had to endure several classes near the Emergency Department during his second year at university studying pharmacology.

That place feels like a vortex of sorts, capable of trapping time as well as memories. Some passages of time are as vivid as if they happened yesterday. Some memories had completely disappeared from my mind. It took the recollections of several people to rebuild that day and the days that followed it. That would be the effect of trauma, I presume.

Your uncle and I arrived at the Emergency Department and were met by your nana, before we were taken through to see your grandad. We were led straight down a hall, turned right, then entered the emergency holding room, the First Responders Unit. It was where the most severely affected patients received immediate care, before being transferred to the Intensive Care Unit.

None of us needed a lesson on the seriousness of the situation, but we still received one when we saw your grandad. He was surrounded by about 10 to 15 doctors and seemed to be connected through tubes, wires and cables to every conceivable medical machine. A breathing tube pumped oxygen that heaved his chest up and down, while the steady beeps of the life support machine were like the soul's rhythm. We prayed this one would not falter.

Even endings have a beginning.

Chapter 24

Every Beginning Has an End

The ABC sports broadcaster adjusted the treadmill and set out running, giving a friendly smile in acknowledgement of the other gym patrons who gazed in recognition of the media identity. It was Tuesday. Mid-morning.

But this was not your grandad.

Glenn Mitchell, your grandad's friend and colleague, was in a similar place at the same time, just a different venue, when his phone rang. He halted his exercise and took the call. Your grandad had been rushed to hospital, he was told. Heart attack. At a gym.

Mitchell looked at his surroundings in disbelief, before packing up his bag and heading towards his car. He immediately phoned Deborah Leavitt, the Local Content Manager – his and your grandad's boss – at ABC Perth and told her he was coming into the office and needed to speak to her. Afterwards, he sped home to see his wife, fellow ABC Grandstand broadcaster and friend of your grandad's Karen Tighe. But home held no respite.

"I knew I wouldn't be able to see Wal or go in there, but I just knew I needed to go down to the hospital," Mitchell said.

"I always remember getting out of the car, walking towards emergency, and you, your mum and Mark were coming straight towards me. I said to Lyn, 'I don't know why I'm here, but if there's anything I can do, please let me know'. Then, we obviously learnt it was more dire than we first thought."

There was something Mitchell could do, actually.

When someone such as your grandad is involved in an incident such as a heart attack, there is a rush for answers, news and information and an enormous number of people who want to receive it all. It was becoming emotionally exhausting and a fulltime job for us, the family, to keep up. WAIS and the ABC – Steve Lawrence and Mitchell – took over.

"Steve and I arranged it and I said to everyone at the ABC, 'No one is to ring Lyn; Steve will ring me with information and I will let everyone know as soon as possible', and either Deborah Leavitt or I would send out an email to everyone," Mitchell said.

We bid farewell to Mitchell at the entry of Sir Charles Gairdner's emergency ward, but it was not long before we returned.

Roanna Edwards laughed. The sports broadcaster with ABC Perth was re-reading a note that had been left on her desk by your grandad the day before – Monday. It read: "R, going to get re-dressed. Have a function at 2:30pm that I thought was 6:30pm". It was signed "WF", in the beautiful script handwriting of your grandad.

Edwards was not supposed to be in the office that day. It was a Tuesday – the sports desk's first day off of the week. But she was leaving for a three-week holiday to America on Friday and was busily going through preparations for her departure and absence.

So, she was equally surprised when she saw her boss Glenn Mitchell hastily walking through the office, dressed in a t-shirt, shorts and sneakers. He appeared distracted and anxious and made his way straight to Local Content Manager Deborah Leavitt's office. Edwards was not deliberately listening to the conversation. Not until she heard a phrase within the first sentence: "Wal has had a heart attack".

Edwards was stunned. The world seemed to become as calm as it was chaotic; everything that was preoccupying her thoughts previously became unimportant, but were replaced by the uncertainty of the news she had just heard.

"He'll be ok," she thought. "He has to be. He's not even that old. And he's as fit as a bloody fiddle."

Mitchell and Leavitt worked together to advise the ABC staff. Edwards was told what was known, which was not a great deal, but none of it was overly promising. Several staff members, understandably, were distraught. A priority for support was put on Russell Woolf. Leavitt knew how close he was to your grandad, but he was yet to arrive at the office. He was on his way, expecting to begin his normal preparations for the Drive show.

Woolf's mode of transport was as fitting as it was comical – a little Vespa motor scooter – which meant he would not hear any radio news of your grandad's condition. It gave Leavitt some level of control and she met him in the carpark, escorting him all the way from the basement to her upper-floor office, to ensure Woolf was not unexpectedly delivered the news by a passer-by in the hallways. It was a thoughtful gesture, but nothing could have softened the blow. Woolf burst into tears.

Edwards turned and re-read the note from your grandad that sat on her desk. There was no laughter that time. She still has that note.

The Intensive Care Unit, from my memory of it, was a row of beds near the central nurses' station; much closer than a normal ward of a hospital, to allow for swift attention if needed. There were no doors to hinder speed, or obstacles in the way.

It was much larger than what we saw, I'm sure, but the path we trod was a repetitive one, with no requirement to move outside it. We would enter the double security doors, which were brandished with all sorts of warnings about mobile phones and electronic devices needing to be switched off, and turn right.

Memory is an interesting organism – ask any police officer attempting to investigate a past event – and can often blend seemingly flawlessly with imagination to the point where reality is lost. So, what the ICU looked like compared to the collective image we remember could be vastly different. Our memory, of course, is shrouded with emotion.

I recall the ward as rather dated: grey-tinged, maybe speckled, lino floors, with predominantly cream coloured walls. Not a nice cream, either; the type that has a yellow tinge to it. The furnishings were a combination of that grey and cream, with blocks of white hugging the banks of beds along the length of one wall.

The room was laid out in an L formation. There were about five beds along one length of the room. Your grandad was positioned a couple of beds down, unconscious, having been placed in an induced coma to help his brain and body heal without the stresses of maintaining themselves in the conscious world. The corridor through which we entered and the nurse's station occupied the other length. Adjacent to the entry corridor was a small meeting room.

The meeting room was where we were taken every time the doctors wanted to provide us with an update. We sat at what felt like old school desks, which had been pieced together to form a larger rectangle. The chairs were not much better. White venetian blinds lined the windows that looked out to the ICU and were drawn closed to signal the commencement of any meeting.

But, as I said, memory is an interesting organism and despite that description being my memory, I'm aware it probably does not reflect reality. Our reality was shrouded in emotion. As it was when we were delivered the news that would change our lives forever.

The blinds had been drawn. In the room was our immediate and extended family members: your nana, uncle and me, your Great Aunties Jill and Sandy with their partners John and Lew, respectively, and your nana's brothers – your Great Uncles – Steve and Les. Steve had your Uncle Mark on his knee, doing his best to console him.

I sat opposite your nana and did not want to be near anyone. I was angry. A psychologist would probably have labelled me as drifting between the first and second stages of grief: denial and anger. I was angry because everyone was talking like we'd lost your grandad already and I was not ready to accept that. It was barely 24 hours after his heart attack, the same heart attack I had insisted to your nana and uncle would not disrupt our lives and "everything will be ok".

"Can we all stop talking like he's dead already. He's still out there," I exclaimed, with equal parts indignation and naivety.

"No, you're right Glen," your Great Aunty Sandy kindly offered. But the conversation continued, as it needed to, because there were important details to discuss in the event death decided to extend from the shadows.

It was Wednesday. We were meeting because the doctors had attempted to draw your grandad out of the induced coma for observation tests, before returning him to the previous state of recovery. We were meeting, because the results from that test had been received.

The rollercoaster carriage jolted as it was released from the boarding platform, then slowly pulled away. Your grandad was sitting alongside your Uncle Mark, white-knuckled in his clutch of the metal safety rail. He had defied all his instincts to volunteer to take his son on the ride. It was the family's holiday to Disney Land with the King family.

Your grandad had seen it as his opportunity to "tick off his turn", because, from what he had observed from the pathway, it appeared to be one of the tamer rides. It was anything but tame, though, and the slow acceleration at the start was swiftly followed by the rushing speeds and ricocheting bounces, twists and turns that usually go with a high-class rollercoaster at Disney Land. Your uncle loved it. Your grandad saw none of it; his eyes were closed the whole time.

It felt like the same rollercoaster we were on in the ICU. It started with a jolt, but was followed by a period of deceptive, seductive calm. A period where we knew little – it was too early to have comprehensive test results – and could do even less. But soon after, time felt like it rushed, then crawled, then rushed again. Life felt like it was bouncing, twisting and turning. Emotional highs were subdued and balanced by lows.

Reality felt lost. It was Wednesday morning and the ride had taken us to a peak. Your grandad was being eased out of his induced coma for observation tests and we were already seeing signs. Signs which seemed positive. He was moving.

At first, it was so intermittent, we couldn't be sure if it happened, or if we imagined it. Nothing big, just a little twinge of the finger. But as the drugs wore off, the movement became more common. More pronounced. More rhythmic. That was the sign I needed.

"See, I told everyone it was going to be fine," I thought.

Then, that sign for your Uncle Mark came in the form of one of the nurses in the ward. He was a mid-to-late 20s man named Walter, middle name Young; your grandad's first name and your nana's surname. It felt too coincidental to be coincidence. Your uncle homed on that connection and looked to the nurse for any shred of hope he could, repeatedly asking if there was "any chance" and cutting him off at, "Yes, but", ensuring there was no room for elaboration. It was enough to keep your uncle going.

Of course, like any rollercoaster, your grandad's eyes were closed the whole time. The first stage of grief is denial.

Graham Moss was driving home early that Wednesday evening, when he reached for the car radio to turn up the volume. It was an evening sports show and they had some news about your grandad. The hosts advised that the hospital had brought him out of the induced coma and "it looks like he's on the road to recovery".

"Thank God," Moss thought. As soon as he arrived home, he texted your nana: "Great to hear the news. Let us know how he's getting on."

Sometimes journalists and broadcasters get facts wrong. This was one of those moments. It wasn't until your nana phoned 10 minutes later that Moss began to fear that, far from being over, the worst was yet to come.

"I don't know what you've heard, but we don't think he's going to pull through," your nana said.

Moss' wife, Robyn, was away at the time. He was left in an empty house with just his thoughts, memories and emotions. They drifted to the first time he met your grandad, sitting in the makeshift office of the Western Australian Institute of Sport on the first floor of UWA's Department of Human Movement and Recreation Studies building.

Moss, a Brownlow Medallist and accomplished footballer, had taken up the role of inaugural general manager for the West Coast Eagles and was working with WAIS' inaugural director, your grandad, to establish dual training ovals on University land in Mount Claremont. The plan was to turn one of them into a mud heap that would help replicate the conditions the Eagles would face on some of the Victorian grounds.

It had been a long friendship. A very enjoyable one, although frustrating at times, as Moss' memories turned to his time as chief executive of the Sports Centre Trust, which controlled the Superdrome, or Challenge Stadium. It brought him in regular contact with your grandad, who had a propensity for pouncing on recently vacated territory in the stadium, staking first claim of it in the name of WAIS.

He recalled the many phone calls of bewildered abuse he would receive from your grandad about Persian rug exhibitions, or arts and crafts shows that had been booked into the main arena, bringing a wealth of funds to the Trust, but revoking access for the day to WAIS's athletes who had basically been gifted that access in the first place. The charge to WAIS barely covered the cost of turning on the lights. He couldn't help but smile; even the frustrating times could be funny when Wally Foreman was involved.

The deafening sound of his thoughts against the silent house became too much and he reached for a bottle of red wine, but he did not get far into it. The voice in his head of his mate was as relentless and as constant as it had been throughout his life. He had to go and see him in the hospital, whether he could access the ICU or not.

"I'm so glad I did," Moss said. "You guys were there, I got to stand beside him, I spoke to your mum and it's the lasting impression that I've got. I'm glad that I got to see him before he officially died and Lyn and I had some close moments then."

The rhythmic twitches of your grandad's finger were like the clicking of the rollercoaster carriage as it hauled itself up its incline. Every click – every twitch – dragged us to a higher state.

That clicking on a rollercoaster is the safety feature of the anti-rollback device. It is a saw-tooth rail that prevents the carriage from slipping backwards, allowing it only to move forward up the lift hill, before plunging at high speeds to its trough. There is no clicking on the descent. Nothing to slow the freefall. That would defeat the purpose of a rollercoaster.

"That twitching is a sign that the brain is damaged," we were advised. Misfiring signals. And while that quote is paraphrased, the impact of the words was the same.

Crash. A freefall descent. Everything we had built our hopes on had been deceiving us. Seducing us. What we thought was a positive sign was, in reality, the worst possible sign.

The results of your grandad's observation tests were showing no sign of brain activity. The best-case scenario, we were advised, was that he would be highly dependent, with little to no mobility or control of his body, with severely impacted and reduced brain activity. The worst-case scenario was that he was already gone, brain dead, and simply being kept alive – or, perhaps being kept breathing, is more accurate – by the machines.

Your nana had been asking repeatedly what seemed to me to be an inconsequential question to any doctor she could find and, until that moment, I hadn't understood why: "How long did the ambulance take to arrive?"

The answer was about 15 minutes.

Almost 10 minutes longer than the human brain can survive without oxygen before it begins to die.

An emotion-charged mob surrounded the team bus and started rocking it back and forth. The people inside the bus were fearful; the people outside were furious. It was Karachi, Pakistan, 1983.

The country held a great deal of pride in its national sporting teams, particularly hockey, in which it had been a dominant force in the world for about two decades. And particularly in 1983, when it hosted the Champions Trophy; a tournament that it had already won twice in the four years it had existed. But pride is a temperamental beast and can turn buoyant confidence into angry indignation in seconds.

The Pakistani men's hockey team turned from national heroes to foes in a 70-minute game. The hosts had been relegated to runner-up by a strong, travelling Australian side consisting of the likes of defender Craig Davies, striker Terry Walsh and the man they called "Grumpy" – Ric Charlesworth, who in that same year would enter Federal Politics as the Labor Party's Member for Perth.

But the Australians were the least of the mob's concern; they instead turned their rage towards their own, furious that the nation's pride could be dented on home soil in such a way. The doors of the bus flew open and the Pakistani players exited, swinging their hockey sticks wildly as they attempted to inch to the safety of their hotel.

Your grandad watched in bewilderment from a distant sidewalk. He had travelled to Karachi with the Australian team as a NINE Network journalist, compiling reports for *The West Australian* as well. It had been a positive trip for him, not just because of Australia's gold medal result, which was the country's first major hockey triumph, but he had also by chance been on the same flight to Karachi as Pakistan's world No.1 squash player Jahangir Khan.

Khan was not only a legend in his sport and a national celebrity, but he was also particularly significant to Western Australians, as the state's Dean Williams had the year before finished runner-up to the Pakistani at the World Open. Your grandad secured an exclusive interview with Khan. Days later, he had been on-hand for Australia's Champions Trophy win and had opted to walk back to the hotel instead of boarding the team bus. He relayed the events of the memorable stroll to the Australian players who he had now become friends with.

Craig Davies, in particular, paid close attention, gripped by the excitement. The same excitement that gripped Davies when he became one of the first employees of the fledgling Western Australian Institute of Sport as its Sports Program Co-ordinator, reuniting him on a more permanent basis with your grandad.

Now, all he could grip was your nana as the tears streamed down his face. Davies had first met your grandad when the former was a player and the latter a journalist in the lead-up to a World Cup in 1981. They became better acquainted at the 1983 Champions Trophy, then lifelong friends through their work at WAIS.

Twenty-five years after that first meeting still felt too soon to be saying goodbye. WAIS's former chairman, Neil McKerracher, had phoned him on the Tuesday and told him your grandad had suffered a heart attack. That he was in hospital and the outlook did not look positive.

Davies, like so many others throughout life, was drawn to your grandad. He had to go to the hospital and did so the next day, meeting us at the couches of the small waiting room outside the Intensive Care Unit security doors. He gripped your nana tight.

Being there was all he could do; it was all many of us could do. Davies had almost not gone, though. He was unsure if he could stomach the reality that would hit through a visit to a hospital ward, particularly an Intensive Care Unit. His former WAIS colleague, Steve Lawrence, had been in the same position and chosen to remain home.

Your grandad, Davies and Lawrence had been the first three fulltime employees at WAIS, but the latter preferred to remember your grandad as the energetic person he was in life. Davies' wife Jenny, though, insisted her husband go to the hospital. He did, but he did so to support our family and chose not to walk through those security doors. Like Lawrence, he preferred to remember your grandad a different way. A way that encapsulated their 25-year friendship, such as the moment that had occurred just four days earlier.

It was the WAIS Annual Dinner and for all your grandad's concerns over his performance, whether those concerns were justified or not, there was one undeniably powerful moment of emotion. It was the induction of Davies to the Hall of Champions.

Your grandad, in a freshly pressed black suit, white shirt and striking red tie, opened the Hall of Champions segment with a trademark joke, this time aimed at the evening's host Basil Zempilas, before acknowledging the passing of one of the Hall's members – surf life saving's Don Morrison. He then moved his acknowledgements around the room, rattling off the names and facts of other Hall members in attendance that night, as they rose from their seats to applause.

It was then time to introduce the new inductees. Your grandad showed the same respect to all three who were introduced to the crowd and had invested as much time in preparation to the first, Paralympic swimmer Priya Cooper, and third, Olympic water polo gold medallist Bridgette Gusterson, as he had the inductee they bookmarked. In fact, given their lengthy friendship, your grandad had probably devoted less time to his preparation for Davies – he knew it all by heart.

But that second presentation held a clear difference in connection between presenter and inductee. A smile spread across your grandad's face as he announced the name, "Craig Davies", before reading out the defender's accomplishments. The interview began in standard fashion, until the discussion turned to Davies' heart issues and related health battles from the 1990s, during which your grandad was a constant source of support. The emotion began to show, first in Davies, then in your grandad, as that discussion drew to a close.

Then, it came flooding out.

"Craig, congratulations on your induction into the Hall tonight," your grandad said. "You mean so much to the people of this organisation, the organisation itself, to hockey and sport generally in this state.

"I have absolutely no qualms in saying that this fellow is the most courageous, most inspirational, the most dignified and decent person that I've ever had the privilege to work with. Craig Davies."

Davies visibly swallowed a lump in his throat and your grandad, who had clearly prepared words to follow the name "Craig Davies", was unable to finish his delivery. The pair hugged and your grandad watched as Davies returned to his seat, incessantly blinking away the tears that refused to stay hidden and applauding for the entire duration of his friend's walk to his table.

It was the last time Davies and your grandad saw each other and the last time they spoke. In the week of the Annual Dinner, your grandad had called Davies, who had left WAIS to return to teaching at Wesley College. He had left a voicemail on Davies' office phone, congratulating and preparing him that they were "going to have a chat on stage". Davies left Wesley in 2010. He kept that voicemail until he departed.

"Why were you and dad so close? What was it that made your friendship so strong?" I asked in the interview with Craig and his wife Jenny for this book.

He immediately choked up. Until that point, we had been discussing facts and history. It was the first time we were discussing your grandad as a person of significance in their lives.

"Maybe I should write this part down," Craig said, as Jenny passed him a box of tissues.

"We thought in similar ways. I had a huge respect for him and he was certainly a role model, a mentor and he taught me a great deal. Perhaps it was through that respect that the friendship developed. He had a great sense of humour and was just great to be around.

"He was a great friend, a great supporter when I was sick, and that friendship meant a lot to me. I think he really influenced a lot of my values and I would like to think I try to fight for what I believe is important, what I believe is right. Wally certainly influenced me there. I just miss him."

Jenny took over as her husband's voice began to falter, but by this time, both were reaching for the tissue box.

"There was a real sense of love and respect," she said.

"He was such a wonderful human being. Those two words come to mind – love and respect – as well as appreciation. He made me feel important and yet I probably didn't feel I should have been important, in the context of what he was dealing with. I loved him and I respected him."

Love and respect led to Davies' visit to the hospital that Wednesday, after being prompted by a phone call the day before advising him that one of the most significant people in his life was lying in a coma in intensive care.

The second phone call came the following day. He found his wife in their bedroom. Tears streamed down his face and he sobbed uncontrollably, struggling with the finality of what he had to tell her.

"He's not coming back."

Chapter 25

Endings Are Contradictions

ENDINGS ARE CONTRADICTIONS: AMONG OTHER things, they are as complex as they are simple. That was the case in your grandad passing away. In the warm, breath of summer lifting him away from this world's grip.

On one hand, there was the complexity of not just his life, but life. Of the clinical, biological factors that had led us to the end. Everything that had to happen – every layer – to lead to finality. The complexity of the life he led. The way in which those around him were forced to deal with the news of his heart attack and the complex ways in which we all did that.

Then, there was the simplicity of it all. Regardless of the complexities that led us there, the result was very simple: your grandad was gone. It took just minutes.

I had returned to our house the night before to collect changes of clothes for myself, your nana and uncle. The hospital was kind enough to allow us to stay overnight, so I volunteered to make the trip home and back again. Mostly because I just needed to get out of that place.

The events of Wednesday had left us emotionally and physically exhausted. The tremors your grandad displayed as he was eased out of the coma were a sign that he was already gone. That the extent of damage to his brain was too extensive for his body to survive. Time, the doctors told us, would not make a difference in situations such as that. Your grandad could be kept in a coma for years and the injuries would not heal, so instead, they needed to see a sign that the injuries were not as severe as first thought. That might give us some hope.

So, your grandad was going to be given one last opportunity to show a sign that he could recover. The machines keeping him alive would be switched off. If he had the potential to recover, he would breathe on his own, which would result in the machines being turned back on and him being given as much time as he needed to heal.

If he did not breathe on his own, it indicated the injuries were too severe and no amount of time would change that. And that was why we were invited to stay at the hospital. To spend a final night with your grandad. To say our goodbyes.

He was not expected to breathe on his own.

ABC sports broadcasters Glenn Mitchell and Karen Tighe sat alongside sound engineer Adam Sallur. It was late Wednesday night, November 1. The building was mostly empty.

Mitchell had received word from your nana about the events of the day and those that were expected to follow. There were no punches pulled about expectations. The ABC and its staff were considered as close to the Foremans as family, as were the WAIS staff.

I hope that the pages that have preceded these ones sufficiently captured the number of people whose lives your grandad impacted. The number of people to whom he devoted so much love, care, support, time and energy. The number of people whom he prioritised over himself. They spanned a country and a lifetime, those people; from the bush to the city.

The ABC recognised early that there was going to be a significant demand to recognise your grandad if the worst was to happen. They recognised that, not only from having known him, but from the flood of talkback correspondents they had already received after news broke of his heart attack.

When death comes to someone who has had that sort of impact on that number of people, there is a great deal of work that needs to be done to bring those people together. And that work was only completed, often unseen and unacknowledged, because of who your grandad was to those people.

The staff of the ABC were among those often-unseen people.

The late night of Mitchell, Tighe and Sallur was the result of hours spent trawling through archived sound recordings, from highlights, to talkback calls, Olympics to speech notes. They went as far back as the ABC Sound Library had available in its archives and began piecing together a montage of your grandad.

"They would have been pulling audio out of the archive and putting things in place to pay tribute to such a remarkable man," former ABC Perth sports broadcaster Roanna Edwards said.

"It seems a bit off when you say it like that, but that's the reality. And it's what keeps everyone functioning. And, most importantly, it's the audio, highlights and montages that let the listeners feel like they're part of the grief – which of course they were."

The trio dreaded to think that the expected would eventuate, but if it did, they were determined to deliver to the audience that craved it the send-off that your grandad deserved.

Streams of white cast by the parking lot floodlights burst through the gaps in vertical blinds, making the family-stay room at Sir Charles Gairdner more a dimly lit blue than dark. It made the improbable – sleeping – impossible.

I was unsure whether I was supposed to sleep, anyway. I was probably supposed to be curled up in the foetal position, sobbing uncontrollably, I thought. Or praying. Or seeing vivid memories of your grandad dance colourful images in front of me, as if they were real. And wasn't there supposed to be music, like, some sort of soundtrack playing at times like this?

Hollywood was the closest I had to explaining the experience of true loss and heartbreak. I was barely out of my teens and the worst heartbreaks I had suffered at that point – losing a girlfriend and the likes – did not really feel comparable in the situation. I had no idea what was supposed to happen, but I knew nothing was happening there.

"Mum?"

"Yes darling?"

Clearly, neither of us were sleeping that night.

"Do you mind if I go and see dad?"

"Of course not, darling. Do you want me to come?"

"No, I'd rather go alone. Love you."

I got out of bed, grabbed my pen and notepad, got dressed and caught the elevator down to the ICU level. I sat with your grandad for about an hour, saying a few awkward words, but writing most of them in a letter. Then I returned to stare at the ceiling and waited for the sun to rise.

There was a sense that life had come full-circle as Anglican priest Keith Wheeler stood at the foot of your grandad's bed, with a Bible in hand. This was the man who, 26 years prior, helped bring our family together when he presided over the marriage of Lyn Young to Wally Foreman. Now, he was helping us say goodbye.

He placed a prayer shawl over your grandad's legs – a blanket sewn and blessed by parishioners of his church – and began the ritual Anointing of the Sick. Then, our family gathered in that bleak room of the Intensive Care Unit to receive the final briefing from the doctors. They would know almost immediately if he was going to breathe by himself, otherwise, we needed to prepare ourselves for the prospect that it could take hours for your grandad to pass away.

We all understood. The doctors left the room and we waited, attempting to fill the excruciating silence with some sort conversation. But we did not need to try for long. The doctors returned within minutes.

"He's going quickly. You might want to come out now," one of them said. We leapt out of our seats and rushed to your grandad's bedside. The prayer blanket had been raised over his chest, but there was little else between us, with all but the monitoring machines having been removed.

I stood on his left, closest to his head. Your Uncle Mark was directly opposite on his right. Your nana was next to me, tears flowing freely by that stage. Either side at his feet were your Great Aunties Sandy and Jill. Sitting on a chair between them was your Great Grandad Eric. Your grandad was surrounded by those who loved him.

Your Uncle Mark glanced out the window for a brief moment, then back to the heart monitor. He felt like it was a scene from a movie as he watched the pulsing signals that formed mountain peaks across the screen get smaller with each jolt. He looked around the patient bay and saw your great grandad in his chair, with a tear in his eye.

I kissed your grandad's forehead, held his hand and gazed, glassy-eyed at his face, praying – begging – for something that was never going to come. In my pocket was the letter I wrote him the night before. And a CD. It was a collection of greatest hits by John Denver, an American folk singer who rose to fame in the 70s and whose music your grandad made me listen to ad nauseum on car rides. The lyrics of one of his most successful songs, "Country Roads", ran through my mind: "Country roads take me home to the place I belong".

The mountain peaks on the screen grew smaller. Smaller. But before they diminished, your grandad's eyes flickered open and with a strength that defied his condition, he looked at those around his bed. Then, his head turned left and he stared into my eyes.

Then, they closed again. Your grandad was gone.

Endings are contradictions, though, because time never really ends. It just moves on. And, as your grandad's time here moved on, our time without him began.

Chapter 26

A Thousand Words Paint a Picture

WORD DID NOT TAKE LONG to spread. Words rarely did when your grandad was involved.

It was one of the intricacies that we, as a family, thankfully did not need to worry about. It was all being taken care of by the ABC, WAIS and the amazing people whose lives your grandad had touched. Who were saddened and near crippled by the news, but who carried on. For him.

Your Great Uncle John began to make the phone calls to the contacts he was provided as your nana, Uncle Mark and I sat in a hospital courtyard, attempting to come to terms with our new reality. We re-joined the extended family in the café a short time later. The logistics had been managed: the ABC and WAIS were advising ahead of time those they needed to, before the broadcaster would make the public announcement ahead of the 4pm news. That was about half an hour away.

The ABC had also been tremendous in proactively managing the requirements of rival news organisations. It was a deliberate, collegiate approach taken by Deborah Leavitt which reflected that same trait she respected in your grandad. The ABC put out information to the media network from the moment your grandad had his heart attack, until the close of the public memorial service. In an equally appreciated show of respect, the other outlets had no issue with the arrangement.

That system was in full-swing Thursday afternoon when Russell Woolf returned a call from the family. He needed clarification on one of your great uncle's instructions. When he had been told that the family wanted him to make the announcement, surely we just meant the ABC, right, and not specifically him?

Your nana grabbed the phone from your great uncle.

"No, Russell. Wally would have wanted you to do it."

The term "Bush Telegraph" is the name given to the phenomenon that is country gossip.

Any event of significance, from a new arrival to a community to the loss of one of its members, has an innate ability to jump fence-lines, cross properties and spread like wildfire throughout a region, simply by word of mouth. And it does so at a speed that would have even the most devoted modern-day Twitter executive in awe. The Bush Telegraph, you could say, was the world's first social media.

Still, Amman, Jordan, would have seemed like a stretch of its powers. It would undoubtedly be one of the last places on Earth expected to receive news of your grandad's death, but it did so at 11am on a blistering hot day.

NINE Network's *60 Minutes* reporter Liam Bartlett felt like his eyes would burn out of their sockets as he glanced out the aeroplane window. He was on assignment in the violence-ravaged Middle East, having moved on from his first assignment in Beirut, Lebanon, where a barrage of Israeli bombs and rockets landed close by, mid-filming.

Bartlett had that year – 2006 – moved from hosting ABC Mornings in Perth, to rival Radio 6PR, then shortly after onto *60 Minutes*. Your grandad had been a close confident for Bartlett in making that decision, given he had experienced similar short-term job hopping in his move from Nine, to the ABC in Adelaide, then back to Perth to take up the directorship of WAIS.

Your grandad was among the last to farewell Bartlett, having been in attendance – and, by all reports, in fine form – at the latter's last supper at Perugino Restaurant in West Perth. He was there among about 20 of Perth's media personalities, including *The Sunday Times'* Billy Rule, Russell Woolf, former 6PR broadcaster Simon Beaumont and even former Liberal Minister Troy Buswell. Bartlett went straight from that dinner to the airport to fly to the Middle East.

Bartlett used his time on the Amman tarmac during refuelling to check his messages. He switched on his mobile phone. A flood of messages began arriving, the first of which was from Nine colleague Michael Thomson, advising him of your grandad's death. He immediately called Thomson.

"I couldn't believe it. I wasn't feeling too good, actually," Bartlett said of the day.

"At that stage, I'd been on a particularly difficult shoot and I was commuting to Sydney, so I hadn't seen a lot of the kids and my wife Claire and I was feeling a bit homesick. I remember saying to Thommo: 'That's sh-t and that makes me feel like I'm over here and what the hell is the point?'

"I was having one of those self-indulgent moments, but it came as a huge shock and I knew I wouldn't be able to get back for the funeral. I remember Mike saying to me, 'Mate, just put your head down and your bum up. Wally was so proud of you getting that gig and he would be all the way with you, just hang in there'.

"It's self-indulgent talking about what I lost, but I think I lost a really great mate who would have been with me all the way into the future. I would have been laughing with Wally for 30 years. I think that's very sad from my own perspective, but I thought it was really sad for your mum and that's who I thought of most of all.

"He was such a vibrant bloke and she was such a young person, physically and mentally, and knowing the sort of relationship they had through all the stories that Wally would tell. They had such a strong marriage, they were such a strong couple. From a family point-of-view, that was what I was thinking of most."

The Bush Telegraph again took flight. Its next stop was two fence-lines away.

"I'll be honest with you, Kim: I'm petrified of the fast bowlers."

Kim Hughes laughed and raised the beer glass to his mouth. The post-training drinks at the Floreat Hotel were nothing if not a source of honest conversation. And as far as an explanation went for your grandad's refusal to play cricket higher than Fourth Grade, he could not fault it for honesty.

"That's what I love about you, Wal; you're a coward, everyone knows you're a coward, you know you're a coward, so it's all ok."

Hughes put the beer glass to his mouth as he turned to continue the conversation, but your grandad was gone. So too was the Floreat Hotel. It had transformed into an empty Dubai hotel room. The beer glass at his lips was replaced by a phone.

"Wally's bloody passed away," Hughes' wife, Jenny, said on the other end of the line.

The former Australia cricket captain cursed, then almost fainted. He had been in the Middle East for a six-a-side competition, "or some bloody useless thing". There was no way he could make it back to Perth in time to farewell his mate. All he could do was remember.

"Lyn and Wal were going to move into the new home and all that sort of thing, the kids were growing up and the next phase of their life was going to be so exciting," Hughes said. "Your dad was, what, 58? Then," he clicked his fingers.

"The other day I heard young Corbin Middlemas say on Sports Talk, 'Right, we've got something to play, because it's six years to the day'. I thought, 'Six years? It can't be'. A lot of those blokes I grew up with – George Young, Dennis Baker, Gary Green – I don't see anymore, just because we've all had kids and your lives change.

"But Wally was a bit of a conduit for us all. If Wally organised something, everyone would come along."

Word took flight again. Its next stop was 3200km away in Athens, Greece.

The idiosyncrasies of a Ken Casellas statistical analysis were as synonymous with an ABC AFL call out of Perth as any of the commentators.

The metring and measure of his delivery was more akin to a drum solo than a stats reading, rising in volume and intensity with every number announced, before dropping and picking up speed for the connecting explanation: THUMP-badoom, THUMP-ba-ba-badoom. TWO tackles, SIX effective handpasses.

Casellas' contributions were like an art form and, like any work of art, it was not defined by a single component, but combined with the elements around it to achieve completion; the drama of the game, the crowd noise and atmosphere through the effects microphone, the skilled descriptions of commentators such as Glenn Mitchell and your grandad and the experienced analysis of the experts such as Ken Judge and Jon Dorotich.

The ABC Perth AFL team might not have been the best work of art in the country – especially in appearance – but they were a band content with making their music. Their art. They enjoyed each other's company and held an immense respect for the sound that each member brought to the ensemble.

But all bands break up. And when they do – especially when not by choice – there is an empty pit left if the stomachs of the remaining members. That pit began engulfing an ever-growing space until it forced Casellas to hunch over, sliding onto the baggage carousel as a makeshift seat in the middle of Athens airport. He held his mobile phone to his ear as George Grljusich delivered the news that your grandad had passed away.

This was a man he had first met in 1972, when your grandad took a cadetship with *The West* and bizarrely replaced another man named Wally Foreman. The pair had reunited throughout their careers and expanded the band with the ABC's football broadcasts.

Casellas could no longer contain the despair of loss that grew inside him. He burst into tears. It was a scene of juxtaposition: he had been on holidays in the Greek islands with his wife Pam, a journalist with *The West Australian* and also a friend of your grandad's, with their cadetships at the paper only a couple of years apart. It was supposed to be happy occasion.

"Pam grabbed the phone and found out and there we were, both crying in the middle of the Athens Airport," Casellas said.

"I cut the holiday short, so I was at the funeral at WAIS. It was amazing the amount of people there. That's an illustration of how I felt about Wally, because I can still remember it now: I collapsed and sat on the luggage carousel at Athens Airport and burst into tears. People, fundamentally, love decent and honest people and that's what it's all about. If you live a decent and honest life and you're straight forward, people hold you in a pretty high regard."

The band had lost its first member. It would lose more as the years went on.

Roanna Edwards' thoughts were racing.

It was Thursday afternoon. She had been given the day off, having been told by Karen Tighe not to bother coming in, "because it wasn't the best place to be". She instead spent the day shopping with her parents, who had driven from the country to support her as she attempted some form of normality.

Just four days prior, she had been filled with excitement about the three-week holiday to the US she was supposed to be leaving for the next day. Now, she didn't even know if she wanted to go. Edwards was in the car with her parents when the phone rang. It was Tighe. She wondered if it could change anything if she just didn't answer the phone.

"Are you with mum and dad, Ro?" Tighe asked.

"Yes," Edwards replied, already choking back tears. "Is he gone?"

"Yes, Ro. He passed away a short time ago and he had his family with him."

There was little else to be said. Tighe was her usual, caring self and did all anyone on the end of a phone could do to ensure Edwards was as well as could be expected, before hanging up. Undoubtedly to make another phone call.

Edwards was told that Russell Woolf would be making the announcement in about half an hour to let the public know, followed by he and Glenn Mitchell hosting a special Drive program dedicated to your grandad. Edwards sat in the back of her parent's car sobbing. The man she had idolised, who had been so caring to her as a trainee, was gone.

"Wally taught me the importance of the listener, how integral regional listeners are to everything at the ABC and he showed me you could be the most successful of men, while always remaining humble and true to your good ol' country foundations," Edwards said, remembering that day.

"The Australian sporting landscape, lost so much the day Wal died. It lost a passionate advocate for athletes. It lost an incredible professional and very talented broadcaster. It lost a warm, wonderful man who, unlike so many in the trade, operated without ego and always with inclusiveness. But for all it lost, we should be grateful we had enjoyed so very much."

Edwards listened to the car radio and waited. Then, Afternoons presenter Bernadette Young introduced an interlude of music with the unrelated, seemingly rushed time stamp of, "You are on 720, the time is eight-to-four", that also betrayed the sense of confusion in her voice.

It was immediately evident – to the broadcaster, as well as the listener – that something was not right. Music began to play.

Pachelbel's Canon will be a song I will never forget.

It is not easily forgotten as a piece of music, let alone as music with significance attached to it. However, despite being arguably the most well-known piece of classical music, its evoking powers are founded in a rather simple structure. The entire piece is only eight bars of music that are continuously repeated, but because a trio of violins play the melody at different stages to create a canon, a beautiful harmony is formed over a cello bass part. It is almost mathematical in its composure.

ABC Perth Local Content Manager Deborah Leavitt selected Pachelbel's Canon as the score for the public announcement of your grandad's death. She made the choice having previously discussed the piece with your grandad. Plus, Johnny Cash did not seem particularly appropriate for the occasion.

It was one of several seemingly rudimentary tasks for Leavitt and the ABC that was anything but rudimentary. In some ways, they had been through the routine before – an event of significance occurs and all the planning and preparation is put in place as a response – but your grandad's passing was different. He was one of their own, who was now gone. That had to be handled as sensitively within the ABC, as outside it.

The planning for the announcement occurred first: Leavitt had received your nana's request that Russell Woolf read out the news and, together with Glenn Mitchell, the three worked out how that would unfold, including playing Pachelbel's Canon – an obscure choice for ABC Local Radio, particularly the Afternoons program – to ensure the listeners' attention was gained and they were prepared for what was to come.

Staff advisory was the next phase – it was to occur at 3:30pm – and included ensuring how to best manage and support Afternoons presenter Bernadette Young, who was on-air at the time other staff were informed.

What to do for the rest of the day's programing was the next consideration, with Leavitt and producer Damien Rabbitt agreeing on clearing the schedule and running a state-wide, Wally Foreman-focused Drive program with Woolf and Mitchell, to allow the public the chance to grieve.

The material that had been compiled by Mitchell, Karen Tighe and Adam Sallur was invaluable and would be played, while even more was sought and developed into a special tribute CD that was placed in ABC Shops. Preparations for a TV special also commenced, with camera crews sent to the homes of identities such as Justin Langer and John Inverarity, then all the way to Bruce Rock to capture the thoughts of your grandad's childhood friends Ray Williams and Bryan Kilminster, as well as shots of the town that had been built to almost mythological status.

It was an enormous amount of airtime and coverage for one man, yet all the plans were approved by the eastern states executives. They might not have known your grandad as well as the locals did, but they understood that Perth had always been a little bit different. A little bit special.

"They understood that it was a local identity, but I think they were quite surprised by the public response and they allowed us to respond to that," Leavitt said.

"I wanted to make sure that it was handled in a way that the family would have wanted and I was concentrating on that, as well as making sure the support was there for the staff, because we were like a family. In places like Perth and Brisbane, they're smaller and so the sense of friendship and camaraderie is strong. And everyone had a Wally story.

"When we were looking at all of those things in terms of the broadcast coverage, it was important, but there was also an appetite; there was an appetite from the public that we felt was compelling and it wasn't our own indulgence. We were really thinking 'Audience First' and I remember the email response was so huge – and we printed them all out for the family to go through – but I can tell you that we never had one complaint asking us why we were going on about it.

"It was the opposite: we had people contacting us asking, 'Can you re-broadcast this', or, 'Can you replay that story again'. I do look back on it all and I feel really proud of what we put to air and that it honoured Wally in a way that was the right way to do it for him.

"He was a very special person in the hearts and minds of a lot of people in WA."

The scene seemed grey, like the ABC was broadcasting in black-and-white again. Like a pall of sadness had been draped over the office. There was no wailing, but there was a sense that the boundary of grief could almost be defined.

That was the way Russell Woolf recalled the moment staff were informed of your grandad's death. There was a lot of hugging and even more tears. To this day, the sense of the room remains with Woolf. And then he had to go on air.

It was an extremely challenging, confusing and conflicting moment for Woolf. Challenging for the obvious reason, that he was not only having to come to terms with the fact his friend was gone, but he had to announce it to the world. Confusing, because "the guy was a rock" and no matter how long the defibrillator took to arrive, no matter how hurt your grandad was, Woolf could not imagine him staying down for anything.

And it was conflicting, because despite the pain, despite never wanting to ever read anything like that out, if it had to be read, Woolf was honoured to be the one to read it. And so he did. He clutched the statement in his hand. The statement that had been sent to the ABC from Sir Charles Gairdner Hospital, on behalf of the family. The statement that your nana insisted he read. And he walked towards the main studio.

Bernadette Young had received a message on her monitor, requesting that she play Pachelbel's Canon as soon as possible, then make her way out of the studio. Deborah Leavitt was waiting for her in the control room. Woolf preferred not to sit in silence, so waited until the final minute before slipping into the studio. He had not thought about what he was going to say, nor had he rehearsed the statement. It would be easier that way.

Another reason Leavitt chose Pachelbel's Canon as the prelude was that its duration was such that it could run for as long as Woolf needed. He entered the studio and lowered the music at 3:59pm.

"On 720 ABC Perth and ABC Radio state-wide. Good afternoon to you, it's Russell Woolf with you, just a minute away from news at four-o'clock," he said, followed by a long pause and an audible inhale.

"And I'm honoured and saddened to be with you at this time. I have an announcement to read out: Sir Charles Gairdner Hospital regrets to announce that much-loved broadcaster and former administrator, Wally Foreman, passed away this afternoon. Wally was brought to the hospital on Tuesday after suffering a cardiac arrest. Wally's wife, Lyn, and sons, Glen and Mark, would like to thank the public for their support over the past two days. They've requested that the media and the public respect the family's privacy at what is, obviously, a very difficult time.

"We'll be bringing you a very special state-wide drive program following the news at four-o'clock today. I'll be joined by Glenn Mitchell for the two hours between four-to-six. Your thoughts are welcome."

Woolf's voice began to quiver and crack as he continued.

"Obviously, we send our love and thoughts to Lyn and the boys and the rest of Wally's family and we'll mark this day down on our calendars – the second of November 2006 – because we've lost somebody that we loved very much, that we worked – and enjoyed being – with. And we're sure that you feel much the same.

"I look forward to your company after the news at four-o'clock on 720 ABC Perth."

It seemed so unfair that it was confusing. So confusing that it could not be true. It had only been a few months earlier that Geoff Hutchison had used your grandad as a sounding board in returning to Perth. Hutchison was living in Melbourne with his young family and with no intention of leaving Victoria.

However, after filling in as host of the Mornings program for Melbourne's ABC 774 and enjoying the experience, he decided it was a role he wanted to pursue more permanently. Shortly after, Liam Bartlett left ABC Perth and the Mornings job at 720 became vacant.

There was one person from whom Hutchison wanted advice: your grandad. He was the man who had been so approachable and given so much of his time when Hutchison was a 15-year-old work experience student from Kalamunda High School, placed with the ABC Sports Department of 1975. He was the man who, later at the NINE Network, pushed for the major broadcaster to give a chance to the young Golden West Network reporter Hutchison, bringing him back up to the city.

The pair had not spoken for more than a decade, but your grandad was "the one person" Hutchison felt he needed to speak to. To ask if he would be capable of doing the job.

"Yep, I'm sure you can," your grandad had replied. "It will be hard and I know you'll be different from Liam Bartlett. It will be exhausting, but I have absolute faith that you would be able to do it."

Hutchison had put the phone down and thought, "How great is this; reuniting with Wally, it's going to be fantastic". It was the "clincher", as he described it. He packed up his family and returned to Perth. At the time of writing this, Hutchison remained as the very successful, well respected and enjoyable host of the Mornings program at ABC Perth.

But that day he felt robbed. Robbed of time and an opportunity that had felt promised to him by fate itself. And it compounded a difficult time for the family, whose son had experienced a bad accident in Melbourne from which he lost sight in one eye. It was followed by the job in Perth, shifting the family at an inopportune time. And then your grandad died. It seemed so unfair.

"We were renting a house in Floreat and I remember walking into the kitchen and telling my wife that Wally had died and I began to cry," Hutchison said.

"Then Hugh came up to me and put his arms around me. I thought, 'This is a kid who a few months ago had one of the most awful experiences you could possibly have'. But that was it. Absolutely shithouse. We were always that close to going out for dinner or something, but we just never did it.

"Life is littered with those types of experiences and always will be. I owe him an enormous debt, particularly at the start, but I'm glad the conversation I had with him about the job was the clincher. What you've lost is profound – absolutely – and what his family and friends have lost is profound, but for me it's a lost opportunity to get back among his world again. It was only a few months, but it was enough to remind me who he was.

"There's a great sadness for me, absolutely a great sadness, that there's this huge gap where I didn't get to see him and then, when I finally got to see him again at the end, I didn't get to spend much time with him. I'd been back four months before he died: to me, it was all about this great return and getting to know your dad again.

"I think if there's one legacy that I would hope your dad had left behind for you, it's that there would be no shortage of mentors of a certain age. If you reflect on the moments that he was a bit remote from you, I think you'll remember the things that you share."

"I look forward to your company after the news at four-o'clock on 720 ABC Perth."

Bryan Cousins barely heard that closing line from Russell Woolf. He had never cried so much in his life and the tears did not stop for about an hour. Cousins had been carting hay on his small farm in Oakford, before returning to his truck for a break and switching on the radio. It was tuned to ABC 720 Perth and it was closing in on four-o'clock.

"I got rung by a couple of radio stations that knew Wal and I were close, but I just couldn't go on, because I knew I'd be that emotional. I went on one – the ABC, with Russell – but that was the only one I did," Cousins said of the day your grandad passed away.

"You have, I suppose, friends and acquaintances, but then you have people like Wal. The real test of any friendship is not when things are going good and his integrity in such a tough time for us to be going through …"

Cousins trailed off, before continuing.

"He was as close a friend as I bloody had. I don't think I've ever known a more balanced and fair person in an industry that's so competitive. There may be guys with integrity, but no-one's integrity was more on display than Wally's was. You just knew everything about him. He gave of himself.

"I remember being at Wally's service and sitting next to a young lady athlete. She was obviously upset by the loss of Wal. Lyn had trained this young girl and she told me this story that she had wanted to do extra training and wanted to pay Lyn, but Lyn didn't want to accept payment. The girl refused to do any training unless she paid Lyn, so she duly did. This was when Wal was director of WAIS.

"After several years of training, she'd become an Australian champion and there was an international meet that she couldn't afford to go to. She said Wally and Lyn turned up one night and said, 'You are going', and all the money she had given Lyn for training, they had put it into a separate little account, with the knowledge they were always going to give it back to her.

"I think that's just the nature of not only Wally, but Lyn, and we forget what a great partnership they were, because Wally might have been the voice on the radio, but they were such a great team.

"He had every quality that you'd want about yourself. If I look at myself and think there's traits I don't have, that I wish I had, Wally would have them. He always took the best view about somebody; if there were two ways to look at something, he always took the way of fairness and benefit of the doubt.

"Life's precious and we never know how long we've got and what's going to happen. I don't think there's any person the community could miss as much as Wally. He had a wonderful life in his 58 years and his passion for sport knew no boundaries."

Russell Woolf exhaled and paused as the news headlines were read out, with the leading story confirming what he had just announced to the world: your grandad had passed away.

What followed was two special hours hosted by Glenn Mitchell and Woolf and filled with a flood of calls, sobs, tears, well-wishes and disbelief, but more importantly memories and laughs for your grandad, as well as his music. There were special guests sharing their thoughts, people such as Bryan Cousins and those guests were accompanied by the recollections of the two hosts.

They were special words, as were the words of the hundred-or-so talkback correspondents who often prefaced their comments with, "I never met Wally, but". And our family is incredibly fortunate that we have every one of them on CD.

"In some ways, I couldn't think of a better thing to do than play a role like that, because we knew how it was going to affect people, that there was going to be an outpouring of love and grief, and we hoped it was going to be quite cathartic for the family, for colleagues, for the community," Woolf said.

"On the second of November, every year, at eight-to-four, I play that back – the music and the statement – and I can't listen to it without crying. I know it sounds weird, listening back to my own voice, but I hear my voice and I hear it faltering and it just takes me back to how shattered we were – all of us.

"It doesn't take a lot for me to cry when I think about Wal still. I don't hide my emotions: I'm not this 1950s bloke, who can't shed a tear. The world's moved on, thank God, and it affected me. I was emotional. My eyes were wet the whole time and I was catching breath in order to stop bawling.

"Then we had that two-hour program and it was just guest after guest after guest; the Premier, his mates, sports administrators and the public. The messages coming through from people, it was the most incredible two hours and it was organic; it wasn't two weeks in the making or anything, it was this instant pouring of love and grief.

"I spoke to Lyn again that night. Your family – your extended family – was very good to me. John, your uncle, drove down to the ABC to thank us for the job that we'd done and the rest of the family at other times. It was all part of the grieving process. It was an event that brought people together. Wal had talked about these people a lot and I felt like I knew all of you, but I guess it was sadly his death that made us all friends and brought us close together.

"When I think of Wal, it's always with a smile, with those tan-coloured trousers, ironed cotton shirt. He was the practical joker, who would always run around and do things in the office. That's what I remember.

"It hurts to think that we've all been starved of that since that day."

Woolf and Mitchell ended the broadcast dedicated to your grandad, but paused to embrace before leaving the studio.

Chapter 27

The Legend from Bruce Rock

More than 3000 people turned out to farewell your grandad at his memorial service at Challenge Stadium on 8 November 2006 – less than a week after his passing. It was reported as one of the largest gatherings for such an event that the state had ever seen.

In death, as in life, people were drawn to your grandad.

That was one of the motivations behind writing this book. Your grandad was an average, fun-loving youth, turned dedicated army officer, turned accomplished journalist, turned leading sports administrator, turned superb broadcaster. He had a reasonably noteworthy public profile and was well-respected. But while that particular set and sequence of accomplishments might have been unique to your grandad, their attributes were not and he was not alone in holding them.

And they, alone, hardly amounted to a packed stadium. So it became a purpose of this project to seek the answers, not only for you, but also for our wider family, as to why that stadium was filled. Why his service was at a stadium in the first place, why the state's media pulled together to help achieve the service and why the Premier of the state requested to speak at it.

And while some of those more public gestures required answers, arguably the more complex questions related to the number of non-sporting, non-media, non-government people who made the effort – took time out of their days – to journey to a venue which, for some, was a substantial distance away, to farewell a man many of them had never met in person.

A purpose of this project was to find an answer to why people cared so much for a simple, humble man. But, as the pages that have filled this story should have explained, there was nothing simple about your grandad. More than a humble farewell was required and we were fortunate that there was an enormous number of people wanting to help achieve that.

And as your grandad's friend and fellow ABC broadcaster Glenn Mitchell stood on the stage at that stadium, in front of those 3000 people, he reflected not so much the opening of the service, as he did the culmination of a lot of work to reach that point. Just as your grandad's service and the enormity of the outpouring of emotion did not reflect an absolute end, but the culmination of a rich, fulfilled life.

Our family had been sitting around your Great Aunty Jill's dining table, planning the service, when we received an offer from the State Government for a State Memorial Service. It was an offer we politely declined, but we welcomed the State's involvement and accepted Premier Alan Carpenter's request to say a few words.

Then came the request from your grandad's close friend throughout life, Dennis Cometti, to deliver a eulogy. Again, we accepted and thanked him for the offer. It was a kind gesture that would have been important for your grandad, given he and Cometti had in the years prior begun reconnecting and meeting on a regular basis, having gone their separate ways throughout their career.

Your grandad had told your nana how much those simple coffee catch-ups had meant to him. Cometti's offer was followed by another, this one from an equally close friend, Graham Moss, for the service to be held at Challenge Stadium.

We had been undecided on a venue at that point but, as appropriate a location as the stadium seemed due to your grandad's attachment to it, the family was racked with concern that we would appear foolish and full of self-importance by hosting a public memorial service at a venue capable of holding thousands of people. We knew your grandad was loved, but we were expecting a few hundred at best. The last thing we wanted was for your grandad's final farewell to turn into an embarrassment.

"Lyn, there's going to be two or three thousand people; Karrakatta won't be able to handle it," Moss had assured your nana. He had spoken to the chairman of the Sports Centre Trust, who agreed the venue should be offered to our family and that there would be no cost attached to it.

Moss engaged the venue's technical services to begin putting the infrastructure together, then worked closely with the ABC on the presentation aspects. He had been on the same page as the broadcaster regarding the expected turnout.

In fact, Local Content Manager Deborah Leavitt not only expected thousands, but was aware from the correspondence the ABC was receiving on a seemingly endless basis that there would be thousands more who wanted to be there, but simply could not make it. Leavitt knew it was going to be more than an average service and would require a little more finesse and preparation.

Arrangements were made with other media outlets on how to best manage the day from a news perspective, before Karen Tighe, Glenn Mitchell, Adam Sallur and Kim Lord – and undoubtedly many more who I am not aware of – began compiling the required audio and visual material, often deep into the nights leading up to the service. The eventual run-sheet included the displaying of numerous photos provided by our family, pauses for the handful of speeches and, of course, several of your grandad's favourite songs. The backing tracks selected for his life.

The correspondence the ABC had received from the public not only gave Leavitt an indication of the numbers expected at the service, but also the need for the service to be broadcast. And it needed to go state-wide. The demand from regional WA was undeniable.

Any broadcast was, of course, going to require broadcasters and, with Mitchell hosting the service itself, that job was asked of your grandad's friend Geraldine Mellet and the man who would eventually take over from him on the ABC Sports Desk, Clint Wheeldon.

The memorial service was a surreal experience for Geraldine Mellet and Clint Wheeldon. The former had initially not wanted to do it and the latter was unsure why he had been asked. Neither could fathom your grandad had gone.

Mellet had known your grandad from before she had even met him. It was her older sister, Jillian, who had been the administrative assistant for the ABC Sports Department in 1975, when your grandad joined George Grljusich and Dennis Cometti and would often phone at obscure hours to be picked up and driven somewhere.

In fact, Jillian was one of an unimaginable number of people whom your grandad contacted the week before he died, for no reason other than to catch up. The lines between fate and coincidence were constantly blurred where your grandad was concerned.

The tales of her sister were then added to through Mellet's own relationship with your grandad in the short period from his return to the ABC that she was the Afternoons presenter, often popping her head over their shared divider when she, as somewhat of a sports philistine, needed authentic-sounding questions for a sports interview. Your grandad was always happy to oblige.

It was those memories and that "great watermelon grin that split his whole face in two and was impossible to resist" that led to her feelings of inadequacy when it came to broadcasting your grandad's service. Mellet was racked with a concern that she could not sufficiently express "what an incredible human being he was in all aspects of his life and work".

"It was when I saw the online tribute page that I knew I need never have worried what I might say," Mellet said. "The public said it all in record numbers of tributes that poured in, hundreds at a time, praising his knowledge, his professionalism, his passion, his sense of humour and even his questionable taste in music.

"It really was an incredible honour to be involved. If ever

someone was genuinely loved it was Wally Foreman, not only by his close-knit family, but by a huge and hurting ABC audience, who wanted those loved ones to know they were surrounded by the hundreds of thousands who would treasure him forever."

For Wheeldon, hosting your grandad's memorial service gave rise to a similar feeling to that which many people were experiencing: it was too soon. Wheeldon had never made any secret of his desire to be a sports broadcaster and had in the years leading up to 2006 made that clear to your grandad, while also leaning on him as a source of stories. He had been preparing to make his case to join the department upon your grandad's expected retirement as a 60-year-old in 2008. That was what your grandad had told him to prepare for.

Now, two years early, he was having to prepare for your grandad departing in a completely different way. Wheeldon's enthusiasm for sport meant he was the natural selection when Glenn Mitchell, Karen Tighe, Deborah Leavitt and Damian Rabbitt were putting together the plans for the service coverage. He was there to complement Mellet's personal relationship with your grandad with his more in-depth knowledge of the state's sporting scene.

He was there to identify the myriad of past and present athletes, coaches and administrators who had filled the section set aside for attendees from the Western Australian Institute of Sport, as well as the hundreds of representatives from the wider sports fraternity scattered throughout the crowd.

They all came together in what was labelled by the media as "a who's who of WA sport, media, politics and business". Together, Wheeldon and Mellet described a two-hour, up-beat service, jumping in to cover each other when their voices faltered, with the reading of emotionally-charged audience comments occasionally becoming too challenging to continue.

They described the scenes of the converted basketball stadium rapidly filling and the people who were filling it, and the hands that struggled to resist clapping to the beat of a playlist of your grandad's favourite music. They paused as Mitchell made his way onto the stage to thank the audience for coming, before advising that your grandad's coffin was about to enter the arena.

They remained paused as the distinct ukulele strumming of Hawaiian artist Israel Kamakawiwo'ole's acoustic medley "Somewhere Over the Rainbow/What a Wonderful World" began to echo through the stadium, before resuming their description of the unfolding scenes; the jarrah casket draped with a Western Australian flag, adorned with a sheath of wheat and swaying in the hands of the six pall bearers, being led by the Anglican priest in crisp, dazzling white robes.

"It was hard and I'd had no real experience as a broadcaster then," Wheeldon said. "I was a journalist and, apart from calling WAFL games for SportFM, that was an unbelievably hard thing to deal with, because there was so much emotion in the room.

"Even now – and I bet you I'm not the only person who does this – I can't even listen to that 'Somewhere Over the Rainbow' song without getting a tight chest and starting to crack up. I'll be walking through somewhere and you can hear that ukulele and straight away the memories transport me back to that day at Challenge.

"One of the real positives, looking back at Wally, was that was the sort of impact he had, because he was so good at what he did. I can't remember who wrote it, but someone said, 'You felt like you knew him, even if you didn't know him'.

"He was always really good to me and I always thanked him for that, because he could have said, 'Who's this young punk from the news department that keeps wandering down once a week for a story'. He could have, but he didn't."

The panting grew heavier. As did the casket.

The want for proper etiquette at such an emotional time had the six mostly burly pall bearers – I was the exception to the category of burly – attempting to suppress their struggles at carrying your grandad. Of course, the more they suppressed, the more difficult it became. A stinging whisper was shot from one bearer over the shoulder of another.

"Pull your bloody side up there, Aitkin," Graham Moss said to Mick Aitken.

Aitken looked at the giant of a man, but returned fire with a glare that indicated he was in as much trouble as Moss was. Your grandad's memorial service was a heart-aching ceremony, but it was also a ceremony for your grandad and that meant a little humour was required. Moss and Aitken, though, felt the joke was on them; like your grandad had "put some lead weights in there to get back at us".

"It was a great service and everything, but the thing I remember the most was carrying the coffin," Moss said.

"God, it was heavy. If I hadn't had one of the funeral directors behind me, I would have dropped it, because I got half way up the aisle and thought, 'Shit, I'm not going to be able to keep doing this'. I had to use two hands and I started to sweat going down the aisle. By the time I got back to my seat, I was a lather of sweat.

"I was sitting through the whole service worrying that I had to carry it back out again. I remember whispering to Mick, 'You've got to take some weight, mate', then the funeral guy behind me put his hands under and took a bit of weight off and I thought, 'Thank Christ for that'.

"We got there, though, and I was really appreciative to be a pallbearer. Wally would have been close friends to quite a lot of people, I would have imagined. I was honoured."

Moss and Aitken were there as representatives of a similar time and friendship. They had come together with your grandad at a period of great excitement and development for Western Australian sport, with all three playing an important part.

Aitken, in particular, had formed a very close bond with your grandad, having found in him an oasis of camaraderie after landing from the UK into a city in which he knew no-one, yet already had a significant number of enemies. He had been appointed the inaugural director of the Western Australian Sports

Federation at the same time your grandad began at WAIS in the early 1980s, with the pair spearheading the Labor Government's assault on the status quo of WA sport.

Just days before, Aitken had been in Queensland on business, having long graduated from his WASF role and bouncing around the world in various positions. It was there that he received the call from a friend advising of your grandad's passing. It was not long after that the follow-up phone call came from your nana, asking him to be a pall bearer.

"You were the best friend he ever made, Mick," your nana told him.

Aitken, of course, dropped everything and flew to Perth.

"I don't say comrades-at-arms lightly, but we were; we had to fight," Aitken said. "If we hadn't of had each other – well, I know for me at least – we would have found that fight far harder.

"I remember the music, of course, the crowd, the eulogies, this overwhelming sense of sadness and – no disrespect to your dad – but the unexpected enormity of the outpouring of feelings that came from everywhere. One of the ironies I think was that your dad was always worried that his style and his character was such that he would rub people up the wrong way.

"He probably never really knew how much he was appreciated, as well as how much he was loved by the people who knew him and liked enormously by the people who didn't. It was that scale of outpouring that was quite overwhelming. It was a very moving experience for us all and I felt so glad to be able to be a part of that, in the saddest of circumstances.

"Fifty-eight and gone. I mean, I'm 65 now and still feel in many ways like I'm 25. It's so hard to understand and I'm sure for family – and friends too – this fact that you never got the chance to say goodbye is something you'll never get rid of. You never got the chance to say how much you loved them.

"It'd be nice if you could have your obituaries and eulogies before you go, wouldn't it? Had Wally known what everybody thought of him, I think he'd have been surprised and humbled, because at the end of the day, he was a man of great strength of opinion, but he was also an ordinary man with a great humility about him.

"He never forgot his roots, he was courteous and polite, friendly.

"If I got a fraction of the outpouring of the love that Wally got when I die, I could look forward to that and I'm glad that his family got the chance to see how much he was loved and still is loved. There's no-one I could talk about more, no-one who has made a more indelible impact on my life personally and professionally than your dad.

"You've given me a chance to reflect on a very, very special man."

The casket hovered over a red carpet that lined the path to the stage that had been setup at the front of the room, continuing its slow – for the pallbearers, painfully slow – march through the masses of people at ground level who had stood in silent remembrance of your grandad.

Every single person that casket passed, who laid eyes on it from afar, or who heard it described on the ABC's broadcast, had a story about your grandad. That was as true for those who had walked to the service, such as the WAIS staff, as it was for those who had driven from the country, and even those who had paid their own way and flown from interstate, such your grandad's fellow ABC broadcaster Drew Morphett.

It was true for people such as Wilma Shakespear, who had been a close ally for your grandad in battles against national bodies in her role as the inaugural director of the Queensland Academy of Sport. Her first reaction had been that "they got the wrong Wally", when she heard the news, before her thoughts drifted to memories of a man with "terrific balance", who could be "deadly earnest" when required, before later swilling red wine and singing country songs in duet with whoever he had roped into joining him.

It was true for people such as Fred Miller, one of your grandad's closest friends from his occasionally misguided youth, during which he often spent more time at the Floreat Hotel than he did pursuing any sort of career. When your career is showered in rat droppings, bonds form quickly. Miller and your grandad, along with their wives, had laughed about those days just a week before, as they shared a Friday dinner. Your grandad had left Fred and Anne Miller's house that night with a warning for his friend: "Get that weight off, Fred, or you won't be around much longer".

It was four days before your grandad's heart attack.

"That's him: he was always thinking of other people," said Miller, who has now joined your grandad. "I think about Wally a lot. So does Anne. He is someone who has had a big bearing on my life, even now that he's gone."

It was true for his colleagues at the ABC, such as Karen Tighe, who was filled with sadness at seeing that casket, but could not help but recall the half-A4 sheet of paper from the office that had been torn and stuck above the Sports Department's newspapers, dressed with the beautiful script writing of your grandad: "You can read our papers, but please don't take them". That sign, to my knowledge, remains above those papers more than 10 years after your grandad's passing.

It was true for the athletes, such as Kylie Wheeler, who would later in the service stand on stage, adorned in her Olympic uniform and deliver a beautiful tribute to your grandad on behalf of all her counterparts who had benefitted from his tireless devotion. Her heart ached over the loss and she was reminded of her own pain from losing her father at a young age, but the thought of your nana's pain equally tore her.

It was true for Tony Davis, the cyclist who had been turned on by his own teammates at the 1988 Seoul Olympics and who would have largely been left by himself in a foreign country if not for the staunch, ferocious support of your grandad. Davis had shunned every officialdom-sanctioned event since Seoul, with only two exceptions; the day of your grandad's memorial service and the 2001 WAIS Annual Dinner that farewelled your grandad from the institute. At the service at Challenge Stadium, he stood watching the casket from the second tier, preferring the shadows of the upper level and overcome with emotion.

"I didn't cry during that Olympic shit, I didn't cry when my parents split up, but I cried that day," Davis said.

And it was true for the hoard of coaches, such as Liz Chetkovich, and WAIS representatives there to remember, not only their inaugural director, but their friend. A friend who had been with them for almost two decades, who had given every bit of himself to help them achieve, but who was now gone.

"The words about Wally are: heart and soul," Chetkovich said.

"He always put his heart and soul into everything. Finding out he died was just absolutely terrible – it still makes me cry. For weeks after, I'd be in the shopping centre with my kids or getting a coffee and I'd start crying."

The tears rolled down Chetkovich's cheeks.

"It was all about Wally and I never got over it. Still – I'm still not over it. That whole sense of devastation just hit me. I don't think when my mum or dad died that it hit me this much; but this is what Wally did to people. That impact when he died was enormous."

The stage approached. It was almost time to rest.

The memories and emotions felt almost alive as the casket continued its rhythmic march. They were flooding out of those who lined the aisles and those who filled the stands, but also those who carried that casket and the family that guarded its front and rear.

Graham Moss and Mick Aitken had joked at the weight of the casket. Particularly given it was your grandad's casket – a man who barely rose above Moss' navel and had never weighed a great deal. Lead weights, they had surmised.

Perhaps in a more figurative explanation, it was the weight of all those memories and emotions, streaming towards your grandad and filling his soul before he said goodbye. Not least of which were the thoughts of those carrying it. The utter confusion and devastation that filled them. Sam Gannon, the former Test cricketer with whom your grandad had been so close since childhood, had received a phone call while in Sydney on business.

"Oh, here we go again," he had thought upon news of the heart attack, "Another chance for Wally to tell a dinner time party story about how he dodged a bullet".

Of course, it did not turn out like that. Instead, there he was, carrying the casket. Their lives had taken them in vastly different directions; your grandad remained in sport and, while Gannon was always passionate about cricket and later became Chairman of the Western Australian Cricket Association, he found his calling in finance. Not a week went by, though, that the pair did not speak.

"I was very emotional. I couldn't believe that I was carrying my little mate down through that group of people," Gannon said.

"I used to go to golf on Saturdays and everyone would be on the practice range hitting balls, talking about Wally's morning program. So the number of people at the service did not surprise me at all. For me, I miss the camaraderie and I miss his laugh."

A great deal of those laughs came at the same place as those shared with many of your grandad's closest friends: the Floreat Hotel. It was where, after his service in Vietnam, Morey Grafton was absorbed into the close-knit group like he had always been among the mates. His time as a private stationed at the Woodside Barracks, South Australia, from 1969 and serving under your second lieutenant grandad was followed by the pair having shared a house on Hastings Street, Scarborough.

Throughout his life, from Woodside to Scarborough, it seemed Grafton was always helping your grandad find his way home. On that day, though, it was not from a bar. And it was for the final time.

The casket's path had finally brought it to the stage. We turned left, before rounding the large projector screen that beamed with your grandad's smile and placed his casket on its holder behind and to the left of the podium. As the spotlights beamed down, brilliantly lighting the dazzling blue of the WA flag and seemingly igniting the wheat that sat upon it, Grafton could not help but think of that often loud, occasionally subordinate second lieutenant who was a cause of constant disruption in the Officers' Bar.

Wally Foreman: once again the centre of attention, with all the Mess Hall watching.

"The previous New Year's Eve, we were at someone's house and Wal was in a reminiscing mood," Grafton said.

"We spent, I don't know, maybe an hour or more with just us two. Occasionally, someone would come up and try to be nice and Wal would make it pretty clear that they weren't wanted. He was in a deeply nostalgic mood, talking about old times. We were a couple of old friends just having a good laugh about things we'd forgotten. I'm really glad we had that, at least.

"His death was a bit hard to comprehend. I have his photograph up in my study, just sitting there, and I often look up at it and say, 'You silly bastard; what have you gone and done?'. It was so bloody unnecessary. He was a good bloke and he was larger than life. You get a lot of blokes who enjoy a beer, who are good company, they go out and enjoy themselves, chase sheilas, tell stories, watch the footy.

"Wal stood out just a little bit differently."

Grafton took his place in the audience, alongside wife Patty. They held each other's hands tightly, wept and openly cried. And, of course, they laughed.

There were several speakers that day. Any service that goes for two hours requires several speakers.

They were there as representatives of the specific points of your grandad's unique journey. Your Uncle Mark and I spoke, as did your Great Aunties Sandy and Jill, while the Rev Keith Wheeler read a note written by your nana. Kylie Wheeler, as mentioned, delivered an address on behalf of the athletes and coaches, while former WAIS Chairman Neil McKerracher spoke of your grandad as a mate, as well as his administrative achievements.

McKerracher spoke of a patient and considerate man, who would make the tough decisions when he needed to, but was never immune to the hardships of those decisions. He would miss your grandad's company, he said, his sense of humour and the genuine care shown for everyone.

"For someone who had a photographic memory of the names and numbers on a football field, he had a very poor memory of who it was who had insisted on opening the last bottle of red the night before," McKerracher had joked.

The impact your grandad had on the state was highlighted by the presence of Premier Alan Carpenter, who, far from feeling obligated to address the audience, had requested the opportunity to do so. It was reflective of the role your grandad played in the state's development over several decades, from working behind the scenes to help the Labor Party establish a sports policy that had WA flourish, to overseeing the development of WAIS into a national powerhouse, and forever playing an important role in engaging and endearing himself to the state's population.

"I still get a bit emotional about it now, but there was a deep sense of shock when Wally Foreman had died at 58 – I'm 59 now – and there's a massive hole where he once was," Carpenter said during the interview for this book.

"Your father was a very significant figure in Western Australia for, actually, quite a long time; a very positive contributor. I had the opportunity to recognise that and I wanted to take it – I did take it – and I'm glad that I did. People recognised that Wally was not just a good person on the radio, but a good person in relation to his own family and everyone he dealt with.

"It's the uniqueness of his background, combined with his personality, then his experience in having had to make decisions, which is very different and difficult. You could have that blend of experience, without the personality, and you wouldn't have had the same result, so it's the blend of all of that over a long period of time then – gone. Then you look around and there's no-one else like him.

"There you go: no-one else like him."

And then there was Dennis Cometti. Cometti strolled to the stage, as large in stature as he was in influence and respect, as a representative of a dream, an era and the moment your grandad finally achieved his goal of entering the media.

Few evoked a wider spectrum of emotions that day than he did, through his anecdotes filled with humour and compassion. Many of those stories have already been repeated in these pages, but it was an address that was memorable to most people in that room as he recalled the moment your grandad began falling for your nana.

"Wal the romantic; Leigh Matthews becoming a Wiggle would have surprised me less," he had said, to rapturous laughter.

Years later, Cometti still felt the loss of your grandad and it was evident that the friendship they had begun rekindling through their regular catch-ups had meant as much to him as they had your grandad.

"We'd all gone a long way into our careers then and we spoke about things that were bothering us, the things we enjoyed, we talked about the kids," Cometti said.

"They were therapeutic for all of us and they were comfortable. They were comfortable. In a world where so much is uncomfortable, they were comfortable. The fun in the life of broadcasting had been lost compared to what we had and there was a lot of, 'Remember the time', and stuff like that. It's nice to want to see someone and I would always look forward to seeing Wally's face

"I remember the day when the word came through; it was one of those shocking things. That's probably one of the things that you and I have in common, is that age when it happened, which was something I mentioned at the funeral.

"You're denied a lot, but in some respects, you're able to take a lot with you. It teaches you a lot of lessons about the way you deal with your own kids and, I think, because you've been deprived, it'll make you a much more caring father. You understand, because you didn't have it, you want to give it to your children."

Cometti's words reminded me of a quote from Mitch Albom's *The Magic Strings of Frankie Presto*: "At a certain point, your life is more about your legacy to your kids than anything else". Would I have even finished writing this book if it was not for you, Charlotte? If I'm completely honest, probably not. At least, not in as much detail as I have.

The enormity of the project had not occurred to me when I first began researching and interviewing and only the motivation of showing you the legacy of your grandad kept it going. I wanted to know more about a father I lost too soon, but more than anything, I wanted you to know him. I wanted to give that to you, because of how much I knew he would have loved you.

Cometti closed his address at your grandad's service with words that remain poignant. They remain as relevant to you as they did to our family that day.

"I can only imagine what Lyn and all the Foreman family must be feeling right now," Cometti had said.

"If my experience is anything to go by, the pain will gradually ease. Having said that, you'll probably think of your dad every day of your life, but more and more he'll become a reassuring thought. In many ways, he'll become a companion.

"You'll be in great company."

Your Uncle Mark had suggested the flag that be draped over your grandad's coffin be that of Western Australia. The previous assumption was that it was going to simply be the Australian flag. Your uncle also suggested the sheath of wheat, as the family grappled with what sort of flowers we should have on display.

Both suggestions were perfect. As simple as they were, they summed up your grandad's life in two images. His start and his end. His passion and his personality.

The service was approaching its end, but there was one more speaker. Your grandad's story had come full circle. His journey had turned him from a boy, who always held a town in his heart, into a man, who a town held at its heart. Then it was time to say goodbye.

The poem that resides in the opening pages of this book, *The Legend from Bruce Rock*, by Mick Colliss, also holds pride of place in the Bruce Rock Council Chambers, regularly becoming a talking point for invited guests. Its position there is a symbol of your grandad's impact on a small country town, as much as its words reflect that town's impact on him.

The opening lines – "Another Aussie icon, a West Australian great, chosen well before his time to walk through Heaven's gate." – were heard at your grandad's service by a strong contingent from The Rock, as they were read by Colliss amidst the darkened Challenge Stadium arena. They were read to an audience of about 3000 and the countless thousands listening on the radio. All for a boy from Bruce Rock.

"It was an awful row of seats," said Kay Djukic, a childhood friend of your grandad's.

"There were heaps of us from Bruce Rock and it was just gut-wrenching. I could cry now, when I think of it. I just had to keep looking down, because I couldn't look up. That could have been any one of us. Any one of us. And we're all too young to die.

"Why did that many people show up? Because he was Wally Foreman. That is the only reason. Wally was everybody's mate; he was loveable, he was cheeky, he was everything. But that many people only came because he was Wally Foreman. And Wally was Bruce Rock.

"If it wasn't for Wally, most people wouldn't even know Bruce Rock exists. Yeah, 99 per cent of them won't ever go there, but if you asked them about it, they'd say, 'That's where Wally Foreman came from'. It's not where I came from, or anybody else, because he gave so much back to Bruce Rock."

About 3000. One of the largest memorial services the state had ever seen.

They sat there, watching, as images of your grandad were beamed from the large screens at the front of the room, framing his trademark grin, his round face and traditional cut of jet black hair, with his narrow eyes having closed too soon. They had stood, moved and clapped along at the request of the wonderfully unique and disarmingly quirky Rev Keith Wheeler, who closed his eyes as he swayed back-and-forth on the stage, not in prayer, but to the rhythm of Johnny Cash's "I Walk the Line".

And they had wept, giving a standing ovation in one final farewell as your grandad's coffin – as heavy as it was – was carried back along that strip of red carpet. It did so to the reflective Australian country song, Slim Dusty's "Lookin' Forward, Lookin' Back". As the song wound to a close, before restarting, all those in attendance delivered a rapturous applause.

About 3000. One of the largest. Why?

Perhaps the answer can be found in your grandad's own words. He had in the early 2000s been asked to deliver a eulogy, just as many people did for him. Your grandad's reflections were for his childhood friend from Bruce Rock, Jimmy Gidgup, and he ended them with the following.

> *That smile, I'll never forget it, and what better way to remember someone than by their smile.*
>
> *To Sue, Darren, Deanna and Daniel, please accept our sincerest sympathy at this very sad time, but be aware that your husband and dad made a huge impression on all of the Foremans, as he obviously did on everyone here today.*
>
> *His achievements and the examples he set in his life are something of which you can always be enormously proud and those examples are examples we can all afford to follow.*
>
> *God bless.*

God bless.

I sat in your Great Grandad Eric's living room, which was still adorned with the furnishings of your Great Grandma Norma. It was 2013; 10 years after her passing. Seven years after the passing of your grandad.

My recorder sat atop the electric heater that struggled to take the bite off the winter chill. We had spoken for about an hour in one of several interviews we did together for this book. We had spoken about his childhood, your grandad's childhood, and all the family had been through. All it had accomplished. All it had lost.

"What keeps you going?" I asked of the man who had lost his wife and his son, yet carried on to see 99-years-old.

"Oh, memories. Without a shadow of a doubt," he said. "I can always go back on some of the naughty things that Wally did and also some of the things that have made me so damn proud to say to my mates, 'He was my boy'."

He was the boy, who grew to the legend, from Bruce Rock.

He was your grandad.

Parents rarely let go of their children,
so children let go of them.
They move on. They move away. The moments that used to
define them – a mother's approval, a father's nod –
are covered by moments of their own accomplishments.
It is not until much later, as the skin sags and the heart
weakens, that children understand; their stories, and all their
accomplishments, sit atop the stories of their mothers and
fathers, stones upon stones, beneath the waters of their lives.

Mitch Albom
The Five People You Meet in Heaven

Appendix

Acknowledgements

A PROJECT THAT CONSUMES CLOSE to six years is bound to involve others and that was certainly true for "The Legend from Bruce Rock". I might be Wally Foreman's son, but I was only 22-years-old when he died and I doubt there are many sons of that age who could write a biography on their fathers unaided.

The difference in my knowledge of dad's life from the time I began this project to the moment I finished it is incomparable. It is a dangerous practice to attempt to mention all of those who helped create this biography and, despite having kept notes of acknowledgment along the way, I fear I have forgotten someone. If I have, I sincerely apologise. Please know that I appreciate everyone who supported me and helped me recreate the story of my dad.

There are also a few specific people whose impact on me or this project was particularly significant in the wake of dad's passing.

Brett McCarthy. A man who has affected my life, despite us having never worked together and rarely seen each other. He was the man who, after dad passed away, phoned me and asked me to pay him a visit at *The Sunday Times*, where he was Editor. There, he helped me plan the next four years of my life in a blueprint that had me wind my way back to that paper. But by that time, he had taken up the position of Editor at *The West Australian*. He re-entered my life with a simple text message: "You should write his biography". Five years later, I replied: "I did. And it was a hell of a story". His words initiated this project and were a constant source of support throughout it.

Glen Quartermain. He ended up with a son half his age that he never asked for, but who he accepted willingly. My sports editor during my employment at News Corp. He fought for me and always had my back, but – oh, boy – would he let me know when I had stuffed up. But more than anything, I remember the moment he pulled me aside at a staff function, in a corner away from the crowd and where no-one could hear. He looked me in the eyes and sternly said: "I employed you because I wanted Glen Foreman. I didn't want Wally Foreman. You deserve to be here. Never forget that". Even since leaving the paper, I've always considered "Quarters" my pseudo father. He helped me become a man capable of being a father to Charlotte and Jon and a husband to Sarah.

Ruth Callaghan. My fiery, red-headed uni lecturer who was not only forced to put up with a moody journalism student, but who also gave her time to support me through an extremely difficult period in my life. It took me a long time to even begin to accept the death of my father, but Ruth's door was always open. And when I phoned her in a frantic state of hysteria on my way to the first interview for this book – my grandad Eric – blabbering that I had no idea what to ask, or where to start, she gave the project its grounding with these simple words: "What you've lost is tremendous, but you've also gained an opportunity that not many people get to experience. You're about to get to know your dad as a boy, as a teenager, as a young adult, as a professional and, finally, as the father you knew. Enjoy it".

Dylan Henderson. My manager throughout my time at Courier Australia. It was my first full-time job and my role was to "strap and pack" magazines off a conveyor belt, before I moved into a cosy administration role. The air conditioning was better than a pay rise. I was sitting in that cosy existence when I received the phone call from mum, telling me of dad's heart attack. Dylan was the first person to hear the news and supported me throughout, even when I didn't show up for work for weeks, with no communication about why. But Dylan was always there. Even when I announced very late in the piece that I intended to leave to go to uni and study journalism, he was there. Dylan asked me to speak at his wedding to Vicki and, in that speech, I said something that still resonates today: "Dylan told me to lift my head up at a time when everyone else said it was ok to keep it down".

James Walker and Darcy White. With the help of others like Mark Davies and Steve Pass, Alex Plant and Lenny Rudeberg, they saved my life. I still remember the week after dad passed away, I answered a knock on the door with a dread of seeing or spending time with anyone. There was James, frozen meals in hand. He asked how I was going and said he didn't want to stay, because he knew I didn't want that. Then he left. A week later, Darcy showed up on the morning of a 35-degree day and pronounced he had nothing on, besides his clothes. Oh, and there was a carton in the car. And we were going to the beach – no protests permitted. They helped me see the path back from a very dark place.

Then, there's "The Legend from Bruce Rock". A project that consumed so much of my life that Charlotte, at just two-years-old, knew and referred to it as "The Book" – "You working on The Book, daddy?," she would ask. It was a question that filled me with pride as much as it did guilt whenever I heard it. This project required so much time and energy that it consumed my family and many others.

First and foremost, I must start with all of those who I interviewed and who gave their time. There were so many in the end, but I guess that's what it takes rebuild the moments of a 58-year long life that achieved as much as dad's did. They were incredibly generous with their time, often sitting with me for multiple hours and on multiple occasions. I know I probably asked stupid questions and tested your patience, but I appreciate it.

I want to specifically thank Tony Davis for taking the time to be interviewed. It was the first time in almost three decades that Tony had spoken about the torturous treatment inflicted on him at the 1988 Seoul Olympics. His story is powerful and he only chose to tell it because of who dad was and the impact he had on his life. Unfortunately, for legal reasons, that chapter had to be removed from the final manuscript. Hopefully, one day we'll get to tell that story, because it deserves to be told.

The final version of the book was only made possible through the efforts of Tim Clarke, who volunteered his experience as a career journalist to objectively edit it. He had the right mix of having known dad and the events in this story, but not so well that his objectivity was compromised. More than anything, he is a devoted family man and when I handed over the draft, saying "I know it needs cutting, but please remember who it's for", he understood.

Karen Tighe and Clint Wheeldon from the ABC were among the most constant sources of support. Not only did they share their kind words, stories and recollections, helping to establish facts and chronology, but they also put up with countless requests for archived audio and vision. They always obliged and were always patient and polite, even when I asked for the same audio on multiple occasions.

So, thereby my thanks also extend to the wider team at ABC Perth, especially Adam Sallur and the team in the library and archives, for their selfless willingness to assist in searching for materials that mean so much to my entire family.

The support and knowledge of Glenn Mitchell was also constant and appreciated. Not only did Glenn lend his support to me – professionally and in this project – but he also did so to dad, through the projects documented in this book and through being an inaugural Wally Foreman Foundation Board Member. His assistance has always been appreciated.

The ABC's Geoff Hutchison and the late Eoin Cameron were their typically amazing selves when I was struggling to find some bloke named "Colin Smith" and wading through an entire phone directory of Smiths clearly was not an option. Their on-air appeal for Colin – dad's Grade 5 teacher – located him within 12hrs. As irony would have it, Colin lived 5min from my house. Geoff's beautiful recollections of dad and his intriguingly intertwined tale of association was also extremely helpful – especially given I arrived 20min late to our scheduled coffee catch up.

WAIS's communications guru Chris Abbott not only accepted, but welcomed my seemingly endless stream of requests for materials and contacts. He is a man passionate about WAIS, who has a firm understanding and opinion on the way the place operates. Dad would be smiling down to see a man like him in an Institute that was so important to him.

The name Robert Hilburn might seem out of place in the back of this book, but the former music editor at the *LA Times* and author of "Johnny Cash: The Life" was kind enough to provide words of advice to this random Australian who popped up out of the blue. I still struggle to believe he took the time to help me overcome one of the most significant crises of confidence in the lifecycle of this project. There would be few better sounding boards for a project like this.

There were also those who helped me understand and describe times and places which occurred long before I was even born. Phil Perry was one of those people; a friend of dad's from Bruce Rock who tracked me down via the ABC. The enormous amount of intricate and seemingly innocuous details he provided made much of the first chapter of this book possible. I didn't have the benefit of living through 1960s Bruce Rock, but Phil enabled me to paint a picture of the time and place.

Another of those people who helped me recreate the past was Bob Lewis. Bob was one of dad's closest friends from his army day, but despite my best efforts I was unable to track him down. Then, he found me. I had almost finished writing the first draft when a random post I made on Facebook in a 3RAR forum found its way to Bob. The amendments and additions he provided around that time of dad's life were invaluable. Not only did he prevent me looking like a complete idiot in my ignorance of military life, but he helped expand the story of a man we both loved and respected.

Barbara Paramor was another of those people. She had compiled the story of her father and fellow crewman Walter Regan, dad's uncle and a man after whom he was named, by the time I began writing this book. She then phoned out of the blue and took the time to provide some crucial information that helped outline the "why" behind dad, not just the "who".

Then there was the entourage of current and/or retired journalists. Many I worked alongside as counterparts and many

I call friends. The careers of Chris Young from Channel 7 and Bob Harnett from Channel 9 spanned the time dad was in the media and, along with Network TEN's Tim Gossage, they helped point me in the right direction when I came to them with random questions. Former Channel 9 Director of News David Stacey and Director's Assistant Caris Edwards hunted through archive footage to find 50-year-old stories by and about dad. And Paul Murray explained what a cadetship in the 1970s entailed and what a posting to Melbourne for *The West* involved in a world without laptops and internet.

Gareth Parker and several other political journalists provided immense help to a journalist who has spent most of his career covering sport. I was completely foreign to the process of tracking down such items as State Record Office documents and my contacts in the arena were limited. I appreciate all the help.

Then, there are a couple of my friends, who might have felt they played little part in creating this story, but they did.

Ashley Storey's talent as a graphic designer, videographer and creativity personified is unmatched and his care for projects devoted to a man he never met has been profound. And Andrew Martin: one hell of a singer, song writer and all-round musician. So talented that not only can he play every instrument known to man, but he also passes that talent on to his students at St Mark's. He was also the first person I thought of and the only one I trusted to describe to me "in laymen's terms" what I was hearing in Pachelbel's Canon – one of the most significant musical pieces now etched my mind.

And, finally, to my family, who I have deliberately left last because my appreciation for them is the most difficult to put into words. I will start with my extended family – my aunties; dad's sisters Sandy and Jill. I understand reliving some of the moments I asked you to would have been painful. I also understand how enormously challenging it would have been to try and remember timelines of events from 60 years ago. I could not have pieced together this biography without that input, care, love and support.

However, there was no-one affected more by my requests for recollections than my mum. I asked her to unbury memories of all kinds – from momentously joyous, to overwhelmingly sad. Many of those memories had been deliberately pushed aside to simply survive; to be there for my brother and I, to see us through the darkness, to help us grow and then to attempt to live her own life. Mum, what you gave through this project was enormous and it changed my life. I truly hope this book, in turn, helps you. And that goes for my brother, Mark, too. I understand the memories were as painful for you to recall as they were me, so thank you for doing so.

Which brings me to my closest family.

Thanks, of course, must go to Charlotte and Jonathon, who provided the inspiration needed to first drive this project, then to complete it. However, neither of those people would be here to have that impact if not for my beautiful wife Sarah. I could write a separate book in thanks to all she has done for me, our family and this project, but I'll keep many of those words between us. Sarah gave as much to this biography as I did, often inventing a reason to take the kids out of the house for chunks of four to six hours, just so I could write. She showed enormous compassion and understanding for the importance of it, despite having entered my life four years after dad passed away.

He would have loved you beyond measure, Sarah. You did more than change my life – you saved it. Thank you for everything.

Thank you to those who read this story and, finally, thank you to my dad. He might have never had the chance to read about his wonderful life, but he didn't need to.

He lived it.

Appendix

Interviews

The following is a list of the interviews conducted to complete the corresponding parts of this book. In addition to the interviews were hundreds of websites, books, newspaper articles and other source material. I have chosen not to list all of those for the simple reason of quantity and that some were dug out of the archives of newspaper publishers and libraries. To list them all would be as impractical as it would be impossible, given the incomplete nature of some of the information of the clippings. In all cases, however, I have attempted to reference those clippings within the text of this book when referring to them.

Part 1

Alan and Mary Hicks; Bryan Kilminster; Ray Williams; Colin Smith; Eric Foreman; Kay Djukic (nee Anderson); Phil Perry; Margaret Robinson; Phillip Perry; Trevor Holm; Trevor Riley; Sandy Shaw; Jill Raynor; Brian Rogers; Daryl Foster; Fred Miller; George Young; Kevin Harrison; Kim Hughes; Lee Hunt; Morey Grafton; Sam Gannon; Steve Heal; Stuart McKeown; Trevor Bickle; Dennis Cometti; Geoff Hutchison; Geraldine Doogue; Paul Murray; Russell Goodrick; David Hatt; Ric Charlesworth; Drew Morphett; Glenn Mitchell; Jillian Mellet; Geraldine Mellet; Noel Kagi, Bob Lewis.

Part 2

Eric Foreman; Sandy Shaw; Jill Raynor; Lyn Foreman; Daryl Foster; Fred Miller; George Young; Sam Gannon; Alan East; Barbara Wilmot; Basil Zempilas; Brian Blanksby; Bruce Elliott; Craig Davies; Daryl Benson; David Hatt; Doug Shave; Graham Edwards; John Bloomfield; Kylie Wheeler; Liz Chetkovich; Lyn McKenzie; Steve Lawrence; Michael Nunan; Mick Aitken; Neil McKerracher; Norman Moore; Ray Turner; Ric Charlesworth; Tom Hoad; Tony Davis; Tudor Bidder; Warwick Hadfield; Wilma

Shakespear; Alan Carpenter; Bryan Cousins; Glenn Mitchell; Karen Tighe; Roanna Edwards; Jillian Mellet; Geraldine Mellet; Peter Sweeney; Mark Foreman.

Part 3

Eric Foreman; Sandy Shaw; Jill Raynor; Lyn Foreman; Dennis Cometti; Geoff Hutchison; Craig Davies; Steve Lawrence; Alan Carpenter; Bryan Cousins; Clint Wheeldon; Dan Lonergan; Deborah Leavitt; Drew Morphett; Glenn Mitchell; Karen Tighe; Roanna Edwards; Ken Judge; Liam Bartlett; Peter Sweeney; Mark Foreman; Russell Woolf.

Part 4

Lyn Foreman; Bryan Kilminster; Ray Williams; Eric Foreman; Kay Djukic (nee Anderson); Sandy Shaw; Jill Raynor; Daryl Foster; Fred Miller; George Young; Kevin Harrison; Kim Hughes; Lee Hunt; Morey Grafton; Sam Gannon; Steve Heal; Stuart McKeown; Dennis Cometti; Geoff Hutchison; Craig Davies; David Hatt; Kylie Wheeler; Liz Chetkovich; Mick Aitken; Neil McKerracher; Ric Charlesworth; Steve Lawrence; Tony Davis; Wilma Shakespear; Alan Carpenter; Bryan Cousins; Clint Wheeldon; Dan Lonergan; Deborah Leavitt; Glenn Mitchell; Karen Tighe; Roanna Edwards; Ken Judge; Liam Bartlett; Mark Foreman; Russell Woolf.

www.ingramcontent.com/pod-product-compliance
Lightning Source LLC
Chambersburg PA
CBHW032020290426
44110CB00012B/617